The Cambridge Companion to Isaiah Berlin

Isaiah Berlin (1909–1997) was a central figure in twentieth-century political thought. This volume highlights Berlin's significance for contemporary readers, covering not only his writings on liberty and liberalism, the Enlightenment and Romanticism, Russian thinkers and pluralism, but also the implications of his thought for political theory, history, and the social sciences, as well as the ethical challenges confronting political actors, and the nature and importance of practical judgment for politics and scholarship. His name and work are inseparable from the revival of political philosophy and the analysis of political extremism and defense of democratic liberalism following World War II. Berlin was primarily an essayist who spoke through commentary on other authors and, while his own commitments and allegiances are clear enough, much in his thought remains controversial. Berlin's work constitutes an unsystematic and incomplete, but nevertheless sweeping and profound, defense of political, ethical, and intellectual humanism in an anti-humanistic age.

Joshua L. Cherniss is the author of *A Mind and Its Time: The Development of Isaiah Berlin's Political Thought* (Oxford, 2013), and of journal articles and book chapters on Berlin, Reinhold Niebuhr, Max Weber, and other twentieth-century political thinkers. He has been a Laurence S. Rockefeller Visiting Faculty Fellow at the University Center for Human Values, Princeton, and a Graduate Fellow at the Center for European Studies and the Safra Center for Ethics, both at Harvard. He is currently an Assistant Professor of Government at Georgetown University.

Steven B. Smith is Alfred Cowles Professor of Political Science at Yale University. He has served as the Master of Branford College at Yale and is the Co-Director of the Yale Center for the Study of Representative Institutions. His book *Spinoza, Liberalism, and the Question of Jewish Identity* (1998) won the Ralph Waldo Emerson Prize from Phi Beta Kappa. His most recent book, *Modernity and its Discontents* (Yale University Press, 2016), has been widely reviewed and the subject of book conferences and panel discussions. He is currently working on a new book called *In Defense of Patriotism*.

Cambridge Companions to Philosophy

Abelard Edited by Jeffrey E. Brower *and* Kevin Guilfoy
Adorno Edited by Thomas Huhn
Ancient Ethics Edited by Christopher Bobonich
Ancient Scepticism Edited by Richard Bett
Anselm Edited by Brian Davies and Brian Leftow
Aquinas Edited by Norman Kretzmann and Eleonore Stump
Arabic Philosophy Edited by Peter Adamson and Richard C. Taylor
Hannah Arendt Edited by Dana Villa
Aristotle Edited by Jonathan Barnes
Aristotle's Politics Edited by Marguerite Deslauriers and Paul Destrée
Atheism Edited by Michael Martin
Augustine 2nd edition Edited by David Meconi and Eleonore Stump
Bacon Edited by Markku Peltonen
Berkeley Edited by Kenneth P. Winkler
Boethius Edited by John Marenbon
Brentano Edited by Dale Jacquette
Carnap Edited by Michael Friedman and Richard Creath
The Communist Manifesto Edited by Terrell Carver and James Farr
Constant Edited by Helena Rosenblatt
Critical Theory Edited by Fred Rush
Darwin 2nd edition Edited by Jonathan Hodge and Gregory Radick
Simone De Beauvoir Edited by Claudia Card
Deleuze Edited by Daniel W. Smith and Henry Somers-HALL
Descartes Edited by John Cottingham
Descartes' Meditations Edited by David Cunning
Dewey Edited by Molly Cochran
Duns Scotus Edited by Thomas Williams
Early Greek Philosophy Edited by A. A. Long
Early Modern Philosophy Edited by Donald Rutherford
Epicureanism Edited by James Warren
Existentialism Edited by Steven Crowell
Feminism in Philosophy Edited by Miranda Fricker and Jennifer Hornsby
Fichte Edited by David James and Guenter Zoeller
Foucault 2nd edition Edited by Gary Gutting
Frege Edited by Tom Ricketts and Michael Potter
Freud Edited by Jerome Neu

Continued at the back of the book

The Cambridge Companion to Isaiah Berlin

Edited by

JOSHUA L. CHERNISS
Georgetown University

STEVEN B. SMITH
Yale University

CAMBRIDGE
UNIVERSITY PRESS

University Printing House, Cambridge CB2 8BS, United Kingdom

One Liberty Plaza, 20th Floor, New York, NY 10006, USA

477 Williamstown Road, Port Melbourne, VIC 3207, Australia

314–321, 3rd Floor, Plot 3, Splendor Forum, Jasola District Centre, New Delhi – 110025, India

79 Anson Road, #06–04/06, Singapore 079906

Cambridge University Press is part of the University of Cambridge.

It furthers the University's mission by disseminating knowledge in the pursuit of education, learning, and research at the highest international levels of excellence.

www.cambridge.org
Information on this title: www.cambridge.org/9781107138506
DOI: 10.1017/9781316481448

© Cambridge University Press 2018 except

Chapter 2 © Cambridge University Press and Henry Hardy 2018

Chapter 15 © Isaiah Berlin 1969, © the Trustees of the Isaiah Berlin Literary Trust and Henry Hardy 2018

This publication is in copyright. Subject to statutory exception and to the provisions of relevant collective licensing agreements, no reproduction of any part may take place without the written permission of Cambridge University Press.

First published 2018

Printed in the United States of America by Sheridan Books, Inc.

A catalogue record for this publication is available from the British Library.

Library of Congress Cataloging-in-Publication Data
NAMES: Cherniss, Joshua L., editor. | Smith, Steven B., 1951– editor.
TITLE: Cambridge companion to Isaiah Berlin / edited by Joshua L. Cherniss, Georgetown University and Steven B. Smith, Yale University.
DESCRIPTION: New York : Cambridge University Press, 2018. | Includes bibliographical references and index
IDENTIFIERS: LCCN 2018026132 | ISBN 9781107138506 (alk. paper)
SUBJECTS: LCSH: Berlin, Isaiah, 1909–1997.
CLASSIFICATION: LCC B1618.B454 C66 2018 | DDC 192–dc23
LC record available at https://lccn.loc.gov/2018026132

ISBN 978-1-107-13850-6 Hardback
ISBN 978-1-316-50305-8 Paperback

Cambridge University Press has no responsibility for the persistence or accuracy of URLs for external or third-party internet websites referred to in this publication and does not guarantee that any content on such websites is, or will remain, accurate or appropriate.

In memoriam Robert Wokler (1942–2006) – amicus Isaiae

Contents

Notes on Contributors	page ix
Acknowledgments	xii
List of Abbreviations	xiii

    Editors' Introduction: Why Berlin? Why Now?   1
    Joshua L. Cherniss and Steven B. Smith

PART I   BERLIN THE MAN   9

1   On Isaiah Berlin   11
    Amos Oz

2   The Life and Opinions of Isaiah Berlin   13
    Joshua L. Cherniss and Henry Hardy

PART II   BERLIN ON PHILOSOPHY, THE HUMAN SCIENCES, AND POLITICAL THEORY   31

3   Berlin, Analytic Philosophy, and the Revival of Political Philosophy   33
    Naomi Choi

4   "The Sense of Reality": Berlin on Political Judgment, Political Ethics, and Leadership   53
    Joshua L. Cherniss

PART III   BERLIN AND THE HISTORY OF IDEAS   79

5   Berlin on the Nature and Purpose of the History of Ideas   81
    Ryan Patrick Hanley

6   Isaiah Berlin on Marx and Marxism   97
    Aurelian Craiutu

7   Privileged Access: Isaiah Berlin and Russian Thought   116
    Kathleen Parthé

8 Isaiah Berlin on the Enlightenment and Counter-Enlightenment   132
   Steven B. Smith

9 Berlin's Romantics and Their Ambiguous Legacy   149
   Gina Gustavsson

PART IV BERLIN AND POLITICS: LIBERALISM, NATIONALISM, AND PLURALISM   167

10 Isaiah Berlin on Nationalism, the Modern Jewish Condition, and Zionism   169
   Fania Oz-Salzberger

11 Negative Liberty and the Cold War   192
   Ian Shapiro and Alicia Steinmetz

12 Isaiah Berlin: Contested Conceptions of Liberty and Liberalism   212
   Alan Ryan

13 Pluralism, Relativism, and Liberalism   229
   George Crowder

14 Liberalism, Nationalism, Pluralism: The Political Thought of Isaiah Berlin   250
   William A. Galston

PART V EPILOGUE   263

15 The Lessons of History   265
   Isaiah Berlin

Bibliography   277
Index   293

Notes on Contributors

Isaiah Berlin was born in Riga in 1909, moved to Petrograd in 1916, and emigrated with his family to England in 1921. He was educated at St Paul's School, London, and Corpus Christi College, Oxford. He remained at Oxford all his life, being successively a Fellow of All Souls College, a Fellow of New College, Professor of Social and Political Theory, and founding President of Wolfson College. He also held the Presidency of the British Academy. As an exponent of the history of ideas he was awarded the Erasmus, Lippincott and Agnelli Prizes; he also received the Jerusalem Prize for his lifelong defence of civil liberties. He died in 1997.

Joshua L. Cherniss is Assistant Professor in the Department of Government at Georgetown University, having previously taught at Harvard University and Smith College. He is the author of *A Mind and Its Time: The Development of Isaiah Berlin's Political Thought* (2013) and of articles and book chapters on Berlin, Max Weber, Reinhold Niebuhr, and Albert Camus. His current work examines the interplay between critiques and defenses of liberalism, problems in political ethics, and the reinterpretation of liberalism as a distinctive ethical temperament or ethos in twentieth-century political thought.

Naomi Choi is Assistant Professor of Political Science at the University of Houston. Her articles have appeared in *History of Political Thought, History of European Ideas, Philosophy of History*, and *The Review of Politics*. She is currently working on her book manuscript, *Political Theory after the Interpretive Turn*, which explores the relationship between scientific inquiry, moral philosophy, and political theory through a sustained examination of the philosophy of Charles Taylor.

Aurelian Craiutu is Professor of Political Science at Indiana University, Bloomington. His most recent books are *A Virtue for Courageous Minds:*

Moderation in French Political Thought, 1748–1830 (2012) and *Faces of Moderation: The Art of Balance in an Age of Extremes* (2016).

George Crowder is Professor in the College of Business, Government and Law, Flinders University, Adelaide, Australia. His books include *Liberalism and Value Pluralism* (2002), *Isaiah Berlin: Liberty and Pluralism* (2004), *The One and the Many: Reading Isaiah Berlin* (coedited with Henry Hardy, 2007), and *Theories of Multiculturalism* (2013). He is currently working on a forthcoming book, to be called *The Problem of Value Pluralism: Beyond Isaiah Berlin*.

William A. Galston is Ezra K. Zilkha Chair and Senior Fellow in Governance Studies at the Brookings Institution. Among his books are *Liberal Purposes* (Cambridge, 1991) and *Liberal Pluralism* (Cambridge, 2002). He also writes a weekly column for *The Wall Street Journal*.

Gina Gustavvson is Associate Professor of Government at Uppsala University and an associate member of Nuffield College, Oxford. She has published articles on Berlin's psychological argument against positive liberty in *The Review of Politics* and *European Political Science Review*, and has also written about the French burqa ban and the Muhammad cartoon controversy. She is the author of a forthcoming book, *The Romantic Strain in Enlightenment Liberalism*.

Ryan Patrick Hanley is the Mellon Distinguished Professor of Political Science at Marquette University. He is the author, most recently, of *Love's Enlightenment: Rethinking Charity in Modernity* (Cambridge, 2017), and editor of *Adam Smith: His Life, Thought, and Legacy* (2016). He is currently completing a monograph on the political philosophy of Fénelon, as well as a translation of Fénelon's moral and political writings.

Henry Hardy is a fellow of Wolfson College, Oxford, and one of Isaiah Berlin's literary trustees. He has edited or coedited eighteen books by Berlin, and a four-volume edition of his letters. He is also the editor of *The Book of Isaiah: Personal Impressions of Isaiah Berlin* (2009), and coeditor (with George Crowder) of *The One and the Many: Reading Isaiah Berlin* (2007).

Amos Oz is an Israeli writer and Professor Emeritus of Literature at the Ben Gurion University of the Negev. His numerous novels include *My Michael* (1968), *Black Box* (1987), *A Tale of Love and Darkness* (2002), and, most recently, *Judas* (2014). His essays include *Jews and Words* (with Fania Oz-Salzberger, 2012), and *Dear Zealots* (2017).

Fania Oz-Salzberger is Professor of History in the Faculty of Law at the University of Haifa and director of Paideia, the European Institute for Jewish Studies in Sweden. Her books include *Translating the Enlightenment: Scottish Civic Discourse in Eighteenth-Century Germany* (1995) *Israelis in Berlin* (2001) and, with Amos Oz, *Jews and Words* (2012).

Notes on Contributors

Kathleen Parthé is Professor of Russian at the University of Rochester. Her publications include *Russian Village Prose: The Radiant Past* (1992), *Russia's Dangerous Texts: Politics between the Lines* (2004), and *A Herzen Reader* (2012). She is currently working a new translation of Herzen's memoir *Past and Thoughts*.

Alan Ryan was Warden of New College, 1996–2009, and Professor of Politics at Princeton. His most recent books are *On Politics* (2012) and *The Making of Modern Liberalism* (2013).

Ian Shapiro is Sterling Professor of Political Science at Yale. His most recent book is *Politics against Domination* (2016).

Steven B. Smith is the Alfred Cowles Professor of Political Science at Yale University. He is the author of *Spinoza, Liberalism, and the Question of Jewish Identity* (1997), *Reading Leo Strauss* (2006), and *Modernity and Its Discontents: Making and Unmaking the Bourgeois from Machiavelli to Bellow* (2016).

Alicia Steinmetz is a Fox International Fellow at Cambridge University, and a PhD candidate in Political Science at Yale University, where she specializes in the history of political thought in the early modern period. Her dissertation explores the role of the imagination in constructing various modern conceptions of autonomy.

Acknowledgments

The editors wish to thank the contributors for their good work and good humor in completing their assigned tasks. We also thank the participants in a two-day conference on Berlin held at Yale University in February 2017, at which versions of most of the chapters comprising this volume were presented: these include, aside from the contributors, Pamela Edwards, Isaac Nakhimovsky, Giulia Oskian, and Marci Shore. We owe debts as well to Amy Gais for her assistance in organizing the conference, and Thijs Kleinpaste for his in preparing the manuscript for publication. At Cambridge University Press, we are grateful to Robert Dreesen, who supported the project from the beginning, and to, Helen Belgian, Jackie Grant, Meera Seth, and Claire Sissen for their work in bringing the project to fruition; we are particularly grateful to Krishna Prasath Ganesan for supervising the complicated work on the proofs and physical production, and Cynthia Crippen for preparing the index, and Cary Cherniss and Thijs Kleinpaste for reviewing it. Special thanks are also due to Henry Hardy, for his various, tireless, and invaluable services to this volume and to scholarship on Berlin more broadly; and to Laura Hartmann, for assistance with the proofs, and for serving as a tireless sounding-board.

Abbreviations

The following works are referred to in the text by the abbreviations listed here, which follow the practice established by Berlin's editor, Henry Hardy. All works are by Isaiah Berlin, unless otherwise noted. The publication date of the edition used is given first, followed by the publication date of the first edition in brackets; full publication details for each work are provided in the bibliography.

A	*Affirming: Letters 1975–1997* (2015)
AC	*Against the Current* (2013 [1979])
AE	*The Age of Enlightenment* (2017 [1956])
B	*Building: Letters 1960–1975* (2013)
BI	Henry Hardy (ed.), *The Book of Isaiah: Personal Impressions of Isaiah Berlin* (2009)
CC	*Concepts and Categories* (2013 [1978])
CIB	Ramin Jahanbegloo, *Conversations with Isaiah Berlin* (1991)
CTH	*The Crooked Timber of Humanity* (2013 [1990])
E	*Enlightening: Letters 1946–1960* (2009)
E+	Supplementary Letters, 1946–1960 (online)
F	*Flourishing: Letters 1928–1946* (2004)
F+	Supplementary Letters, 1928–1946 (online)
FIB	*Freedom and Its Betrayal* (2014 [2002])
HF	*The Hedgehog and the Fox* (2013 [1953])
IBLT	Isaiah Berlin Literary Trust
KM	*Karl Marx* (2013 [1939])
L	*Liberty* (2002)
MSB	Isaiah Berlin Papers, Department of Special Collections and Western Manuscripts, Bodleian Library, University of Oxford
PI	*Personal Impressions* (2014 [1980])

PIRA	*Political Ideas in the Romantic Age* (2014 [2006])
POI	*The Power of Ideas* (2013 [2000])
PSM	*The Proper Study of Mankind* (2014 [1997])
RR	*The Roots of Romanticism* (2013 [1999])
RT	*Russian Thinkers* (2008 [1978])
SM	*The Soviet Mind* (2016 [2004])
SR	*The Sense of Reality* (2019 [1996])
TCE	*Three Critics of the Enlightenment* (2013 [2000])
UD	Isaiah Berlin and Beata Polanowska-Sygulska, Unfinished Dialogue (2006)

EDITORS' INTRODUCTION

Why Berlin? Why Now?

Joshua L. Cherniss and Steven B. Smith

Isaiah Berlin (1909–97) was a central figure in twentieth-century political thought, his name and work inseparable from the larger revival of political philosophy, and the related analysis of political extremism and defense of democratic liberalism, that followed World War II. His classic essay "Two Concepts of Liberty" remains a staple of courses in political theory, while "The Hedgehog and the Fox" has furnished a durable metaphor for discussing the temperaments and philosophies of politicians and intellectuals. Berlin's many essays on the history of ideas, principally in the period between the French and Russian Revolutions, did much to promote interest in this field in the English-speaking world. While his interpretations of individual thinkers, and characterization of the central struggle between Enlightenment and Romantic thought, bear the marks of the ideological struggles and academic standards of their time, and have accordingly been challenged by later historians (and now are seldom accepted without considerable qualification), they continue to provoke further reconsiderations of these topics – and provide, if nothing else, the foil against which scholars continue to pit themselves.

Perhaps Berlin's most profound influence, as some of the chapters of this volume confirm, has been his articulation of a pluralistic conception of ethics, which began to be recognized as a significant, and challenging, position in moral and political philosophy. Since Berlin's death, debates about the nature, cogency, and validity of Berlin's pluralism – and the sustainability of his linkage between pluralism and liberalism – have continued to grow. So has interest in Berlin's life and intellectual career, fueled by the ongoing publication of unpublished writings by his editor, Henry Hardy, which has furnished scholars and general readers with an increasingly complete record of Berlin's thought. This still-growing body of work has inspired a truly global readership, with Berlin's work translated into numerous languages. There has been particular interest in Berlin among readers and scholars in Latin America and East Asia, particularly Japan, China, and South Korea, the latter two of which have recently hosted conferences on Berlin's work; Berlin is also commemorated with an annual conference in his native Riga.

While Berlin's most cherished commitments and allegiances are clear enough, much in his thought is ambiguous – and controversial. Controversy has raged, particularly, over the relationship between Berlin's commitment to liberalism, and his assertion of ethical pluralism, and over the meaning and validity of the claims involved in Berlin's pluralism. Berlin is also, appropriately, a subject of political controversy. Both his own political position and the political (or ideological) implications of his ideas have been hotly debated. He has been both praised and attacked as an intellectual Cold Warrior – and for the relative mildness of his anticommunism. Berlin's reformulation of liberalism has been charged with contributing to the growth of a "thinner," more morally neutral, unambitious, and dispiritingly "negative" form of liberalism, even as it has also been criticized for tying liberalism to a controversial moral doctrine and ideal of character. The coherence of Berlin's championing of a "negative" conception of liberty, understood strictly as the absence of interference, and his support for the welfare state, have also been questioned. Some have associated Berlin (for better or worse) with libertarian theory and neoliberal politics, while others have found in his pluralism resources for critiques of an unqualified embrace of the free market.

One challenge any reader of Berlin confronts concerns the question of genre. Berlin wrote in a variety of registers: from the Oxford analytical style early in his career, to studies in the history of ideas, to "personal impressions" or *éloges* written in the manner of the great French funeral oration. His preferred genre was the essay. Other than his early biography of Karl Marx, all of Berlin's later works were essays, many of them individual pieces written for occasional purposes. This was perhaps deliberate. To use Pascal's distinction, philosophy was for him more a matter of the *esprit de finesse* than the *esprit de geometrie*. He understood that philosophy was a matter not simply of logic, but of persuasion. Among philosophical writers of the last century, he is rivaled only by Michael Oakeshott as a master of English prose. He was capable of painting on a broad canvas as well as working in miniature. His work often took the form of intellectual portraits of key figures in the history of political thought, from Vico and Herder to Machiavelli, Marx, Tolstoy, and de Maistre, as well as notable contemporaries such as J. L. Austin, Chaim Weizmann, Franklin Roosevelt, and Winston Churchill.

This raises another important set of questions. Was Berlin a philosopher at all, and does his work have traction beyond the period of the Cold War in which it arose? Our answer to both of the above is "yes." Although Berlin never wrote a comprehensive tome on politics to rival works such as Locke's *Second Treatise of Government* or Rawls's *A Theory of Justice*, we believe that his work was instrumental in the revival of political theory at a time when it had been declared all but moribund. Like another contemporary, Leo Strauss, Berlin's essays often took the form of a commentary on other authors, yet he used this medium to engage the central philosophical problems of his time. These include the problem of liberty and coercion, the issues of determinism and responsibility, the philosophy of the social sciences, the themes of monism and pluralism, the conflict between Enlightenment and romanticism, and the role of nationalism and Jewish identity. The chapters included in this volume testify to the wide range of Berlin's philosophical, political, and literary interests, but rather than focus on his interpretation of particular figures in the history of ideas, we have preferred to highlight the general themes that these writings were intended to illuminate.

This volume is divided into four parts. Part I contains accounts of "Berlin the Man." This includes a biographical portrait by Joshua Cherniss and Henry Hardy (Chapter 2) which provides an overview of Berlin's life and work, situating it within his Russian, Jewish, and British contexts. Underlying Berlin's multifarious intellectual concerns, they argue, is a kind of "humanism" that gave voice to the primacy of freedom of choice, a recognition of the conflict of basic values, and an emphasis on the irreducible uniqueness of the individual. In Part II, "Berlin on Philosophy, the Human Sciences, and Political Theory," Naomi Choi (Chapter 3) examines the underappreciated role of the Oxford analytical movement in shaping Berlin's thought. Although Berlin was never a logical positivist, his questions were often framed in response to the dominance of positivism in the interwar period. Berlin's repudiation of the belief in the efficacy of scientific method to solve the problems of ethics and politics was central to the late-twentieth-century revival of political theory in which he played so notable a part. Joshua Cherniss (Chapter 4) explicates Berlin's account of political judgment, and shows how this account contributed to, and was motivated by, Berlin's opposition to scientistic reductionism and abstraction in the study of, and programs of technocratic control in the ruling of, human beings and societies. Cherniss also explores Berlin's account of good political judgment in action – and his distinction between very different types of successful, or "great," political leaders – through an examination of Berlin's discussions of those individual leaders to whom he devoted extensive discussion: Winston Churchill, Franklin Roosevelt, and Chaim Weizmann.

Part III is titled "Berlin and the History of Ideas." Ryan Patrick Hanley (Chapter 5) traces the continuities between Berlin's work as an analytical philosopher and his later self-definition and work as a "historian of ideas," as well as Berlin's reasons for making this shift. Through an explication of Berlin's conception and practice of the history of ideas, Hanley argues that this shift was "a political decision – albeit in a very particular sense." Berlin's practice of the history of ideas was also connected to his political thought in that both reflected similar (though distinct) conceptions of human understanding: the "sense of reality" and "political judgment." While Berlin's approach to the history of ideas, on Hanley's account, reflected views on both the demands of historical understanding, and the purpose of studying past ideas and thinkers, he neither thought extensively about, nor programmatically stated, nor rigorously deployed, any particular "method," there is no "Berlinian" approach to the history of ideas or the interpretation of texts. Berlin's interpretations were, instead, guided by his personal, intuitive response to individual thinkers, with whom he engaged as partners in a conversation about political and moral issues. These personal responses, amplified by the ideological conflicts of his time, sometimes produced skewed or simplified presentations of thinkers – such as Rousseau or Hegel – whose ideas were far more complex and rich than Berlin allowed. But his sensitivity to the interplay of ideas and personal circumstances could also produce brilliant insights. And Berlin's accounts were, above all, never dull.

Berlin's political commitments certainly inflected his response to Marxism and to Russian thought – though he was never the dogmatic "Cold Warrior" that some readers have perceived. Aurelilan Craiutu (Chapter 6) shows how Berlin acknowledged Marx as a major interlocutor and epoch-making force in history and took a strong interest in the founders of Marxism (if not in the Marxist theorists of his own day). Yet Berlin was drawn in the end to Herzen, whom he saw as a better guide to the events of the twentieth century. Craiutu's chapter highlights some of the reasons why Berlin could never have been a Marxist, the most important being his commitment to pluralism and his opposition to determinism in history. Kathleen Parthé (Chapter 7) discusses Berlin's early exposure to the language, culture, and history of Russia, including some of the events of 1917, which he witnessed first-hand. This Russian background gave him "privileged access" to some of the leading personalities who shaped Russia's evolution and to the ideas they embodied. His two great loves were the Moscow intelligentsia circles of the 1840s and the Russian poets of the Soviet era, especially Akhmatova, Pasternak, and Mandelstam, and he celebrated their unconditional love for artistic and personal freedom with an eloquence that has not been surpassed. Berlin brought his deep knowledge of Russia's intellectual and cultural history to his study of the USSR, and of positive and negative liberty.

Steven Smith (Chapter 8) examines the role that the Enlightenment and Counter-Enlightenment play in Berlin's thought, how each holds up a mirror to the other. He argues that the Enlightenment and its romantic *doppelgänger* represent "two ends of a chain": the first focused on certain universal human values, the second on an appreciation of moral and political variety. Smith concludes that this tension – this unresolved and fruitful tension – provides the West with its peculiar vitality. Gina Gustavvson (Chapter 9) explores the role of European romanticism in Berlin's political theory. Berlin, she argues, believed that the romantic revolution could be summarized in terms of two main movements. One is the step from a monistic to a pluralistic understanding of values and human existence: the belief that values are created rather than found. The other shift consists in the ascent of a "new set of values" in the realms of moral and political life: the unbounded expression of the will, self-realization, sincerity, and dedication. She argues that the romantic insights into value pluralism inspired his own anti-utopian liberalism, but the celebration of the unfettered will was something he urged liberals to avoid, since it risks leading to the infamous inversion of liberty into tyranny.

Part IV is titled "Berlin and Politics: Liberalism, Nationalism, and Pluralism." Fania Oz-Salzberger (Chapter 10) develops Berlin's controversial ideas about nationalism, and especially his lifelong adherence to Zionism. Berlin's ideas about Zionism, Oz-Salzberger writes, grew out of his own family history. He thought of Zionism as a liberal and humane alternative to the "pathological" forms of European nationalism. Zionism was unique among nationalisms because, rather than foreclosing choice, it actually increased the scope of negative liberties. Henceforth, Jews could exercise a choice between country of birth or ancestral homeland, between diasporic Judaism and life in a Jewish state. Connecting Berlin's thought and political commitments in a different way, Ian Shapiro and Alicia Steinmetz (Chapter 11) frame Berlin's analysis of liberty within the context of the Cold War. Drawing on the wealth of new evidence that has become available due to the publication of Berlin's letters, they show that Berlin's defense of negative liberty was indeed rooted in the antipathy for the Soviet Union that he shared with such contemporaries as Friedrich Hayek, Karl Popper, and George Kennan. But Berlin's account was distinctive in that he also explored the underlying insecurities that rendered people susceptible to positive liberty's allure. This exploration left him skeptical that negative liberty would triumph once communism collapsed unless the sources of that insecurity could be addressed.

Alan Ryan (Chapter 12) also addresses Berlin's account of liberty, offering both a sketch of Berlin's famous essay "Two Concepts of Liberty," as well as his own dissent from Berlin's analysis. Ryan dissents from Berlin in holding that there is one correct, basically positive, conception of liberty, and finds Berlin's discussion of liberty to be in crucial respects insufficiently political. Ryan brings out the force of this latter criticism through a comparison of Berlin's essay with the liberalism of Benjamin Constant, arguing that Constant was more attentive to the institutional face of liberty and the practice of active citizenship to protect the private freedoms prized by liberals. He concludes that Berlin's articulation of liberalism is valuable in giving voice to an attractive and wise liberal sensibility and temper, but that this needs supplementing with a greater engagement with the concrete challenges of politics.

George Crowder argues that Berlin's idea of value pluralism – that basic human values are multiple, potentially conflicting, and "incommensurable" – has been one of his most controversial. Among several issues, an especially vexed question is whether Berlin's pluralism is consistent with his liberalism. Pluralism seems to point to a multiplicity of legitimate political choices of which liberalism is at best only one, not superior to any other. Crowder finds several responses to this problem in Berlin's writing, but he argues that none of these is wholly satisfactory. He concludes that stronger links between pluralism and liberalism will build on Berlin's work but go beyond it, and he sketches some possibilities along those lines. William Galston (Chapter 14) argues that Berlin offers a principled account of the relation between pluralism and liberalism. Berlinian pluralism provides a platform against both dogmatic libertarianism with its embrace of laissez-faire economics, and against radical relativists who see no way of resolving basic conflicts of values. For Berlin, value pluralism provides a "rational basis" for distinguishing between defensible and indefensible regimes. These regimes may not always be liberal, Galston argues, but "they will be broadly consistent with at least the minimal requirements" of liberalism.

The volume is sandwiched between two remarkable essays. One is a personal recollection of Berlin by the celebrated Israeli novelist Amos Oz (Chapter 1), who recalls his first meeting, as a budding 29-year-old author, with Berlin in 1969 at his home in Oxford. The other is a little-known lecture – "The Lessons of History" (Chapter 15) – by Berlin himself, dating from 1966.

As should be clear from the above, and from the chapters that follow, Berlin's work often inspired admiration rather than discipleship. He not only pointed to the inability of systematic theory to do justice to a complex reality, but followed through with this insight by adopting an unsystematic, even impressionistic approach. Berlin was incapable of the sorts of scholarly rigor (or pedantry) and theoretical sophistication (or obfuscation) at which others excelled; he was also uninterested, in principle, in delivering the final, conversation-ending verdict on the topics he discussed. Yet examination suggests that not only was Berlin a significant figure in the intellectual history of his time, his work continues to have much to tell contemporary readers – about liberty and liberalism, the Enlightenment and Romanticism, the perils of monism and wisdom of pluralism, as well as, more broadly, about the practice of political theory, history, and the social sciences, the ethical challenges confronting political actors, and the nature and importance of practical judgment for both politics and scholarship. One of Berlin's many friends – the Yale Slavic scholar Victor Erlich – summed it up admirably: Berlin, he concluded, "managed to tackle with incisiveness and subtlety some of the most vital moral–political themes of our time. No one has made a more eloquent and nuanced case for pluralism"; and few have written about the history of ideas with, as Erlich added, such "generosity of spirit" (Erlich 2006, 167–8). Berlin's work constitutes a sweeping and profound defense of political, ethical, and intellectual humanism in a virulently anti-humanistic age.

Perhaps most importantly, Berlin emphasized the significance of political judgment as the central virtue of political theory. As several of the chapters emphasize, Berlinian political theory was less about building architectonic systems based on justice, rights, or even liberty than about a careful attention to the conflict between even the most basic political goods. Politics, on his account, was not so much a war between good and evil as between rival goods, and a matter of choosing the lesser of two (or more) evils. This could be achieved not by developing a systematic theory of the good life or the good society, but through honing the art of political judgment. It was the art of practical rationality that distinguished not only the great statesmen of the past but also the great political thinkers, from Aristotle to Machiavelli to Tocqueville. We think it best to conclude by letting Berlin speak in his own voice:

The quality I am attempting to describe is that special understanding of public life (or for that matter private life) which successful statesmen have, whether they are wicked or virtuous – that which Bismarck had . . ., or Talleyrand or Franklin Roosevelt, or, for that matter, men such as Cavour or Disraeli, Gladstone or Ataturk, in common with the great psychological novelists, something which is conspicuously lacking in men of more purely theoretical genius such as Newton or Einstein or Russell, or even Freud.

What are we to call this kind of capacity? Practical wisdom, practical reason, perhaps, a sense of what will work and what will not. It is a capacity . . . for synthesis rather than analysis, for knowledge in the sense in which trainers know their animals, or parents their children, or conductors their orchestras, as opposed to that in which chemists know the contents of their test tubes, or mathematicians know the rules that their symbols obey. Those who lack this, whatever other qualities they may possess, no matter how clever, learned, imaginative, kind, noble, attractive, gifted in other ways they may be, are correctly regarded as politically inept. (SR 58–9)

PART I

BERLIN THE MAN

I

On Isaiah Berlin

Amos Oz

When I first came to Oxford, Sir Isaiah Berlin was 60 and a light unto the nations. I was a 29-year-old budding writer. I had a letter of reference. I telephoned, received an invitation to Headington House, showed up, and the luminary himself opened the door. As I took off my coat Berlin boomed, "Would you like to live forever?" It was very un-British of him, very Dostoevsky.

Astonished, but knowing I was being tested, I replied: yes, but only if both the head and the body are in good order, and only if those dearest to me would live forever too. Isaiah put his arm around my shoulder and said, "Welcome to my clan." He later added that he would really like to live forever, not because it was so good around here, certainly not, but because it is incessantly interesting.

In another conversation, Isaiah gifted me his distinction between an intellectual and an "*intelligent,*" member of the intelligentsia. The intellectual – mostly a western term – is a person comfortable with the fact that there are more questions in the world than answers. The *intelligent* – Russian, Slav, Jewish – is absolutely sure that he must tirelessly seek an answer to each question. This observation was no less important to me than the more famous (and partially overlapping) distinction between fox and hedgehog. In my mind, Isaiah Berlin was a full-fledged intellectual in the upstairs of his personality, and an Eastern European *intelligent* on the ground floor. This is why he so thoroughly understood both types.

Unlike many thinkers of the nineteenth and twentieth centuries, and perhaps akin to most eighteenth-century *philosophes*, Isaiah Berlin did not philosophize in a tight-lipped, teeth-grinding sort of way. He felt no need to pour his wrath onto others or onto the existing order, but meted out his ideas calmly, at times with a certain smile. A fox studying hedgehogs, at home in philosophy, poetry, history, and politics, he loved gossip, knew how to keep his distance, and always remained engaged. His sarcasm was biting, sometimes hurtful. But he never embarked on an obsessive crusade. His taste in ideas, like his taste in people, was diverse. But diversity, for Isaiah, never meant moral or aesthetic relativism.

He remained deeply suspicious of anyone pretending to teach us once and for all what is the good, and insisting on opening our eyes if we fail to choose it. I learned from him that the good is tricky to define, but anyone can sense evil. Truth is slippery, but even a child knows that a lie is a lie. Berlin also taught me that one could be national without being nationalist, and be patriotic without loathing or condescension for the patriotism of others. You can be a Zionist without ignoring Palestinian justice. There is a line between human compassion and sweeping "Christian" forgiveness. In politics, Thou Shalt Not Romanticize.

Then there was his understanding that the tragic and the comic are not two planets, as they teach us at school, but two windows on the same world. This insight, I think, came from Berlin's Jewish and Eastern European roots. In an age of utopias and dystopias, he subverted both. He was a skeptic and, unusually for skeptics, an optimist. A sober judge of mankind and, unusually for sober judges, a man of great *joie de vivre*. He not only insisted on personal freedom of choice, but redefined it; not only redefined it, but enjoyed it tremendously.

Oxford usually calmed down his Jewish–Slavic storminess, and covered it with the gown of amused skepticism, light-handedness, irony, and caution. He was particularly cautious about what he loved most: ideas. Michael Ignatieff quotes Berlin's erstwhile student Larry Siedentop: "He liked to venture out into the Romantic irrational by day, but always returned to the Enlightenment at nightfall."[1] This is marvelous. Had Isaiah Berlin lived here in Israel in our times, he would have advised us to steer clear of Jerusalem, of Jerusalemite ideas. Tel Aviv, kibbutz, synagogue, yes. Holy hubs and utter convictions, no.

Finally, Berlin's use of Kant's "crooked timber of humanity" speaks directly to the art of storytelling. If human nature could be chiseled or rectified, not a single novel would ever be written. Our natural crookedness is not only the seed of liberty, but also the sap of literature.

---

[1] Ignatieff 1998, 250.

2

The Life and Opinions of Isaiah Berlin

Joshua L. Cherniss and Henry Hardy

I

Isaiah Berlin ought never to have been born; nor, once born, ought he to have lived out his natural lifespan.

In the spring of 1907, in the Baltic seaport of Riga (at that time the capital of Livonia, a governorate of the Russian empire), Marie Berlin, née Volshonok, wife and first cousin of Mendel Berlin, a successful middle-class Russian Jewish timber-merchant, gave birth to a stillborn daughter, after a prolonged labour that nearly killed her. During her convalescence one of her doctors told her she would never have more children. Nevertheless, on 6 June 1909, she was successfully delivered of a son, named Isaiah ('Shaya' to his family and friends) after his childless adoptive great-grandfather. Isaiah's birth was difficult, too, and the forceps used to extract the baby left him with a permanently damaged left arm. Marie had no further offspring.

More than one narrow escape followed. In 1915 the family evaded Russian anti-Semitism in Riga, and the advancing Germans, by moving to the small town of Andreapol', halfway from Riga to Moscow, on one of Mendel's timber estates, and then in 1916 to Petrograd, as St Petersburg was then called; in 1920 they evaded the Bolsheviks by returning to Riga, then capital of a newly independent Latvia, as Latvian citizens. Berlin himself used to say that he would have blown his own brains out sooner than remain trapped in the USSR. The family's final emigration, to England in 1921, prompted by Latvian anti-Semitism, and made possible by an accident of business regarded by Mendel as 'an act of providence' (BI 301), saved them from extermination by the Nazis in Riga in 1941, when most of their near relations were murdered. By this slender thread hangs the long and happy life of one of the most arrestingly exceptional of twentieth-century British figures.

Before coming to England, Isaiah had been educated by Hebrew tutors. His parents were both directly descended from Shneur Zalman, founder of Lubavitch Hasidism, and they both, especially his mother, took their Jewish heritage very seriously. Isaiah was brought up to know the traditions of conservative Judaism, a culture with which he too identified strongly if unselfconsciously, despite an absence of religious belief. On arrival in England in early 1921, his family lived at addresses in Surbiton and environs while Isaiah attended a normal English preparatory school for the rest of that calendar year; and from January 1922 in Kensington, London, while he attended St Paul's School, at that time in Hammersmith.

In 1926 Mendel, still a citizen of Latvia, applied for British nationality for his family, observing, in words that might well also have been used by his son, that he had 'become sincerely attached to this country and its institutions'.[1] The application was not granted until October 1929, after a renewed application earlier that year, apparently timed to avoid Isaiah's call-up that September for military training with the Latvian Army – another happy escape. By this time Isaiah had for a year been an undergraduate scholar at Corpus Christi College in Oxford, where he took firsts in Greats (classics) in 1931 and in PPE (politics, philosophy and economics) in 1932.

Berlin used tellingly to endorse Karl Wolfskehl's remark that 'People are my landscape.'[2] This was so for Berlin in life, in thought, in every conceivable way. He was fascinated by the idiosyncrasies of persons, positive and negative – both for their own sake and for what they told him about human nature. Human nature, indeed, was always the focus of his attention: its capacity to display enormous individual and collective variety despite crucial constancies across time, place and culture; its strengths, its weaknesses, its quirks, its needs, its liability to great good and to hideous evil. His relations to other people were the centre of his life: 'the longer I live the more passionately convinced I become that personal relations are all in all'.[3] And his intense absorption in people manifested itself in a famous conversational ebullience, a pyrotechnic cascade of scintillating talk that captivated his audiences, singular or plural, making them feel preternaturally alive, gifted beyond their real abilities, the centre of his attention while it was upon them, privileged observers of an extraordinary intellect in full flood.

His unusual talents and disposition were apparent from his earliest years. He himself played down his prominence at St Paul's, but we can recognise the adult Berlin in the memories of his school contemporary Arthur Calder-Marshall:

Isaiah encompassed within his polymathia continents of gossip .... His talking in a way shocked me, because it was like playing an instrument – not in pursuit of truth or beauty or for anything except sheer pleasure – like a fountain.... He was, it seemed to me, more interested in thinking than in thought. ... At St Paul's Hammersmith there were

---

[1] Mendel Berlin, Memorial to the Home Secretary, 25 January 1926, National Archives (London), HO 144/10471 C575009.
[2] 'Menschen sind meine Landschaft', cited in Schuler 1940, 51. Cf. B 359 ('only the human landscape matters') and note 2, and E 451 ('the only landscape I like is human beings').
[3] Letter to Katharine Graham, 4 November 1974 (copy in IBLT archive).

corridors running hundreds of yards, down which Shaya, an adolescent peripatetic, would discourse below the busts of Plato, Socrates and Cicero .... I now recognise these as the fledgling flights of a supreme Kulturphilosoph.[4]

The same characteristics belong to Berlin's written work, much of which, at any rate in his maturity, began life by being dictated. He defined an intellectual as someone who wants ideas to be as interesting as possible, and by this criterion was himself a consummate member of this class. His natural medium was the essay, and his essays are seductive invitations to the life of the mind, making much professional academic writing seem pale and uninspired by comparison. His focus was always on what made the ideas he was explaining seem exciting, important, timeless, relevant to basic issues of human life – not on mere scholarly detail.

This intellectual personality had the defects of its merits. Although he deeply respected exact scholarship, he was not an adept practitioner of it. His interest in his topic was too headlong to allow for scrupulous checking of references and quotations – even of facts – and his texts required careful editorial attention if they were to be shorn of their most obvious shortcomings. He once said, with characteristic modesty and generosity, that the editing of his essays had 'turned what were mere belles-lettres into scholarship'.[5] Of course, some insights are more easily conveyed in belletrist mode, and Berlin's unacademic literary style could pay rich dividends. Nevertheless, his accounts of the history of ideas, even when provided with a scrupulous scholarly apparatus, often fall short of the standards of accuracy and methodological refinement set by later, more self-conscious and exacting, scholars. His essays are saved – and their continuing value is confirmed – by their intellectually enlivening effects upon the reader. Few writers have so vividly conveyed the 'lived-through' (e.g., CTH 61; A 15, 208; RT 20, 94; SR 269; TCE 430) and life-changing quality of thought, the drama and power of ideas – or their dangers. Those who do not understand these ideas, or their origins, can become their victims. Describing the twentieth century as 'the most terrible century of any in the history of the Western world', he wrote:

it is ideas which have done it all[6] – not, as some historians would like to believe, social conditions, the factors involved in social or political change or development, the relationship of economic classes, the effect of technology on culture. In my view it is ideas – Marxism, Fascism, National Socialism – ideas born in the heads of individuals who bound their spell upon a mass of credulous followers: it is these ideas in the end, and these individuals, who are responsible. (A 540–1)

Indeed, for all his temperamental ebullience, Berlin's was a mind haunted by fear – and galvanised by an appalled reaction to the horrors of his time, above all

---

[4] Arthur Calder-Marshall to Henry Hardy, 3 April [sc. May] 1991, IBLT archive.
[5] Quoted in Patricia Utechin to Henry Hardy, 12 December 1997 (copy in IBLT archive).
[6] An allusion to Voltaire's 'Les livres ont tout fait' ('Books did it all'): Voltaire 1877–85 [1771], x, 427.

the depredations of Nazism and Stalinism. The enduring focus of his intellectual activity was effectively decided by a formative early experience. Aged seven, he was out walking with his governess on Vasil'evsky Island in Petrograd during the 1917 February Revolution. He saw a tsarist policeman, white-faced with terror, being dragged off by a lynch mob, almost certainly to his death. From that moment he loathed Communism and all its works, and was inoculated against its attractions, which seduced many of his friends and contemporaries in the 1930s. More broadly, he always ascribed his lifelong horror of violence, especially when ideologically inspired, to this episode, which was one of the oldest and deepest sources of his mature liberalism. This too is surely one of the principal roots of his visceral antipathy to the conviction, wherever it may be found, that there is only one answer to the ultimate questions of life, that it has to be imposed on all who do not recognise it, and that any means to the remaking of reality in accordance with this final solution are justified, indeed demanded. Towards the end of his life, as his restatements of his views became more wintry and more concentrated, this abhorrence of totalitarian certainty stood out starkly as the core of his outlook. It is well summed up in a Shakespearean 'motto for a sober philosophy' dreamt by his friend J. L. Austin: 'Neither a be-all nor an end-all be.'[7]

The most important intellectual influence in Berlin's later youth came from his mentor Solomon Rachmilevich ('Rach', 1891–1953), a Russian Jewish polymath and Menshevik social democrat, born in Riga like Berlin, and living in exile in London, where he worked as a legal adviser to the timber trader Lionel Schalit. It was in the London house of the Schalits, friends and associates of the Berlins, that the teenage Isaiah met Rach. Rach became a close friend, and a 'dominant influence' (Berlin's term)[8] on the young Isaiah, who told his biographer that he was 'the first person who gave me a taste for ideas in general, interesting ideas *telles quelles*'.[9] Rach taught him about everything – about philosophy, especially Kant and the post-Kantians, about music, about physics and mathematics, about Karl Marx, about Russian literature. He was a tough critic who accused Berlin of intellectual laziness, enjoining him to show more 'political, moral and cerebral passion',[10] but recognising his ability 'to warm, to enlighten, and to whet the appetite',[11] and referring to 'the important work which you are predestined to write'.[12] He wrote to Berlin in English, but spoke to him in Russian, a crucial factor in preserving Berlin's fluency in the language, as well as his lifelong interest in Russian literature and culture. The appearance of 'Mr S. Rachmilevich' in the list of acknowledgements in Berlin's book on Marx (KM xxxv) is the tip of a very large iceberg, and it is no

---

[7] Austin 1958, 278 note 16: 'I dreamt a line that would make a motto for a sober philosophy: *Neither a be-all nor an end-all be.*'
[8] Interview of Berlin by Michael Ignatieff, 30 November 1988 (IBLT archive, MI Tape 6).
[9] Ibid.   [10] Rachmilevich to Berlin, 29 October 1935, MSB 104/191.
[11] Rachmilevich to Berlin, 14 November 1935, MSB 104/203.
[12] 26 May 1950, MSB 123/116.

exaggeration to say that, without Rach, Berlin's intellectual course – indeed, his whole life – might not have taken the direction it did.

Berlin's transition from undergraduate to professional academic was far from automatic. After his final exams in Oxford he was interviewed unsuccessfully for a post in journalism and joined the Middle Temple in London, where barristers were trained, with a view to a possible legal career. But Oxford reclaimed him when, in late 1932, he was appointed by R. H. Crossman to a lectureship in philosophy at New College. Shortly thereafter he was successful in the All Souls fellowship examination, becoming the first Jewish fellow of the College. He remained an Oxonian for the rest of his days. Despite his position at the heart of the British establishment, he always felt an outsider in his adoptive country, and it was primarily Oxford that gave him the sense of home he needed.

The next decisive event in his life, which again had repercussions for his whole career, was an invitation in 1933 from the editors of the Home University Library, a series of introductory books for the intelligent general reader, to write an account of the life and thought of Karl Marx. He was not the editors' first choice: they had already been turned down by Harold Laski, Sidney and Beatrice Webb (jointly), and Frank Pakenham (later Lord Longford). Berlin already knew a good deal about Marx from Rach, but he had read little of his work, and accepted the commission as the only way to force himself to read more by and about a man whose ideas he knew to be of world-historical importance. His wide reading for the book led him to Marx's predecessors, the *philosophes* of the eighteenth century, especially as filtered through the works of the Marxist theoretician Georgy Plekhanov. So it was that the intellectual storehouse on which he drew from that time onwards was built and furnished.

While at All Souls Berlin also became the centre of a group of brilliant young philosophers, including A. J. Ayer and J. L. Austin, who met regularly in his rooms. Ayer defended the then novel programme of logical positivism; Berlin and Austin subjected it to probing criticism; the approach to philosophical problems that emerged came to be known as 'Oxford philosophy', and was later the focus of philosophical activity in the University.

While he played his part in the undoing of logical positivism, Berlin continued to work on Marx, finishing the book – still in print today, in its fifth edition – in 1938. (It was published the following year, shortly before the outbreak of war.) He then accepted a philosophy fellowship at New College, resigning his All Souls fellowship a year before its expiry. When war came, his damaged arm barred him from military service, and his foreign origins from an administrative post in London, and he continued teaching. But in the summer of 1940 a bizarre development took him to the USA. His friend Guy Burgess, who was working for the British intelligence organisation MI5 (but also, unbeknownst to Berlin, as a Soviet spy), offered him the chance to travel with him to Moscow as a press officer at the British Embassy. They set off via the

USA, but soon after they arrived Burgess was recalled in mysterious circumstances, and Berlin was told his services were no longer required in Moscow. In due course Berlin was given work in New York for the Ministry of Information, summarising American press reports on the war, as part of the task of persuading the USA to abandon its neutrality. After Pearl Harbor achieved this objective in December 1941, Berlin was moved to the British Embassy in Washington to run the Political Survey Section there, remaining in post until April 1946. He drafted the weekly reports sent to London in diplomatic pouches under the name of the British Ambassador, which impressed and amused Winston Churchill, among others. This led to the famous episode – often recounted by Berlin – in which Churchill, hearing from his wife that Irving Berlin was visiting from America, insisted on meeting him. Churchill spent a bewildering, increasingly frustrating lunch with his guest, realising only afterwards his confusion of Irving with Isaiah – and that he had been conversing with the American author of *White Christmas*.

During these years in the States he made a number of close and lifelong friends, including leading New Dealers such as Benjamin Cohen and Edward Prichard; intellectuals such as the young, politically engaged historian Arthur Schlesinger, Jr; journalists and publishers such as Joseph Alsop and Philip and Katherine Graham of the *Washington Post*; and foreign service officers such as George Kennan and Charles Bohlen. He returned regularly to see them, often in association with visiting professorships.

In 1945 Berlin was seconded to the British Embassy in Moscow to report on post-war relations with the Soviet Union. He was in Russia from mid September 1945 to early January 1946, meeting many Russian writers, including Boris Pasternak. In November he visited Leningrad (as it then was), and paid a famous night-long but chaste visit – and thereafter at least one further visit, possibly several – to the poet Anna Akhmatova, forming a lasting bond with her which she invested with tremendous mystical significance. The Russian intelligentsia of the nineteenth and early twentieth centuries, whether represented by Marxists such as Plekhanov, mystics such as Aleksandr Blok, or Westernisers such as Herzen and Turgenev, had long evoked a sympathetic response in Berlin. But his post-war encounters with Akhmatova, Pasternak and others transformed this sympathy into a sense of personal solidarity with the intelligentsia of his native land, which inspired and informed a series of deeply felt essays on their work (eventually collected as *Russian Thinkers* in 1978), and inflected his articulation of liberalism, giving it a distinctive tone and emphasis.

His witnessing of the effects of Stalinism also reinforced his staunch anticommunism. He helped to formulate the idea, developed by American friends such as Bohlen and Schlesinger, of the 'Non-Communist Left' (F 522; E 28, 134; UD 118). He kept direct political agitation at arm's length – not least because he feared the impact that any anti-Soviet pronouncements might have on those he had met in Moscow and Leningrad, and on his remaining family in the Soviet Union. Indeed, an uncle was arrested and interrogated by the KGB as a result of Berlin's visit to the USSR, and died of a heart attack when he later saw one of his torturers on the street. Nevertheless, Berlin was central to the international community of anticommunist intellectuals that formed around the Congress for Cultural Freedom, and the various publications and conferences it funded, including *Encounter* (co-edited for many years by his lifelong friend, the ex-Communist poet Stephen Spender), in which many of his essays on the nineteenth-century Russian intelligentsia first appeared.

In 1944, on a transatlantic flight in a wartime bomber, Berlin had, according to his later account, undergone a final and definitive Damascene conversion from philosophy to the history of ideas, following a sobering conversation with the US logician H. M. Sheffer that undermined his faith in philosophy as a route to knowledge. He decided he wanted to know more at the end of his life than at the beginning, and, in the wake of his work on Marx, he increasingly transferred his allegiance to this new discipline, not much practised in Oxford at the time. He continued to publish philosophical work of importance until at least 1950, when he returned to All Souls as a research fellow, but his heart was no longer in a field which, he felt, was incapable of cumulative progress, or of addressing the vital issues of social and political morality which had preoccupied the Russian intelligentsia, and increasingly pressed on Berlin. His study of Marx, the ideological debates of the 1930s, and the excitement of observing American politics at close hand, as well as the horrors of the war, his brush with Stalinism, and the moral resilience of its surviving victims, had gradually transformed someone who had previously described himself as 'not a very political thinker',[13] preparing him to become one of the most distinctive and influential proponents of liberalism in his time.

Among the first fruits of Berlin's deep engagement with Russian thought was an essay, originally published in an academic journal in 1951, which became better known two years later, in an expanded form, as *The Hedgehog and the Fox*, taking its new title from a line by the Greek poet Archilochus: 'The fox knows many things, but the hedgehog knows one big thing.'[14] In the guise of a study of Tolstoy's view of history, Berlin introduced one of the major themes, and antinomies, in his thought, contrasting, in effect, monistic and pluralistic approaches to life. Tolstoy, he maintained, aspired to the monistic vision of the 'hedgehog', who 'knows one big thing', while being constitutionally unable to forswear his naturally vulpine sensitivity to plurality. Much of Berlin's work can be seen as addressed to a battle between the one and the many in the sphere of the intellect, and there is never any doubt where his own sympathies lie. This emerges canonically in his 1958 inaugural lecture as an Oxford professor, 'Two

---

[13] Berlin to Mendel Berlin, autumn 1935 (F+).
[14] Archilochus fragment 201 in West 1989. Cf. HF 1/2. The essay is also in RT and PSM.

Concepts of Liberty',[15] especially in the section entitled 'The One and the Many', though anticipations of it can be found as far back as his lectures of the 1930s, and in essays from 'Democracy, Communism and the Individual' (1949, published in POI) to *Historical Inevitability* (1954, republished in L).

The Hedgehog and the Fox appeared at the beginning of a golden age for Berlin, which spanned, roughly, the twenty-five years from 1950 until his official retirement from Oxford University in 1975. These were the years when the major essays in political theory, the philosophy of history and the history of ideas for which he is best known were published. It is not an incidental fact that on 7 February 1956, after a four-year courtship, he became the third husband of the beautiful, wealthy, aristocratic French Jewess Aline Halban, née de Gunzbourg, and stepfather to her three sons by her two former marriages. Berlin's marriage, with its base in an elegant mansion in Oxford, was the foundation stone of his life from that day forward.

It was in 1957 that he became Oxford's Chichele Professor of Social and Political Theory, and he was knighted in the same year. The pressure that he felt, as a professor whose chair bore that title, to expound positive political doctrines of his own increasingly weighed on Berlin, whose work centred on strictly political and social issues only for a relatively short time; in the 1960s and 1970s his attention became more exclusively focused on the history of ideas, understood as embracing all the many facets of high culture – philosophy, literature, music, art – as well as political theory and social studies.

It was therefore with some relief that Berlin resigned his professorship and, in 1966, took office as founding President of Oxford's Wolfson College, a new college for graduates, especially in the sciences, whose growth and development he regarded as 'the greatest success story of our time' ('The Pursuit of the Ideal', CTH 1), even though he himself had little scientific expertise. For Berlin, this move was an expression of gratitude to Oxford for all it had done for him, as well as a lifeline thrown to those holders of university posts who, lacking fellowships at undergraduate colleges, had been relegated to the margins of university life; it also gave rein to a previously untapped talent for fundraising, and to his skill in political intrigue. In 1971 he was appointed to the British monarch's extremely select Order of Merit, and in 1974 elected President of the British Academy (a four-year term), the pinnacle of his country's academic achievement in the humanities. His Presidency of Wolfson ended on the Ides of March, 1975.

Public recognition, sometimes fretfully borne (he was initially inclined to reject his knighthood, accepting it only under pressure from his mother, and after her death declined the offer of a peerage), buoyed Berlin up through a difficult period when his brand of moderate, gradualist and resolutely anti-Marxist liberalism came under sharp attack from the young radicals of the 1960s – attacks whose echoes are still heard today. The republication of his

---

[15] In L and PSM; 'The One and the Many' is section VIII.

scattered essays (which brought his value pluralism, of which more below, to centre stage), combined with the vindication, in the late 1980s and 1990s, of his rejection of Soviet Communism and of his insistence on the continuing power of nationalism, led to a revival of interest in, and a degree of adulation for, Berlin in the final decades of his life – a period which also saw him receive the Jerusalem, Erasmus, Agnelli and Lippincott Prizes.

During his golden quarter-century the publications flooded out. His final purely philosophical papers settled accounts with logical positivism, rejecting its levelling, reductionist, somewhat authoritarian account of language in favour of greater sensitivity to the variety and messiness of human experience, and the richness and unsystematic nature of human responses to that experience. Despite his own account of the discontinuity between his work as a philosopher and the more historical work that followed, the same intellectual personality, with the same or related preoccupations, can also be discerned in his later work: an opposition to oversimplification (or Procrusteanism, to borrow a favourite, and appropriately gruesome, classical allusion of his), a defence of variousness and complexity, and an understanding but critical attitude towards the desire for certainty and symmetry that drives rationalist and reductionist projects.[16]

II

It is impossible within the present compass to do justice to all Berlin's multifarious writings. He wrote about a wide range of thinkers – Russian, German, Italian, French, British – sensitive to the uniqueness of each, but also mining their writings for perceptions of more general human application. Personal uniqueness was also, perhaps more, to the fore in his series of 'personal impressions'[17] of his contemporaries, from Churchill to Akhmatova, which might indeed be regarded as case studies in individual difference, but which also bring to the table insights from which anyone may profit. Under both these headings his astonishing gifts of imaginative identification are given full rein, to the point where the boundary between Berlin and his subject becomes permeable, leaving us unsure whether we are being addressed by one or the other or both. This is especially true of his depictions of the radical Russian thinker Alexander Herzen, perhaps his greatest hero, and a figure with whom he clearly had much in common. Herzen unleashed

a rapid torrent of descriptive sentences, fresh, lucid, direct, interspersed with vivid and never irrelevant digressions, variations on the same theme in many keys, ... quotations real and imaginary, verbal inventions, ... mordant personal observations and cascades of vivid images ..., which, so far from either tiring or distracting the reader by their

[16] Cf. Choi, Chapter 3 in this volume.
[17] Berlin to Henry Hardy, 2 October 1978: 'I have thought of a better title for vol. 4 [of *Selected Writings*] than any of the previous ones: *Personal Impressions*.' Hardy 2018, 79.

virtuosity, add to the force and swiftness of the narrative. The effect is one of spontaneous improvisation: exhilarating conversation by an intellectually gay and exceptionally clever and honest man endowed with singular powers of observation and expression.[18]

Berlin might well have been describing himself. Some have been less complimentary than others about this ventriloquistic talent, arguing that it distorts the figures being inhabited. As Ernest Gellner put it: 'Machiavelli, Vico, Herder, Tolstoy all ... come out looking suspiciously alike – Niccolò Berlini, Giambattista Berlino, Johann Gottfried Berliner and Lev Nicolaevich Berlinov.'[19] There is something in this.

Berlin's intellectual energies were not devoted solely to the history of ideas. Calder-Marshall was right: he was a true *Kulturphilosoph*, and his writings reflect the breadth of his interests. He was passionate, and extremely knowledgeable, about music, and wrote a number of musical essays and reviews, from his undergraduate years onwards, as well as serving on the board of London's Royal Opera House for many years. He translated three works by Ivan Turgenev; surveyed the progress of world culture for the *Encyclopaedia Britannica* in three successive years (1950–2); reviewed many books; and wrote about the Soviet Union, about Zionism and Israel, about political ideas in the twentieth century, historical inevitability, political liberty, equality, European unity, why history is not a science, why philosophy and political theory are necessary, whether knowledge is bound to liberate, Giambattista Vico's concept of knowledge, J. G. Herder's relationship with the Enlightenment, Verdi's 'naivety', Hume's and Kant's unwitting influences on German anti-rationalism, the tortured responses of Disraeli and Marx to their Jewish roots, Machiavelli's proto-pluralism, Turgenev's indecisiveness, why nationalism does not die, the Counter-Enlightenment (a term Berlin was responsible for popularising), romanticism (a never-to-be-completed study of which occupied his later years), utopianism, Marxist and non-Marxist socialism, the purposes of education, and, of course, the Russian intelligentsia. This list is far from complete, but perhaps begins to convey the variety of his subject matter. The limitations of his knowledge of science probably make the term 'Renaissance man' inapplicable, but a humanist polymath of wide and voracious reading he most certainly was. He also talked volubly on radio and television, becoming known by that means to a wide highbrow public in his heyday.

---

[18] Compare Tolstoy's equally apt description of Herzen as reported by Petr Alekseevich Sergeenko: 'a not very large, plump little man, who generated electric energy. "Lively, responsive, intelligent, interesting," Lev Nikolaevich explained ..., "Herzen at once began talking to me as if we had known each other for a long time. I found his personality enchanting ... I have never met a more attractive man. He stands head and shoulders above all the politicians of his own and of our time."' Sergeenko 1911, 13–14.

[19] Gellner 1995, 56.

One strong theme does emerge from this cornucopia, and that is his lasting concern with the critics of the Enlightenment. He saw himself as fundamentally on the side of the Enlightenment and its campaign against 'dark mysteries and grotesque fairy tales (the fruit of indolence, blindness and deliberate chicanery) which went by the names of theology, metaphysics and other brands of concealed dogma or superstition, with which unscrupulous knaves had for so long befuddled the stupid and benighted multitudes whom they murdered, enslaved, oppressed and exploited' (AE 113–14). He wrote: 'The intellectual power, honesty, lucidity, courage and disinterested love of the truth of the most gifted thinkers of the eighteenth century remain to this day without parallel. Their age is one of the best and most hopeful episodes in the life of mankind' (AE 29; POI 62). But he was more fascinated by its enemies, who seemed to him to identify crucial weak spots in its armour, to provide ammunition against its more extreme manifestations, to stand up for the individual and the particular, what Kipling had called the 'toad beneath the harrow',[20] against the *grands simplificateurs*[21] – among whom he included those champions and heirs of the Enlightenment who sought to apply the methods of the natural sciences to all human knowledge and experience. This unifying leitmotif lies behind a number of his books, including *Vico and Herder, Against the Current, The Crooked Timber of Humanity, The Magus of the North* (a study of the obscure German pietist J. G. Hamann, who for Berlin was the first and most uncompromising foe of all that the Enlightenment stood for), and his 1965 Mellon Lectures, *The Roots of Romanticism*. Some key soldiers in his Counter-Enlightenment army have already been named, but we should add Joseph de Maistre and Georges Sorel – and the many romantic thinkers whose decisive break with the monistic tradition of Western thought Berlin examines in *The Roots of Romanticism* and elsewhere.

III

No one, to our knowledge, has ever talked of 'Berlinism'. Indeed, there is something deeply paradoxical in the idea of such a label when applied to the thought of a man who abhorred over-simple solutions, did not seek (indeed longed not to have) disciples, and was never a flag-waver for any kind of straightforward blueprint for humanity. He often quoted Kant: 'Out of the crooked timber of humanity no straight thing was ever made.'[22] He was an advocate of complexity, nuance, nice distinctions, untidiness, unique individuality, which made him a natural opponent of all the usual '-isms'. But

---

[20] TCE 433: the epigraph to Rudyard Kipling's poem 'Pagett, MP' (1886) begins 'The Toad beneath the Harrow knows / Exactly where each tooth-point goes.' Kipling 1902, 43.
[21] The phrase 'grand simplificateur' and the word 'simplificateur' itself were coined by Sainte-Beuve in 1852 to describe Benjamin Franklin: Sainte-Beuve 1853, 142.
[22] Kant 1912 [1784], 23 line 22.

it would be a mistake to conclude from this that he offered no message, no vision of or interpretative framework for the world which might be taken up by others. Any receptive reader of his work will become aware of a number of linked attitudes which, taken together, characterise his outlook, and are related in a non-random fashion. He was a peerless exemplar of a recognisable approach to life, an identifiable way of being human.

If there is a single existing label that can be applied to this congeries of beliefs, it might be 'humanism', but this is a promiscuous term, 'a label on too many bottles' (to use an image of Berlin's own),[23] and needs to be given a more precise focus. Berlin's thought resists summary, and any second-hand account must fall woefully short of his own remarkable way with words. As his friend Noel Annan observed, 'He will always use two words where one will not do' (PI 451). But the attempt can be made.

Essential to Berlin's humanism is the idea that human beings are by nature free to choose their own path through life. Freedom of choice, which he sometimes calls 'basic freedom' (A 345, 518; POI 222) is, for Berlin, a central characteristic of the human condition (and built into the language in which we talk about human beings). To the extent that it is thwarted or narrowed, humanity is denied and degraded. It is by deploying this creative freedom that we construct our identities, which are partially inherited or bestowed, but which can always, within limits, be freely adapted. Freedom of the will, and the political freedom that depends on it, are the principal subjects of the essays from the 1950s that are collected in the volume he regarded as his most important, *Four Essays on Liberty* (1969), now absorbed into the expanded collection *Liberty* (2002).

Political freedom has many aspects, chief among which are the 'negative' freedom of not being interfered with or blocked by other human beings, and the 'positive' freedom to be in charge of or make something of ourselves, to pursue positive goals. For Berlin, both 'negative' and 'positive' liberty are vital – if also sometimes treacherous – human ideals, deriving much of their value from their contribution to nurturing the basic human freedom to make choices between different actions or beliefs, different courses and styles of life. These two kinds of freedom are the subject of 'Two Concepts of Liberty'. In this powerful tract Berlin inveighs against the tendency of totalitarian thinkers to commit the 'monstrous impersonation' (FIB 197; L 180; PSM 205) of making positive liberty an instrument of enslavement, by positing an alleged collective 'real self' whose expert representatives – namely themselves – know better than we do ourselves, individually, what our proper goals should be. Here, and always, Berlin defends the individual as the true locus of moral decision and activity as against authoritarian collectives that attempt to assume the role of moral guide (see L 179ff). The main unspoken example that drives the argument is Soviet Communism (though Berlin was later at pains to insist that he had not been

---

[23] Ignatieff 1992. Berlin applied the metaphor to the word 'liberal'.

thinking of Communism alone, but of the various dictatorships and totalitarian movements that overshadowed much of Europe during his youth),[24] and it is this lecture above all, together with 'Historical Inevitability', that gave Berlin a reputation as a Cold War thinker, though his message is of far wider import.

Though Berlin fully accepts the importance of positive liberty, the stress in his inaugural is on the defence of negative liberty in politics, and implicitly of the liberalism of which it is the fundamental component. Negative freedom is a *political* value; but it is valuable, in part, in affording individuals protection *against* the demands of political life, against pressures towards social usefulness and civic virtue which may bear down too heavily.[25] Berlin's liberalism is marked by a strong sense of the importance of safeguarding a private sphere in which those who cannot attain, or do not wish to pursue, recognition, success or satisfaction in public, can live privately with dignity and pursue their own most cherished goals. This may be seen as a rationalisation of luxuries for, and irresponsibility by, the privileged and the negligent; or, alternatively, as the defence of a basic level of decent existence for the marginalised, the cowed, and those whom Judith Shklar, Berlin's fellow Riga-born Jew – reflecting the same experiences that had shaped Berlin's outlook – called 'permanent minorities'. In Berlin's liberalism, an ebullient embrace of variety and expressiveness always sat side by side with a sober awareness of danger and suffering akin to that recognised by Shklar's 'liberalism of fear'.[26]

Closely related to Berlin's championing of negative liberty, albeit in contested ways that have led to a flood of controversy, is his recognition that the ultimate values that govern human behaviour and aspiration are irreducibly multiple. That is, they each have their own distinctive character which cannot be cashed out or translated into the terms of other values, still less a single super-value such as utility or pleasure, let alone a deontic principle such as dignity or autonomy. This is what Berlin called 'pluralism' (L 216–17 etc.), and what subsequent writers tend to refer to as 'value pluralism'. His exposition of this view, opposed as it is, for him, to centuries of philosophical searching for monist coherence, has given us some of Berlin's most resounding, indeed moving, sentences:

Everything is what it is: liberty is liberty, not equality or fairness or justice or culture, or human happiness or a quiet conscience. (L 172)

The world that we encounter in ordinary experience is one in which we are faced with choices between ends equally ultimate, and claims equally absolute, the realisation of some of which must inevitably involve the sacrifice of others. (L 213)

If, as I believe, the ends of men are many, and not all of them are in principle compatible with each other, then the possibility of conflict – and of tragedy – can never wholly be

---

[24] See letter to Frederick Rosen, 17 July 1991, A 423–8 at 425.
[25] Cf. Ryan, Chapter 12 in this volume, and Rosenblum 1987, 74–6.   [26] Shklar 1964, 224.

eliminated from human life, either personal or social. The necessity of choosing between absolute claims is then an inescapable characteristic of the human condition. (L 214)

When ends or values come into conflict, there is sometimes no uniquely right way to resolve the conflict between them. This applies not only within and between the separate values of an individual or group, including those that are common to all humanity, but also to the constellations of value that we call cultures, yielding 'cultural pluralism' (CTH 62, 68; A 59, 415), versions of which Berlin encountered especially in the writings of Vico and Herder. In 'Two Concepts', and in later summaries of his views, the emphasis is on conflicts between values within an individual breast; in Berlin's work in the history of ideas it is cultural pluralism that comes to the fore; but the pluralist logic is similar. Different individuals, groups, cultures, nations will make different decisions, often in line with their existing value-structures and attitudes, and one decision cannot necessarily be gainsaid by those who make another. This predicament gives our freedom to choose a special importance: we deploy our free will to form our own moral personalities, on our own recognisance, taking responsibility for becoming the people we are.

The centrality of choice is a link, too, to another basic tenet of Berlin's humanism: his defence of a specifically and uniquely humanistic form of knowledge or understanding, and, linked to this, of the autonomy and importance of the humanities. Human beings are not to be understood or treated only from outside, by analogy with the objects of the natural sciences such as trees and rocks, or even other animals, but also from inside, as beings with purposes and forms of understanding that cannot be left out of account in the explanation of their lives. This is humanism as anti-scientism, a rejection, especially in the realm of human behaviour, of the view that scientific explanation must apply everywhere. Since we are humans ourselves, we have access to a source of knowledge radically different from that of the scientist, namely imaginative empathy, and only if we deploy this capacity to its fullest degree will we have a chance of making sense of what other humans are and do. Humans are indeed objects in the world, subject to the same natural laws as any physical objects, but that is only part of the story, and it is the other, distinctive, part that matters most. It is this inside view, as Vico taught, that makes our internal understanding of humanity deeper than our external knowledge of the natural world. And the inner world that it reveals is what makes us most importantly different from one another. Human knowledge and the human sciences are, as the neo-Kantian German philosophers who influenced the young Berlin had insisted, 'idiographic', concerned with understanding the full, unrepeatable uniqueness of individuals and events, and not with subsuming individuals and events under general, universal, predictive laws, as the natural sciences do.[27] The tendency of contemporary social science to ape

---

[27] Windelband 1894. See also Bambach 1995, 57–81, 83–102; Beiser 2011, 365–441; Beiser 2014, 133–57.

natural science in this regard, which Berlin deeply deprecated, expressed an antagonism, and posed a threat, to freedom: for human freedom was bound up with the unpredictability of human actions, the irregularity of human character and conduct.

The search for uniformity, predictability and order also runs counter to central features of human self-understanding. Berlin certainly believed in a central core of characteristics, needs, aspirations, limitations and potentialities shared by all humanity, and this core plays an important role in his thought, providing standards against which all human behaviour can be evaluated, and defining the boundaries of what can count as a human value – the 'human horizon', as he called it (CTH 12, 314, 316; PSM 10). However, far from being homogeneous or seeking homogeneity, humans define themselves to a large extent by difference. This is the essence not only of individual identity, but also of the cultural belonging alluded to above. The fact of value pluralism opens the way to the construction of a wide variety of collective identities, and it is partly in terms of these identities that we tether ourselves in the world. For Berlin, the need to belong to a culturally differentiated group of persons with whom one feels at home is as basic in human nature as the need for food, drink, shelter and sexual fulfilment. If all the cultures of the world were run together into one, Berlin said, 'this would not be one universal culture, but the death of culture'.[28] This may be a contestable thesis, but it is certainly Berlin's.

Cultural membership does not mean that individuals cannot define the meaning and shape of their lives for themselves. On the contrary, cultural variety can furnish a richer range of resources for unpredictable individual self-fashioning – as well as offering a haven for those individuals who feel vulnerable in the face of freedom, which, Berlin always insisted, though precious, was 'not at all cosy' (E 656). The existence – and protection – of a variety of cultures, nations, and human associations was valuable not only in promoting variety, but in rendering (as he wrote of the creation of the State of Israel) 'the greatest service that any human institution can perform for individuals', securing their 'right to choose as individuals how they shall live – the basic freedom of choice, the right to live or perish, go to the good or the bad in one's own way, without which life is a form of slavery' (POI 222).[29]

In his own case there was a tripartite cultural belonging: Russian, British and Jewish. The last of these went together with an unwavering devotion to the Zionist cause, though coupled with disappointment at the behaviour of successive Israeli governments, especially towards the Arab minority in Israel. For Berlin, the foundation of the modern state of Israel was one of the clearest refutations of historical determinism, as well as a demonstration of the

---

[28] Gardels 1991, 10.
[29] Berlin's views on nationalism, and the ambiguities both of these views in themselves and of their relationship to pluralism, are explored by Crowder (Chapter 13), Oz-Salzberger (Chapter 10), and Galston (Chapter 14) in this volume.

effectiveness of great men in history – in this case of Israel's first president, his friend Chaim Weizmann. For this reason, and because it offered individual Jews the choice between living as members of a *sui generis* minority in the diaspora and living as members of a majority culture in Israel (and, not least, because it offered a refuge from persecution), Berlin celebrated the founding of the Israeli state. But he resisted repeated calls to emigrate to Israel himself: his life was in Britain, above all in Oxford. Neither did his appreciation of the need for, and accomplishments of, Israel blind him to Israel's shortcomings – such as the use of terrorism in establishing the Jewish state, the growing power and increasing militancy of its ultra-Orthodox communities, and, above all, successive Israeli governments' expansionist policies and mistreatment of Israel's Arab minority. Always a liberal, left-wing Zionist, Berlin became increasingly critical and worried about Israel's policies under the governments of Menachem Begin and Yitzhak Shamir, and lent his support to organisations promoting peace and human rights in Israel, especially Peace Now.

Related to freedom of choice and anti-scientism is Berlin's strong anti-managerialism. Managerialism is a scientistic approach to human society, with roots in the Enlightenment, that tries to regiment and control behaviour by a series of manipulative techniques which downgrade or ignore human freedom, autonomy and variety. Taken to its extreme it becomes the ruthless control of whole societies by the fear, ideological propaganda and brainwashing notoriously perpetrated by Communism, and caricatured in Orwell's *1984*. But it is also present in insidious ways even in less totalitarian societies, in the form of repressively homogenising social planning and organisation, against which Berlin felt it a vital task of his time to warn:

> What the age calls for is not … more faith, or stronger leadership, or more scientific organisation. Rather is it the opposite – less Messianic ardour, more enlightened scepticism, more toleration of idiosyncrasies, more frequent ad hoc measures to achieve aims in a foreseeable future, more room for the attainment of their personal ends by individuals and by minorities whose tastes and beliefs find (whether rightly or wrongly must not matter) little response among the majority. What is required is a less mechanical, less fanatical application of general principles, however rational or righteous, a more cautious and less arrogantly self-confident application of accepted, scientifically tested, general solutions to unexamined individual cases. … Since no solution can be guaranteed against error, no disposition is final. And therefore a loose texture and toleration of a minimum of inefficiency, even a degree of indulgence in idle talk, idle curiosity, aimless pursuit of this or that without authorisation … will always be worth more than the neatest and most delicately fashioned imposed pattern. (L 92–3)

Such attacks, combined with his championing of 'negative' liberty and critique of 'positive' liberty (clarified and moderated in the important introduction he wrote for the publication of *Four Essays on Liberty* in 1969), have led to the perception by many of Berlin as a champion of laissez-faire and the minimalist state. This was not his position. As a young man he had been identified with the left at Oxford; then and after the war he was a supporter of the Labour Party.

If he was too much of a liberal ever fully to embrace social democracy, he was too committed to social equality and the alleviation of material misery – and too sceptical of the market as a panacea – ever to embrace the new right. Though he described himself as 'extreme left of the right, extreme right of the left' (A 378), Berlin's sympathy for the Russian populists and his lifelong admiration for Herzen suggest that his emotional affinities were more with the left – as does his declaration, later in life, that he admired and would follow the guidance of his contemporary James Meade, a Keynesian economist who advocated a fusion of liberalism and socialism that would ensure, among other things, a more egalitarian distribution of property through government intervention, including a guaranteed basic income for all. To the end of his life, Berlin remained an admirer of Roosevelt's New Deal and Attlee's post-war Welfare State as the most hopeful and humane political achievements of his time.

Above all, Berlinian humanism is an outlook, a cast of mind and temper, which appreciates and prioritises humanity, understood in two quite distinct but related senses. In one sense, 'humanity' refers to the mass of actual, unique, complicated human beings, as they have lived, struggled and created over the course of history. This is what 'the crooked timber of humanity' is about. Berlin believed the study and understanding of this humanity, in all its facets, to be among the most absorbing and worthwhile of human activities; it was certainly his own most vital preoccupation. And this was expressed by an interest in and appreciation of individuals that eschewed and defied formulae and abstractions – even the formulae and abstractions of a thinner, blunter 'humanitarianism'. In its second sense, 'humanity' refers to sensitivity to human beings in all their uniqueness and difficulty, recognition of their dignity and vulnerability, a compassionate but clear-eyed perception of their striving and frailty – and horror and indignation at their mistreatment by one another. Having humanity, in this sense, is what makes one a *humane* person. Berlin himself was gifted with it, in a way in which few great thinkers are. His was not the most systematic or fully worked out interpretation of politics and of human values of his time – but it was, to echo his own phrase, among the truest and most humane.

IV

All these aspects of 'Berlinism' raise complex questions, and have generated reams of discussion, reflected in and enriched by the subsequent discussions in this volume. But it is hardly surprising that the search for an overall understanding of what humanity amounts to should be a permanent, open-ended quest. Here it has been possible only to gesture at some of the main landmarks in Berlin's own reports from the front line.

These reports are rich and various and detailed, and repay careful study. It was only during Berlin's retirement that it became fully apparent how extensive and wide-ranging his explorations had been. He was a reluctant publisher, and for much of his life enjoyed a false reputation for writing little. When Berlin was appointed to the Order of Merit, his friend Maurice Bowra wrote: 'Though like Our Lord and Socrates he does not publish much, he thinks and says a great deal and has had an enormous influence on our times.'[30] In fact he had published a great deal, as we have seen, but often in obscure places, and it was not until the appearance of a substantial series of thematic collections of his essays, the first of which appeared in his sixtieth year, that a true measure of his achievement could be taken. He had also written or said much that he had not published at all, and the best of this material was included in further volumes that appeared after his death, as did an authorised biography by Michael Ignatieff that drew on extensive conversations with its subject, and a generous four-volume selection of his revealing, virtuoso letters.

Now at last the whole edifice is before us, making possible the kind of overall assessment and explication that this volume attempts. If we are right, the man in question was truly exceptional, one of a kind, a gift to humanity; with faults, certainly, like any member of his species, and far from being all things to all men, but a worthy bearer of the prophetic name given him by his parents in Riga in 1909.

---

[30] Maurice Bowra to Noel Annan quoted in Annan 1971, 53.

PART II

BERLIN ON PHILOSOPHY, THE HUMAN
SCIENCES, AND POLITICAL THEORY

3

Berlin, Analytic Philosophy, and the Revival of Political Philosophy

Naomi Choi

INTRODUCTION

The importance of Isaiah Berlin in the twentieth century goes without saying. The significance of his contributions to intellectual history and political theory – for example, on the antagonism between Enlightenment and "Counter-Enlightenment" thinking, on the idea of liberty – and his advocacy of liberal values in conjunction with value pluralism is taken for granted. Until recently, it was commonplace for scholars to focus exclusively on Berlin's postwar writings on these topics. If his earlier work on analytic philosophy was mentioned at all, it was often glossed as a separate preoccupation of his before he settled into his role as political theorist and historian of ideas. Since Berlin's death in 1997 and the lifting of his personal injunction against the publication of his unrevised writings during his lifetime,[1] his full-time editor, Henry Hardy, has worked to bring the full corpus of his works to press, dramatically improving our ability to appreciate and assess his contributions. Berlin's early engagement with Oxford philosophy, beginning in the 1930s, is one of the areas of Berlin's oeuvre that repays closer examination.

But first, there are several possible explanations for why scholars have long neglected his earlier writings in philosophy. If we seek to understand not just the meaning, but also the significance of his earlier philosophical writings, then we ought to dispense with the best of these reasons. For a start, one culprit might well be Berlin himself, since a great deal has been made of his own claim to have given up philosophy for the history of ideas (CC xxv–xxvii). If ever there were grounds for discounting the writings in question, it might be to heed the author's own telling narration of his exit from the discipline – at once self-effacing and dismissive about the enterprise. Berlin attributes his early doubts about pursuing philosophy to a 1944 conversation with the Harvard logician H. M. Sheffer, according to whom progress was possible

---

[1] Hardy 1999, vii.

only in such subfields as logic and psychology. Berlin concluded that he lacked the passion to pursue pure philosophy, doubting both his ability to ever make any original contributions, and the possibility of learning anything new in his lifetime (F 497–9). The discipline of the history of ideas did not present these challenges.

To accept uncritically Berlin's own story of his departure from philosophy, however, would be tantamount to committing an anachronistic fallacy about what it once meant, but no longer means, to "do philosophy," strictly speaking. Moreover, specifically what Berlin departed from for the history of ideas was *analytic* philosophy (which, of course, remains alive and well in the discipline), not the philosophy of history (which he never did abandon). Furthermore, Berlin's initial foray into "philosophy proper" constituted an important voice in the discourses that helped to shape "Oxford philosophy," and has turned out to be quite prescient in many ways. To understand the rise of analysis, arguably the most powerful philosophical movement in the twentieth century in the Anglophone world, in its historical context, beyond scrutinizing whether its origins lie with Russell, Moore, or Frege, we must notice the major shift of the center of philosophical activity from Cambridge in the 1920s to Oxford by the 1960s, and thus the importance of Berlin's place in it.

There is also another, sociocultural, explanation for why Berlin is famous for the arguments he made after the war, and why almost all scholarly attention has revolved around those arguments that made him famous. It is not a coincidence that from the early 1950s onward, when the defense of liberalism and the idea of value pluralism started to occupy a central place in Berlin's thinking, the specter of totalitarianism continued to loom over Europe and America, and with it growing anxieties about extremist and fanatical possibilities of all stripes. The antidotal qualities of Berlin's arguments against Nazism and Stalinism resonated with many readers in the twentieth century, and this awareness shows few, if any, signs of waning. To infer, however, that Berlin's earlier thought had little or no significant impact in his day, or on his later thought, or to assume that the latter can be sufficiently understood without proper attention to the former, would be tantamount to committing the anachronistic fallacy.

The purpose of this chapter is not directly to address the historiographical questions about the nature of Berlin's oeuvre as a whole, or to probe the questions of whether the development of his ideas displays greater continuity or discontinuity, is marked by coherence more than by fractures and shifts, and so forth. Those are important questions whose answers are matters of judgment best left to the intellectual historians. The aim of this brief chapter is at once more limited and broader in scope. It builds on the claim of established interpreters of Berlin's philosophy who have already begun to address this particular lacuna in Berlin studies, and who each severally, yet collectively, argue that we must take a more comprehensive view of the development of Berlin's ideas in order fully to understand his intellectual contributions.[2]

This chapter clarifies how Berlin's earlier arguments in the burgeoning field of analytic philosophy reveal the earlier roots of both his liberal political theory and his antinaturalism when it comes to the human sciences. Those earlier writings help to properly situate his epistemological concerns and his preoccupation with value pluralism as about the complex and variable character of any lived human life; and with how we might properly capture and not cause damage to it. The antireductionist position that Berlin initially staked out between Idealism and Oxford Realism not only simultaneously opposed their new empiricist challengers, but has also continued to have a profound and indelible impact on political philosophy ever since.

ANTIREDUCTIONISM BETWEEN OXONIAN IDEALISM AND REALISM[3]

Like much of the British Empire in the aftermath of the First World War, philosophy in Britain also underwent a tumultuous period of revision and reconstruction in the interwar years.[4] Absolute Idealism, which purported to have obliterated empiricism and which had dominated philosophy departments since the 1860s, came under fierce attack. At Cambridge, Bertrand Russell's new logical instrument for the analysis of objective phenomena evolved into his "logical atomism"; and G. E. Moore rejected the monistic holism of F. H. Bradley's Idealism in favor of an extreme form of pluralist atomist realism, or "conceptual realism." Despite all of their skepticism about Idealism's "woolliness," Realists such as Moore and Russell nevertheless tended to remain committed to the establishment of metaphysical truths. Moore's 1898 dissertation was rooted not in common sense or empiricism, but in Platonic realism. He sought to describe the specific philosophic purposes of the use of linguistic expression and its rule-governed connections with other expressions by way of implication, exclusion,

---

[2] See Arie Dubnov's intellectual biography: Dubnov 2012. Joshua Cherniss also develops the idea of continuity between Berlin's earliest concern with intercultural and intersubjective understanding and communication in his prewar philosophical work, and his postwar political thought, as well as his later writings on ethical pluralism and historical understanding (Cherniss 2013). Jamie Reed shows how Berlin's early critique of philosophical reductionism runs seamlessly through to his later writings against metaphysical rationalism; see Reed 2008. Carla Yumatle works from the opposite end to show how Berlin's late normative antireductionism on ethics and politics presupposes his earlier arguments on semantics, truth, and ontology; see Yumatle 2012, 672–700.
[3] See Berlin and Hampshire, "I'm Going to Tamper with Your Beliefs a Little" (n.d.).
[4] By most accounts, philosophical activity in Britain stalled significantly during the interwar years. Analysts continued to make quiet and steady progress at Cambridge, but they didn't garner much attention at Oxford until the 1930s with Price's return from Cambridge, and until the subsequent excitement and activities of the "second generation of analytic philosophers," including Berlin and his peers, dispelled the general quiescence in philosophy of the 1920s and 1930s. See Wokler 2001.

presupposition, and so on.[5] Unlike Moore and Russell, the Oxford Realists were not trained mathematicians or scientists. John Cook Wilson, who was the Chair of Logic from 1899 until his death in 1915, was the leading spirit of the Realist revolt at Oxford against the Idealism of Bradley and Bernard Bosanquet that dominated philosophy prior to World War I. Cook Wilson was taught by T. H. Green and Jowett at Balliol, but soon revolted against his teachers, and inspired the next generation of Oxford Realists, referred to as the "Cook-Wilsonians." Unlike the Cambridge Realists, these were predominantly Aristotelian scholars who, in the venerable Oxford tradition, read Literae Humaniores. Their attack on Idealism was rooted in respect for ordinary language, and the ordinary usage of terms, a theme that was echoed by Austin in the 1930s, according to whom the student of logic must aim to determine the normal use of an expression.

The intellectual shortcomings of British Idealist philosophy (which the Realists were genuinely interested to point out) were amplified by the changing cultural and political trends in Britain during the World War I and post–World War I era. By the mid-twentieth century, Hegel's organic metaphor of the state came to be widely viewed as a precursor to fascism and totalitarianism, and was roundly condemned for promoting authoritarian views on freedom, and an aggressive, warlike stance in foreign relations that exerted absolute control over people.[6] British philosophers and historians also began to take aim at the ultra-nationalist views of Fichte and the antimoralist ideas of Nietzsche, along with the Hegelian doctrine that deified the state as the supreme type of human organization, alleging that the latter effectively fueled German war machine by identifying liberty and personal rights with the law, showing contempt for democracy, and upholding war as a necessity. In this context, embracing the political critique of so-called "continental philosophy" meant condemning post-Kantian German thought as a philosophically inadequate and politically aggressive source of all that was corrupting Europe. The British backlash against German thought and culture extended also to the British Hegelians of the nineteenth and early twentieth centuries; Idealists who followed Hegel, such as Bosanquet, Bradley, J. H. Muirhead, and Ernest Barker, all came under fire.

When Berlin began his studies at Corpus Christi College, Oxford in 1928 he read classics and ancient philosophy (Greats) as well as philosophy, politics, and economics (PPE), and was influenced early by the British Idealists.[7] In step with the changing intellectual culture of his time, Berlin was then immersed in

---

[5] Meinong and Brentano had the parallel inspiration on the Continent, but at Cambridge, Moore led the revolt against Idealism, with Russell swiftly following in his footsteps.

[6] Akehurst 2010, 16–52.

[7] For an account of Berlin's even earlier intellectual development as "a young boy from Riga," as well as a useful warning against the reductionist determinism of trying to excavate the earliest childhood memories and experiences to explain a subject's worldview, see Dubnov 2012, 17.

the Realism of Moore and Cook Wilson.[8] In 1932, when Berlin was elected to a Prize Fellowship at All Souls, he began teaching philosophy as a lecturer at New College, and joined a new generation of rebellious empiricists at Oxford that included the young A. J. Ayer, J. L. Austin, D. G. C. MacNabb, A. D. Woozley, and Stuart Hampshire. Throughout the 1930s he actively participated in these weekly evening discussions with his friends and colleagues that would mark the beginning of "Oxford philosophy" as something distinct from "philosophy at Oxford."[9]

In the words of Bernard Williams, Berlin "was never a positivist," but was "seriously interested in philosophy at a time when philosophy's most pressing questions came from positivist directions" (CC xxx–xxxi). His formative intellectual experiences in the 1930s and 1940s occurred as he engaged with the full-blown rebellion against Idealism by his friends and fellow philosophers, and grappled with their preoccupation with logical positivism and linguistic analysis.[10] The philosophical agenda of Berlin's prewar group was largely set by logical positivism, led by Ayer, in conjunction with phenomenalism, thanks to the popular lectures of H. H. Price, who was responsible for putting the problem of perception at the center of Oxford philosophy in the 1930s. They discussed issues in perception and verificationism, e.g. sense-data, the possibility of *a priori* truths which are not analytic (i.e. propositions that appeared necessarily true or false but were apparently not reducible to rules or definitions), the logical character of counterfactual statements, and problems about the nature and criteria of personal identity, not to mention the problem of knowing other minds. The group concerned itself with the conditions under which sentences have a meaning; the connections between meaning and verification (construed in terms of sense perception); and, most fundamentally, with an empiricist view of science that regarded natural science as the paradigm of knowledge and scientific theory as a generator of all actual and possible observations.

Like his philosophy peers at Oxford, Berlin was initially drawn to the vigorous antimetaphysical empiricism of the logical positivists, which tried to deflate Idealism's overblown view of philosophy as capable of establishing fundamental, necessary, absolute, and abstract truths. With the Realists, Berlin rejected the metaphysical pretensions of the Absolute and the unknowable obscurity of "Spirit."[11] Surely, if the Absolute encompassed

---

[8] Both attacked Idealism head on, though they did so differently. For a fuller historical narrative, see Hacker 1996.
[9] See Berlin and Hampshire, "I'm Going to Tamper with Your Beliefs a Little" (n.d.), 9–10.
[10] Berlin's interest in philosophy and the history of ideas predates his arrival at Oxford, due in part to the influence of his friend and Russian–Jewish mentor Solomon Rachmilevich. Rachmilevich, who was educated at several German universities, first introduced Berlin to the ideological quarrels of Russian history and to Kant and German philosophy after Kant.
[11] In the early twentieth century, British Idealists had to contend with the central problems in Hegel's philosophy that Feuerbach identified, beginning with his 1839 essay, "Toward a Critique of Hegelian Philosophy."

everything in the universe, then it couldn't explain anything. This mysterious entity, with its conception of a systematic order and its teleological view of the universe, was a confused and baffling notion, at best. Worse, a causal link could be posited between German aggression in the twentieth century and the nineteenth century philosophies of Hegel, Nietzsche, and the Romantics, as a direct source of fascist ideology. In ethics, the Idealist notion of the Absolute was exemplified by an imperative of universal self-realization, of man's "true" nature against his empirical, and individual, self. The British Idealists subscribed to the idea of the telos of man within the larger purposive order as that which transcends the instincts and ends of the "empirical" self. T. H. Green identified the most complete possible satisfaction of man's actual nature to consist in the good of society as a whole, which in turn benefited not the empirical individual self, distinct from other selves, but universal reason, which was thought to be shared by all.[12]

Along with his fellow new empiricist philosophers, Berlin was deeply concerned with the nature and authority of knowledge, and was therefore thoroughly suspicious of metaphysical claims. However, their stringent demand for clarity, precision, and the rigorous scrutiny of arguments, above all, also entailed a technocratic view of philosophy, which for Berlin would require putting on blinders that could leave dangerous political beliefs unexamined, and worse, relegated all moral and aesthetic statements to the status of mere "emotivist" utterances of "like" and "dislike."[13] Therefore, while Berlin extolled the virtues of clear argumentation and a commitment to piecemeal reasoning, he was nevertheless deeply discomfited by the new empiricist forms of philosophy that tried to curb the excesses of Hegelian speculation by unrealistically imposing some singular unified method of logico-linguistic analysis. Despite the excesses he saw in Hegelianism, Berlin saw its appreciation for historical perspective and, more broadly, the role of personal and cultural purposes in human conduct as grounds for approval.[14]

Ayer, as well as Austin, led the new empiricist generation of Oxford philosophers who revolted against the entire traditional conception of philosophy as a source of knowledge about the universe. And it is precisely in the space between Ayer's and Austin's irreconcilable points of view that we can see the significance of the particular humanistic and interpretive view about linguistic meaning and its relation to ethics that Berlin forged (PI 156–76).

---

[12] Although Berlin singles out T. H. Green among the Hegelians as a liberal, his fear of the totalitarian elements in Hegel's thought led him, famously, to worry about the possible justification, in the name of liberty, of the abandonment of reason by dictatorships that seek to mold and shape people into obedience.

[13] Emotivism was also referred to colloquially as the "Boo–Hurrah" theory. Ayer laid out the meta-ethical view of emotivism, which was developed into a systematic value judgment theory by Stevenson. See Stevenson 1944.

[14] Suffice it to say that Berlin's relationship to Idealism would remain complex. See "My Intellectual Path," POI 4; Berlin 1952b.

Ayer synthesized the Cambridge analysis of Russell, Moore, Ramsey, and the early Wittgenstein, and adopted the Vienna Circle's interpretation of sense and meaning.[15] Berlin reports that Ayer's paper on Wittgenstein's *Tractatus* delivered to the Jowett Society in 1932, to which he replied, was not only the first public discussion of Wittgenstein's work in Oxford, but also "the opening shot in the great positivist campaign" (PI 159). Ayer combined the classical British empiricism of Hume with Price's work on perception, and accepted the Vienna Circle's view that all significant propositions are either tautologies (logical or mathematical propositions) or else empirically verifiable, which together constituted the sole subject matter of philosophy as logical analysis. At Berlin's urging, Ayer began to write up his ideas in 1934 and immediately became one of the leading exponents of logical positivism, the central tenets of which he formulated as: (i) the principle of verification; (ii) the dismissal of metaphysics as nonsense; (iii) the reduction of all empirical propositions to subjective experience; and (iv) ethical noncognitivism or emotivism in morality.[16] Ayer asserted that all genuine philosophical propositions were either logical tautologies, the truth of which could be ascertained through examination of the meanings of their constituent terms, or statements verifiable by the sense-data of actual or possible experience. All propositions that failed to satisfy either of these two criteria had no philosophical value, and were at best "pseudo-propositions."[17]

From the very start, Berlin opposed each of the tenets of logical positivism, and his philosophical inquiries reveal his deep frustration with the reductionism and narrow scientism that Ayer and the logical positivists propounded. Although Berlin was always drawn to empiricism, he became frustrated with the abstract and ahistorical approach of Ayer, which forced an unrealistic restriction on the enterprise of philosophy, and he found himself increasingly drawn to the historically and culturally richer discipline of the history of ideas.[18] As it was then taking shape, Oxford philosophy need not be practiced as a moral vocation. Philosophy should be disentangled from political outcomes, and need not be judged for its consequences or its omissions. In 1939, the same year that saw the publication of Berlin's essay on "Verification," in which he fundamentally disagreed with the philosophical endeavor to reduce all semantic explanation to a privileged category of basic

---

[15] Ayer gave his first Oxford lecture course in 1933, on the *Tractatus*, and the same year, during the annual summer joint sessions of the Mind Association and the Aristotelian Society, the journal *Analysis* was founded, and quickly became the mouthpiece for the younger philosophers, not only from Oxford but also from Cambridge and elsewhere.

[16] Ayer 2001, 35.   [17] Ayer 2001, 36.

[18] In the 1930s, Berlin exhibited interest in a wider range of thinkers than his philosophical peers. Cherniss has found that Berlin's surviving lectures from this time include references to such figures as Schopenhauer, Max Scheler, and Nicolai Hartmann. See Cherniss 2013, 9, note 56. In addition, several commentaries recount Berlin's frustrations about philosophy in the 1930s; see Bowra 1966, 12–16; and Ayer 1977, 98.

propositions, his first book also appeared – a well-researched study of *Karl Marx*, in print to this day and now in its fifth edition. In several other essays penned after "Verification," Berlin continued to develop his deep resistance to the reductionist tendency in the operative idea of positivism, not only due to fear that it could become intellectually oppressive, but also because of his belief that it was fundamentally misguided in principle.

Berlin's chief objection to Ayer's standard of meaning, premised on the translation – or the reduction "without residue" – of any philosophically genuine sentence to a set of propositions describing the individual sense-data of actual or possible experience, was that this position constituted far too strong a restriction on the scope of what could be considered legitimate philosophical inquiry. For Berlin, the principle of verification identified meaningfulness solely with verifiability. As such, it constituted too narrow a criterion of the meaningfulness of a proposition. Logical positivism rested on this erroneous standard of meaning, on the notion of an ideal language that did not correspond to linguistic usage, and consisted of propositions solely about some basic category of experience. Thus, for Berlin, the principle of verification attempted to restrict what philosophy could legitimately say, with the further unwarranted consequence of turning any potential philosophical disagreement into a mere procedural problem. Verificationism served, in effect, to reduce and distort, rather than explain or translate, the initial statement in question. The new empiricist drive for clarity and precision, which, Berlin acknowledged, had once played "a decisive role in the history of modern philosophy, by clearing up confusions [and] exposing major errors," nevertheless needed "to be abandoned or else considerably revised, if it is to be prevented from breeding *new fallacies* in place of those which it eradicates" (CC 15, emphasis added).

In an unpublished 1940 lecture series entitled "Introduction: Induction and Logic," Berlin expounded his philosophy of language, bringing together his piecemeal critiques from the 1930s. He called attention to the deeper underlying "fallacy of reduction" inherent, for instance, in the conceptions of linguistic meaning held by both Ayer and Russell. His problem with Ayer's logical positivism, as well as Russell's logical atomism, had to do with "reducing things which are different from one another by violent means in order to conform to an ideal itself founded on a fallacy."[19] He explicitly traces the commitment of these philosophers to constructing a logically perfect language, in order to model the basic structure of reality by means of basic propositions or units, back to Hume's empiricist analysis of experience, and refers to the legacy of Humean empiricism as the "great fallacy with which we shall have to contend throughout the twentieth century."[20] Berlin rejected the

---

[19] Berlin, "Introduction: Induction and Logic," 7.
[20] Ibid., 51. Hume's empiricism and skepticism attracted Berlin, but he would remain wary of any unqualified imperialism on the part of Newtonian science, because of its disastrous effects on

assumption that the meaning of our statements about reality can be given directly by our procedures for finding out about it, and maintained that the demand for certainty is self-defeating. Berlin could not accept the logical positivist claim that there was only a single criterion of meaningfulness. He rejected not just the means of logical reduction, but also its aim, and the very notion that we can access linguistic meaning by correlating words with bits of reality such as sense-data or atomic facts.

The conception of meaning that Berlin advanced looks instead to a subject's immersion within a particular context of understanding, and to the individual's capacity for multiple levels of recognition – in particular, the capacity to recognize situations appropriate for words to have the meanings they do.[21] Berlin's view readily acknowledges the irreducibility of propositional meaning, and not only accepts, but calls for, the recognition of the coexistence of multiple criteria of semantic meaning. Rather than providing another singular principle of verification as an alternative to that offered by logical positivism, or demanding a different form of translation of propositions in order to render them verifiable, Berlin argued that it was logically impossible for any single formal criterion – or hard and fast rule – to secure the meaning of any statement. Such an antireductionist conception of linguistic meaning might have aligned Berlin more closely with J. L. Austin, who opposed Ayer's philosophy of meaning, and led the opposition to logical positivism's sense-datum terminology. After all, in 1935, Berlin and Austin gave a joint class on a book by the Harvard positivist pragmatist C. I. Lewis, *Mind and the World Order*, in which Berlin argued against the verification principle and against pure Carnapian logical positivism.[22] According to Austin, the meaning of an utterance was best explained in terms of how it was used in the context of ordinary circumstances.

Berlin was certainly in agreement with Austin's view that logically perfect languages, such as Ayer's, were unacceptable, since they depended on clear-cut dichotomies that didn't always exist; and that the drive for clarity and precision could serve to obliterate rather than to elucidate the important distinctions that ordinary language was used to describe.[23] Berlin was impressed, for example, with Austin's refusal of all doctrinaire approaches, including those of the

---

ethics and moral philosophy. Berlin doubted Hume's claim that human beings were much the same everywhere at all times, and objected to what he saw as the conservative implications of Hume's account of justice.

[21] Ibid., 67–70.

[22] Cherniss credits Berlin's engagement with Lewis's work as the source of his adaptation of Kantian ideas to a pragmatic empiricism, and as one possible source of Berlin's pluralism. See Cherniss 2013, 9.

[23] See Austin's first published contribution to philosophy, "A Priori Concepts," in *Proceedings of the Aristotelian Society* supplementary volume 18, 1939, which expresses much of his positive doctrine against the pure Carnapian logical positivism of Ayer, and also the logical atomism of Russell. See also his more developed later work, Austin 1962.

metaphysical Idealist moral philosophers, the new empiricist logical positivists such as Ayer, and the phenomenalists such as Price; and Berlin shared Austin's penchant for treating problems, instead, in a piecemeal fashion, "seeking to establish the truth about particular questions, not promote a new orthodoxy."[24] Like Berlin, Austin viewed the use of language as central to human activity, and the study of its use as an important preliminary to the pursuit of philosophy itself. The two were in general agreement that to say anything about the world inevitably requires invoking things other than immediate sense-data. Reducing meaning to what could be verified in terms of propositions constructed solely on the basis of real or possible sense-data – and restricting philosophy only to what can be said via such methods of verification, without doubt or fear of being mistaken – was to condemn us to silence. Insofar as ordinary language was sufficient for most everyday purposes, Austin's proposal for the careful and imaginative charting of the uses and implications of ordinary language might have sufficed to meet Berlin's notion of what should constitute philosophy's main purpose. Ordinary language might not serve as an infallible guide, but it would not systematically mislead by construing experience in abstract and ahistorical terms that distort, instead of convey, human reality. However, Berlin's issues with the reductive tendencies of new empiricism didn't end with his disagreement with Ayer's logical positivism; he could no more countenance Austin's more generous conception of linguistic meaning and more open-ended conception of philosophy.

What Austin urged was the study of the actual use of language – the careful analysis and charting of the distinctions and nuances involved in asserting and assessing any proposition, whether that is an ordinary descriptive claim or a normative judgment. Berlin concluded that although philosophy as ordinary language analysis was less exacting than Ayer's logical positivism, it nevertheless failed to deal with the question of authority, leaving questions of morality utterly vulnerable to a wide range of relativistic worries. The linguistic analysis movement was incapable of dealing with questions such as why, even if the analysis of our moral language were correct, this should license us to think that it has jurisdiction in our society, let alone how the moral language of one society could have any kind of jurisdiction over another society. In this way, in Berlin's view, Ayer and Austin each directly and systematically challenged the meaningfulness of statements about morality and undermined the philosophical basis of normative ethics. In fact, Berlin would later recall that ethics and morality were hardly ever discussed by their prewar group, and even when they were, this served only as a brief respite before they resumed their usual concerns.[25]

---

[24] Cherniss 2013, 7.   [25] See Berlin, Hampshire, Murdoch, and Quinton 1955, 495–521.

PHILOSOPHY AND THE HUMAN SCIENCES

Berlin left Oxford only briefly, during the war, when he served from 1940 to 1942 in the British Information Services in New York City, and from 1942 to 1946 at the British Embassy in Washington, DC (from where he drafted weekly reports), including a visit in 1945–6 to the Soviet Union, where he met with persecuted members of the Russian intelligentsia, including the poets Anna Akhmatova and Boris Pasternak. Returning to Oxford after the war, Berlin continued to teach and write on philosophy throughout the later 1940s and early 1950s, but he also acquired a more public profile as a leading commentator on the intellectual dimensions of the developing Cold War. His writings began to drift away from his early philosophical concerns toward the history of ideas, perhaps following the lead of his first book, back to the history of Marxist and socialist theories, and the Enlightenment and its critics. His election to a research fellowship at All Souls in 1950 allowed him to devote himself more fully to his historical, political, and literary interests, which lay well outside the mainstream of philosophy as it was then practiced at Oxford.

Given the developments of Oxford philosophy throughout the '30s and '40s, and his intellectual disagreements with both Ayer and Austin, it is not difficult to see why Berlin might have thought that his own deeper concerns about morality and ethics, and with "conceptual truths" that are bound up with experience but are not themselves experienced, might be more fruitfully pursued beyond the narrow confines of the discipline of Oxford philosophy as it was then taking shape. Berlin's expressed views about the enterprise of philosophy help to explain why he left for the history of ideas, as well as why he ultimately took issue with Austin's ordinary language approach as demonstrating an insufficient grasp of the purpose of philosophy.[26] The history of ideas allowed him to uphold and defend, and to further explore, what first led him to reject verificationism – that is, his view of the complexity and heterogeneity of human life. Commentators have referred to Berlin's understanding of this complexity as his "awareness of the protean character of individual experience, belief, and commitment," noting it as the source of his "anti-procrustean liberalism."[27] It is remarkable how Berlin's earlier writings from the '30s and '40s already evinced the same concerns as his more mature view of the nature of philosophy contained in his later writings in the '60s. He had already expressed the same concern with how philosophy ought to capture, and not reduce, the complex nature of particular human subjects in moral and political circumstances, as when he later argued for why

---

[26] The broader task that Berlin sought to claim for philosophy is elaborated in three essays published in the early 1960s: "History and Theory: The Concept of Scientific History," "The Purpose of Philosophy," and "Does Political Theory Still Exist?" – all in CC.

[27] See Allen 2004.

the human sciences (including philosophy) are an enterprise distinct from the natural sciences.

Berlin may have departed from the discipline of philosophy proper, but his emigration was only a titular one in many ways, and he never gave up his campaign against reductionism. Berlin's 1950 essay, "Logical Translation," is widely regarded as his final contribution to the specific field of analytic philosophy, but it was there that he expanded the target of his critique from the specific logical positivist or atomist positions to a broader range of ideas and philosophical assumptions.[28] What Berlin saw driving the logical positivist's claim that a statement must be capable of being translated into a single, proper, type of proposition in order to be true or genuinely meaningful was not a desire for an accurate perception of reality, but rather a reductionist drive, which motivates many more offenders, not just his new empiricist contemporaries. He called this the "Ionian Fallacy," or the erroneous assumption that everything is made out of, or can be reduced to, or understood in terms of, one and the same substance or type of entity. Berlin identified the same fatally flawed correspondence model of truth operating in two different, yet equally erroneous, approaches to the forcible assimilation of all propositions: (i) the "deflationary" approach, which sought to assimilate all propositions to one true type, and (ii) the "inflationary" approach which posited entities corresponding to all statements, thus "creating" or asserting the existence of things that Berlin believed didn't exist at all. Behind this fatal consequence, moreover, according to Berlin, was the impulse to cling to the dualism of "good" and "bad" propositions, driven by the hopeless pursuit of security through the search for certainty, or the belief "that there must be a group of propositions, tested and found indestructible, which forms the minimum gold reserve without which intellectual currency cannot be exchanged" (CC 101).

In "Logical Translation," Berlin emphatically wrote that "words mean, not by pinning down bits of reality, but by having a recognised use, i.e. when their users know how and in what situations to use them in order to communicate whatever they wish to communicate; and for this there are no exhaustive formal rules" (CC 103–4). But Berlin had already made this very same point in an unpublished 1934 lecture on "Matter," naming contemporary logical positivists alongside several of the Pre-Socratics as well as the sixth century Thales of Miletus, who each sought a singular unified answer to the question of the nature of the material world.[29] Berlin opposed myriad philosophical attempts to reduce the ordinary thought and experience of normal human beings to doctrines that did violence to what people actually thought and meant. He noticed the same new empiricist reductionist drive of the logical positivists manifest in the human sciences, as well as in moral philosophy.

---

[28] Pears 1991, 31–9.   [29] See Berlin 1934.

For Berlin, philosophy – as distinct from those questions to which there are empirical answers – is about how to inquire into things that cannot be objects of empirical knowledge. Like neo-Kantians Heinrich Rickert and Wilhem Windelband, Berlin insisted on the fundamental difference between the natural and the human sciences. Berlin remained staunchly opposed to the positivist belief that the natural sciences are the paradigmatic form of knowledge that the human sciences should seek to emulate. Following Vico and Dilthey, he thought that the natural and the human sciences fundamentally differed in the very nature of the subject matter that they studied; and, echoing Rickert, Berlin insisted that the type of knowledge each sought made different methods, standards, and goals appropriate to each. He classed philosophy as part of the human sciences, as separate from the natural sciences, and as having a unique status in that not only are the answers to philosophical questions in question, but also the means for arriving at answers; and the standards by which to evaluate and judge whether an answer is plausible, are not – nor can they be – known in advance (CC 11). He concludes his 1961 essay "The Purpose of Philosophy" by summarizing this purpose as "to assist men to understand themselves and thus operate in the open, and not wildly, in the dark."[30] Philosophy, importantly, includes reflection upon and inquiry into "life-forming moral values,"[31] which Berlin took to be both multiple and incommensurable. For Berlin, values may be tragically irreconcilable, but they constitute a real part of human nature, and so should not be understood as mere subjective projections or simply a reflection of how some people happen to use words.

The idea that moral statements have no meaning other than as expressions of emotional attitudes was, for Berlin, an absurd way of rendering and accounting for the way we actually make and understand ethical judgments. For the same reason, he remained skeptical of the conventionalism entailed by Austin's ordinary language analysis, which sought to recast the entire task of philosophy solely as the analysis of linguistic usage, and jeopardized the prospects for properly understanding both values and their import. To focus exclusively on usage was systematically to neglect the importance of history, to deflate questions about the objectivity of what is regarded as truth or knowledge, and to diminish questions about the validity of human experience in different eras and cultural situations. For Berlin, it was a mistake to seek to fix on any single criterion of meaningfulness, some single paramount standard or common currency that could provide the basis for unproblematic translations; and attempting to do so artificially flattened controversies and conflated the past with the present. Both Ayer's and Austin's views of philosophy were method-driven in that whatever subject or explanandum their respective methods could not handle unproblematically was automatically rejected as an irrelevant or illegitimate topic for philosophy.

---

[30] CC 14.   [31] The phrase is from Hardy 2000.

Berlin's opposition to verificationism and his antireductionist claim that philosophy had a larger task is in many ways a return to an Idealist sense of the importance of history, imagination, and insight.[32] The claim of the unity of knowledge and the knowing subject only needed advancement and defense because of the new empiricism's epistemology that implicitly – if not explicitly – divorced what is true (i.e. what could be validly deduced from discrete premises) from interpretation, which necessarily makes reference to and relies on further interpretations. In this vein, Berlin was deeply influenced by R. G. Collingwood at Oxford, who reinforced Berlin's Kantian belief in the importance of the basic concepts and categories in terms of which human beings organize and analyze their experience, which implied a much broader view of philosophy than any of the new empiricist models of experience would allow. Collingwood fostered Berlin's interest in the history of ideas and introduced him to founders such as the Italian historian, philosopher, and jurist Giambattista Vico, and the German philosopher, theologian, and literary critic Johann Herder. It was in the spirit of Collingwood that Berlin condemned the modest role that logical positivism attributed to philosophy as "secretary to science and obituarist of metaphysics" (CC xxxii).

Berlin's view of philosophy took seriously Kant's distinction between matters of fact and the structures or categories in terms of which facts are made sense of. But rather than take categories to be prior to or independent of experience, Berlin held the Collingwoodian view that the ideas through which we make sense of the world are closely tied up with our experiences, shaping and being shaped by them, which renders them logically prior both to the acquisition of empirical information and deductive reasoning. And since experience varies from one time and place to another, so, for Berlin, do basic concepts. Berlin opposed the verificationist assumption that concepts are unchanging as either immature or possibly dangerous. Such a notion was immature when philosophers were led to withdraw from political philosophy because they were not yet cured of a certain conception of metaphysics, as Wittgenstein would have it, despite their proclamations against metaphysics. Similarly, the assumption that concepts were unchanging could be dangerous when social reformers sought to impose abstract ideas on particular societies without regard for local details or the "spirit of the age."

In "The Concept of Scientific History" Berlin argued that the natural and the human worlds must be studied differently because of the relationship between the observer or thinker and his object of study.[33] The human sciences are peculiar in having a subject matter that is of the same nature as the

---

[32] For a broader exposition of some of the Idealist themes that developed through the twentieth century, see Bevir and O'Brien 2003, 305–29.

[33] He contrasts the dispassionately objective scientific method in history with an empathetic approach that he developed in particular through his writings on Vico. See "The Concept of Scientific History," in CC. See also "Historical Inevitability" (1954) in L.

investigator. While the natural sciences study the physical world of nature dispassionately and objectively from without, the human sciences study the world that human beings create for themselves and inhabit – from within their cultures. To study human life, Berlin thought, we cannot divest ourselves entirely of the experience on which we base our judgments; rather, we must begin from our understanding of other human beings in the "thick" sense of what it is like to have motives and feelings. To understand human actions, according to Berlin, we must follow the empiricist commitment to lived experience, but should also bear in mind that access to that experience is available not through the natural sciences alone but through the "inside view" of people's goals, beliefs, and values, which requires an insightful kind of understanding with a vitalist account of behavior.

For this reason, the human sciences could not be conducted in the same way as the natural sciences, because the latter seek to establish general laws based on similarities and regularities which, by categorizing events into types, can explain whole classes of phenomena. In contrast, the whole point of the human sciences is to understand the unique particulars of human life in and of themselves, which requires the study of history and of personality. What Berlin saw as necessary for such a task is *Verstehen,* or imaginative understanding. This kind of understanding is based on a knowledge of humanity that can only be derived from direct experience, by interaction with others, and not merely from introspection. In keeping with his general "inside view" approach to the explanation of human conduct, which eschewed the detached and impersonal methods of the natural sciences, Berlin favored an empathetic stress on the values, purposes, and world-views of the actors themselves. Against the conventional analytical technique of constructing arguments and counterarguments in the quest for certainty, Berlin preferred a historical style that traced ideas to their origins in the work of key thinkers whose personalities were shown to be as important as their logic. And it was this capacity to recapture the view of past cultures and convey a powerful sense of the reality of the past that Berlin salutes in Vico and Herder.[34]

Philosophy as the means of understanding the concepts and categories of human experience must entail a broader range of tasks that are more historical and more culturally rich than the new empiricist wave of analysis could allow. More than that of his Realist predecessors, and against that of his new empiricist, positivist peers, Berlin's thought was marked by a deep historical awareness, and by a concern for cultural and philosophical diversity. Moral or

---

[34] Berlin's notion of a historical "sense of reality" referred to the importance of an intuitive feel for the way particular observations and ideas fit within a plausible overall picture. No fixed method that could be set in advance could accomplish the transmission of a historical sensibility that would set ideas within their context and would reach beyond the immediate context to connect the past with the present. See "The Concept of Scientific History" and "Does Political Theory Still Exist?" (both in CC).

ethical theory, moreover, for Berlin, was directly connected to interpersonal understanding, the capacity to communicate with others, and the belief that people could understand and be understood by others, so as to be able to establish that such belief was justified. Throughout his life, Berlin was concerned with the problem of understanding between persons, as well as with the validity of moral judgment across lines of difference – whether between individuals with opposed beliefs, or between those divided by membership in different cultures, classes, or nations.

Berlin rejected as fallacious the belief in any foundational source of knowledge that could provide philosophy with a firm basis of certainty. The misguided pursuit of absolute certainty is a major theme of his later writings on intellectual history, ethics, and political theory. For example, in his 1960 essay on the issue of why a science of history is conceptually impossible, he writes of the complexity of the human world, observing that the many strands that make up human experience are "too many, too minute, too fleeting, too blurred at the edges" to be investigated in isolation (CC 156). Berlin had already attributed the early analysts' erroneous reductionist drive to a psychological need for certainty, and here he reiterates his view that absolute certainty is an impossible ideal, for the kind of certainties on which the unfolding of human lives depend, and "the vast majority of the types of reasoning on which our beliefs rest, or by which we should seek to justify them if they were challenged, are not reducible to formal deductive or inductive schemata, or combinations of them" (CC 149). Decades later, in a piece on his intellectual path posthumously published in the *New York Review of Books*, Berlin would recount the impact of this very idea on his overall thinking: "One of the intellectual phenomena which made the greatest impact on me was the universal search by philosophers for absolute certainty, for answers which could not be doubted, for total intellectual security. This from the very beginning appeared to me to be an illusory quest" (POI 4–5).

Berlin's early philosophical writings contain an important keystone to his thought. They reveal just how important the idea of heterogeneity – which accounts for his skeptical stance about reductionism in any guise – was to him from the very start. His antireductionism led him to reject the technocratic stance that mistakenly claims a unity of method, and presupposes agreement over *ends*, which is to take as settled what ought instead to be an achievement – a discursive, interpretive, interpersonal achievement. This is a theme that recurs in his writings on the distinction between the natural and the human sciences, and the need for *Verstehen* when it comes to the history of ideas. The same resistance to the reductionism of the new empiricists that made him suspicious of verificationism and phenomenalism, with their logical deductions, their linguistic abstractions, and their quest for certainty, led Berlin in his later writings on ethics and politics to oppose utilitarian moral and political philosophy and other forms of ethical monism, and to fear the despotic and totalitarian effects of attempting to unify and harmonize human values, especially in politics. From the 1950s onward, he embarked on a defense of liberalism that would assume a central place in his intellectual concerns for the rest of his life, producing a steady stream of lectures, essays, and broadcasts on the political theme of the modern betrayal of freedom. His defense of liberalism, which defined the issue in the twentieth century in the Anglophone world, went hand in hand with his philosophy of human sciences. Both grew out of his preoccupation with the nature and role of values and moral beliefs in human life, which led him to develop the idea of value pluralism that became prominent in the 1980s and after. Throughout his career, Berlin's concerns were all of a piece, and the significance of this Berlinian position can be seen in the wider postwar context of the development of political theory in the Anglophone world.

POLITICAL PHILOSOPHY'S DEATH AND REVIVAL

Logical positivism's answer to normative concerns was to advocate a deflationary emotivism, according to which the claims of ethics, morality, aesthetics, and theology were pseudo-statements: neither true nor false but meaningless, at best mere statements of subjective taste. The rise of modernist empiricism in the twentieth century engendered the technocratic drive of logical positivism in philosophy, and went hand in hand with the emergence of other positivist empirical movements such as behaviorism in the social sciences. Together they promised the systematic scientific study of society and offered remarkable transformations in how moral and political concerns could legitimately be addressed. All the while, this took the air out of the disciplinary space in academic departments for more historically minded, developmental studies of political ideas and institutions, or more comprehensive reflections on values as they might concern students of politics.[35] It remains a commonplace to speak of the late twentieth century *revival* of political philosophy in the Anglophone world. However, to celebrate its *re*-birth is also to cite its antecedent death; and among its most famous obituaries is that of Peter Laslett, who in 1956 declared that "for the time being anyway, political philosophy is dead."[36]

There are probably several stories that could be told about why a narrative of death and resurrection came to define Anglo-American political theory's self-image in the twentieth century, but a few specific circumstances stand out. World-historical events and shifts in the cultural and political landscape help

---

[35] See Adcock and Bevir 2007; cf. White 2004.
[36] Laslett 1956, viii. Leo Strauss expressed related concerns about the decline of traditional philosophic wisdom brought on by the rise of scientism and historicism when he declared political philosophy to be "in a state of decay and perhaps of putrefaction, if it has not vanished altogether"; Strauss 1959, 17. In America, Judith Shklar set out to study how political theory's "disappearance had come to pass"; see Shklar 1957, vii.

to explain why theories of "political and social relationships at the widest possible level of generality" seemed to slow to a trickle by mid-century. Both the attempt to comprehend the horrors of Nazism and growing fears about nuclear annihilation no doubt made the neat Western images of political order on a grand scale seem less relevant, if not obsolete. And where Marxist ideas prevailed, their orthodox forms served only to nail shut the coffin by declaring political theory nothing more than class ideology in a different guise. Among the numerous factors contributing to the quiescence, however, the modernist empiricist philosophical movements of logical positivism and ordinary-language philosophy, and the twin deflationary effects of emotivism and conventionalism on normative issues, were no less profound.[37]

Berlin answered Laslett's indictment by recording his own worries about the continuing life of political theory in an essay titled with a rhetorical question: "Does Political Theory Still Exist?"[38] He called attention to the absence of works of grand theory and political reflection on a par with those of Hobbes, Locke, or Rousseau, but argued that this absence should not be construed as conclusive evidence of the death of the discipline. But whatever the accuracy of the funerary proclamations, and whatever its cause of death, everyone knows that analytic philosophy did eventually recover an interest in political philosophy. Moreover, there is widespread agreement that Rawls is to be credited for single-handedly resuscitating political theory from its moribund postwar condition.[39] But while this Rawlsian revival might have made Berlin's concerns about the endangered life of political theory seem antiquated, the opposite has in fact turned out to be the case.

Berlin's critique of formalism and reductionism, and his warnings about a technocratic conception of politics, has taken on renewed relevance through the echoes of admirers of his work such as Charles Taylor and Bernard Williams, writing precisely against Rawls's methodological assumptions. Understanding Berlin's critique makes it possible to see how Rawls and Taylor exemplify distinct modes of postanalytic liberal theorizing, which emerged in the late twentieth century out of two very different responses to the challenge of analytic philosophy's discursive beginnings.

Rawls sought to emulate the formalism of modernist empiricists such as Ayer, Carnap, and other members of the Vienna Circle. He devised a liberal political theory within a decision-making framework that helped him to minimize the interpretive challenges of articulating liberal values in diverse cultural conditions. Taylor's thinking, on the other hand, reflects the approach to political philosophy that was earlier shaped by his Oxford teachers, Berlin as well as Hampshire,

---

[37] Mark Bevir has detailed the shared themes and dilemmas comprising "modernist empiricism": see Bevir 2011 and Bevir 2006, 583–606. See also Bentley 2005.
[38] See "Does Political Theory Still Exist?" in CC.
[39] Others, such as Quentin Skinner and Sheldon Wolin, have also been viewed as saviors, but much less so. Recent examples include Richard Arneson: see Arneson 2006, 45–64, and Moon 2004.

through whom Oxford philosophical writing on ethics and politics remained broadly humanistic and interpretive despite the rise of analysis.[40] In taking up the critique of modernist empiricism rooted in an earlier debate about the prospects of political philosophy in the wake of analysis, Taylor is best read as bringing the insights of an "interpretive turn" to bear on the question of how a theory of liberal political values might be constructed and defended. Like Berlin, Taylor urges us to resist "Procrustean" attempts to confine and reduce thinking about complex problems to a single, restrictive approach or solution.[41]

Berlin continues to be most famous for his arguments for the plurality of values against the supposition of ethical monism, utilitarian or otherwise, which he thinks is deeply erroneous concerning the nature of morality and human experience. The error lies in supposing that all goods, virtues, and ideals are compatible, and that all desirable human ends can be united into a harmonious whole without loss or conflict. Moral monism, in short, is false to human experience because human values – goods such as liberty and equality that exist and can be known objectively – by their very nature conflict. Though these values may be universal, they can be "incommensurable" in that each is so distinct and has its own character and force that makes it impossible for translation into the terms of any other. Berlin extolled value pluralism as both the truer and the safer view of the deep nature of morality.

The skepticism that both Taylor and Williams later came to express about establishing a foundation to moral philosophy was already well articulated by Berlin in 1953 in the contrast he made famous in his essay "The Hedgehog and the Fox," quoting the archaic Greek poet Archilochus's enigmatic statement that the fox knows many things but the hedgehog knows one big thing.[42] Two opposing kinds of intellectual disposition are described: that of the systematizing hedgehogs who seek to relate everything to a single vision (e.g. Plato and Hegel), and that of the unsystematic foxes who celebrate "a vast variety of experiences and objects for what they are in themselves" (e.g. Shakespeare and Montaigne). Berlin sees himself as a fox, standing in favor of flexibility against the single-issue fanaticism of the hedgehog. Of course, his defense of multiplicity and variety can itself paradoxically be seen as single-minded, in that his insistence on value pluralism is a persistent, if sometimes implicit, theme underlying nearly everything he wrote. But setting Berlin's arguments about value pluralism against the wider backdrop of his interpretive view of the human subject makes clear his core belief that moral theories can never reflect the complexities of human life, insofar as they tend to systematize and abstract from it how human agents experience life.

---

[40] I have argued this at length elsewhere: see Choi 2015, 243–70.
[41] On precisely the issue of the different styles of the politics of recognition and the variety of solutions to the challenge of democratic inclusion, Taylor states, "there are not too many things that one can say in utter generality. Solutions have to be tailored to particular situations"; Taylor 1999, 163.
[42] See "The Hedgehog and the Fox," RT 24.

CONCLUSION

We should be skeptical of any claim that Berlin's early writings somehow contain the seeds of everything valuable that he ever wrote, or that his overall position can be explained by reference to its formative analytical themes alone. But there can be no doubt that his intellectual formation in the interwar years was a crucial background against which his postwar liberalism developed, and that his political theory both grew out of and gave greater voice to several of those key ideas. Berlin's early opposition to reductionism powerfully expressed his conception of the humanistic purpose and promise of philosophy. The space between Idealism and empiricism, in which Berlin developed his views against both logical positivism and ordinary language, provided an early distillation of key ideas that Berlin continued to work on even as he left the discipline proper. While we need not take as incorrigible Berlin's own retrospective account of his intellectual journey, it is not surprising that, near the very end of his career, reflecting on its beginnings, he says unequivocally that his earlier attitude to verificationism "has remained with me for the rest of my life, and has coloured everything else that I have thought" (POI 3). This self-description seems borne out in his antireductionism against logical positivism and scientific naturalism, as well as ethical monism. Motivating Berlin's arguments for rejecting the "principle of verification" against the reductivist drive of logical positivism's view of meaning and knowledge from the late 1930s onward and his advocacy of *Verstehen* was his conviction that not everything can or should be reduced to a single model, theory, standard, or ideal.

Berlin's early philosophical writings articulate his moral vision for philosophy, an approach that allows the possibility of conceiving of the status quo in alternative, possibly multiple, ways. He eschewed the empiricist demand for certainty and instead favored an interpretive epistemology that locates facts, beliefs, and knowledge interpretively from within our "thick" ethical concepts, which are nonetheless frail in the context of the existence of alternatives. Trying to secure such epistemological claims only makes sense against a commitment to an interpretive ontology of the human subject. Berlin acknowledged and appreciated the social aspects of identity and selfhood, along with the uniqueness and historically specific nature of particular human experience, which he upheld through his anti-utopian belief in the plurality of values in human life – all convictions which, though not always properly understood, would come to define his legacy as one of the most famous liberal thinkers of the twentieth century, if not *the* most famous.

4

"The Sense of Reality": Berlin on Political Judgment, Political Ethics, and Leadership

Joshua L. Cherniss

His sensitivity to the power of general ideas and appreciation for the value of community and culture notwithstanding, Isaiah Berlin was an individualist in outlook. Individual freedom – the protection of the individual from trampling, bullying, humiliation, terror – was for him *primus inter pares*, the most personally precious of the many divergent goods that constituted the moral world. His intellectual approach, too, was individualizing: few political theorists have framed so much of their work through the study of individual thinkers. For Berlin, individuals were both the subject and the medium of thinking, and human personality the most interesting subject of thought.

This shaped Berlin's political outlook – both in his commitment to the protection of the "negative liberty" of individuals, and also in his sympathy for romantic aversions to "everything cold and instrumental, impersonal and unlovely" in politics.[1] Berlin recognized that history was not merely the story of "what Alcibiades did and suffered" (PI 14, quoting Aristotle, *Poetics* 1451b11). But he was fascinated by the imprint of individual character on politics; and he approached politics, as his perceptive reports on the American political scene during World War II demonstrate, in terms of the relationships and personalities of individuals. This encouraged a certain lack of interest in the *institutional* face of politics – one that has puzzled some readers, frustrated others, and led one of Berlin's professorial successors to harsh rebuke.[2] While neglect of institutions may constitute a shortcoming in a political theorist, Berlin's focus on the interplay between individual personality, sensibility, and judgment, and his related concern with politics as an ethical experience, are among the most distinctive, and potentially fruitful, features of his thought for students of politics. Despite this, these features have seldom received close attention from scholars of Berlin's work.[3]

---

[1] Rosenblum 1989, 207.   [2] Waldron 2013. Cf. Ryan, Chapter 12 in this volume.

[3] The most notable exception to this neglect is Hanley 2004; there is also a perceptive discussion in Allen 1998. Berlin has occasionally been invoked in discussions of political judgment (e.g. Tetlock

Berlin's approach reflected a first-hand exposure to politics unrivaled distinctive by nearly all political theorists of his time (and subsequent generations). He was directly involved in some of the major events of his time: the efforts to bring America into World War II, the drafting of the UN Charter and the Marshall Plan, and the struggle to establish the state of Israel. An intimate of Chaim Weizmann, familiar with many of the founding generation of Israeli politicians, Berlin was more than once offered leading positions in the Israeli government; he moved among leading politicians, diplomats, and journalists in Cold War Britain and America, and was even unwittingly consulted by President Kennedy about how to interpret Russian action on the eve of the Cuban Missile Crisis.[4] Berlin was no Machiavelli: he did not seek power, either directly or through the ear of a prince.[5] But his experience gave him a unique perspective from which to reflect on the realities of political leadership. At the same time, Berlin's approach to politics was marked by a romantic tendency to focus on individual leaders (or "great men"). If his writings usefully supplement many political scientists' focus on institutions and processes, many of his accounts of politics miss opportunities to examine the importance of the interactions *among* groups of individuals united in political movements, the interplay between whose personalities shape the course of those movements.[6]

Berlin's concern with political judgment and leadership also reflected three overarching preoccupations that shaped his thought. The first was the nature of human understanding, which involved Berlin in polemics against scientism or positivism (which held only "scientific" knowledge to be valid), as well as a rejection of a solipsistic relativism (which held interpersonal understanding and evaluation to be impossible). The second, reflecting Berlin's engagement with Marxist thought and with polemics among nineteenth-century Russian radicals, concerned the questioning and defense of the significance of human action in history. The third – also reflecting a characteristically Russian theme, as well as the circumstances of Berlin's own times – concerned the relationship between politics and morality, and the dangers of and possible alternatives to both "utopian" absolutism, and "realist" cynicism as political approaches. For Berlin, personal judgment represented a form of understanding opposed to the positivist model dominant in the social sciences: a form of understanding that was both *individualizing*, seeking to grasp situations in their unique specificity

---

2006), but goes unmentioned in one of the few recent studies of political leadership by a political theorist (Keohane 2012).

[4] Ignatieff 1998, 239–41.

[5] Invited to present at a seminar for the president and leading members of the Kennedy administration, Berlin first declined – and then, having relented, chose to speak about nineteenth-century Russian thought (Ignatieff 1998, 241–2).

[6] There are notable exceptions: e.g. his discussion of the relationships among Marx, Bakunin, and Lasalle in KM, or his evocation of the passionate arguments among Russian revolutionary activists in the essays collected in RT.

rather than in terms of general regularities or laws, and *individualized,* reflecting the distinct personal experiences, circumstances, values, and gifts of the individual, as opposed to the more impersonal or "objective" model of the ideal scientific observer. Judgment emerges as a significant historical factor if, contrary to determinist and materialist analyses, individual choices do matter in history – and if these choices reflect perceptions and beliefs distinct from, and not wholly determined by, material interests. And judgment for Berlin represents a mode of engaging with the world which brings together questions of efficacy and of desirability or rightness – thus bridging politics and ethics, and avoiding both an amoralism which ignores values, and an idealism which ignores realities. His insistence on the importance of political judgment also reflected Berlin's pluralism, which held that many situations require choices between competing values which, those values being theoretically incommensurable, cannot be based on the application of some doctrine or formula.

This chapter first summarizes Berlin's account of the nature of human understanding and judgment, as well as his critique of determinism and scientism. Next, it explores Berlin's discussions of political leadership, and his portraits of individual statesmen. The exploration of Berlin's judgments of these figures leads to a consideration of his views on the relationship of morality and politics.

I UNDERSTANDING, PERCEPTION, AND THE SKILL OF POLITICAL JUDGMENT

Berlin published little explicitly devoted to the topic of political judgment: two of the most important sources for his views on the subject were lectures, which would have gone unpublished without the intervention of Berlin's editor, Henry Hardy.[7] Much of what he did have to say about *political* judgment reflected, and was sometimes conflated with, a larger concern with the nature of human knowledge – more particularly, the nature of humanistic as opposed to scientific knowledge.[8] If the defense of liberty and a particular liberal spirit against authoritarian theories and impulses was central to Berlin's political thinking and writing, and the defense of pluralism against monistic theories and impulses was central to his ethical thought, the critique of a reductionistic scientism and defense of humanist modes of understanding were central to his thinking about epistemology, history, and intellectual inquiry broadly. (Often, in Berlin's work, these all seem to be one and the same project.) Berlin objected to those who, "hypnotised by the magnificent progress of the natural sciences," sought

---

[7] Only a relatively short piece on the subject ("Realism in Politics") was published by Berlin under his own steam (in the *Spectator* in 1954); it has subsequently been reprinted in POI 163–72.
[8] On this, see Choi (Chapter 3) and Hanley (Chapter 5) in this volume, as well as Hanley 2004 and Hanley 2007.

to establish a "science of society" which would supplant humanistic, historical, interpretive approaches to understanding human experience (CC 140).

As an empiricist committed to at least some elements and manifestations of modern skepticism and scientific method, Berlin did not denigrate or demonize scientific inquiry, as did many "Counter-Enlightenment" thinkers. Modern science had succeeded in explaining and establishing a great deal, and what science could explain and establish, it should. Nevertheless, he cautioned that "a great deal cannot be ... grasped by the sciences," and that to seek to treat human experience *wholly* scientifically was "one of the most grotesque claims ever made by human beings" (SR 60, 25; cf. L 19–20, 26–7). Following Vico, Herder, and Dilthey, Berlin defended the validity of a humanistic approach to history which aimed at understanding human action from within. History could not be written "in a purely behaviouristic way, i.e. causally," dispensing with "motives, purposes, frustrations, ideal ends, miseries & splendours of vice & virtue & achievement & failure."[9] The "historical sense" involved "concentrated interest in particular events or persons or situations as such, and not as instances of a generalisation"; historical writing should aim to "convey differences more than similarities, to paint a portrait of a unique, absolutely specific set of events and persons" (CC 180; FIB 107).

Another central theme in Berlin's writings on history, which undergirded his focus on political leadership, was his discussion of the question of determinism, which he identified as "the most celebrated question of all" concerning human nature (L 4) – and which was, in any case, an issue particularly close to his heart.[10] In the controversial "Historical Inevitability" (1953), Berlin did not assert that determinism was false, but only that accepting it as true would require a drastic revision of our understanding of human action and of our own experience. Following Kant, Berlin insisted that belief in free will – the ability to make genuine choices for oneself between alternative courses of action, either (or any) of which one *might* have made in a genuinely possible counterfactual situation – was necessary to the very idea of morality (or, the moral worth of actions).[11] To genuinely and consistently hold that individuals *could* not have acted other than they in fact did would require a complete rejection of our present practices of praising, blaming, holding responsible – indeed, of judging human conduct generally.

So drastic a change in the way we think about and relate to one another (and ourselves) could be justified, Berlin believed, only if the case for determinism was conclusive; and, in his view, it was not. While it was impossible to prove

---

[9] To Myron Gilmore, December 26, 1949, E 151.
[10] E.g. "anything that upsets careful predictions, the general assumption that vast impersonal forces are guiding our faltering footsteps in directions unknown to us ... pleases me immensely. There is no limit to my pleasure in the unforeseen and fortuitous ... [which] really spring from the heart of the Russian intelligentsia – like everything else that I believe" (to Nicolas Nabokov, June 25, 1970, B 425).
[11] On Berlin's debt to Kant, see the evidence presented in Cherniss 2013, 101, 190–4.

that human choices were not determined by antecedent causal factors lying outside the will of the agent, most philosophies of history that attributed human action to the influence of "vast impersonal forces" struck Berlin as decidedly unconvincing (see L 4–5, 21, 27–30). The attempts of deterministic philosophers of history (and social scientists) to explain behavior and events struck Berlin as unconvincing; and their attempts to make *predictions* based on their deterministic theories were, Berlin pointed out (not without relish), almost uniformly unsuccessful. In fact, he alleged, belief in historical and sociological determinism was not truly scientific, but rather "pseudo-scientific," resting on "immense, unsubstantiated images and similes," and reflecting a fearful desire to escape the anxiety of freedom and responsibility. Historical determinism was an "alibi," through which, "by directing our gaze towards the greater wholes, we make them responsible in our place" (L 162, 165, 163, 131, 164).

Berlin's argument provoked many, often sharp, critiques – not all of which were directed at what Berlin had actually said.[12] The fault lay not entirely with the critics (or with whatever impersonal forces were impelling them forward); for "Historical Inevitability" was prolix in its argument, and undiscriminating in its targets: what Berlin means by "determinism," which variants of determinism are most central to his argument, and which thinkers are the main exponents of the views he is attacking are not always kept clear. What does seem clear, stepping back from the thicket of arguments, is that Berlin was particularly concerned with those who saw history forming some unalterable "pattern" and conforming to inflexible laws of development; and with the related belief that individuals and groups never have a genuine choice between alternative courses of action – that all choices are really made ahead of time by impersonal forces, so that individual judgment and will have no genuine force (see L 5, 26–7, 85, 97–8). These views came together in the conviction – nightmarish to Berlin – that there is always "one and only one direction in which a given aggregate of individuals" is traveling, in which they are driven by "quasi-occult impersonal forces" (L 85). It appears to have been this, more than the belief that our actions have identifiable predetermining causes beyond an autonomous human will, that was the true target of Berlin's writings against determinism. His goal was not to defend a particular metaphysical theory, but to vindicate the significance of individual personality, and human beings' capacity, and responsibility, to make choices, and to judge the choices of others, in undertaking action, even if we must also modestly acknowledge the limits of our wisdom and capacity for control.

This argument had ideological implications – and a clear ideological motivation – insofar as determinism was widely recognized as a central tenet of Marxism, and hence of communism (even though communism was also shaped by the Bolsheviks' rejection of the rigid determinism of orthodox

---

[12] Berlin's response to these criticisms can be found in L 4–30; for a cataloging of the critiques, see Harris 2002.

Marxism). Like many of his contemporaries (most prominently, Raymond Aron and Karl Popper), Berlin advanced a critique of historical determinism as part of an anticommunist polemical program – though it should be noted that all three men directed their anti-deterministic critique against other philosophies and ideologies, and that, if their political opposition to communism motivated their attacks on determinism, it was also the case that their skepticism about deterministic philosophies of history was a significant inspiration for their rejection of communism.[13] But to reject determinism could also open the door to utopian aspirations (of the sort Marx and Engels had savagely critiqued, and from which they had struggled to free socialism). If nothing was predetermined, was not all possible? Berlin did not think so; but explaining why this wasn't the case, and, still more, how one could *know* (or at least, come to reasonable hypotheses about) what was and was not possible, took some work.

This was the question with which Berlin began one of his most significant discussions of practical – including political – judgment. "The Sense of Reality" (1953) begins by asking what it means to dismiss certain aspirations or plans as utopian, anachronistic, "escapist," and "unrealistic" because they are unsuited to the conditions of present-day society, which set definite limits on what can be done. Berlin first acknowledged – indeed, emphasized – "the limits of free human action – the barriers imposed by unalterable and little alterable regularities in nature, in the functioning of human bodies and minds" (SR 1–6, 9), before going on to push against an excessively restrictive picture of human freedom of action. A "sense of reality" points to the limited possibilities of action, but also enables actors to move as freely as possible within those limits. Belief in "iron law[s]" of historical development had been "broken" by the tumultuous events of the twentieth century, which made it "clear that men of sufficient energy and ruthlessness could collect a sufficient degree of material power to transform their worlds much more radically than had been thought possible before." Lenin, Stalin, and Hitler had demonstrated that "human beings are a good deal more plastic than was hitherto thought, that given enough willpower, fanaticism, determination – and no doubt a favorable conjunction of circumstances – almost anything, at any rate far more than was hitherto thought possible, can be altered." "Realism," then, should not be equated with acceptance of such "laws." Indeed, it was belief in "iron laws" of history or society that was at the heart of failures of realism: for such schemata "oversimplify the complex texture," the "shapeless living reality of human lives" (SR 12, 14, 16–17, 38–9). A genuine sense of reality allows for the perception of the unexpected, of opportunities to move in new and different directions rather than rigidly following the path laid out by past developments. Good practical judgment requires not only knowledge of facts, but also an

---

[13] On Berlin's critique of Marxism, and his affinities with Aron and Popper, see Craiutu, Chapter 6 in this volume.

imaginative capacity to see possibilities; and an ability to integrate knowledge and imagination in a way that disciplines and sobers the latter, while giving fresh perspective and direction to the former.

"The Sense of Reality" is largely concerned with historical understanding. But in the final section Berlin draws out the *political* implications of his account. "[W]isdom in statesmen," he asserts, is a matter of being able to grasp, and respond effectively to, the most practically salient features of the infinitely complex texture of reality, without having consciously and comprehensively grasped reality in full. This requires "an element of improvisation, of playing by ear, of being able to size up the situation ... for which no formulae, no nostrums, no general recipes, no skill in identifying specific situations as instances of general laws can be a substitute" (SR 40–41). The capacity for improvisation requires both a mastery of the available knowledge, of the "rules of thumb" (SR 51) derived from past experience; and a capacity to innovate, to find one's way where no path exists, to take a leap in the dark – and find one's footing on landing.

Berlin returned to these themes in "Political Judgment" (1957), which takes up the question "What is it to have good judgment in politics?" He begins the essay by asserting what such judgment is *not*: it is not a matter of the sort of knowledge aimed at by the sciences – "systems of verified hypotheses, organised under laws, that enable one, by the use of further experiment and observation, to discover other facts, and to verify new hypotheses" (SR 51). Instead, good judgment consists in a personal quality of "exceptional sensitiveness" – which Berlin likens to the possession of "antennae." This "perceptual gift" is not a mystical quality, but "something perfectly ordinary, empirical, and quasi-aesthetic," which is developed through experience; a "semi-instinctive" skill – "like the the ability to read without simultaneous awareness of the rules of the language" (SR 56–7, 63). To deploy a related metaphor, the good politician is like a person who writes well – elegantly, even eloquently – without self-consciously or rigidly following the laws of grammar.

Such "practical wisdom" consists, in part, of a capacity for "synthesis rather than analysis," "integrating a vast amalgam of constantly changing, multicoloured, evanescent, perpetually overlapping data," in a way that allows one to see how different elements "hang together" in a "total pattern." While political judgment is thus synthesizing, it is also particularistic; it never loses a sense of the uniqueness and distinctness of different entities and events. The "merit" of great politicians is that "they grasp the unique combination of characteristics that constitute this particular situation – this and no other," "the character of a particular movement, of a particular individual, of a unique state of affairs, of a unique atmosphere, of some particular combination of economic, political, personal factors." But in addition to these features, common to good political judgment and the "sense of reality" more generally, political judgment involves seeing situations "pragmatically ... in terms of what you or others can or will do to them, and what they can or will do to others or to you." In addition to a practical or pragmatic *orientation*, political judgment requires a capacity to make practical *estimations* – or, a "sense of what will 'work', and what will not," "an acute sense of what fits with what, what springs from what, what leads to what" (SR 56–9, 63).

Berlin's account of political judgment is reminiscent of Aristotle's notion of *phronesis*, or practical wisdom: a shrewd sense, based in experience, irreducible to rules or theorems, of the right thing to do in a given set of circumstances. Like Aristotle, Berlin suggested that a certain amount of vagueness or imprecision in discussing judgment is inescapable, since it is only possible to achieve that degree of precision which the phenomenon under investigation allows.[14] Also like Aristotle, Berlin depicted judgment as a faculty that is properly concerned with particulars, rather than universals. In this he departed from Kant, to whom he was in other respects deeply indebted; he also did not connect judgment to impartiality or universality, as both Kant and Arendt[15] did. Berlin *did*, however, resemble Kant in seeing judgment as an *active* and *synthesizing* capacity – rather than a capacity for merely recreating or reflecting an external reality.

Berlin was suspicious of claims to possess a "key" to how to act, or how to go about deciding how to act. There was, he insisted, no set of propositions from which good judgment can be deduced or derived, or to which it can be reduced. Instead of precepts or protocols, political actors must rely on dispositional qualities, which are not easily taught, but nevertheless can be cultivated: "sympathy, interest and imagination," "sense of timing, sensitiveness to the needs and capacities of human beings" (SR 25, 41). The tendency to approach politics with the assumption that all problems were solvable, and that the means to solving them was through the possession of the proper theoretical or technical knowledge – "here is the disease, and if the doctor is well enough informed, he has the cure" – was an often fatal conceit.[16] This critique of the search for a key to political judgment was tied to a more immediate intellectual and political agenda: to combat not only the attempt to impose a "scientific" model of understanding on the study of human beings, but also the technocratic project of subjecting society to the control of scientific experts who would secure human happiness and virtue through "social hygiene," the "reorganization" of human life based on "systematic" knowledge, and the deployment of technology, including techniques for forming and modifying human mental habits and behavior (SR 34–5). Such technocratic rule threatened to cramp human existence and crush individuality.[17] It was also

---

[14] Cf. Hanley 2004, 330–2; Smith 2012, 84–8. For Aristotle's influence on Berlin, see Cherniss 2013, 3, 6–7, 18–19.
[15] See Arendt 1993, 197–264; Arendt 1994, 313; and Arendt 1982, *passim*. For Kant's identification of (aesthetic) judgment with a "*sensus communis*" see Kant 2000 [1790], section 40, 173–6.
[16] Berlin, "The Lessons of History," Chapter 15 in this volume, 270.
[17] See e.g. L 55–93; POI 273–84.

bound to fail, Berlin insisted, because it refused to recognize the limitations of scientific or technical knowledge and the complexity of individuals and societies. The resulting failures would produce still more evils, as the frustrated social planners sought to force their plans on to a reality which the plans failed to fit (SR 38–9, 65–6).[18]

Berlin's skepticism about the ability of theory to guide practice, and his opposition to scientism, significantly resemble his contemporary Michael Oakeshott's critique of "rationalism in politics." Berlin was loath to admit the affinity (just as he was reluctant say a good word about Hannah Arendt, another thinker who defended the merits of judgment as against scientific rationalism or positivism [see e.g. Arendt 1993, 241–2]).[19] He sought to distance himself from what he regarded as Oakeshott's obscurantist irrationalism and conservatism, peppering his discussions of judgment with criticisms of (unnamed) doctrinaires on the right for their defense of prejudice, mystical intuition, or unthinking "common sense" (SR 39–40, 43–4, 61–2).[20] While there was an element of political wariness (and personal animus) at work here, there were also significant intellectual disparities between the two men. Berlin did not endorse Oakeshott's view that habituation within a larger tradition of practice is the necessary precondition for developing skill or forming understanding; he did not identify rationality or morality with an "idiom" which furnishes "knowledge of how to behave appropriately in the circumstances," or with "coherence" with a tradition of sentiment or an ongoing "practice."[21] Oakeshott's account of judgment at times seems to rule out the possibility of a genuine revolutionary – one who breaks drastically with established modes and habits – possessing good judgment. Berlin, for all his aversion to revolutionary violence, recognized and respected good judgment in revolutionaries where he found it. And he appreciated the radical potential of judgment, which can seize on unexpected opportunities and discern when novel rather than traditional political forms may be (most) effective. Berlin also did not target, as Oakeshott did, the very conception of politics as problem-solving, and he was less sweeping in his criticisms of reformist projects in politics (as distinct from those who pursued such reformist projects with a dogmatically theoretical, technocratic, and/or authoritarian mindset) than was Oakeshott: not only did he celebrate Franklin Roosevelt, he defended the British welfare state to the end of his days.

---

[18] For the importance of this theme in Berlin's political thought, and its immediate historical context, see Cherniss 2014a. On the connection between epistemological "scientism" and political authoritarianism, see Scott 1998.
[19] On the other hand, Berlin acknowledged that his account resembled his Oxford colleague Gilbert Ryle's distinction between "knowing that" and "knowing how," with which Oakeshott's views also show affinity (SR 41–3; Ryle 1945–6).
[20] For Berlin's anxiety about being identified with conservative "obscurantists" see Berlin to Myron Gilmore, December 26, 1949, E 150–2; to Noel Annan, January 13, 1954, E 422–3.
[21] Oakeshott 1991, 101.

The two men's intellectual styles were also tellingly different. Oakeshott ultimately sought to offer an anti-"rationalist" account of rationality, a sort of anti-theory theory of political understanding. Berlin did not. In keeping with his belief that the objects and operation of political judgment are irreducibly particular, that judgment can be perceived, apprehended, and understood as it is practiced by individuals in particular cases but not translated into or grasped through a general theory, he did not advance a systematic account of practical judgment. Instead, he offered vivid portraits of the distinctive temperaments and leadership style of individual figures.

II THE VISIONARY AND THE VIRTUOSO: POLITICAL LEADERS AND LEADERSHIP

Berlin often framed his portraits of political leaders as depictions of "political greatness." To be great, on Berlin's account, is to take "a large step, one far beyond the normal capacities of men, in satisfying, or materially affecting, central human interests." Great individuals "permanently and radically" alter "the outlook and values of a significant body of human beings" in ways that previously seemed impossible, or at least improbable (PI 59). This is not to say that great political leaders act alone, or can control the consequences of their actions: they are dependent on the action of others, and captive to the vagaries of events and unintended consequences. But they imprint a personal impression on the world, leaving it different from what it was, and from how it would have been in their absence.

Berlin began his analysis, in characteristic fashion, by noting that there were "at least two types of political greatness" (POI 227). These closely resemble his famous distinction between single-minded "hedgehogs" and multi-focal "foxes" (RT 24–5).[22] "Hedgehog"-like politicians – whom we may term political *visionaries* – are possessed by a "bright, coherent dream," free of "doubts or hesitations." They often fail to understand people or events, and succeed, when they succeed, through "concentration of willpower, directness and strength," inspiring, hectoring, manipulating, or coercing others to fit into the patterns that they see in their minds' eyes, dominating history by ignoring its complexities. Such leaders may rise to "noble grandeur"; they may also be monsters. Even when they are benevolent, there is something inhuman about such "vehement, fanatical crusaders" who, "armed with a doctrine ... in place of humanity and realism," are "morally proof against human considerations," and emotionally remote from "the sufferings of the human beings upon whom they inevitably trample." Absorbed in their visions, and determined to translate them into reality, such politicians "know not what they do (and do not care

---

[22] "Chaim Weizmann's Leadership," in which Berlin set out his typology of leaders, appeared in 1954, the year after "The Hedgehog and the Fox" was published (though the original essay from which the latter grew appeared in 1951).

either)." It is this, indeed, that sometimes allows them to overcome "enormous odds." Their conviction, focus, and determination can free them from doubts and hesitations that afflict others, making them "exceptionally, dangerously effective." By virtue of their very resistance to reality, they are sometimes able to transform the world to an unforeseen degree (POI 227–9; 234; PI 43, 67; SR 12–14, 63).

The second type of great politician – the "political virtuoso" – is particularly gifted with a capacity for political judgment. Such politicians possess "antennae of the greatest possible delicacy," which give them a sense of "what to do and when to do it" in order to achieve their ends – ends which reflect what large numbers of their fellow citizens are thinking and feeling, often dimly and inarticulately. Leaders of this second type have a keen sense of "precisely where the shoe pinches," "where life presses on them most heavily," and convey "a sense of understanding their inner needs, of responding to their own deepest impulses." They accordingly inspire not awe, but confidence and affection. Berlin clearly was drawn to leaders of this second type; many of the examples he typically used to illustrate it – Lincoln, Masaryk, Roosevelt, and Weizmann – were figures he regarded as morally good as well as politically great (PI 43–4, POI 229–30; cf. SR 56–7).

Berlin's distinction between visionary and virtuoso leaders, like that between hedgehogs and foxes, or positive and negative liberty, may seem to be obviously – perhaps tendentiously – normative: what presents itself as an analytical distinction appears to really be an oblique strategy of advocacy. Yet (as with his other, more famous dichotomies) Berlin's evaluative stance toward the two types of leader he describes is more complex and nuanced than it first appears. The characterization of the "visionary" politician just quoted carries with it, to be sure, implicit or explicit moral censure. But Berlin qualified his criticism, acknowledging that visionary politicians could be not only successful, but admirable. Indeed, when one turns to the first of Berlin's portraits of individual leaders, one finds him praising a statesman he explicitly identified with the visionary type: Winston Churchill (see e.g. POI 231). Churchill's strength lay in the impregnability of his "bright, heroic vision"; blind to halftones, resistant to change, "he does not mirror, he affects others and alters them to his own powerful measure" (PI 7, 18, 20). Through the "sheer intensity of his eloquence" and force of personality, Churchill "bound his spell" upon his fellow citizens, who "went forward into battle transformed by his words." (PI 19). He *created* a new mood around him, rather than accurately perceiving the one that was there. It was this that allowed him to rally his beleaguered nation when it most needed rallying.

The second great exemplar of political leadership to whom Berlin devoted extended discussion, Churchill's friend and ally Franklin D. Roosevelt, was a politician of a very different quality: not a visionary but a pragmatist, not an aristocrat but a democrat – indeed, "the most genuine and unswerving spokesman for democracy of his time" (PI 15). Roosevelt's was a demotic virtuosity: the capacity to understand, identify with, and respond to the aspirations, needs, and ideals of "humble people" in ways that made them feel understood, respected, and protected (PI 15; cf. POI 230). His capacity to inspire rested not merely on charisma, but on the trust and confidence that he evoked in his followers, which rested on a perception that he understood the ideals and needs of his people and had their best interests at heart. And even if Roosevelt did play on his constituents' sentiments, he did not (with some notable exceptions, on which Berlin remained silent) seek to dragoon or tyrannize them. He had the skills of a demagogue, but he eschewed base demagoguery and so was able to protect American democracy against demagogic temptations. And his sharp awareness of his fellow citizens' needs, hopes, virtues, and limitations kept his politics grounded. By virtue of his perceptual gift, the naturally ebullient, optimistic Roosevelt was able to avoid the folly of arrogant, and the fury of disappointed, utopianism (see PI 37–49).

Yet the buoyancy that allowed Roosevelt to free his followers from fear and despair reflected a lack of the depth, the sense of the tragic, that Churchill possessed. "[M]agnificent virtuoso" though he was (PI 44), Roosevelt was averse to "probing beneath the surface." He recognized similarities, but was impervious to differences; he saw possibilities, but was sometimes blind to dangers. Churchill was "more serious, more intent," felt more keenly the "eternal differences" between people that would make a new, cosmopolitan order difficult to attain (PI 23–4, 27). This allowed him to strike chords that lay beyond Roosevelt's grasp: "Roosevelt might have spoken of sweat and blood, but when Churchill offered his people tears, he spoke a word which might have been uttered by Lincoln or Mazzini or Cromwell, but not by Roosevelt" (PI 17). On the other hand, Churchill was "frightening" in his imperviousness to aspects of reality that contradicted his vision. There was in him something of the "fanatical vision" and "blindness and stubborn self-absorption" that Berlin noted in Woodrow Wilson, another political visionary (PI 16–17, 43). And if Roosevelt lacked depth, he possessed the political virtuoso's sensitivity to reality "developed to the point of genius," and was able to sense "the tendencies of his time and their projections into the future to a most uncommon" or "uncanny" degree: "The inner currents, the tremors and complicated convolutions" of his time "seemed to register themselves within his nervous system with a kind of seismographical accuracy" (PI 15).

Read in conjunction with his essays on political judgment, his portraits of Churchill and Roosevelt reveal that Berlin held both political "hedgehogs" and "foxes" to have both merits and weaknesses. These portraits usefully undermine the stark distinction that Berlin drew between "virtuoso" and "visionary" leaders in his more abstract discussions: Churchill's and Roosevelt's success was due to the fact that the former was not completely blind to the real needs and aspirations of his countrymen, while the latter was able to look beyond immediate exigencies to more audacious hopes. At the same time, these portraits also underline the necessary imperfection of all political leaders – but not in a disparaging or demeaning way, which denigrates the subject and undermines any sense of politics as a (potentially) noble activity. Berlin sought to highlight the real gifts and achievements of Churchill and Roosevelt – and, in so doing, vindicate the reality, possibility, and importance of political heroism. But by acknowledging crucial limitations of both men, and using each as a foil to highlight the virtues and weaknesses of the other, he suggests not only that no politician is perfect – and that success depends in large part on the (fortuitous) "fit" between a leader's personal qualities and the circumstances – but also that the very virtues which make a given politician capable of doing great things are inseparable from limitations, faults, even vices. Berlin's essays, read in conjunction, vividly illustrate what Edward Shils called "the complexity of virtue."[23] Berlin thus points to a more realistic appreciation of political leadership, against both over-critical cynicism and uncritical hero-worship (the former of which often reflects a simplistic reaction against the simplicity of the latter).

The statesman whom Berlin knew most intimately, and about whom he wrote most extensively, was Chaim Weizmann. Where Churchill and Roosevelt preserved their political communities in the face of trial and disaster, Weizmann brought a new community into being. In doing so he showed how visionary and pragmatic dispositions might be blended – and political efficacy and moral integrity balanced. Weizmann was certainly a statesman of the "virtuoso" type: "On good terms with reality," he was "above all things an empiricist," free from "fanaticism and intolerant, utopian idealism." Yet he combined his realism with a visionary power reminiscent of Churchill. He held firm to the belief that "moral force, if ... competently organised, always defeated mere material power": as he remarked to Berlin, "Miracles do happen, but one has to work very hard for them" (PI 72, 95–6; Berlin 1970, 18–20). Acting as if he were a statesman with the power of a nation behind him, he was able to impel others to act as if this were true – until, in effect, it became true. Weizmann's apparently visionary tendencies proved to be in tune with reality: one can sense Berlin's relish when he writes that "it turned out that history conformed to Weizmann's vision, compounded of hard-headed common sense and deep historical emotion, and not to the normal categories of the 'realists'" (PI 86–7). Even more than the depictions of Roosevelt and Churchill, Berlin's tribute to Weizmann suggests how vision and virtuosity might be brought together in ways that enrich both.

---

[23] As Shils explains, recognizing the complexity of virtue requires an understanding that "no virtue stands alone, that every virtuous act costs something in terms of other virtuous acts, that virtues are intertwined with evils, and that no theoretical system of a hierarchy of virtue is ever realizable in practice" (Shils 1997, 52).

III AGAINST THE CURRENT: INTEGRITY, HUMANITY, AND THE VIRTUES OF "FAILURE"

Berlin's presentation of Weizmann as an exemplar of political greatness may appear to raise a puzzle. Like Machiavelli in his discussion of Cesare Borgia, Berlin chose to hold up for praise a figure whose political career ended in what may be regarded as failure.[24] Though his dream of establishing a Jewish state was realized, Weizmann's ideals were ultimately "set aside" by the nation which he had dedicated his life to creating; he died a bitter man, experiencing the honors his country granted him as an inadequate substitute for genuine power. Berlin does not seek to evade this point; he notes, even emphasizes Weizmann's disappointment.

As with Machiavelli's use of Borgia, we may take this as an indication that, as Berlin acknowledged, success requires not only skill, but also luck (SR 49). However, I wish to suggest that Berlin makes a deeper, more uncomfortable point. Weizmann's very virtues – his "excessively clear sense of reality," his moderation and rejection of the tools of fanaticism, extremism, demagoguery, and brutality – ultimately became handicaps in a political context marked by polarization, intransigence, and violence (POI 236). But it was these very qualities that were the basis of Weizmann's earlier, crucially important achievements. His personal power, his ability to command devotion and inspire others to act, rested on the moral authority of his cause and personal conduct. Weizmann, at the height of his career, occupied the curious position of a world statesman without a state. It was only because they found his moral case irrefutable – particularly when presented with the dignity and integrity which his personal bearing lent it – that gentile leaders were inspired or embarrassed into cooperating with him. A more fanatical, or more cynically "realistic" figure would have been easier to dismiss (PI 60, 63–4, 84, 86–7).

One response to Berlin's stress on the way in which changing circumstances render the same qualities advantageous or damaging to a politician's effectiveness is to conclude that the greatest of political virtues is adaptability.[25] The most virtuosic – and, in general, the most successful – politician, on such a view, is the one who can change her spots in response to the circumstances. Yet Berlin seems to resist this conclusion. If moral authority is sometimes a crucial part of a politician's effectiveness, changeability with regard to principles and persona may be self-undermining. Success is, furthermore, not the only or the primary criterion for judging a politician. Integrity and nobility may have their own intrinsic claims. If these qualities may be political disadvantages in some contexts, they also seem desirable

---

[24] See Machiavelli 1985 [1532], ch. 7.
[25] The competing merits of adaptability and constancy are also a major theme in Machiavelli: see Machiavelli 1985 [1532], Ch. XVII, p. 68; Ch. XXV *passim*; Machiavelli 1996 [1531] Bk I Ch. 6; Bk II, Ch. 29; Bk. III, Chs. 9, 22, 31.

qualities for a politician to possess from the perspective of subjects who fear the oppression and betrayal that a morally ruthless politician may inflict upon them.[26]

In judging a politician's success (or lack thereof), moral considerations are not extraneous: "success" means more than "climbing the greasy pole." The successful conquest of power may leave behind a bitter heritage of violence, distrust, cynicism, and opportunism. Heroic failure may bequeath a better legacy, furnishing richer soil in which others may plant and nourish the seeds of freedom and political flourishing. Viewed in a broader historical perspective, those who fail in their own time may prove the more influential, and more beneficial, political figures. Furthermore, the qualities, stances, and actions desirable in a political leader depend not only on immediate circumstances, but also on the goals that she or he pursues. In Weizmann's case, even if greater fanaticism, brutality, or cynicism had allowed him to be more politically effective at certain junctures, the crucial question would remain: effective to what end? Weizmann's moral vision was, in fact, essential to both the definition and the achievement of his political project. He did not simply desire power for himself or his nation. Rather, his political life was dedicated to enabling his fellow Jews to "live a life worthy of human beings, without betraying their own ideals or trampling on those of others" (PI 76). The embrace of more ruthless policies and a more brutal morality would have betrayed and undermined the cause for which Weizmann was striving. To win power in such terms, and with the effects that such a conquest of power would likely have, would have been a larger defeat.

These reflections raise the larger question of how Berlin believed political actors should respond to the often conflicting claims of personal morality and political efficacy.[27] Berlin respected the gifts of, and recognized the need for, political virtuosi; he did not take them for granted or cavil at their invariable failings. But his heart was with Herzen, Turgenev, Hess, Vico, Herder, even Hamann – the misfits, the losers, the "toad[s] beneath the harrow" trampled by the march of history; those who went "against the current," whose integrity did not allow them to simplify or sell themselves, worldly failures, prophets unarmed and without honor in their own lifetimes and lands. And he rejected

---

[26] One implication of this – which Berlin did not pursue, though his discussion of Roosevelt's distinctively *democratic* political greatness suggests it – is that the personal qualities desirable in a democratic leader, or desirable from a democratic normative perspective, may be closer to notions of personal ethical goodness than is the case for other political systems or norms. For a kindred argument, see the account of "democratic constancy" in Sabl 2001.

[27] This question – a perennial of political reflection, invariably posed by political action – has been addressed in e.g. Machiavelli 1985 [1532]; Weber 1948a [1919]; Walzer 1973; Hampshire et al. 1978; Hampshire 1989; and Williams 2005. Berlin wrote directly about Machiavelli; his affinities with Weber's perspective are apparent (and discussed by Crowder in this volume; see Chapter 13). Hampshire and Williams were among his closest friends; Walzer's work has many affinities with Berlin's (and reflects the personal influence of Hampshire).

those "realists," contemptuous of idealism, who hard-headedly embraced political necessity or the "march of history," who admired the toughness and effectiveness of "world-historical individuals," prophets armed and lethally effective in imposing their visions on the "human material" within their grasp (see L 343).

This picture of Berlin as a critic of "realism," juxtaposed with his insistence on the importance of a "sense of reality" about politics, and in light of his reputation as a critic of "utopianism,"[28] calls for clarification. Berlin distinguished between two senses of "realism": a correct perception of reality, free of emotional distortions and doctrinal presuppositions, related to the "sense of reality"; and a "more sinister" sense – the sense in which people used the term when they "explain[ed] away some unusually mean or brutal decision" by admitting, often with false regret, to being "realists." In this latter sense, "realism" was a euphemism for being "harsh and brutal, not shrinking from what is usually considered immoral, not swayed by soft sentimental moral considerations" (POI 163; FIB 104). This latter sort of "realism," applied to social or political inquiry, held that the job of the inquirer was not to judge the phenomena under investigation as good or bad, nor to "express likes and dislikes," but simply to show why certain actions had been regarded by their authors as necessary under the circumstances. From this standpoint, "Lies, cruelty, terrorism, brutality" appeared "normal"; criticism of such actions was sentimental and foolish.[29]

Such "realism" was a powerful current in postwar thought, and a major target for Berlin and other postwar liberals.[30] Its claims to intellectual superiority hinged on equating a single-minded focus on power, and an amoral perspective on politics, with a correct perception of reality. Berlin's insistence on the difference between the two senses of "realism" was part of his polemic against this "realist" tendency, as were his attacks on theories of "historical inevitability," which he alleged underwrote the "realist" worship of success and contempt for failure, and his insistence that politics involves a contest not only of interests but of ideals, and that complete moral "neutrality" in the study of history was neither possible nor desirable.[31] He also reacted against this sort of "realism" in his sympathetic accounts of thinkers who went "against the current," his deployment of a language of moral appraisal in his discussion of individuals and events,[32] and his highlighting of the "idealistic" elements in the outlook of successful politicians, so as to show how a certain sort of personal decency plays a role in the most admirable sort of political greatness. Thus, he declared that (after ensuring Allied victory) the "greatest service to mankind"

---

[28] See Aarsbergen-Ligtvoet 2006, ch. 2; Jacoby 2005; Walzer 2013.
[29] Burnham 1941, 153–4; cf. ibid. 8, 206, 272, 273, 285.
[30] For a brief summary, see Cherniss 2013, 112–13.
[31] See L 95–165 and *passim*; ibid. 166–8; Berlin 1950a, 1961, 1962a.
[32] Cf. Hanley 2004, 333.

rendered by Roosevelt – "the most benevolent as well as the greatest master" of the art of politics in modern times – was to show that "it is possible to be politically effective and yet benevolent and human; that the fierce left- and right-wing propaganda of the 1930s, according to which the conquest and retention of political power is not compatible with human qualities," but demands the sacrifice of self and others "upon the altar of some ruthless ideology, or the practice of despotism," was "simply untrue" (PI 44, 48).

This opposition to vulgar or doctrinaire realism, which informed all of Berlin's discussions of leadership, came to the fore in his characterization of Weizmann. Berlin knew that Weizmann was no moral paragon, and did not portray him as one: he acknowledged that Weizmann was apt to manipulate the feelings of his associates, appealing to them when it suited his purposes, and dropping them when they ceased to be useful to him.[33] Weizmann, like Churchill and Roosevelt, was willing to dirty his hands to a degree – as, Berlin maintained (without relishing the fact), all responsible politicians must be. But Weizmann remained essentially "morally decent ... civilised and ... humane" (PI 81). There were limits to which he was willing to dirty his hands, and moral principles he would not compromise. He

> did not attempt to save his people by violence or cunning – to beat them into shape, if need be with the utmost brutality, like Lenin, or to deceive them for their own good, like Bismarck ... He never called upon the Jews to make terrible sacrifices, or offer their lives, or commit crimes, or condone the crimes of others, for the sake of some felicity to be realised at some unspecified date, as the Marxists did; nor did he play upon their feelings unscrupulously, or try deliberately to exacerbate them against this or that real, or imaginary, enemy, as extremists in his own movement have frequently tried to do. He wished to make his nation free and happy, but not at the price of sinning against any human value in which he and they believed. (PI 76)

These ethical scruples were not contrary to the sense of reality which was at the root of Weizmann's political shrewdness. To the contrary: they were inseparable from it. Both reflected the same freedom from "that streak of bigoted rationalism which breeds belief in final solutions for which no price ... can be too high" (PI 72).

Berlin's accounts of statesmen are thus not morally neutral – as befits one who attacked the goal of "neutrality" in the study of human affairs. He was concerned with showing not only what made them great, but what allowed them to use greatness to good ends. When it came to studying past thinkers, Berlin was fascinated by those with whom he disagreed. But in discussing political leaders, he was drawn to – or, perhaps, could only bear to discuss at length – those of whom he approved; his discussions of those he despised or feared could be incisive, but were rarely lengthy or in-depth. The leaders on

---

[33] This reflects tensions in Berlin's own relationship with Weizmann, on which see Dubnov 2012, especially 186–7.

whom he focused represented what he regarded as morally worthy causes – indeed, the political causes that had mattered most to him: the British tradition of political liberty, and Britain's struggle for survival in World War II; the cause of democracy itself in the 1930s, and more narrowly, the progressive, pragmatic, mildly social-democratic liberalism embodied in the New Deal, which represented Berlin's own deepest political sympathies; and (liberal, democratic) Zionism. And, at least on Berlin's account, all had pulled back from the temptation of embracing brutal immorality in the pursuit of their goals.

His encomium to Weizmann, and his similar tributes to Churchill and Roosevelt for eschewing the demagogic temptations to which their political gifts opened them, reveal the extent to which Berlin was concerned not only with political greatness, but also with the relationship of greatness to goodness in politics. Greatness, Berlin acknowledged, is not the same as (either personal or political) goodness. It can enslave, as well as liberate.[34] Morally dubious motivations and actions invariably play a part in the pursuit of political power. Thus, Berlin acknowledged that "only those people can govern great nations who love power – who enjoy it"; he reflected that most of the politicians he had known had appeared "brutal" in some respects.[35] But success, again, is not the only criterion. Whether a political leader's achievements are beneficial or harmful – whether they effect emancipation or enslavement, the alleviation and diminution of suffering or its extension and intensification – is just as important.

Berlin was not a political moralist in any simple sense. That he rejected the particular brand of "vulgar realism" being peddled in the interwar and postwar years does not mean that he categorically rejected the more sophisticated and discomfiting "realist" argument that the personal qualities and conduct that conduce to ruling well are different from those that are personally (or morally) virtuous. As his essay on Machiavelli makes clear, Berlin recognized an insurmountable tension between political efficacy and moral integrity (see AC 33–100). But he also maintained that *both* of these values make irrefutable demands on us; *and* that, if the goals of political striving have any moral worth, some degree of decency and integrity are both in tension with, *and integral to*, the success of that striving, since "evil means destroy good ends" (RT 299). He accepted that one could not seek and exercise political power without moral compromise – and that this made the world of politics tragic and morally dangerous. But he rejected the belief that political responsibility demands the abandonment and repudiation of personal decency – a belief attractive to those who cannot bear the guilt of having violated their consciences, and so seek the excuse of necessity, or who lack the strength or courage to act decently or

---

[34] *Pace* Hanley 2004, 333, where greatness, as such, is said to liberate.
[35] Berlin to Rowland Burdon-Muller, September 7, 1964; B 205–6; to Bernard Williams, October 13, 1971; B 468.

honorably, and are eager to see decency and honesty as signs of weakness or cowardice – a belief that has inspired and excused many lies, and the spilling of much blood (cf. AC 265; L 86, 131, 160).

CONCLUSION: THE MORAL AND POLITICAL SIGNIFICANCE OF GOOD JUDGMENT

Berlin's writings on leadership and judgment are largely neglected, in part because their focus on individual leaders is deeply unfashionable. In democratic times, it smacks too much of a "great man" view of history.[36] (Matters are not helped by the fact that in writing on political leadership Berlin did focus almost solely on *men*.) It also appears insufficiently rigorous and conducive to generalization – that is, insufficiently "scientific." And it may appear tendentious if, against Berlin (and with Tolstoy, and many Marxist theorists), we conclude that "individuals are largely irrelevant to the course of history;" from such a perspective, it will seem "deluded" to focus on studies of their temperaments and actions.[37]

To this last doubt we can offer two brief responses. First, it seems implausible to discount *completely* the importance of individual judgment, choices, and leadership qualities as (sometimes decisive) factors, alongside more "impersonal forces," in history. It is by no means obvious (to take an example close to Berlin's heart[38]) that any leader in Churchill's position, and from Churchill's background, would have elected to fight on against Germany in 1939–40; or that any leader in his position, pursuing his policies, would have been equally successful in rallying Britain to withstand the physical and emotional ordeal of that period. On the other side of the battle lines, the Weimar Republic may in retrospect appear a lost cause. But would the Nazi Party have had the success it did, and would Germany have embarked upon the path of genocide and total war, had Hitler died on the battlefield in World War I, and the Nazis thus been deprived of his powerful demagoguery, and the world spared his racial and historical fantasies? Or, had Lenin been prevented from reaching the Finland Station in 1917, and had Trotsky failed to escape exile to Siberia in 1907, would the Bolsheviks have seized the upper hand in the Russian Revolution?[39]

A second line of argument relies on the fact that political theory, as it is (and has long been) practiced, rests on the assumption, as Melissa Lane has argued, that "political action is inescapably normative." If this is the case, "the theorizing of political action must attend to the practical predicament of

---

[36] On the difficulty of discussing leadership in a democratic context, see Keohane 2012, 155–93.
[37] Lane 2011, 147.   [38] See e.g. CIB 148; UD 55.
[39] Such counterfactuals pose deep problems for causal inquiry, which point to the importance of judgment not just for political actors, but also for historians and social scientists. See Hawthorn 1991.

moral agents deciding how to act," even if it is acknowledged that this includes various constraints on individual action. To this we may add that the fact that we simply do experience politics in terms of some degree of (limited) individual agency is important, not only to the very endeavor of political theory, but also, as Berlin's friend James Joll noted, to "all democratic political theory with its emphasis on 'responsible government' and the 'accountability' of ministers," as well as in ordinary democratic political practice, in which leaders are attacked, and in which their opponents seek to hold them accountable, for their actions. And if we do persist in thinking about and engaging in politics in this way, then, as Lane writes, "the study of historical agents – who faced the demands of agency, however great the constraints on their performances, and the unintended consequences of their actions – cannot help but be instructive."[40]

In going against contemporary political and intellectual currents, Berlin offers a warning about the limitations not only of accounts of history that deny significance to individual agency, but also of approaches to politics which look solely to the rules and internal logic of institutions, or to the strategic logic of (abstracted models of) human interaction, to explain events and secure goals. He offers a reminder that individual figures have a capacity to seize control of and shape movements; to upset, even topple, institutions, or bend their rules to the individual leader's will – for good or ill: the achievements of Gandhi and Nehru, Gorbachev and Havel, Martin Luther King, Jr. and Aung San Suu Kyi, as well as Churchill, Roosevelt, and Weizmann, attest to this power; so do the examples of Lenin, Hitler, Stalin, and Mao (or others we might name).

Berlin's writings on individual leaders also go against contemporary scholarly practice, and invite charges of falling prey to a "great man" view of the world, in being largely "studies in praise."[41] Berlin's approach may be judged intellectually insufficient for lacking critical edge, and failing to contribute to a deeper critique of familiar political and social practices. This line of objection again reflects a broader feature of Berlin's intellectual approach which, while it imposes limitations, also has its own virtue – one rare in much academic work. While Berlin certainly did not lack powers of sharp critical judgment, his more characteristic mode was that of appreciation. This appreciation was not uncritical or undiscriminating; as his friend, the historian John Clive, observed, Berlin's "praise is at no time indiscriminate, and never excludes definition and refinement."[42] Both the processes of discrimination, definition, and refinement and the impulses of appreciation and the willingness to praise, were directed at the same end: to identify and convey not only what made an individual (or work, or event) unique, but what made him or her (or it) valuable – those characteristic features which contributed to human life in all its rich variety and fertile complexity. This

[40] Joll 1979, 99; Lane 2011, 147–8. [41] Annan 2014, 442. [42] Clive 1981, 35.

capacity for appreciation is of value for historical understanding. As the historian Fritz Stern noted, "it is a fairly rare quality for historians to understand greatness, and greatness of a person and greatness of achievement"; Berlin was such a rare case.[43]

Another likely reason for the neglect of Berlin's writings on judgment and leadership is that these unsystematic essays leave many questions open and unexplored. It remains unclear just how seriously Berlin intended, and how far he would push, his distinction between virtuoso and visionary leaders; or how far historical understanding, political judgment, and correct moral discrimination are the same, and how far (and in what ways) they differ. Beyond warning against the blinding effects of dogmatism and reliance on *a priori* theory, Berlin does not take a strong stance on the question of how good judgment is to be cultivated (in contrast, for example, to Aristotle's identification of prolonged habituation in a practice as the necessary route to acquiring *phronesis*). Nor does he offer a philosophical exploration, either of the formal conditions and nature of practical activity (as Oakeshott did in his later work[44]). Nor did he attempt to emulate Machiavelli in exploring how to think about particular dispositions and political tactics. And he did not consider – or, at least, did not pursue and develop – the important thought, which has a natural affinity with his pluralism, that different qualities, styles, and capacities might be demanded in different circumstances, and in different institutional settings and roles.[45]

But even these apparent defects may reflect a valuable feature of Berlin's approach, which rejected *theory* as a guide to action, because theories, as such, require abstraction from the unique features of individual situations and persons, while political judgment requires attention to just such ungeneralizable particular features (SR 36–9). Berlin offers no pat conclusion about what distinguishes good from bad leadership, nor does he prescribe a formula for how to achieve political greatness, because one of the main points that he makes is that political success, or political greatness, is not amenable to formulae.[46]

---

[43] Fritz Stern, in Dworkin, Lilla, and Silvers 2001, 195. Such appreciation of individual greatness may be both unfashionable, and *especially* valuable, in a democratic culture. This, at least, was the view of Tocqueville, who associated an emphasis on individual agency, and therefore personality, with "aristocratic history," and a more impersonal approach with "democratic history." Tocqueville anticipated Berlin in expressing the fear that a tendency to see history as guided by "vast impersonal forces" (L 94, quoting T. S. Eliot) would undermine commitment to individual freedom; sustaining an unfashionably "aristocratic" historical imagination in democratic times might be needed to preserve a measure of human freedom rather than completing human prostration (Tocqueville 2010 [1835–40]), vol. II, part I, ch. 20.

[44] See Oakeshott 1975. [45] For an argument along these lines, see Sabl 2001.

[46] Berlin's attitude seems kindred to that expressed in Saul Kripke's remark on the "cluster concept theory of names": "The only defect I think it has is probably common to all philosophical theories. It's wrong. You may suspect me of proposing another theory in its place; but I hope not, because I'm sure it's wrong too if it is a theory" (Kripke 1980, 64).

This aspect of Berlin's account of political judgment was, as noted earlier, explicitly linked to a critique of a "scientistic" approach to understanding. But Berlin's targets extended beyond scientism and the technocratic project in politics, and his work has relevance beyond the circumstances in which it took shape. One of the goals of many leading moral theories is to do away with the need for difficult, fallible, subjective (in the sense of being individual and potentially idiosyncratic) situational judgments, by providing some formula, metric, or rule for resolving moral questions; once this is assimilated, moral choice is a matter of calculation, or the application of some general rule or principle(s).[47] Berlin's view of moral, as well as political, judgment stands opposed to such calculative, rule-oriented models of moral agency. This opposition was partly intellectual, based on a conviction that reliance on formulae was inadequate for correctly perceiving and addressing the difficulties of particular situations. But it was also ethical, reflecting a normative vision of what good moral agency is. The attempt to escape from the difficulty, uncertainty, and imprecision of judgment into general principles, theories, and rubrics seemed to Berlin dishonest and irresponsible, a surrender of an individual's capacity to be a truly thoughtful, responsible moral agent.

At its most agonized and admirable – as in the case of Tolstoy, the fox who wanted to be a hedgehog, the perceptually gifted artist who sought to be a seer, the skeptic who longed to believe, whose striving only left him "a desperate old man, beyond human aid, wandering self-blinded at Colonus" (RT 92) – the attempt to escape into doctrine was noble, and tragic. In most cases, it was not so noble, but relatively harmless. In the worst cases, it was neither noble nor harmless – and less tragic than horrific. To act as if one possesses a key to all questions, a blueprint that can be imposed directly onto life, is "an appalling and gratuitous handicap" to political action, which "leads to avoidable suffering" (SR 66). Even worse, those who have blinded themselves by adherence to dogma will often seek to impose their vision on – that is, to blind – others. This led to the "*a priori* barbarities of Procrustes" (L 216): "The less the application of ... formulae yields the expected results, the more exasperated the theorists" – or visionary politicians – "become, the more they try to force the facts into some preconceived mould; the more resistance they encounter, the more violent are the efforts to overcome it, the greater the reaction, confusion, suffering untold, the more the original ends are lost sight of " (SR 39).

Berlin's writings point to the importance of an *ethics* of judgment; and his essays on Churchill, Roosevelt, and Weizmann advance an ethical project, reflecting the conviction that the examples of great political leaders show how it may be possible to see beyond the distortions of doctrine and abstraction –

---

[47] For a discussion of this theme drawing on very different theoretical sources, see Satkunanandan 2015. For an influential, powerful argument for the importance of general principles and insufficiency of judgment, see Kant 1991 [1793].

and the loss of freedom that these inflict. For Berlin, the defense of political and social freedom was linked to a practice of what we might call, adapting a similar phrase that he quoted from Herzen (RT 103), *seeing freely*, approaching the world without blinders, seeking to apprehend it without forcing it to fit preconceived theories.

This is not to say that one must, or can, think wholly free of presuppositions or theories. Berlin acknowledged that *all* thought relies on unexamined or incompletely examined presuppositions, and involves some degree of generalization or abstraction, some amount of comparison of a given set of conditions with prior expectations based on some underlying picture of the world, however inchoate, tentative, or loose. What is important in cultivating good judgment is, first, how *valid* these presupposed models are, whether they allow one to perceive, imagine, synthesize, and judge accurately, in a way that does not "do violence" to reality. Second, and connected to this, is the *way* in which ideas are held. Good judgment requires the cultivation of practices or habits of looking at the world and evaluating one's own assumptions and convictions which allow one to avoid (or, if need be, cast off) blinders. This requires "direct confrontation with the concrete data of observation and introspection" in order to test our presuppositions about them – and ensure that we do not "ignore something that [we] know directly of human nature and thereby do violence to what we are, or what we know, by forcing it into the Procrustean bed of some rigid dogma" (CC 210).[48]

Hence, the larger ethical and political significance of Berlin's reiterated insistence on the value of skepticism or fallibilism, humility or modesty – and, at the same time, the combination of curiosity, irony, and proud refusal to simplify or repress one's perceptions, to "deny what one knows to be true." It was this capacity to look at the world freely that Berlin celebrated in his portrayals not only of political leaders, but also of artists such as Turgenev, historians and philosophers such as Montesquieu and Meinecke, and social critics such as Herzen and Moses Hess. For all the differences of their roles, vantage-points, and commitments, such figures shared a distinctive combination of respect for reality with imaginative freedom: a capacity to look beyond the present and the familiar, to perceive creatively, and to dream realistically.

---

[48] Berlin is here discussing not political judgment, but political theory. This requires a caveat. In the case of theory, *analysis* of these underlying concepts and categories is crucial (PSM 76), whereas practical judgment involves *synthesis* of experience rather than the analysis of theoretical models. Furthermore, Berlin depicts political judgment as involving or requiring a *pragmatic*, action-oriented perspective – an evaluation of all data in terms of its relevance to possibilities for action; this is not the case for theoretical reflection. Introspective testing of our presuppositions plays a role in both political judgment and political theory; but Berlin suggests that it is more central to theoretical reflection, and that an *excess* of introspection may be a handicap in practical action.

This is a demanding description. It reflects an unfashionably heroic vision, which may be uncomfortable for those firmly committed to contemporary liberal democracy. His writings on leadership may be seen as placing Berlin among those defenders of liberalism who suggest, disturbingly, that liberal democracies have need of qualities of character that they often hold in suspicion, and have difficulty producing.[49] Yet the "aristocratic" element of Berlin's celebrations of Churchill and Weizmann must be placed beside his praise of Roosevelt's distinctively democratic political talents. Berlin was preserved from unambiguous affirmation of aristocratic or democratic temperaments, pragmatism or idealism, visionary or virtuoso leadership, by his awareness of complexity and contingency – and by his pluralism, which in itself pointed to the importance of judgment. The absence of (valid) principles, rules, or decision-procedures to settle conflicts between values left individuals – whether leaders deciding matters of public policy, or private individuals deciding matters of personal conduct – to fall back on the resource of judgment. And such judgment, which is nuanced and context-sensitive, could show the way to balancing competing claims, smoothing conflicts, and even combining discordant values in a skillful compromise in a way that general principles could not.[50] At the same time, strong monism represents a barrier to the exercise of good political judgment, while a pluralistic mindset or disposition (whether or not it was based on or accompanied by a theoretical articulation of pluralistic ethics) conduces to a recognition of judgment's importance, and care in exercising judgment.[51]

Neither the vision of the "hedgehog" nor that of the "fox," neither "aristocratic" nor "democratic" styles of leadership, guarantee either success or moral goodness. All carry with them disadvantages and dangers: there is something lost in, and imperiled by, the triumph of any approach to politics over its alternative. Berlin's account of leadership is thus not only pluralistic, but *tragic*, pointing to the necessity and inevitability of imperfection, risk, and loss. For all its celebration of human greatness, it is humbling, pointing to the partiality and insufficiency of any unconditional conclusion. But it is not, obviously, neutral. It represents a vigorous repudiation of the project of replacing the art of practical, situated judgment with "scientific" or categorical postulates. And it reflects a moral passion which affirms decency and humanity over the inhuman power and glory pursued, and sometimes achieved, by the politically avaricious, ambitious, and visionary.

Berlin's writings on political judgment and political leadership sought to illuminate phenomena which he believed to be widely recognized, but little understood. But they were also aimed at combating, or curing his audience of,

---

[49] See Hanley 2004, 333, 337.
[50] See Smith 2016, 287–8. On the importance of contextual judgment to responding to conflicts of values, see Crowder (Chapter 13) in this volume.
[51] See Khilnani 2009, 276.

two different – but, in Berlin's mind, linked – pathologies: a tendency to rely on doctrine; and a tendency to disregard a sense of *humanity* in thinking about political action – both in the sense of disregarding human understanding, and in the sense of disregarding humane sentiments. Those who enter politics, Berlin suggests, should be politicians, with all the pragmatism and readiness to compromise and to forego the satisfactions of personal purity that being a politician entails; but, amidst all their political activity, they should not cease to be both human and humane. Good political judgment, and great political leadership, may be detached from human goodness. But they are also important resources for preserving an element of goodness, of "decent respect for the opinions" – and the "deepest interests," the lives and freedoms – "of mankind" (Berlin 1970, 21; PI 80). Without the capacity for and exercise of good judgment and, on occasion, great leadership, such human goodness will be imperiled. And it is, Berlin maintained, human goodness that political judgment and political leaders should seek to serve.[52]

[52] I am grateful to audiences at Exeter, Oxford, and Yale (particularly Teresa Bejan, Ross Carroll, William Galston, Iain Hampsher-Monk, Kei Hiruta, Isaac Nakhimovsky, Fania Oz-Salzberger, Alan Ryan, and Edward Skidelsky) for their responses to talks related to this chapter; to Aaron Garrett, Michael Lesley, and Nancy Rosenblum, for discussion of ideas presented here; and to Cary Cherniss, Laura Hartmann, Henry Hardy, and Steven B. Smith for comments on the text.

PART III

BERLIN AND THE HISTORY OF IDEAS

5

Berlin on the Nature and Purpose of the History of Ideas

Ryan Patrick Hanley

Isaiah Berlin began his career as an analytical philosopher, yet he became famous as a historian of ideas. In a revealing radio interview, Berlin explained the motivations behind this shift. Recalling a transatlantic plane flight of 1944, Berlin professed that it was in the course of that flight that he came to the conclusion that "philosophy was a most marvellous subject," but yet "not for me," insofar as it failed to "produce the kind of intellectual excitement" that he thought necessary to sustain intense and extended research. On the other hand, Berlin's encounters with various nineteenth-century Russian thinkers whom he'd "always dabbled with a little" had begun to generate a different sort of excitement. In his own words: "I thus became terribly interested in the history of these thinkers, because I thought that they were relevant, not only to the modern world, but to the human condition in general." And it was on the basis of this interest, Berlin reports, that he came back to Oxford to tell his "startled colleagues" his decision, a decision that was "not very well received" – namely, that "I didn't really wish to go on doing philosophy, but wished to turn myself into a historian of thought" (F 488–9).[1]

Berlin's account is remarkable; few are the academics who willingly give up a bright career in the field of their original training to pursue new life as a specialist in an area that, as Berlin says, "was not a subject much encouraged in England, then or now" (F 489).[2] Yet for the present purposes, what is chiefly interesting in Berlin's account of his shift is his justification of it on the grounds that study of the history of ideas is in fact "relevant" both "to the modern world" and "to the human condition in general." But what exactly does this mean?

---

[1] All quotations in this paragraph are from the transcription of Berlin's February 1979 Belgian Radio interview as it appears in F. Compare this account with that given in CC, xii.
[2] In this context see also Bernard Williams' lovely account of this transition, which rejects the notion that Berlin simply turned his back on philosophy for history: "Rather, he turned from a form of philosophy which ignored history to a form of philosophy which did not ignore history" (Williams 2001, 92). For recent development of this claim, see Ryan 2012, 67–8.

In what exactly does the "relevance" of the history of ideas for the present consist, and how exactly does Berlin's practice as a historian of ideas illuminate this relevance? What follows aims to elucidate these aspects of Berlin's understanding of and contributions to the study of the history of ideas. And, in so doing, it chiefly aims to demonstrate that Berlin's turn to the history of ideas is ultimately best understood as a political decision – albeit in a very particular sense.

Berlin's turn to the history of ideas was not political in either of two familiar senses. It was certainly not political in the sense of being prudent; as noted earlier, in practice Berlin stood to gain little – and in fact risked losing much – by turning his back on Oxford philosophy at the very time that Oxford's star shone so brightly in the philosophical universe. It was also not political in the crude sense of being shaped by contemporary politics. During the 1940s Berlin had of course been directly involved in politics in wartime and post-wartime Washington and New York, but it would be a mistake to trace his academic shift directly to this activity.[3] His personal involvement in politics during this period did, however, contribute to his heightening sense of the significance of certain political and ethical issues which in time would become part of his historical interests, as we will see. But for now, the key point is that Berlin's turn to the history of ideas emerged from his concern to understand the relationship of the past to the present in such a way that this very understanding might help clarify the nature of the principal political problems faced by his own age.

In Berlin's hands, study of the history of ideas illuminates the relationship of past to present in two politically salutary ways.[4] First, comparison of past ideas to present political thinking can often reveal the discontinuities between present and past. That is, careful study of the history of ideas can help to reveal the differences in the ways in which past thinkers thought and spoke – and the sorts of questions they thought and spoke about – when set next to the ways in which we today think and speak about political problems. Clarifying these discontinuities is of great political value insofar as it helps us to understand which of our problems are unique to our age, and thus admit, and perhaps even demand, solutions unique to our age. On the other hand, the comparison of past ideas to present political thought is also capable of revealing the continuities that elsewhere join present and past – that is, the ways in which past political thinkers not merely anticipate but also define the very concepts and categories through which we understand the political problems that we continue to

---

[3] On Berlin's time in New York and Washington, see Ignatieff 1998, 97–134. For helpful analysis of how these experiences relate to the development of his political thought, see especially Cherniss 2013, 53–87.

[4] By demonstrating the specific ways in which Berlin understood the study of the history of ideas to be politically useful, what follows aims to develop in productive ways the wide appreciation of Berlin's general concerns on this front; see e.g. Kelly 2002, 44–5; Cherniss 2014b, xxiv; Hanley 2007, 178–9.

struggle with today. Clarifying these continuities is of political value in its own right insofar as it helps us understand which of our political problems in fact transcend our age and are best regarded as manifestations of problems that all ages must grapple with, and as such demand recognition as perennial problems of the sort that do not admit of a final solution. This sense of the two ways in which the study of the history of ideas can be politically valuable, I hope to show, both ties Berlin's activities as a historian of thought to his activities as a political theorist, and marks him as a unique and potentially useful voice in our efforts today to explain and to justify the unique enterprise which is the study of the history of ideas.

Berlin's approach to the history of ideas is also valuable for a second reason. Berlin sought to explain not only *why* the history of ideas should be studied, but also *how* it should be studied. On this front, his contributions to the history of ideas are especially valuable for their illumination of the utility of three particular tools in the intellectual historian's toolbox. These include, first, facility at what he called "political judgment"; second, possession of what he called a "sense of reality"; and third, capacity for sympathetic engagement with one's subject "from the inside." All three methods Berlin thought indispensable to historians of ideas. Moreover, his appreciation of the utility of each of these three tools to the historian was itself the product of his own historical researches on various thinkers from the past who had themselves pioneered and perfected these skills. In this sense, Berlin's early forays into the history of ideas introduced him to several of the key methods that he would himself later apply in his own practice as a historian of ideas.

Berlin's corpus thus offers several largely unexplored resources to historians of ideas engaged in articulating the why and the how of their field. Yet it also needs to be noted at the outset that, for all his many writings on the history of ideas, Berlin failed to provide – indeed, never sought to provide – any methodological statement akin to those that govern the practices of other contemporary approaches to study of the history of ideas. As a result, uncovering Berlin's justifications for and methods of studying ideas and their history must necessarily take the form of reconstruction. The reconstruction offered here is largely drawn from his political and historical writings from 1947 to 1953. The reasons for this are threefold. First, this is clearly the period in which Berlin understood himself to be transitioning from philosophy to history.[5] As a result, focusing on these texts allows us to see Berlin at work in the midst of his transition, as opposed to the retrospective and justificatory account that he gave three decades later in the radio interview quoted at the beginning of the chapter. Second, this period was crucial to Berlin's development not only as a historian of ideas, but as a political thinker as well.

---

[5] Berlin is explicit on this in the radio interview: "And so in 1950 I stopped being a professional philosopher and devoted myself, so far as I could, to the history of Russian ideas in the nineteenth century" (F 489).

Our appreciation of this fact has only grown since the publication in 2006 of his *Political Ideas in the Romantic Age* – a manuscript originally developed in preparation for his Flexner Lectures at Bryn Mawr College in 1952, and which has been recognized as a sort of *Grundrisse* in which Berlin first worked out many of his signature contributions to political theory.[6] Third, these texts tend to be much less well-known than Berlin's later writings, and my hope is that focusing on them here will reveal them to be rich if underexplored sources of insight into his project as an intellectual historian, and complement without duplicating other contributions to this volume.

THE HOW OF THE HISTORY OF IDEAS: THREE ESSENTIAL SKILLS

As noted earlier, Berlin's practice as a historian of ideas was particularly noteworthy for the degree to which it was animated by his use of three methods or tools: "political judgment," the "sense of reality," and sympathetic understanding. Moreover, Berlin's appreciation of the value of these skills (the second and third in particular) owed in large part to his historical research, and specifically his studies of the way in which various past thinkers had themselves employed these methods. What follows aims to explain what Berlin understood each of these tools to consist in, and why he thought they were especially valuable to historians of ideas.

We begin with political judgment, a topic to which Berlin returned several times in his essays from the period that is our focus. Berlin initially introduced this concept not with reference to historians of political thought, but with reference to political scientists and politicians. His essay devoted to political judgment indeed uses possession of such judgment to distinguish the methods of understanding employed by statesmen from those employed by social scientists. Thus, in response to the question of "what is it to have good judgment in politics?" he wonders:

But what is this knowledge? Is it knowledge of a science? Are there really laws to be discovered, rules to be learnt? Can statesmen be taught something called political science – the science of the relationships of human beings to each other and to their environment – which consists, like other sciences, of systems of verified hypotheses, organised under laws, that enable one, by the use of further experiment and observation, to discover other facts, and to verify new hypotheses? (SR 50–1)

Berlin's formulation of this problem clearly draws on his engagement with several different questions that he had been dealing with at the time in various intellectual capacities; indeed, one hears ready echoes here of his analytical work on verification, of his skepticism toward the propensity to import methods of the natural sciences into the human sciences, and of his esteem for those statesmen of genius who show themselves to possess a form of political

---

[6] See e.g. Wokler 2008, 349; Cherniss 2014b, xxiv.

understanding, which he calls "wisdom" and "political skill" (POI 233; SR 25, 32, 33, 46, 47).[7] Berlin himself wrote extensively on the preeminent exemplars of this skill in his own age, particularly lauding Roosevelt and Churchill and Weizmann for their capacities on this front.

Yet for all its utility to the statesmen, the capacity for political judgment was also of great utility to the student of political thought. Some sense of this utility can be gleaned from Berlin's political writings of this period. Several of these essays, if little known today, reveal Berlin to be no mere student of political judgment, but also a practitioner of it in his own right. Especially revealing on this front are the three cultural and political survey essays that Berlin had been commissioned to write for the Encyclopedia Britannica during this period. In 1938 Britannica inaugurated a tradition of annually publishing a *Book of the Year* chronicling major developments of the preceding twelve months. In the early 1950s it fell to Berlin to write the synoptic essays that introduced the yearbooks for each of the three years from 1949 to 1951. The essays are of interest for several reasons, but for our purposes they are most useful for how they show Berlin at work exercising his own political judgment in order to define and clarify the most pressing political problems of his time. The essays themselves leave little doubt as to what he understood the chief challenge of his own age to be. In the first essay he thus forthrightly says that "the most important single factor in 1949 was, of course, the continuation of the battle between the creeds – between Marxism and its various enemies – the greatest since the Reformation and its aftermath" (Berlin 1950b, xxii). In the essay he goes on to explain why this was a particular problem: "Everywhere the doctrine of social responsibility was gaining ground at the expense of self-assertive individualism and liberal humanism alike" (Berlin 1950b, xxvii). Berlin's concerns on this front only intensified after the invasion of South Korea; thus, his essay for the following year's book reiterates even more pointedly that "in short the question of one's attitude toward the USSR and communism became the central social and personal issue of the time" (Berlin 1951, xxiv). Matters hardly abate after that; hence, in his third Britannica essay, even in calling attention to "the revival of religion" as "a central issue of discussion," Berlin reiterated the threat posed by communists who "preached a fanatical counterrevolution of their own" (Berlin 1952a, xxii–xxiii). And Berlin would extend this theme in his other published writings of the period. Thus, in his "Political Ideas in the Twentieth Century" – to which we will have reason to return in the following section – this conflict is also the dominant center, with Berlin proclaiming that "the new factors violently opposed to the humanist psychology of bourgeois civilization is to a large extent the history of political ideas in our time" (L 61). And Berlin's *Foreign Affairs* article (published under the pseudonym "O. Utis") of this period concludes by insisting that Stalinist communism, "being dominant over the lives of some eight hundred million

---

[7] See also e.g. Hanley 2004, 327–39; and Cherniss, Chapter 4 in this volume.

human beings, is the most important, most inhuman, and still the most imperfectly understood phenomenon of our times" (SM 111).

From all of this it is abundantly clear that in the period in which Berlin was making his shift from philosophy to the study of the history of political thought he regarded the struggle over communism as by far the most decisive political issue of his age. This bears mentioning not because we need reminding of Berlin's credentials as a Cold Warrior, but because of the degree to which his most explicitly political essays of the period were so deeply concerned to isolate and identify what Berlin understood to be the preeminent political issue of his day. And of even greater significance is the fact that Berlin's concern with this particular issue animated to a great extent his labors, and indeed shaped his focus as both a political theorist and as a historian of political ideas in this period. This is especially evident in his political theory. The dominant category in Berlin's political theory in this period is authority. Berlin's BBC radio lectures of 1952 (published as *Freedom and Its Betrayal*) began by insisting that while "Moral and political philosophy are vast subjects," with a "certain amount of exaggeration and simplification" we can "reduce the questions to one and one only, namely: Why should an individual obey other individuals?" (FIB 1). The same claim would be the point of departure for his Flexner Lectures that same year: "The central issue of political philosophy is the question 'Why should any man obey any other man or body of men?'" (PIRA 21).

For all its obvious reductionism, Berlin's isolation of the core question of political philosophy is interesting for at least three reasons. First, while Berlin is today famous as a theorist of liberty, his early engagements with political theory emerged as an expression of concerns over not freedom, but its opposite.[8] Second, Berlin's interest in authority and obedience as a central question was at the very least stimulated if not determined by his engagement with contemporary political reality, and Marxism and communism in particular. Third, Berlin's interest in the concept of authority in the period was in large part what drove him to study the specific historical thinkers and ideas on which he trained his focus in the period in question. Put slightly differently, Berlin's own exercises of political judgment can be seen as a tool which helped him to narrow down from the vast field of history those thinkers and ideas which he considered to be most worthy of study insofar as they can best help us to clarify the relationships between our most pressing political problems and the ways in which these had been treated in the past (SR 17–19).

Berlin's efforts as a historian of ideas to grapple with the relationship of past to present was also significantly aided by a second skill. Throughout his writings of the late 1940s and early 1950s, Berlin returned again and again to this skill, which he himself was prone to call a "sense of reality." Berlin's interest in the sense of reality emerged as a way of trying to make sense of a certain way by

---

[8] Joshua Cherniss has pointed out to me that Berlin's shift on this front is consistent with similar shifts made in the writings of several of his Oxford predecessors, including Green and Bosanquet.

which human beings have historically sought to understand their world and their surroundings. What is especially significant about the sense of reality is the way in which it constitutes an alternative to other more familiar ways of understanding that were then especially ascendant. Two of these Berlin found especially troubling, and his familiarity with each is directly traceable to his early forays into historical studies. The first was the notion that social phenomena can be usefully understood via the same methods that had proven fruitful in the natural sciences – an idea whose origins Berlin was prone to locate in the thought of the materialists of the French Enlightenment. The second was the notion that the study of historical phenomena can best be understood as a working out of certain "inexorable" laws, in accord with a sort of determinism – an idea whose origins Berlin often traced to the thought of Marx and his epigones. Both approaches to the study of social behavior Berlin found tragically misguided, insofar as they impose categories on human beings that are alien to their natures, and also insofar as they thereby preclude recognition of what he saw as the distinguishing feature of human beings.[9] This concerned their capacity for freely chosen autonomous action – which itself, as Berlin was fond of noting, was at once the fact that made morality possible and the fact that justifies preference for individual liberty over coercion. Indeed, one of the principal themes of Berlin's political theory of this period was to demonstrate the specific political consequences of the alternative, insisting in no uncertain terms that

So long as the opposite assumptions are made by those who believe in radical reforms of human society, in the name – falsely invoked – of science and reason and unbiased observation of nature, human beings will continue to be offered up to theories and abstractions, a form of idolatry – and of human sacrifice – colder and more destructive than the more intelligible follies of previous generations.[10] (POI 172; cf. SR 49)

But what positive alternative did Berlin offer to these methods of studying reality, and how did it shape his practice as a historian of ideas? The answer to the first question lies in his articulation of the "sense of reality." For Berlin, the sense of reality consists principally in the capacity of certain thinkers and observers to forge synthetic and imaginative connections between discrete data, thereby rendering the sum of the data intelligible as a coherent and interconnected whole. At times Berlin was prone to call attention to the prominent role of "synthesis" in this process, and to emphasize its contrast with approaches that privileged "analysis" (SR 37–8, 58–9). He himself was prone to describe this process as a form of "pattern formation." Yet this is an idea that has to be handled carefully, especially with reference to Berlin's thought

---

[9] Berlin would in time develop these objections into a larger critique of historical determinism and scientific history more generally; see e.g. his 1960 essay "The Concept of Scientific History" in CC. I examine this critique in Hanley 2007; see also Gray 1996, esp. 77–81.
[10] Berlin's critical attitude toward the determinist approach to the study of history is also evident in Berlin 1950a.

at the period; many are the places where Berlin calls attention to the political dangers inherent in the project of various "Messianic preachers" and "dogmatic thinkers" to impose upon innocent peoples their "belief that there is one great universal pattern, and one unique method of apprehending it" (SR 53). Pattern construction and imposition of this sort Berlin considered anathema. The pattern construction that he admired was of a different sort altogether – not one that ran roughshod over those seemingly idiosyncratic or eccentric exceptions to the rule, but rather one focused precisely on noting these, valuing these, and attempting to integrate them into a whole capable of embracing them. Hence his claim that

Judgement, skill, sense of timing, grasp of the relationship of means to results depends upon empirical factors, such as experience, observation, above all on that "sense of reality" which consists in semi-conscious integration of a large number of apparently trivial or unnoticeable elements in the situation that between them form some kind of pattern which of itself "suggests" – "invites" – the appropriate action. (POI 170)

Indeed, this notion of pattern detection is the dominant metaphor that runs across Berlin's descriptions of the sense of reality in this period. The judgments that shape the sense of reality begin in "scrupulous observation, accurate knowledge of facts, but it is more than this: it is a form of understanding and not of knowledge in the ordinary sense" (SR 28) – a process that begins by seeing "the half noticed, half inferred, half gazed-at, half unconsciously absorbed minutiae of behaviour and thought and feeling" which too often escape scientists, but proceeds to a recognition of "pattern qualities – what else are we to call them?" that we come to "absorb into our picture of what goes on, and the more sensitively and sharply aware of them we are, the more understanding and insight we are rightly said to possess" (SR 29).

Berlin clearly admired this capacity. But why, exactly? And how did he think it was of benefit to historians? Berlin's contemporaneous writings on the great statesmen of his day – again including Roosevelt, Churchill, and Weizmann, among others – call attention to the practical political utility of such a capacity. Yet Berlin was also explicit that "historians of ideas, however scrupulous and minute they may feel it necessary to be, cannot avoid perceiving their material in some kind of pattern" (L 55). Berlin thus thought a sense of reality was indispensable, and in some sense even inescapable, for historians, and indeed for reasons that lie at the heart of his own project as a politically engaged historian of ideas. Understood as a form of pattern construction, the sense of reality enables its possessor to conceptualize systems as wholes, and indeed to see the guiding inner thread that binds seemingly discrete data together. But the key fact here is that what holds true for the statesman trying to make sense of the mass of data that lies before him in the present also holds true for the historian trying to make sense of the mass of data that lies before him as he surveys the past. Historical intelligibility depends on such a capacity; Berlin himself was fond of noting that "a mere recital of facts is not history."

Historical narrative proper requires a facility at setting such facts "in the concrete, at times opaque, but continuous, rich, full texture of 'real life' – the intersubjective, directly recognizable continuum of experience" (SR 32). And herein lies the significance of the sense of reality for the historian of ideas. If indeed a key contribution of the history of ideas to our understanding of the present is a capacity to reveal both continuities and discontinuities, this promise can never be realized in the absence of the synthesis and pattern detection that the sense of reality makes possible, and without which all past thought and action must necessarily appear a mere string of unrelated and unintelligible discontinuities.

A third crucial methodological skill for the historian of ideas concerns what Berlin calls the "inside view," and which we today might associate with what Berlin himself occasionally called "sympathetic" understanding. As with political judgment and the sense of reality, Berlin's interest in this "inside view" was distinctly shaped by his early historical research, in this case his work on Marx and the eighteenth-century French materialists. For all these differences that separate Marx from the *philosophes*, what united their enterprises, on Berlin's view, was the belief that human beings could be studied, like any other natural or physical phenomena, from the perspective of a detached observer. Berlin questioned this view. Wholly aside from the issue of whether certain aspects of human beings can be productively understood in the same way as we seek to understand physical phenomena, Berlin thought attempts to understand human behavior solely via the methods of detached observation deprives us of one of the greatest advantages that we have as observers of ourselves – namely, our capacity for sympathetic identification with our subjects as a result of our shared humanity.

Across his writings, Berlin frequently returned to this contrast between these two methods of studying human beings. He offers one of his clearest statements of this contrast in a later autobiographical essay, and ties it specifically to historical understanding.

In thinking about the past, we go beyond behaviour; we wish to understand how human beings lived, and that means understanding their motives, their fears and hopes and ambitions and loves and hatreds – to whom they prayed, how they expressed themselves in poetry, in art, in religion. We are able to do this because we are ourselves human, and understand our own inner life in these terms. We know how a rock, or a table, behaves because we observe it and make conjectures and verify them; but we do not know why the rock wishes to be as it is – indeed, we think it has no capacity for wishing, or for any other consciousness. But we do know why we are what we are, what we seek, what frustrates us, what expresses our inmost feelings and beliefs; we know more about ourselves than we shall ever know about rocks and streams. (POI 8–9)

Here Berlin presents the core of the notion that we possess a certain insight into our "inner life" (POI 9) that enables us to understand human beings more intimately than we can understand objective external phenomena. And importantly, Berlin here traces his awareness of this capacity to his study of Vico. Yet Vico was hardly Berlin's sole source of inspiration on this front. In his later work the same idea would often find expression in his writings on Herder, and in the writings of the period that are our focus here, Berlin credits Hegel with it, explaining that "History is the story of human creation, human imagination, human wills and intentions, feelings, purposes, everything which human beings do and feel" – a fact that itself explains "why the understanding of history is an 'inside' view, whereas our understanding of tables and chairs is an 'outside' view" (FIB 87).[11] In short, as human beings studying the morality and history that human beings have created, we do ourselves a grave disservice if we fail to take advantage of our unique imaginative capacities for understanding these phenomena in our capacity as creators of them. And concomitantly with this, Berlin also expressed deep skepticism that there was in fact any other alternative to so doing – that we are in some sense capable of occupying a neutral space by which we might observe human phenomena. In his words, "there is no Archimedean point outside ourselves where we can stand in order to take up our critical viewpoint" – indeed, "we have no outside vantage-point from which dispassionately to observe and identify it all" (SR 20, 31; L 58). In this sense, our capacity for sympathetic inner understanding is not just a powerful tool that we possess; with regard to the question of inner and outer perspectives, it may be all that we possess.

THE WHY OF THE HISTORY OF IDEAS: PROBLEMS POLITICAL AND PHILOSOPHICAL

Berlin's accounts of the methodological tools indispensable to the historian of ideas answers our question of how he thinks the history of ideas should be studied. But this leaves unanswered another question: why should the history of ideas be studied at all? This is hardly an idle question in Berlin's time or ours. Today, in an age of ever-increasing academic specialization and, especially in the social sciences, ever-increasing preference for quantitative methodologies, historians of ideas have often been relegated to the margins (if not pushed out altogether) of fields ranging from economics and political science to philosophy and history. And as Berlin's own autobiographical comments attest, the history of ideas was sufficiently marginal in his own day that turning to it required some justification. What justification, then, did Berlin in fact provide, and of what use might it be to historians of ideas today?

Berlin's case for the study of the history of ideas rests on the belief that such study (especially when prosecuted in accord with the methods examined in the previous section) can help reveal the relationship of past ideas to present problems in two ways of direct benefit to those concerned to address such

---

[11] I examine Berlin's use of this approach to history in his later work in Hanley 2007, 168–72.

problems.¹² First, careful study of the ideas of the past and their relationship to the present will often reveal discontinuities separating past thought from present conditions. Awareness of these discontinuities is valuable insofar as it can help us identify precisely which problems are unique to our age, and thus demand solutions that cannot be supplied by past thought and to which we need to apply our own ingenuity. Second, careful study of the ideas of the past and their relationship to the present can often reveal something quite different – namely, the continuities that connect our problems and modes of thinking to those of seemingly remote ages. This would seem to point in the inverse direction of the other task of the history of ideas, yet, like that other task, it results in conclusions of value to the present. For just as the awareness that some political problems are new to our age suggests the degree to which they require to be addressed by modes of thinking endemic to our age, the awareness that some problems are not new to our age – and have in fact been perennial problems across the ages – suggests the degree to which such problems are intractable and indeed unsolvable through political action of any sort. The political payoff – if we can even speak that way – of the study of the history of ideas thus lies in its capacity to help us distinguish which of our contemporary problems are capable of being solved through political action, and which of our political problems are problems endemic to our condition as human beings, and for which any attempt to solve via political "final solutions" must necessarily come only at our peril.¹³ Put slightly differently, and in Berlin's own terms, study of the history of ideas can help us to distinguish political problems from "philosophical problems," which are such that there are "no obvious and generally accepted procedures for answering them, nor any class of specialists to whom we automatically turn for the solutions" (POI 43). These philosophical problems are quite simply "a permanent element in the history of human thought," for which we equally quite simply cannot arrive at "answers which settle the matter once and for all, so that the problems do not crop up afresh in each generation" (POI 46, 44). As Berlin understood it, the tragedy of the Enlightenment thinkers, for all their other genuine virtues, lay in their propensity to conflate these two sorts of problems. And it was on these grounds that Berlin set himself, as both a political theorist and a politically

---

¹² It is worth noting, at least parenthetically, that Berlin had little patience for crude attempts to cherry-pick ideas or examples from history and attempt to apply their lessons to contemporary problems – an exercise he dismissed as producing only "a very thin, generalised residue, and one far too unspecific to be of much help in a practical dilemma" (SR 56; see also 1).

¹³ Given my claims here, it again deserves notice, at least parenthetically, how resistant Berlin was (especially in his writings of this period) to what he saw as the ascendant notion that ideas were to be valued solely on the basis of their "social usefulness" – a tendency that he feared, were it to become widely embraced, would "mean a rapid end of all the liberal arts and sciences" and "the gradual atrophying of disinterested creative impulses" ("The Intellectual Life of American Universities," in E 753).

engaged historian of ideas, the task of ensuring that our age not fall victim to the same deception.

Berlin's writings on the history of ideas from the late 1940s and early 1950s variously employ versions of both discontinuous and continuous approaches to the conceptualization of the relationship of past to present. These two approaches are especially evident in two texts from this period: "Political Ideas in the Twentieth Century" and *Political Ideas in the Romantic Age*. These texts – as their very titles suggest – together reveal the degree to which Berlin was engaged in this period in an attempt to understand the relationship of past to present. Yet each text, in its own right, sought to illuminate these two different yet complementary and politically salutary ways of understanding this relationship, with the romantic age manuscript exemplifying the continuities approach, and the twentieth-century essay exemplifying the discontinuities approach.

We begin with the discontinuities approach. The dominant emphasis of the "Political Ideas in the Twentieth Century" essay is on the uniqueness of the specific challenges endemic to the mid-twentieth century – hence Berlin's claim at the end of its introduction that "the remarks that follow deliberately ignore the similarities in favor of the specific differences in political outlook which characterize our own time, and, to a large degree, solely our own" (L 58–9). Berlin himself explicitly characterizes these differences as "discontinuities":

The student of the political ideas of, for example, the mid-nineteenth century must indeed be blind if he does not, sooner or later, become aware of the profound differences in ideas and terminology, in the general view of things – the ways in which the elements of experience are conceived to be related to one another – which divide that not very distant age from our own. He understands neither that time nor his own if he does not perceive the contrast between what was common to Comte and Mill, Mazzini and Michelet, Herzen and Marx, on the one hand, and to Max Weber and William James, Tawney and Beard, Lytton Strachey and Namier, on the other; the continuity of the European intellectual tradition without which no historical understanding at all would be possible is, at shorter range, a succession of specific discontinuities and dissimilarities. (L 58)

In continuing, Berlin explains that only the "casual observer" will be prone to think that "every idea and movement typical of our time is best understood as a natural development of tendencies already prominent in the nineteenth century" (L 61). The truth is that "there is a barrier which divides what is unmistakably past and done with from that which most characteristically belongs to our day," and indeed "the familiarity of this barrier must not blind us to its relative novelty" (L 61).

Elsewhere in the essay Berlin makes clear why he thinks it so important that we recognize these discontinuities and resist the temptation to gloss over the ways in which present differs from past. Specifically, to fall victim to this temptation is to deprive ourselves of the capacity to recognize what might be unique in our situation. It is in this vein that Berlin insists that indeed it is precisely as a result of "the historical approach" that "the very sense of contrast and dissimilarity with which the past affects us provides the only relevant background against which the features peculiar to our own experience stand out in sufficient relief to be adequately discerned and described" (L 58). And as Berlin's writings on statesmanship and political understanding make clear, effective political intervention in the present is impossible without precisely an appreciation of these "features peculiar to our own experience" and a sense of how they hang together; in this vein, Berlin frequently insists that in politics "what matters is to understand a particular situation in its full uniqueness, ... the unique combination of characteristics that constitute this particular situation – this and no other" (SR 56). To fail to appreciate the unique features of our age – a task that by its very nature requires both the political judgment that grasps the present and the historical understanding that perceives whether and how this present differs from the past – is necessarily then to deprive ourselves of any hope of being able to address our unique problems.

At the same time, Berlin recognized that there was also significant political utility in what seems on its face a diametrically opposed approach. This approach – which we might call the "continuities" approach, in contrast to the "discontinuities" approach – is on particular display in *Political Ideas in the Romantic Age*, as well as in Berlin's BBC lectures of the same year. In fact, Berlin introduced his radio lectures by explicitly invoking the continuities approach in order to justify his turn to his subject. The thinkers on which he meant to focus in the radio programs, he thus explained, were "all born in what might be called the dawn of our period," and "the earliest thinkers to speak in a language which is still directly familiar to us" (FIB 1–2). And herein lies their significance. For all the greatness of many other more ancient thinkers, they yet remain "divided from us by history," and for us to read them, "they need a kind of translation." The six thinkers of the late eighteenth century on which he proposes to focus, however, "speak a language which still speaks directly to us" (FIB 2). Moreover, not just their language but their questions are familiar to us; in this vein Berlin even goes so far as to say that "what makes them worthy of our consideration" is precisely that "It is our period and our time which they seem to analyse with astonishing foresight and skill." As he understands it, it is precisely because they were so "hostile to liberty" that we are bound to them: "There is hardly any need to add that in the twentieth century this became the most acute of all problems" (FIB 6). But the key point here is that Berlin thinks that we stand to gain much from studying our problem in the form in which they present it; indeed, part of the justification of the turn to the past on this front is that "the problem is often best examined in this pristine form, before it gets covered over with too many nuances, with too much discussion, with too many local and temporal variations" (FIB 6).

Political Ideas in the Romantic Age itself begins from this same standpoint, though it goes on to develop this claim on new levels of theoretical sophistication. Thus, like the BBC lectures, *Political Ideas in the Romantic Age* begins by observing that the thinkers that are its focus presented us with "the basic intellectual capital on which, with few additions, we live to this day" insofar as "Social, moral, political, economic discussion has ever since occurred in terms of the concepts, the language, indeed the images and metaphors which were generated during that period" (PIRA 1).[14] Berlin admits that caution is needed here – "few activities are more dangerous to the cause of historical truth than the attempt to find a fully grown oak in the acorn" – but, for all that, it remains the case that in the romantic age "the issues debated were literally identical with those which stir individuals and nations in our own time" (PIRA 3). Hence the justificatory refrain that sounds across his introduction: insofar as the ideas of the romantic age "transformed our world" and "The controversies of our age are the direct product" of this revolution and its "clash of values," it is the task of the politically engaged historian of ideas "to assess its intrinsic importance and its vast consequences" (PIRA 20, 17, 14).

Political Ideas in the Romantic Age thus explicitly justifies its enterprise on the grounds that our political present is constituted by the concepts and categories of the past. Yet there is also another more subtle claim being made here – one that strikes at the heart of Berlin's own understanding of the nature of both intellectual history and of political philosophy. Indeed, one of Berlin's key aims here is to define political philosophy against certain rival interpretations. Political philosophy, we are told, has "a province of its own," no matter how obscure it may seem to some, and Berlin thinks it a duty "to the cause of lucidity and truth to try to indicate what this province is" – and indeed to counter those who "pretend either, as some have done, that it is a province of epistemology or semantics – that nothing useful can be said unless and until the ways in which words are used in political argument have been properly compared and contrasted with other ways of using words," as well as those others who tell us "that politics is part of a larger whole" and "can and must be studied within that whole or not at all" (PIRA 24). Against these positions – positions still familiar today – Berlin insists that the true province of political philosophy lies somewhere else altogether:

It is a platitude to say that each age has its own problems, its own experience, its own imagery and symbolism and ways of feeling and speaking. It is a lesser platitude to add that political philosophy derives its intelligibility solely from the understanding of such change, and that its perennial principles, or what seem to be such, depend on the relative stability and unchanging characteristics of human beings in their social aspect. If the supersession of eighteenth-century doctrine, which evaluated everything unhistorically, by a more historical or evolutionary point of view has any value, it should teach us that each political philosophy responds to the needs of its own times and is fully intelligible only in terms of all the relevant factors of its age, and intelligible to us only to the degree

---

[14] See also Cherniss 2014b, xxiv–xxv; Cherniss 2013, 135ff; Wokler 2008, 352–3.

to which (and it is a far larger one than some modern relativists wish to persuade us that it is) we have experience in common with previous generations. (PIRA 15)

At least two important points are being made here. First, Berlin is clearly aware of the degree to which political ideas demand to be understood in the first instance as responses to or interventions in specific political controversies intrinsic to the age in which they were generated – that is, that political thought is, in the first instance, and as we would say today, context-specific. But that said, Berlin also takes another step, arguing that even if the generation of ideas is context-specific, the intelligibility of such ideas is context-transcendent, requiring the historical interpreter's capacity to appreciate the degree to which these various ideas remain unified and connected by their shared origin in the minds of human beings whose nature exhibits "relative stability and unchanging characteristics." Appreciating these connections is no easy task he admits, insofar as "the presuppositions of one age and culture are sometimes so difficult to grasp for those brought up in a different one." The fact remains that this intelligibility is not beyond human beings, capable as we are of "the exercise of a specific kind of moral imagination" (PIRA 15).

But in what precisely does the specifically political benefit to exercises of moral imagination of this sort consist? What exactly do we stand to gain today from seeing these "perennial principles"? The answer consists in the fact that it is this capacity that enables us to distinguish political problems that demand political action from perennial or philosophical problems that are incapable of being solved via political action.[15] It is hardly an exaggeration to say that Berlin thought that the propensity of the twentieth century to confuse these types of problems constituted the source of many of its worst political tragedies. Berlin believed this conviction – that "[t]here is a solution to social problems, as to all other real problems clearly conceived" – was the faith that animated the totalitarian movements of the twentieth century, all founded on the conviction that they had "the correct answers" to the questions (PIRA 28, 62, 330; FIB 4, 29, 68; SR 49, 307; POI 6, 21, 49, 61–2). It was on these grounds indeed that Berlin himself professed his preference for that skepticism (exemplified by Hume, among others) which doubts "the possibility of obtaining final and absolute solutions" to problems that by nature do not admit of such (L 76).[16] It is ultimately on these same grounds that Berlin can help us see that the study of the history of political thought, whatever other

---

[15] It should be noted that Berlin also regards certain types of non-philosophical political problems as perennial as well; see e.g. his claims in his writings on socialism that "the notion that the concentration of power or wealth in the hands of a minority of a community leads to the exploitation of, and injustice to, the majority, is almost as ancient as social thought itself" – a "social protest" that is indeed "heard in every generation" ("Socialism and Socialist Theories" in SR 96–9).

[16] On the important question of Hume's influence on Berlin, see esp. Wokler 2008, 359–60; Cherniss 2013, 8; Hanley 2004, 330 n5.

benefits and pleasures it might bring, has the potential to do us the inestimable service of preempting such tragedies by clarifying which problems do and do not admit of final solutions.

CONCLUSION

Berlin wrote extensively in and about the history of ideas. He was, however, not a methodologist, and he failed to produce a methodological manifesto that future historians of ideas might follow in their own right. At the same time, his writings offer signposts sufficient to enable us to reconstruct the essential elements and implications of his approach. It is an approach that rests in the first place on the capacity to utilize a set of skills to which Berlin was introduced in the course of his own historical research: the political judgment exhibited by statesmen from Bismarck to Churchill, the sense of reality lacked by the eighteenth-century French materialists and by Marx, the imaginative sympathy pioneered by Vico and Herder.

Yet Berlin was not only to explain how to do the history of ideas, but also why it was worth doing at all. Among the substantive and methodological lessons of *Political Ideas in the Romantic Age* is the notion that our political present has been constituted by our romantic past, and that these connections can be perceived by interpreters possessed of sufficient sympathy and imagination. At very nearly the same time that Berlin was emphasizing the ways in which these continuities might best be seen, he was in other texts emphasizing the radical discontinuities between past and present. On the face of it, of course, these two approaches seem at odds. Yet Berlin saw them not as contradictory, but as two sides of the same coin. The value of the history of ideas lies precisely in the way it can help us distinguish which of our problems are continuous and which are discontinuous with those of the past, and it is the task of historians of ideas to be able to communicate to those entrusted with political decision-making the wisdom that consists in knowing the difference.

6

Isaiah Berlin on Marx and Marxism

Aurelian Craiutu

A SURPRISING INTELLECTUAL DIALOGUE

In a conversation with the Iranian philosopher Ramin Jahanbegloo from three decades ago, Isaiah Berlin gave a memorable justification of his approach to the history of political thought. "It is absurd to accept either Maistre or Helvétius, to swallow them whole," he claimed. "One must read both. One must read both Tom Paine and Burke. This is the way to learn something. Nothing is more fatal in ethics or politics than a few simple ideas, as universal keys, however noble, fanatically held" (CIB 72). Because Berlin disliked reading people of roughly the same views as himself, he enjoyed confronting and measuring his opinions against those with whom he disagreed or who stood against his own (liberal) beliefs and who could reveal the weak points in his own doctrine.

One of the thinkers with whom he had an extended intellectual dialogue while also taking distance from his political message was Karl Marx. Although Berlin was as anti-Communist as only a Russian who witnessed the Russian revolution and its bloody aftermath could have been,[1] he took time to read and reflect on Marx, whom he acknowledged as a major thinker and epoch-making force in history. Yet, the author of *The Communist Manifesto* exercised only a marginal direct influence on Berlin; maintaining his distance from Marx, Berlin turned instead to Vico, Herder, Turgenev, and Herzen in his search for explanations of the important forces at work in the history of the twentieth century. It may seem, then, all the more surprising that Berlin's first book was *Karl Marx: His Life and Environment*, originally published in 1939 (the book has remained in print ever since; its fifth edition was published by Princeton

---

I would like to express my thanks to Joshua Cherniss, Dan Cole, Henry Hardy, Jeffrey Isaac, Rafael Khachaturian, and Steven Smith for their comments on previous drafts of this chapter.

[1] See Ryan 2013, 65, and Ignatieff 1998, 70–1. See also the following statement from Berlin: "First of all, I couldn't help being affected by the existence of the Soviet Union, I was never attracted by Marxism, nor by the Soviet regime ... I did have memories of the Soviet regime, which were not happy.... There were a great many executions – there was a terror" (CIB 9).

University Press in 2013). References to Marx, socialism, and Marxism are scattered throughout Berlin's writings, most notably in the essays collected in *The Sense of Reality* (most of which were written in the 1950s) and *The Power of Ideas* (where we find one of the later reflections on Marx dating from 1975). The other relatively late piece that contains a brief discussion of Marx is the essay on Disraeli, Marx, and Jewish identity from *Against the Current* (originally published in 1970), in which Berlin takes up the issue of identity in Marx's thought and offers a quasi-psychological account of his embrace of the cause of the proletariat. Moreover, occasional references to Marx and Marxism can be found in an important autobiographical essay, "My Intellectual Path" (republished in *The Power of Ideas*), in which Berlin comments briefly on the monist core of Marxism, while its failure to foresee the rise of nationalism is touched upon in two other essays: "Nationalism: Past Neglect and Present Power" (from *Against the Current*), and "The Bent Twig: On the Rise of Nationalism" (included in *The Crooked Timber of Humanity*, originally published in 1990). Marx's name also appeared in two interesting dialogues of Isaiah Berlin with Ramin Jahanbegloo and Steven Lukes that, taken together, offer an excellent introduction into his political thought.

The main catalyst for writing the book on Marx seems to have been serendipity, since Berlin did not initially intend to write on him. It was the Home University Library which commissioned him to do the book in 1933, after other, more prominent scholars had declined the offer. Yet, there was most likely another reason that motivated Berlin to undertake the study of an author with whom he had, after all, few affinities. As he acknowledged, unlike some of his radical colleagues on the Left at that time, Berlin had no particular interest in Marx's teachings and had read only a limited amount of his writings. Yet, since the influence of Marxism was on the rise among many undergraduates and younger professors in Oxford and beyond, Berlin was convinced that a serious engagement with Marx's ideas could be profitable in order to test the validity and strength of his own liberal commitments.[2] Subsequently, he set out to read about Marx and Marxism. As Michael Ignatieff remarked, "the reading he did between 1933 and 1938 provided Berlin with the intellectual capital on which he was to depend for the entire of his life."[3] "I thought that if I never wrote about him I would never read him," Berlin confessed (CIB 11). He forced himself to read Marx extensively, partly in German, partly in English and Russian.[4] Berlin, who was notoriously weak at economics, struggled with Marx's economic theories, and found *Das Kapital* in particular quite difficult and at times, unreadable, which explains why he never managed to fully grasp Marx's economic theories. Yet, he still wanted to understand "what it was like

---

[2] See Arie Dubnov's discussion of Berlin's relations with the Left in Oxford in the 1930s (Dubnov 2012).
[3] Ignatieff 1998, 71.
[4] See Cherniss 2013, 30–44. On Berlin's approach to Marx, also see CIB 28.

to be Marx in Berlin, in Paris, in Brussels, in London, and to think in terms of his concepts, categories" (CIB 28) and why his following was growing everywhere.

After Berlin began reading Marx, he became interested in his forerunners, the *philosophes* who made for "wonderful reading" (Berlin 1998, 73). Therefore, he immersed himself in the writings of the radical *philosophes* such as Helvétius and Holbach, and then turned to the utopian socialists (Saint-Simon, Charles Fourrier, Robert Owen), before discovering G. V. Plekhanov, whose polemical and fearless style charmed him (he went so far as to declare him a first-rate thinker!) and whom he considered the "true father" of Russian Marxism. After reading Marx, Berlin went back to French thinkers such as Proudhon, and forward to the Russian forerunners of the Revolution. As he was researching his book, his most important discovery was Alexander Herzen, who, along with Ivan Turgenev, became one of his intellectual heroes for the rest of his life. Those readings, Berlin acknowledged, exercised a much stronger influence on him than the writings of Marx or Engels, which explains why his interest in the founders of Marxism was always, *toutes proportions gardées*, secondary compared to his appreciation for Herzen, whom he saw as a better guide to the events of the twentieth century than Marx.

Out of the encounter with Marx's ideas and his predecessors and contemporaries came a book that scarcely resembled any other study written before about the author of *Das Kapital*. It was a fitting starting point to a long and distinguished career as historian of political ideas. To comprehend Marxism, Berlin believed, it was necessary to examine the context in which the doctrine appeared and developed, something that he tried to do in his book. As Joshua Cherniss[5] has pointed out, Berlin's study of Marx was important not only for the ideas discussed in its pages – from monism, scientism, and the Enlightenment to rationalism, determinism, and utopianism – but also because it definitively put history – and in particular, the history of ideas – at the core of Berlin's method and thought.

Four decades later, in the preface to the fourth edition of the book, Berlin acknowledged that when he wrote the first edition, he was "perhaps too deeply influenced by the classical interpretations of Engels, Plekhanov, and Mehring" (KM xxx), as well as by the critical biography of E. H. Carr, *Karl Marx: A Study in Fanaticism*, originally published in 1934. By the mid-1970s, Berlin's understanding of some central concepts in Marx's writings had changed, and he admitted that he would have written a different book following the publication of *Grundrisse*, which altered his interpretation of Marx's science of society and the relation of ideas to institutions and the forces of production.

In the mid-1930s, as he sat down to write his book, Berlin was determined to avoid yet another hagiography or ideological demolition of the tenets of Marxism. His subject was not the superhuman hero who appeared to some on the Left as the new Messiah, but rather a down-to earth, "poverty-stricken

---

[5] Cherniss 2013, 40.

chief of a non-existing sect, burrowing away in the British Museum, author of works none too familiar to professional socialists, let alone to the educated public" (SR 147–8). This man lived a great part of his life in obscurity in London, and was "by temperament a theorist and an intellectual [who] instinctively avoided direct contact with the masses" (KM 2).[6] As a writer, Berlin claimed, Marx was often "turgid, clumsy, and obscure in detail,"[7] but he always managed somehow to make clear the central points of his doctrine to friends and enemies alike. Moreover, belonging to the elite of those for whom theories and ideas are often more real than facts, Marx was not very introspective and took surprisingly little interest in real persons or states of mind or soul. His mind, as Berlin affirmed, was "unsentimental" but endowed with a profound sense of injustice and an acute sense of living in a hostile world, arguably intensified by his Jewish origin. Like other intellectuals, Marx was "haunted by a perpetual feeling of insecurity, and was morbidly thin-skinned and jealously suspicious of the least signs of antagonism to his person or his doctrines" (KM 95). His difficult character did not escape his friends or enemies, to whom Marx often appeared, in Bakunin's own words, as a fanatical authoritarian, "as intolerant and autocratic as Jehovah" (KM 101).[8]

In Berlin's eyes, Marx resembled an ancient prophet performing a task imposed on him by heaven with the inner tranquility derived from his belief in the bright future which he felt called to bring forth. His strong will and genius for simplification helped him remain to the end of his life a warrior engaged in a holy war against the bourgeoisie and endowed with a sacred mission: defeating the enemy. As a result, Berlin noted (KM 8), Marx behaved like "a commander, actually engaged in a campaign, who therefore does not continually call upon himself and others to show reason for engaging in a war at all, or for being on one side of it rather than the other." Worth noting here is Berlin's approach, which shows the extent to which his method of studying Marx was neither ideological nor philosophical, but presupposed an engagement with Marx's personality and temperament. The fact that Berlin examined Marx's intellectual and political achievement first and foremost through the lenses of the latter's personal style and proclivities did not mean that he paid no attention to ideas. In fact, Berlin did take the latter seriously into account, even if he never properly managed to grasp Marx's economic ideas. As such, Berlin's

---

[6] This may be an unfair characterization since Marx was very involved in the organization of the First International. See also Berlin's description of Marx's living conditions in London (KM 180–1).

[7] In his essay on Plekhanov, "The Father of Russian Marxism," Berlin made the following comment about Marx's writing style: "Marxist writings are not among the clearest or most readable in the literature of socialism. It was not only Keynes who found himself physically unable to plod through *Das Kapital*; and if Lenin had not radically altered our world, I doubt whether his works would be as minutely studied as they necessarily are" (POI 158).

[8] Also see the portrait of Marx by Paul Annenkov, as quoted in KM 98.

book on Marx and his environment anticipates and exemplifies his distinctive approach as a historian of ideas in his later work, in which he explored the *forma mentis* and personality of the thinkers whom he found interesting or intriguing, from Herder and Vico to Maistre and Hamann.

MARX'S ACCOMPLISHMENTS

Although Berlin was skeptical about the main tenets of Marx's doctrine, he did not shy away from acknowledging his achievements, which were considerable whether one agrees with his principles or not. Even if many of Marx's ideas may have come from others' writings, his synthesis was nonetheless remarkable and original (Berlin also noted that Marx often refused to properly acknowledge his intellectual debt to his contemporaries).[9] While Marx was not a revolutionary and did not take any personal part in the revolutions of his time, he was, on Berlin's account (POI 150), a teacher and ideologue like no other, who fought with words for a cause which was justified by the allegedly inexorable laws of history. Berlin singled out Marx's single-mindedness, which he regarded as both a virtue and a limitation. Marx's success and appeal owed a lot to the fact that he saw the world in stark Manichaean terms, black-and-white contrasts, friends and enemies. Hence, Marx had a clear idea about whom he could rely upon, whom he had to fight against, and why his party was ultimately destined to triumph over its opponents.[10] As a result, Berlin remarked, as soon as Marx reached the conclusion that the building of a communist society could only be achieved through a worldwide revolution led by the proletariat, he devoted his entire attention to the organization of this class, which he sought to motivate and educate for this monumental task.

Berlin was particularly interested in understanding the reasons for the success of Marxism, which achieved greater influence than any other rival doctrine of its age, such as Comtean positivism, utilitarianism, and Christian socialism. He began with an examination of the role played by ideas and theories in Marx's works.[11] Among them, Berlin thought that the most prominent and significant one was his philosophy of history, the source of all of Marx's philosophical beliefs. It owed a great deal to Hegel, who had previously sought to highlight a discernable pattern and intelligible goal in history. Berlin was particularly struck by the claim that Marxism alone could fully account for the evolution of human history and predict the shape of the future. Marx applied his entire energy to discovering the laws that govern the

---

[9] See Berlin 1998, 72. It must be added here that Marx did acknowledge his debt to Hegel and Feuerbach, even if he approached them critically.

[10] It might be worth noting here the extent to which this view of Marx anticipated – and perhaps shaped – Berlin's later diagnosis of totalitarianism as an expression of monism.

[11] On this issue, see Berlin 1998, 71. Also worth noting is Berlin's somewhat surprising claim that the most original and influential contribution of Marx was "the celebrated doctrine of the unity of theory and practice" (SR 153).

behavior of individuals in society and creating the movement designed to transform their lives in conformity with these laws. He believed that rational individuals could understand the laws and factors at work in society if they did not let themselves become deluded by ideologies. If Marx borrowed the theory of stages of history from Hegel, along with the ideas of conflict, tension, and a new synthesis, he developed the Hegelian concept of the Spirit and his logical apparatus into a full-fledged theory of history as class struggle under the influence of French historians such as François Guizot (1787–1874), the author of the influential *History of Civilization in Europe* (1828). The result of all this, as Berlin noted, was to split mankind forever into two worlds engaged in a ruthless war against each other and incapable of reaching a compromise.

Second, Berlin attributed Marx's success to his successful identification of the interests of a particular class (the proletariat) with the interests of the entire mankind. This dichotomy between the forward-looking proletariat and the backward-looking bourgeoisie served to identify the agent of progress and its enemy that, according to Marx's later followers, had to be vanquished and exterminated because it represented the reactionary class. It also led Marx to claim that the engine of history has always been and will continue to be class struggle, for which no one is responsible other than the unfair division of labor in modern society. And it emboldened him to make a daring prophecy, namely that all previous classes were bound to wither away because they represented particular interests of society, and that the future will belong to the proletariat alone because it represents the interests and aspirations of the *entire* mankind. This allowed Marxism to articulate a gospel of liberation that spoke directly to the immediate interests of the proletariat; through its prophetic side, it also gave hope and a sense of direction to millions of disenfranchised or exploited individuals.

In his later writings on Marx,[12] Berlin argued that Marx's idealization of the proletariat was itself "the idealized image of a man craving to identify himself with a favoured group of men who do not suffer from his particular wounds" (AC 356). On this reading, what made Marx identify himself with the proletariat was his personal "need to find [his] proper place, to establish a personal identity" (AC 358). It was an attempt on his part, after having been cut off from his original establishment (the Jewish community), to replant himself "in some new and no less secure and nourishing soil" (AC 358), to find "firmer moorings," even if he had to reinvent himself and work with a stylized image of the proletariat.

It is fair to say that this psychological reading of Marx was a more prominent feature of Berlin's later analysis of Marx and did not feature extensively in his 1939 book or in his discussions of Marx in the early postwar period. However, what remained a constant theme in Berlin's interpretation of Marx is the fact

---

[12] This shift in emphasis reflects Berlin's growing interest in nationalism which assumed much greater prominence in the 1960s and 1970s.

that he always viewed Marx as "a herald and a prophet, speaking in the name not of human beings but of the universal law itself, seeking not to rescue, nor to improve, but to warn and to condemn, to reveal the truth, and above all, to refute falsehood" (KM 7). Marxism, Berlin pointed out (SR 164), managed to "liberate its adherents from the old ... 'bourgeois' morality" more effectively than any other doctrine, including Nietzsche. What Marx and his successors succeeded in doing, Berlin pointed out (SR 187–8), "was to translate the sense of human atomisation, of the dehumanisation of which vast impersonal institutions, bureaucracies, factories, armies, political parties were at once a cause and a symptom, ... into an inevitable phase in human development," which, Marx predicted, would end with the advent of communism, whose justification and outline he offered in *The Communist Manifesto*.

Third, on Berlin's account, Marx put his finger on something that others either did not see as clearly as he did, or missed completely. Even if most of the premises on which his economic doctrines rest have been refuted by marginalist economists (beginning with Carl Menger and continuing with Stanley Jevons and Léon Walras) who replaced Marx's labor-based theory of value and price with a new marginal utility theory, the part of Marx's doctrine which has survived and grown, according to Berlin (KM 265), was his theory of the evolution and structure of capitalist society. In particular, Marx highlighted and commented upon "the concentration and centralization of control of economic resources; the increasing incompatibility between Big Business methods of production and older methods of distribution and the social and political impact of this fact; the effect of industrialization – and science – on the methods of war; and the swift and radical transformation of ways of living that all this would cause" (KM 234). No one else perceived as sharply as he did the magnitude and consequences of these historical transformations that changed the face of Europe over the span of several decades.

Fourth, Berlin emphasized the organizational genius of Marx, who grasped the salience of the social question in the nineteenth century and attempted to do something about it. Both the theoretical base and the practical side of later versions of Marxism (as well as Leninism, which drew inspiration from Marx) were directed toward the minute organization of all human energies in order to eliminate unjust inequalities and practices on the largest possible scale. What singles Marx out in the history of political thought, Berlin went on, is that he alone was capable of laying down the foundation of a powerful worldwide mass movement of the Left. Marx formulated a simple agenda and set clear goals "with specific indications of the type of action to which they were meant to lead" (SR 185). Thus, with the substantial help provided by Engels, Marx managed to create "a new ecumenical organisation, a kind of anti-Church, with a full apparatus of concepts and categories, capable, at least in theory, of yielding clear and final answers to all possible questions" (SR 149–50). It is perhaps also worth noting, at this point, that Berlin's picture of Marx as creator of an "anti-Church" resembled and anticipated other characterizations of

Marxism as a secular religion *sui generis*. A few years later, after visiting the Soviet Union, Berlin explicitly referred to Marxism as "a school of religion" (F 626) whose rituals, even if they did not mean much to individuals any longer, were nonetheless mandatory and could not be easily abolished or abandoned at will.

In this regard, it mattered a great deal that Marx took a long-term (revolutionary) perspective that sought to change the entire organization of the capitalist world; he refused to create an organization only to purse short-term reformist ends. Aspiring to unleash a worldwide revolution, he paid a lot of attention to training the proper cadres for it, entirely dedicated to their noble cause, by giving them a clear consciousness of their soteriological mission, power, and role in history. Not surprisingly, Berlin wrote, Marx was "a man of war" entirely committed to creating "an organisation with a clear and intransigent doctrine" (SR 185, 184). He deftly exploited the advantages derived from identifying a specific enemy (the bourgeoisie) and savior (the proletariat), and drawing a clear distinction between the forces of evil (darkness) and good (light). "What was original in Marx's analysis," Berlin commented (SR 165, 169, 176), "was the notion of bourgeoisie and proletariat as historical categories, due to arise and to vanish at specific historical stages." He started a "holy war" which gave the poor and the exploited not only hope, but something specific to do in order to change the conditions in which they lived. It was this organization for a ruthless struggle between classes and the promise of a happy ending that energized the masses and elicited unbound enthusiasm from Marx's followers – above all, Lenin.

In Berlin's view, even if many of Marx's ideas were not original – as already noted, he freely borrowed themes from thinkers as diverse as Hegel, Stirner, Ricardo, Sismondi, Guizot, Feuerbach, and Saint-Simon – he had the genius of synthesis, aided by his notorious single-mindedness in the pursuit of a sacred goal to which he was prepared to sacrifice anything. Because he lacked eclecticism and intellectual flexibility – traits that incline one toward moderation – Marx's views and analyses of contemporary society were bold and uncompromising; he never felt compelled to justify his opposition to the bourgeoisie, nor was he interested in assessing the merits or defects of the latter. Instead, he simply took for granted that he and the proletariat were on the right side of history. Marx's views were at all times clear cut and deduced from premises which, Berlin remarked, admitted no ambiguity in their conclusions. The consciousness of being a warrior and his belief in the scientific laws of history explain the almost complete absence from *Das Kapital* of "explicit moral argument, of appeals to conscience or to principle, and the equally striking absence of detailed prediction of what will or should happen after the victory" (KM 8). The declared priority was winning the class struggle against the bourgeoisie, a point on which Marx differed in both focus and intensity from other democratic reformers and utopian socialists, whom he disparaged and attacked constantly.

All this, Berlin concluded, accounts for the appeal of Marx's theory of history, society, and revolution. Although he described *Das Kapital* as "an original amalgam of economic theory, history, sociology, and propaganda which fits none of the accepted categories" (KM 220), Berlin viewed *The Communist Manifesto* as "the greatest of all socialist pamphlets ... a document of prodigious dramatic force ... an edifice of bold and arresting historical generalizations, mounting to a denunciation of the existing order in the name of the avenging forces of the future" (KM 153–4). Berlin also regarded *The German Ideology* as "philosophically far more interesting than any other work by Marx," and thought that it represented "a submerged, but a most crucial and original stage of his thought" (KM 114). In Berlin's view, the main appeal of Marx's synthesis comes from the fact that, contrary to its avowed claims, it is by no means an empirical theory based on facts. In reality, the core of Marx's theory of history – the famous Marxist doctrine of movement in dialectical collisions derived from Hegel – "is not a hypothesis liable to be made less or more probable by the evidence of facts, but a pattern uncovered by a non-empirical, historical model, the validity of which is not questioned" (KM 147). This is far from being an insignificant detail. Because Marxist theories of society, history, and revolution are not falsifiable in the proper sense of the term, they will always remain appealing to those who prefer to dream of a perfect future society and tend to be perpetually discontented with the present.[13]

Equally important, Marx sought to offer a new and superior understanding of history from the perspective of a privileged Archimedian point, in terms of a single set of universal laws capable of explaining the past and predicting the future. As such, Marxism offered a total system and plan of action and life that "gave the workers a concrete programme, and more than this, a total *Weltanschauung*, a morality, a metaphysics, a social doctrine" (SR 170) aimed at wrestling political power away from the enemy and directing it to advance its own interests and needs. The promise and prospect of "a complete unity of wholly rational beings leading lives of frictionless co-operation towards universally accepted and harmonious ends" (SR 152) proved extremely appealing to those whom history had condemned to poverty and solitude. Unfortunately, history was not on their side. Marxism was based on a Promethean belief that once the right class is in power, all human problems will somehow be miraculously solved, after a period of transition led by the vanguard party and marked by the dictatorship of the proletariat. This proved to be a costly illusion once the proletariat won power in Russia, and the charisma of the Revolution of 1917 disappeared soon afterwards, only to be replaced by the ruthless dictatorship of "the vanguard of the proletariat" under Lenin and Stalin's leadership.

---

[13] Also see AC 356–60.

MARX'S LIMITATIONS

The list of Marx's limitations drawn by Berlin was equally long, and it repeated most of the critiques previously leveled by others at the author of *Das Kapital*. To begin, Marx did not possess the qualities of a great popular leader or agitator, and he lacked eloquence, psychological insight, and emotional receptiveness. Uninterested in the character of persons outside his immediate range, he had a hard time socializing and entering into personal relationships. Engels was his only close friend, apart from his own family.

Second, in Berlin's view Marx was a false prophet who suffered from an acute (and unjustifiable) form of metaphysical optimism.[14] He (and Engels) predicted many things, from the falling rates of profit, the waning away of the state, and the concentration of the ownership of industry and land in private hands, to the decline in the standard of living of the proletariat – none of which happened in the end. He was equally wrong about the timing, causes, results, and economic effects of political revolutions. Perhaps more importantly in Berlin's view, Marx failed to understand the force and appeal of nationalism and religion, which subsequently proved to be much stronger than the power of socialism. Marx's exclusive focus on the emergence of classes and class war led him to mistakenly believe that nationalism and religion are mere temporary and reactionary phenomena that would be superseded in the future society once the proletariat takes the reins of power. Committed to the cause of internationalism, and believing that workers in all countries should unite, Marx took no interest in nations and questions of national identity. He saw mankind in black-and-white terms, divided into exploited workers led by a vanguard of the proletariat on the one hand, and, on the other hand, the capitalists and their allies holding on to the means of production. "This tenet," Berlin noted (CTH 265), "became a dogma for every school of Marxism ... The belief that nationalism was a reactionary bourgeois ideology was tantamount to the belief that it was doomed." Marx (and Engels) would have been surprised to discover that in the twentieth century, socialism and communism were most successful only when they allied themselves with nationalism, abandoned internationalism, and expressed appreciation rather than contempt for national values and symbols.[15] What they failed to grasp was that Marxism had the best chance of success not in the developed industrial Western societies, but in the less developed agrarian (peripheral) ones, where the intensity of class struggle was low compared to the West and nationalist movements were strong. Finally, Marx did not take seriously into account non-Western cultures and had a dismissive attitude toward them, displaying a curious form of Orientalism avant la lettre. It was probably this contemptuous stance of the founder of Marxism toward nationalism that made Marx's followers blind to the fact that in many regions around the globe, usually located in the periphery of the "civilized" world, nationalism often had an

---

[14] See CIB 21.   [15] See SR 192 and CTH 265–6.

emancipatory and progressive dimension that also furthered to some extent the cause of the working class.

Third, on Berlin's account, Marx's single-mindedness proved to be a liability in the end as it made him rigid and intolerant to critique and disagreement. He disliked and dismissed anyone who did not completely accept every word he uttered; not surprisingly, he never admitted any valid criticism of his mistakes.[16] Marx displayed not only harshness toward his enemies, whom he suspected of concocting plots and conspiracies everywhere, but also surprising aggressiveness and jealousy toward his fellow socialists, with whom he often quarreled and sought to crush. For example, he regarded Bakunin as "half charlatan, half madman" (KM 100), distrusted and envied Lasalle's outstanding organizational skills, and accused Proudhon of "intellectual immorality" (KM 108). Marx also found surprisingly few supporters among trade union leaders, who were open in principle to his message but were ultimately uneasy about his harsh personality. The idea that no compromise was possible with one's opponents became a major tenet of most forms of Marxism and Leninism, and separated them from the more humanistic branches of the Left that veered toward social democracy and less radical forms of socialism.

As a political moderate, Berlin was also taken aback by the fact that Marx was excessively critical toward those on the Left who believed that a compromise and a peaceful reconciliation of interests with the bourgeoisie were both possible and desirable.[17] The existing institutions of the bourgeois society, Marx confidently declared, could not be reformed and were destined to perish; the only real and important thing was the war between two incompatible classes, as a prelude to a radiant future that promised to bring about a complete break with the past. For him, gradualism and moderation were the most dangerous of all heresies because they presented a distorted view of reality and failed to perceive the enemy for what he really was – that is, a class destined to be eliminated forever from the scene of history.

Consequently, Berlin affirmed, Marx chose to stick to an apocalyptic vision of capitalism which other socialist thinkers such as Eduard Bernstein did not embrace. He was too confident that the intensification of class war would bring about more and more economic and social tensions that would lead in the end to the ultimate explosion of capitalist societies in the Western world. Because Marx underestimated the value of gradualist approaches, his theory did not have any room for progressive social policies and concessions to labor unions given and enacted by the capitalists.[18] As a result, Berlin reminded us, Marx did

---

[16] See CIB 122.
[17] "He neither offered nor invited concessions at any time, and did not enter into any dubious political alliances, since he declined all forms of compromise" (KM 9).
[18] Berlin noted that the development of social-democratic regimes in the West owed a lot to Marx, for the reformist measures were made possible by the pressure from hardcore Marxists.

not foresee the subsequent evolution of social democracy in Western Europe, nor could his theory account for the gradual evolution of capitalist society into moderate forms of socialism under persistent but peaceful pressure from below. Between *The Communist Manifesto* and Bernstein's *Evolutionary Socialism* (1899) there were not only major differences in tone and focus. The core message of Bernstein's book, aimed at justifying the possibility of a gradual transformation of capitalism in tandem with the more progressive members of the bourgeoisie, fundamentally differed from the revolutionary radicalism of Marx, which confidently proclaimed that capitalism was simply doomed by the laws of history.

WHY BERLIN COULD NEVER HAVE BEEN A MARXIST

Berlin could have never been a Marxist in the proper sense of the word, for several reasons. They have to do with the core of his political vision based on his unflinching commitment to pluralism and freedom, and his principled opposition to monism, determinism, and all forms of Procrusteanism.

In the eyes of someone like Berlin, who believed in the possibility of rational argument among individuals of different philosophical outlooks and political persuasions, Marx's historicist and revolutionary doctrine had to appear alien, to say the least.[19] For Marx challenged an old belief in the existence of a set of values common to the entire mankind, values that create bridges and allow for communication among human beings regardless of their ethnic, racial, or political background. Once class consciousness becomes dominant and takes center stage, it is no longer possible for people to believe in timeless ideas and see the world through the eyes of those who belong to a different class, nation, or religion.

Berlin could have never become a Marxist or a communist because he was aware that people share several important things in common, in spite of the existence of significant differences between their values, principles, and interests.[20] He rejected Marx's attempt to divide mankind into those who can (and deserve to) be saved because they are on the "right" side of history and the losers destined to be sacrificed because they are on the "wrong" side of history. This idea was "a terrible new weapon" (SR 175) that justified violence and terror "on a scale hitherto attained only by fanatical religious movements" (SR 176). Moreover, a liberal thinker such as Berlin, who admired the Kantian idea of human dignity and human rights, could find little common ground with someone like Marx, who was a notorious critic of the concept of individual rights. The latter notion rests on the assumption that there are certain values and goods that all human beings share beyond their class membership and religious and national identities. Marx consistently denied this claim.

---

[19] On Marx's historicism, see POI 146–7. [20] Also see CIB 38–9.

Whether or not Berlin's account of Marx rendered full justice to his complex subject is an open question.[21] Some of Marx's defenders argued that there are places in his writings where he appears to embrace a more gradualist and compromising strategy in pursuing the destruction of capitalism. Berlin tended to dismiss such claims when he didn't ignore them completely. To the extent to which understanding Marx amounts first and foremost to making sense of his attempt in *Das Kapital* to provide an allegedly scientific basis for his theory of the inevitable collapse of capitalism, it might be said that Berlin probably missed his target to a certain degree. Nor is it clear what position he took in the longstanding debate on the young versus the old Marx, and whether or not the young Marx should receive priority over the more mature thinker. One might argue that Berlin's book gave more weight to the early Marx than had been the case in the English-language scholarship up to the moment when he wrote his book. As such, Berlin's study of Marx and Marxism may be seen as occupying – both chronologically and substantively – a space between an older, more positivist reading of Marx, and the Hegelian–Idealist interpretation made possible by the rediscovery and publication of Marx's early works, and encouraged by the Western Marxists' desire to save the founder's ideas from the subsequent violent excesses of Lenin and his overzealous disciples. Moreover, at times, such as when he discussed monism and the idea of a perfect society, Berlin presented some of the ideas of Marx in such a way that the whole conceptual frame curiously resembled his own much more than Marx's. What cannot be denied, however, is the seriousness with which Berlin treated his subject, or the measured respect he showed to Marx's ideas as well as to the ideas of other Marxist thinkers such as Plekhanov. Aware that powerful ideas have major consequences, Berlin pleaded for "a sharply critical approach" to doctrines which were "swallowed whole by the fanatical Marxist sectaries" (E 100).

For obvious historical, political, and biographical reasons, Berlin's views on Marxism were never those of an impartial spectator, especially in the context of the Cold War, when capitalism was attacked by prophets of extremity from all sides and impartiality was not a legitimate option for the friends of the open society. Although he was a man of the Center-Left not blind to the imperfections of capitalism, Berlin could never forget the magnitude of the tragedies of the twentieth century in which the regimes that invoked and spoke in the name of Marx's ideas played a major part. Berlin's famous visit to the Soviet Union in 1945 strengthened his skepticism toward Marxism and his loathing of

---

[21] I commented on Berlin's anticommunism in connection with his political moderation in Craiutu 2016, 85–98.

Stalinism, about which he entertained no illusions.²² In a letter to the editor of *The New York Times* on June 30, 1949, Berlin pointed out "the errors and distortions in which Marxism abounds," and stressed "the incompatibility between any form of democratic belief and Marxist doctrine" (E 100).²³ In another important letter to Alan Dudley on March 17, 1948, he listed several key reasons that made him differ from Marxists (as well as fanatical anticommunists). Among them, Berlin mentioned his belief that cooperation is possible among classes and class struggle was not inevitable, and the idea that "such concepts as truth, goodness, justice, kindness, compromise etc. are not disguised forms of class interests, but genuinely common to different classes, individuals and societies" (E 46). Although Berlin refused to play the role of a propagandist, his writings on Marx and Marxism must be seen as an exercise in intellectual history written by someone who was to become a major representative of Cold War liberalism.

Furthermore, Berlin's longstanding interest in ideas and his belief in their power put him at odds with Marx, the defender of historical materialism who believed that the mental and religious life of individuals is entirely determined by the material conditions of the societies in which they live. On Marx's account, the dominant factors in any society are not ideas, but the struggle for survival and for satisfaction of basic needs. Moreover, as already mentioned, he did not believe in the existence of universal, timeless truths about individuals and societies in general. Ideas, Marx famously argued, always follow and reflect the changing material needs of society; hence, he believed that it would be an error to refer to timeless ideas. *Pace* Marx, Berlin refused to admit that ideas are mere epiphenomena dependent on their social and political contexts. He argued instead that it is people's ideas, along with their emotions, hopes, and fears, that influence moral codes, political priorities, economic structures, and modes of behavior. Ambitious ideas regarding the best form of government and the good life generate powerful controversies on what is just, right, possible, and desirable. These ideas and ideologies, Berlin insisted, are never mere reflections of the material conditions in which people live; they originate in people's hearts and minds, as personal expressions of their own views, values, aspirations, and principles. A caveat might be in order here. Berlin was no naïve idealist, to be sure; while he rejected Marxian materialist reductionism, he also stressed that ideas reflect political, cultural, and economic conditions, even as

---

²² For an excellent example of Berlin's views on Stalinism, see the article that he wrote under the pseudonym O. Utis, "Generalissimo Stalin and the Art of Government," published in *Foreign Affairs* (SM 92–111). Berlin's letters from that period are also worth rereading in this context (they are collected in F and E). Of particular interest is the letter Berlin sent to Angus Malcolm on February 20, 1946 (F 625–7) in which he compared the atmosphere in the Soviet Union to that of a severe type of English public school.

²³ Berlin went on to add that "if Marxism were to be refuted, which I believed to be both possible and desirable, it must first be understood" (E 100).

they also acquire a force of their own that can change those conditions in unpredictable ways.

Second, Berlin's interpretation of Marxism depicted the latter as a monist doctrine committed to the twin assumptions that "[t]here can be only one true answer to any given problem, ... one social policy or way of life that is rational in any given situation" (SR 155), and that "all human ends are, in principle, harmonisable and capable of satisfaction" (SR 151).[24] This Platonic ideal, Berlin insisted, was a leap of faith that he could never make; consequently, he rejected the possibility of the very notion of a perfect society that lies at the core of Marxism and which promises precisely such a harmony of values and principles.[25] Marx, Berlin argued, was neither a pluralist nor a moderate: he was a monist radical who always interpreted the world "in terms of a single, clear passionately held principle, denouncing and destroying all that conflicts with it" (KM 19). His intellectual system, Berlin argued, was a "closed one, everything that entered was made to conform to a pre-established pattern" (KM 19–20) even if it was justified by recourse to experience and history.

The idea that there is always one single correct agenda or policy to be determined as such by the members of a "privileged priesthood" who see themselves as the infallible depository of truth turns Marxism into an inflexible doctrine, "a bold and startling combination of absolute authority and evolutionary morality" (SR 160, 162). This helps explain, in Berlin's opinion, the illiberal and dangerous side of Marxism as illustrated by the doctrine of the necessary dictatorship of the proletariat and the required intransigence toward dissenters. This doctrine affirms that the ends justify the means and encourages people to judge reality based on what theory says while ignoring the evidence on the ground. This is, in Berlin's view (POI 16–17), a corollary of the unbridled monism at the heart of the Marxist doctrine that paves the way to extremism and fanaticism; it is also what "Marxism has in common with some of the great dogmatic Churches of the world" (SR 164). All this is visible in the case of Leninism, which justified many violent acts on the grounds of the requirements of the revolutionary movement. But it is not limited to Lenin's case, to be sure. It can be found wherever and whenever truth is regarded as the authority of one privileged group over all others, as something that can be discovered only by an elite whose authority may not be challenged by the laymen. In reality, Berlin affirmed, truth is something that no individual can ever fully possess, and it is never the monopoly of any single group; it can be approximated or intimated only through conjectures and refutations.

---

[24] Also see the description of what Berlin called "The Platonic Ideal" given in "The Pursuit of the Ideal" (CTH 6).
[25] Values and principles such as liberty and equality, justice and mercy, clash and cannot be perfectly harmonized with each other. This is both empirically and theoretically impossible. See Berlin's critique of monism and his endorsement of pluralism in POI 6–8, 14–17.

Third, Berlin could not have been a Marxist because he was deeply skeptical toward any form of historical determinism (POI 25) which affirms that history obeys inexorable and necessary laws from which there is no escape for individuals: "to think that there exists *the* pattern, *the* basic rhythm of history ... that is to take the game too seriously, to see in it a key to reality. Certainly it is to commit oneself to the view that the notion of individual responsibility is, 'in the end', an illusion" (L 106–7). As a deterministic doctrine, Marxism fosters the erosion of the notion of individual choice and may lead people to believe that they are not responsible for their own actions. History – Berlin liked to repeat a sentence of one of his favorite authors (Herzen) – has no predetermined libretto or endpoint; it is and will always remain unpredictable and open-ended. "I believe in pluralism and do not believe in historical determinism," Berlin affirmed (CIB 34). "I do not believe in a libretto of history ... Although of course there are great impersonal factors which determine the shapes of the lives of individuals and nations, I see no reason to see history as an autobahn from which major deviations cannot occur" (CIB 35).

Fourth, Berlin's interest in diversity and his commitment to the idea that values and human goals are plural, incommensurable, in rivalry with one another, and sometimes incompatible made him implacably opposed to Marxism, which flatly rejects these ideas. Berlin claimed that there is an implicit antiliberal and antipluralist bias in Marxism which has always sided with homogeneity and unity against diversity, pluralism, disagreement, competition, and strife among values. Berlin saw Marx as continuing the tradition of thought initiated by Plato, and continued by Spinoza, Helvétius, Rousseau, and Fichte whose theories of static perfection affirmed the possibility of suppressing all conflicts in society once and forever. Pluralism, Berlin claimed, is more faithful to the complex nature of the human condition than determinism because it respects human creativity, diversity, spontaneity, conflict, and luck. Moreover, it is a safer political principle because it provides guarantees for disagreement and dissent and shows that the search for moral certainty is illusory in an ever-changing, imperfect, and uncertain world. Trade-offs between our values and priorities are always necessary and unavoidable if we are to prevent tragic situations and avoid inflicting suffering upon other individuals.

Furthermore, there is a fifth reason why Berlin could have never been a Marxist: his conception of freedom was significantly different from Marx's. The latter, Berlin believed, amounted to a great perversion of the ideal of freedom by giving "unlimited power to any person or body which feels itself in possession of the right rule for the government of men" (PIRA 177). Marxism failed to treat people as ends in themselves, or paid lip service to Kant's famous principle; thus, it justified denying individuals the right to deliberately and freely choose their own path in life (PIRA 192–4). Against Marx and his followers, Berlin insisted that respecting individuals' fundamental right to be treated as ends in themselves and as unique persons is a pillar of our Western liberal civilization that may not be tampered with under any circumstances.

This is the basis of what some of Berlin's interpreters called his anti-Procrusteanism,[26] at the core of which lies a simple idea – namely, that human beings should never be coerced into following patterns of behavior and thought imposed from above. It was Marxism that proclaimed that select members of the vanguard must be allowed to begin their work of building a perfect world free of the sins of the past and that there should be no limit to what they may undertake. No sacrifice will be seen as too costly, no human life will be seen as too precious in the pursuit of such an ideal. Gas chambers, labor camps, induced famine, show trials, civil wars, and genocides could all be justified in the name of distant goals and ends, or in light of emergency circumstances that require exceptions to the rule. Once the eggs are broken and the habit of breaking them becomes entrenched in society, it will become virtually impossible to stop it, and the outcome will be an endless series of brutalities, sacrifices, brain-washing, and exterminations.[27] "Man must be free," Berlin believed (PIRA 144), "uninterfered with, acting by his own volition, pursuing ends which are his, and solely his, for motives which are his own, in ways which he perceives to be best." Any attempt to mold human beings "like children or animals leads logically to Auguste Comte, Marx and Lenin. Once you know what has to be done, you can do it by persuasion or by force and that denies basic human rights – above all of choice – lack of freedom of choice means dehumanization" (CIB 71–2).

This was one of the main reasons why Berlin felt attracted to Herzen rather than to Marx. Herzen was, in Berlin's own words (POI 121), "the rarest of characters, a revolutionary without fanaticism, a man ready for violent change, never in the name of abstract principles, but only of actual misery and injustice." Many things separated Herzen from Marx, including their temperaments and character – Herzen found Marx "personally unbearable" (POI 111) – but one idea stood out above all. It was Herzen's refusal to admit that one has the sacred duty to sacrifice oneself upon the altar of a greater cause, be that Progress, the Proletariat, Equality, Nation, or Revolution. All doctrines which attempt to justify such sacrifices in the name of big principles, Herzen (and Berlin) thought, were irrational vestiges of the past, to be regarded as "crimes or lunacies" (POI 114) that threaten human dignity. Distant ends confidently proclaimed by the prophets of a bright future are particularly dangerous because they are terrible delusions which tend to bring about tyranny. Berlin shared Herzen's skepticism toward all theories that minimize the role of individuals, tend to limit their freedom and repress their desire for self-expression and capacity for choice. For that reason alone, he could have never been an orthodox Marxist, as some of his colleagues on the Left turned out to be.

---

[26] On this issue, see Cherniss 2013 18–19 and Allen 1998.   [27] See PSM 13–14 and POI 27–8.

IN LIEU OF CONCLUSION

Berlin occupied, as he once put it, "the extreme Right Wing edge of the Left Wing movement, both philosophically and politically."[28] This witty comment sheds light on the political moderation that made him immune to the temptation of Marxism and dichotomic thinking.[29] His critique of Marx overlapped to a certain extent with the interpretations of two other prominent contemporaries, Raymond Aron and Leszek Kołakowski. Much like Berlin, they took Marx's ideas very seriously and carefully studied them before finally coming out against them. No one who is seriously interested in Marx today can afford to ignore their seminal exegeses. It would not be an exaggeration to say that Aron is probably a better guide than Berlin when it comes to Marx's economic and social thought, while Kołakowski, the author of *Main Currents of Marxism*, is a more comprehensive guide on Marxism's complex intellectual sources and branches. What is really interesting to note is that these interpreters of Marx, who produced three major studies of Marxism, believed in political moderation while being anticommunists, each in his own personal way, but without ever becoming fanatical in their commitments.[30]

Therefore, it would be helpful to end this chapter by summarizing Berlin's position on communism, which has occasionally raised a few questions among some of his more skeptical readers. While he denounced in unequivocal terms the cynicism, high costs, and moral corruption brought about by the Soviet regime, Berlin firmly refused the posture of a propagandist in the ideological battle against the Soviet Union and its satellites.[31] A critic of Lenin's ruthless practices and philosophy of action, he did not shy away from praising Plekhanov and Herzen, which seems to confirm the claim that he may have been more nuanced on Marxism than has been believed.[32] Be that as it may, Berlin's version of anticommunism was influenced by his profound distrust of the zealotry, ideological simplicity, and political fundamentalism which dominated the politics of the Cold War. At the same time, he lacked the fervent zeal of those who saw themselves engaged in an all-or-nothing crusade against communism[33] and refused to accept that the answer to communism was a counter faith, equally fervent and militant. There was, he warned his anticommunist friends, no point in defeating their side, "if our beliefs at the end of the war are simply the inverse of theirs, just as irrational, despotic, etc." (E 351). He felt compelled to try a different path.

---

[28] Berlin as quoted in in Cherniss 2013, 80.
[29] I commented on Berlin's political moderation in the context of Cold War liberalism in Craiutu 2016, 71–111.
[30] On Aron and Kołakowski's political moderation, see Craiutu 2016: 34–70, 190–5, 226–8.
[31] On this issue, see Berlin's important letter to Alan Dudley from March 17, 1948 (E 44–8).
[32] See, inter alia, Cherniss 2013, 30.
[33] All this came to the fore in a memorable letter Berlin sent to Herbert Elliston on December 30, 1952 (E 349–52).

At the very end of his important essay "Political Ideas in the Twentieth Century," Berlin wrote:

> What the age calls for is not (as we are so often told) more faith, or stronger leadership, or more scientific organization. Rather it is the opposite – less Messianic ardour, more enlightened skepticism, more toleration of idiosyncrasies, more frequent ad hoc measures to achieve aims in a foreseeable future, more room for the attainment of their personal ends by individuals and by minorities whose tastes and beliefs find (whether rightly or wrongly must not matter) little response among the majority. What is required is a less mechanical, less fanatical application of general principles, however rational and righteous, a more cautious and less arrogantly self-confident application of accepted, scientifically tested, general solutions to unexamined individual cases (L 92).

It is no accident that Berlin recommended "less Messianic ardour, more enlightened skepticism, more toleration of idiosyncrasies" in the fight against communism at a point in time – the 1950s! – when many of his contemporaries on both the Left and the Right called for the opposite, namely more intransigent partisanship, more faith, less skepticism, and no compromise. The age, he believed, did not need more political radicalism; in reality, it called instead for more political moderation, a virtue for courageous minds which requires prudence and judgment far more than enthusiasm and passion.

This was *not* a lesson that Berlin could have learned from Marx. The latter never accepted, to use a favorite expression of Berlin (from his essay on Churchill in 1940), that life ought to be seen through many windows, none of which is absolutely clear or opaque, and none of which is without some merit of its own. Marx believed instead that we should uncritically embrace a single doctrine and a new faith which promises to bring about an earthly paradise when the time is ripe. That was supposed to be the only window which could give us a full and undistorted view of the real world. Berlin begged to disagree. The encounter with Marx's (and others') ideas had taught him valuable lessons about the dangers of monism and ideological intransigence that he could never forget.

In the end, however, there was no ambiguity about where Berlin stood on Marxism. It is no accident that in his moving message for his twenty-first century readers (Berlin 2014), Marx's name did not appear at all. Berlin knew Marx well, but, true to his own method, he had also read many others, including Herzen, Turgenev, Herder, Mill, Maistre, Hamann, and Vico, all of whom opened fascinating windows through which he could contemplate the world around him. He knew well that ideas fanatically held are always fatal in politics, and that the road to Hell is often paved with good intentions.

7

Privileged Access: Isaiah Berlin and Russian Thought

Kathleen Parthé

Isaiah Berlin's links to Russian thought evoke the notion of "privileged access," which involves more than an account of the people he met and the events he witnessed.[1] There is his famous ability to empathize with figures from the past, none more so than members of the nineteenth-century Russian intelligentsia – writers, critics, and activists – whom he propelled into public view with a series of groundbreaking essays from the late 1940s through the 1960s. There is Oxford, where, for many decades, he had great swaths of time in which to read and think about Russia, with occasional visits from such luminaries as Akhmatova, Likhachev, Rostropovich, and Shostakovich. There are his journeys back to Russia and to Israel, where he encountered many Russian-born residents, from President Chaim Weizmann to his cousin Yitzhak Sadeh (who fought in both the Russian Revolution and the Israeli War of Independence). Finally, there is the exposure, early on, to the Russian language, the key that opened many doors.

Only twenty-four years old when asked to write a book on Karl Marx, Berlin embarked on a six-year odyssey that led, among other places, to the London Library, with its shelves full of Russian books, where "by pure accident [I] stumbled on Herzen ... I took one volume, and never looked back" (F 67–8). As proof of Herzen's argument for the role of chance in human affairs, it was serendipity that led the young scholar to a pre-eminent figure in Russian *kruzhki* (discussion groups) of the 1830s and 1840s. Building on his earlier reading of Tolstoy and other authors of Russia's Golden Age, Berlin made a permanent move to this political and cultural "neighborhood," becoming an eloquent publicist for his "friends."[2] Later, chance encounters led him to meetings with Boris Pasternak and Anna Akhmatova.

---

[1] Roger Hausheer, in his introduction to *The Proper Study of Mankind*, refers to the "network of connections" that made Berlin "a privileged observer of, at times an active participant in, some of the major events of the day" (PSM xxiv).

[2] Kelly 2013, 112.

Before completing the Marx project, Berlin wrote "A Sense of Impending Doom," comparing modern English poetry with revolutionary-era Russian verse; rejected at the time by *London Mercury*, the article appeared posthumously. In it, he argued that analogies with Russia are inevitably profitable, "since everything in its history is so much more dramatic and exaggerated than anything anywhere else," and because Russian writers have conveniently left "a complete record" of their state of mind during various eras (Berlin 2001, 11–12).[3] The exceptionalism of Russians – as the most dramatic and talkative of people – made bringing Russia into broader discussions necessary and relatively easy. Years of intensive reading endowed Berlin with an "intellectual capital on which he was to depend the rest of his life"; he also added to this capital for decades to come.[4] The subject of the commissioned book was Marx, but its pages include Herzen, Bakunin, Nechaev, Plekhanov, and Lenin; there is no doubt where Berlin's loyalty lay in Marx's skirmishes with Bakunin (KM 217–19, 244–8, 256, 261). This was the first of many texts that acquired, in Berlin's hands, a "distinctively Russian cast."[5]

Correspondence from the late 1930s demonstrates that the euphoria Berlin felt when discussing Russian personalities and ideas was becoming a permanent state of mind.[6] By 1937, Alexander Herzen's name shows up frequently, as first among "my noble 19th century Russians," whose reactions to people and events had begun to shape Berlin's own. By the following year, Berlin was certain that there was no one he would like to resemble more than Herzen. "If anyone were alive now who talked as he must have done – vide the memoirs of others about him – one wd [sic] never listen to anyone else" (F 258–9, 279–80). By age sixty, he called his "fellow-feeling" for Herzen at the point of "lunatic self-identification" (B 388).[7] When asked to compare Tocqueville and Herzen, Berlin speculated that the latter, at least, would have joined the Resistance during World War II because he was the braver of the two (CIB 180). What Berlin likely did not know is that one of Herzen's great-grandsons, Jean Rist, was in the Resistance, and was killed by retreating Germans in 1944. In Herzen, Berlin had found "a perfect surrogate, an authentic Russian figure, lauded as a hero by the Soviets themselves, who could 'speak out' for those who could not, without risk or fear of reprisal."[8] Lenin's 1912 centenary tribute was the imprimatur allowing Soviet scholars to study and publish Herzen's work.

Aileen Kelly sees Berlin's notion of empathy emerge in his introductions to Herzen's *From the Other Shore* and *My Past and Thoughts*.[9] The former impressed Berlin with its insistence that human beings not be sacrificed to

---

[3] Cherniss 2013, 24–6. [4] Ignatieff 1998, 71. [5] Cherniss 2013, 30. [6] Dabney 1998, 31.
[7] Berlin showed no interest in the fact that Herzen was, in fact, half German, perhaps agreeing with Karl Marx's observation in the notes to *Das Kapital* that Herzen was "half Russian, but a total Muscovite" (as cited in Gurvich-Lishchiner 1987, 466).
[8] Harris (forthcoming), ch. 1.5. [9] Kelly 2001, 18.

abstractions, and that, absent a libretto, we must make our own moral choices and accept what comes with courage and dignity.[10] The latter book he declared to be the best nineteenth-century autobiography; it remained for him a "monument to the civilized, sensitive, morally preoccupied and gifted Russian society to which Herzen belonged" (PSM 499–524). For those familiar with Berlin's writing, the Herzen memoir offers much that seems familiar: an aristocratic taste for individual freedom, lengthy digressions on colorful characters, unsystematic reading, and a writing style that has "the effect of spontaneous improvisation" (PSM 507).

In his studies of the Russian intelligentsia, Berlin gravitated toward figures such as Belinsky and Herzen, whose values he shared and whose fearlessness he admired, and he avoided those with whom he felt uncomfortable, in particular Dostoevsky, who "unnerved" and threatened to dominate him: "One suddenly finds oneself in a nightmare, one's world becomes obsessive, turns into something sinister … It's too strong, too dark, too terrifying" (CIB 173). Such affinities and antipathies reveal the extent to which Berlin sympathized with liberal and indeed radical critics of authority, and against traditionalism and conservatism. He reacted more intensely to Russian ideas and actions than to most other subjects of study, exploring these topics confidently, intuitively, and joyfully, reading the writers' personal letters with as much interest as if they had been sent to him. Writing to thank Pasternak's sister Josephine for the gift of one of their father's paintings, Berlin spoke of "the consuming personal self-identification" with which he looked on "everything to do with Russia in the 19th century which extends exactly to 1918" (E 628–9). He conceived a "desire to promote a vision [of Russia] that had strong roots in the past and offered hope for the future."[11] This meant, in effect, taking the side of the Westernizers in the debates of the nineteenth-century intelligentsia.

When World War II began in September 1939, Berlin was awaiting the publication of *Karl Marx. His Life and Environment*. Not called up because of his damaged arm and foreign birth, he was disappointed when a plan hatched by Guy Burgess for them to work in the Moscow Embassy was scuttled by the Foreign Office; he was apparently unaware of suspicions attached to Burgess at this point (A 118–20). In a letter of June 21, 1940, to the Foreign Office, Berlin described Russia as "the subject which absorbs me the most," and added that he hoped to serve his country in the USSR, perhaps by establishing relations with literary circles there (F 302–4). Instead, he was ultimately ordered to New York to track American sentiment toward the United Kingdom. Transferred to Washington at the beginning of 1942, Berlin's background in Russian studies

---

[10] Berlin agreed with Herzen on the absence of a program going forward, a precise libretto; he also joined Herzen in believing that there were still patterns to be seen in past and present events. Carefully observing these patterns – and finding the right metaphors to explain them – help us to see the choices that lie before us (SR 27–30, 56–7; CC 141). Cf. Herzen 1956.

[11] Harris (forthcoming), ch. 1.5.

enriched weekly dispatches sent back to the Foreign Office, and gave him access to Soviet expert Charles Bohlen, Embassy colleague Donald Maclean (another member of the Cambridge spy ring, unbeknownst to Berlin), Russian Jewish émigrés, the composer Nicolas Nabokov, the former Provisional Government official Alexander Halpern, and Soviet visitors to Washington such as Andrei Gromyko (F 302–4, 311–96, 455, 463, 481, 493, 532, 550–2).

Reports drafted by Berlin, and sent out under the ambassador's name, were subsequently published as *Washington Dispatches 1941–5*. The analysis of the wartime alliance included frequent observations about the Soviet Union, especially the "disturbing obscurity" of Soviet speeches and actions that made it difficult to read their intentions.[12] Did Russian successes in 1943 mean that a secret deal was being made with the Germans? Did Moscow really have nothing to do with the murder of 10,000 Polish officers at Katyn? What was Stalin's attitude toward frontiers? A May 1945 dispatch, written by Berlin from the UN Conference in San Francisco, notes that the American press, unwisely, saw US–Soviet disputes as a zero-sum game, and viewed the Russian delegation in San Francisco as "so many strange visitors from Mars, concerning whom so little is known and whose behavior is so inscrutable that any information, however trivial, is so scarce as to be immensely interesting and valuable as such."[13]

When his language skills came to the attention of Sir Clark Kerr, British Ambassador to the USSR, Berlin was, at long last, invited to Moscow. He compared himself to all three of Chekhov's "sisters" in saying "to Moscow, to Moscow," although he knew little about what the new post would entail. To the Warden of New College, he claimed that the Foreign Office believed him "uniquely qualified" to advise on pressing issues, and write a dispatch on foreign policy to "act as a corrective" to officials obsessed with US policy toward Russia (F 550, 558, 563, 570, 573, 582–3).

Details of Berlin's stay in Moscow are known from contemporary letters and his later accounts of Akhmatova and Pasternak, and from confidential reports, circulated at the time and published in full only in 2004. Robert N. Harris calls it "one of the most erudite memoranda ever to land on a desk at the British Foreign Office," although probably more culturally based than they had anticipated.[14] "The Arts in Russia Under Stalin" begins with the caveat that "few analogies from the West are of use" and that "the present is particularly unintelligible without at least a glance at previous events," a task Berlin is eager to undertake (SM 1). Beginning in 1920 (the year he left Petrograd), Berlin describes the literary and artistic battlefield leading up to the terror of 1937, changes wrought by the war, and the situation he encountered in the fall of 1945. While conditions had eased up, writers were still viewed as persons to be watched "since they deal in the dangerous commodity of ideas" and "it is only

---

[12] Nichols 1981, 154–9, 173, 180–4, 235.   [13] Nichols 1981, 554–5.
[14] Harris (forthcoming), ch. 1.5.

by talking to writers and their friends that foreign visitors (including the author of this memorandum) have been able to obtain any degree of coherent insight" (SM 11). In Berlin's mind, the introductions to Akhmatova and Pasternak led him to the writers they read and revered, back through the generations to the free thinkers of an earlier age. Pasternak, for example, had known Leo Tolstoy, and was present, along with his father, at Tolstoy's deathbed. Berlin's new acquaintances gave him a clearer view of the lines of cultural development that had begun a century earlier and survived the immediate aftermath of the Revolution, but which had been severely damaged by the Soviet government.

Berlin witnessed the growing nationalism and suspicion of the West months before vicious attacks commenced on Akhmatova, Zoshchenko, Yiddish cultural figures, and many others. There was little new of intellectual interest because "the authorities, who would eagerly welcome invention and discovery in the technological field, do not seem aware of the indivisibility of freedom of inquiry" (SM 12, 16). Soviet theater audiences were so eager for an authentic experience that they reacted to productions of Shakespeare or Griboyedov "as if the play was drawn from contemporary life." The most striking aspect of Soviet culture was the gap between the receptivity of the Soviet people and "the inferiority of the pablum provided" (SM 21–2). A "nucleus of ageing but articulate intellectuals" maintained the standards of the prerevolutionary intelligentsia, and, despite the desperate situation, were capable of "gaiety, intellectual as well as social ... and a sense of the ridiculous." Berlin's hope was that the vitality and curiosity of the Russian people would lead to "a new flowering of the liberated Russian genius" (SM 21–3, 24–6).

The second report, "A Visit to Leningrad," records Berlin's brief return to the recently liberated city of his childhood. The intelligentsia lived a more threadbare life than their counterparts in Moscow, and even eminent writers' days "were still semi-obsessed by household needs" (SM 27–8, 39). The search for reading material led Berlin to the Writers' Bookshop on Nevsky Prospekt, on the site of a famous establishment run by Alexander Smirdin a century earlier; connections made there brought Berlin to the apartment of "an eminent literary personage" (Akhmatova is not named). Without knowing it, Berlin may have been sent to Akhmatova by the bookstore's manager to draw out anti-Soviet comments (SM 32, 36, 37).

Berlin's correspondence reinforces the impression that this was a pivotal moment in his life; we see how well he used his time, as every point of access led to another person and another conversation, most notably in literary spheres. He experienced the sensory overload familiar to first-time (and even repeat) visitors to Moscow who are fluent in Russian; Pasternak remarked, disapprovingly, on Berlin's state of exhilaration while visiting a country where everything was in fact "appalling." Berlin understood how well some visitors were treated during the Thaw years, and advised a Tolstoy granddaughter on what kind of reception to expect (PI 391; E 546, 16). Listening to what people were saying on the street and in the theater made Berlin realize that he "had forgotten that such emotions & expressions existed"; these conversations "are unlike anything to be heard anywhere else on earth" (F 591–5, 618). In Berlin's writing on Russia, it is virtually impossible to unravel the various threads: personal, cultural, political, and intellectual. One can only say that he experienced all things Russian with great intensity, a quality that is conveyed in the many essays written in the years following this initial visit to Moscow, which have survived the "aging" process to which so much Russian analysis is subject.

Berlin, apparently, did not intend to live off his knowledge of foreign affairs, but sometimes, like the "taxi" he claimed to be, he was summoned to a policy-related destination; he believed that his background, experiences, and many-sided reading had given him insight into how Russia worked. "Why the Soviet Union Chooses to Insulate Itself" is the fruit of an invitation to speak at the Royal Institute of International Affairs (Chatham House) in June 1946. He distinguished between an American desire to be "isolated" from international responsibilities, and the Russian desire to be "insulated" from outside interference. Official Russia was not concerned with borders, but "something more intangible," with building their society "in an imaginary race against time and in a ring of jealous enemies." Misreading the USSR's motives, the British annoyed the Russians "without frightening them" (SM 85–91). Modestly describing his "fugitive impressions" at the beginning of the talk, by the end Berlin clearly had found his voice.

Well into the 1950s, Berlin was asked to comment on Soviet behavior, most famously by the journal *Foreign Affairs* (L 55–93; SM 92–111; SM 122–56). For their mid-century issue, they commissioned "Political Ideas in the Twentieth Century," and Berlin responded with a manuscript that brought together what he had read and thought since the 1930s. While addressing broad philosophical issues, the epigraph is from Trotsky and the text is saturated with Russian examples, from Turgenev's Bazarov and Dostoevsky's Shigalev to the 1903 Second Congress of the Russian Social Democratic Party, which "altered the history of our world" (L 68–87). Berlin was fascinated by the deep roots of communist ideology, and in his writing he freely employed examples from literature, a source underutilized by other contemporary Russia experts.

Stalin's unpredictable behavior, a frequent subject of the wartime dispatches, was the theme of Berlin's essay "Generalissimo Stalin and the Art of Government" for *Foreign Affairs* in 1952. Worried that statements made under his name could harm friends and relatives living there, he insisted on the pen name "O. Utis" (SM xxx–xxxvii; E 239–41, 255–7). He began by asking: why does the Soviet Union alternate between "periods of quiescence and crisis," between thaw and freeze, which "puzzle not merely the outside world, but Soviet citizens," especially Party members who need to adjust their actions accordingly? What Berlin calls the "zigzag movement of the Party line" was Stalin's solution for preserving the USSR from problems that destroyed revolutionary regimes in the past, as popular enthusiasm gave way to corruption and cynicism. When revolutionary fervor goes too far and society's needs are not met, a regime can run out of scapegoats, although, as Berlin noted, "there can never be enough victims to expiate a crime which no one has committed." Stalin's invention was the political equivalent of "artificial rubber or mechanical brains ... an artificial dialectic" (SM 93, 96–7, 9).

Permanent wartime mobilization "alone enables so unnatural a form of life to be carried on." Unless one accepts these zigzags as deliberate, Soviet behavior is difficult to understand and predict (SM 107). Berlin wrote in 1950 that the authorities prevented provocative questions from being asked; by 1952, the Soviet government saw that it "cannot do without a minimum knowledge of what is being thought" (L 76; SM 99–100, 106). What would happen when the "master of manipulation" was gone? Would the State fall, having no goal other than self-perpetuation? The author advises paying attention to the artificial dialectic, which represented an even greater disdain of freedom "than that which Dostoevsky endowed his Grand Inquisitor" (SM 111). Was Berlin's line of argument an embarrassing "illusion,"[15] or a major insight into how power actually works in Russia?

For a talk given at Haverford College in February 1952, "Marxist versus non-Marxist Ideas in Soviet Policy" (SM 161–76), Berlin reiterates some points made the same year in *Foreign Affairs*, but with fascinating additions, wedding his deep knowledge of the onslaught of Western ideas in the nineteenth century to the interpretation of contemporary foreign policy. He is eloquent about the rigorous logic used by Russians before and after the Revolution. "They are sometimes apt to start with peculiar premises, and argue them through to a weird conclusion. But what they haven't much of is common-sense control. That is to say, when they are faced with facts, they simply ignore the facts," and "when faced with the choice between observing facts and acting upon hypotheses, they act on hypotheses" (SM 162, 175).[16] They collect lots of data, but few are bold enough to make sense of it; "and so it is that huge masses of information come in unweighted, unanalysed, and some very peculiar little things emerge, since the conferees at the Kremlin don't know what sort of weight to attach to a given set of raw facts" (SM 173).

In 1957, Berlin was asked for a post-Stalin update by *Foreign Affairs*, which appeared as "The Silence in Russian Culture" and "The Soviet Intelligentsia." He had, in the interim, traveled to Moscow and Leningrad, recording his impressions in "Four Weeks in the Soviet Union," first published in *The Soviet Mind*. Eleven years on, Leningrad was much improved, and he was told that contact with foreigners was allowed, especially in the cultural sphere. A literary scholar at Pushkin House said that going back to past horrors was unthinkable "save in so far as in Russia nothing was unthinkable." Berlin met senior government and Party officials who fawned on their superiors and bullied

---

[15] James 1998. [16] See also Parthé 2004, 117–20.

everyone else (SM 112–14, 119–21). Pasternak gave him a copy of *Doctor Zhivago*, to be delivered to the poet's sisters Lydia and Josephine in Oxford, prior to publication in the West. Berlin described staying up all night to read it, and said that no novel except *War and Peace* had affected him as strongly, with its scenes from 1917 Petrograd that he, too, had witnessed (E 539–42; SM xxvii–xxviii).

Berlin wrote two appreciations of *Doctor Zhivago* for the *Sunday Times* (republished in SM xxvi–xxix), and another piece that was first published in *The Soviet Mind* (SM 80–4). In 1958, amid turbulence surrounding the book's appearance abroad and the author's Nobel Prize, Berlin called the novel "a literary and moral event without parallel in our day" – the very terms in which Belinsky praised works in critical surveys. It was a matter of regret that both sides used *Doctor Zhivago* as Cold War propaganda, because it was a "poetical masterpiece in the central tradition of Russian literature, perhaps the last of its kind" (SM xxvi). In 1995, he recounted two trips made to Peredelkino in 1956, where he witnessed disagreements within the Pasternak family over publication (SM xxix). Berlin compares Pasternak to Tolstoy in his final decades: controversial at home but famous abroad, who joined no movement but whose work was imbued with "a sense of the artist's responsibility" to speak the truth. Pasternak's un-Soviet language "reminds one painfully of what it once was to be a great man" (SM 81–3).

Shortly after the 1956 trip, Berlin wrote to a friend that there had been "*no real change*" and the same "terrifying body of toughs" was still in charge (E 541). He says this in "The Silence in Russian Culture" (the first part of what is now called "Soviet Russian Culture"), which traces the importation of ideas from the West beginning in the 1830s; in Russia, such ideas assumed "fantastic shapes" and became "fighting faiths" all the way up to the Revolution, before Bolshevism became a "compulsory" way of life (SM 122–7, 130). In the 1930s, the regime focused on harnessing creativity and knowledge to the task of perpetuating itself, as writers became "engineers of human souls," a phrase which terrified Berlin. Citing "Mr. Utis" (i.e., himself) from five years earlier, Berlin says that even without Stalin, the system survived, "organized not for happiness, comfort, liberty, justice, personal relationships, but for combat" (SM 13–24).

Additional observations appeared in *Foreign Affairs* as "The Soviet Intelligentsia" by "L." With Stalin dead, "a set of rules and regulations" had taken his place. There was a thriving new "ersatz intelligentsia," but the government barely tolerated real intellectuals; they were thought necessary for a great nation's reputation, but still deeply suspect (SM 147–9, 152–5). In the nineteenth century, all Russian literature had been an "indictment of Russian life"; now, a few pre-Stalin figures survive as "semi-mythical creatures from a fabulous but dead past." Such was the state of a cultural enterprise that had once inspired its own people and had gained a wide international readership (SM 156).

Foreign policy analysis was never more than a by-product of Berlin's interest in Russia's intelligentsia and literature. He saw a clear link between the Western ideas – ingested and transformed in Moscow and Petersburg – and political currents leading to the upheaval of 1917 and beyond. The chance to say something new and more culturally based about how Russia had reached its present state was irresistible, and, following his 1946 return to Oxford, Berlin pursued this passion over the course of at least fifteen years, his own "remarkable" decade-and-a-half. He wrote, translated, taught at home and abroad, lectured everywhere, and worked to establish Russian Studies in England on a firmer footing (F 564–5, 577; E 122).

In "The Man Who Became a Myth" (POI 95–105), Berlin launched his postwar study of the Russian intelligentsia with Vissarion Belinsky, the creator of social criticism and the center of cultural and political debates that began in the 1830s. On the centenary of Belinsky's death, Berlin wished to present this mythic figure and fearless "conscience" of his generation to a larger audience. For Belinsky, ideas and texts were "events, matters of life and death, salvation and damnation," to which he reacted with a passion that Berlin found immensely attractive (PI 95, 100). The following year brought another centenary essay, "Russia and 1848," in which Berlin explained how the tumult of revolutionary Europe reached the quiet backwaters of Russian life under Nicholas I. By 1848, Belinsky had died, Herzen was living abroad, and Moscow professor Timofey Granovsky was largely silent, but Russians used this time of "enforced insulation" to develop political ideas on their own; the result was a critical mass of practically minded revolutionaries in the decades that followed (RT 1–23).

From the beginning, Berlin identified with members of the Russian intelligentsia, irrespective of whether he had met them personally (e.g. Pasternak, Akhmatova, Chukovsky, Marschak, Eisenstein, Brodsky, and Sakharov) or only through their works, whether they shared his twentieth century or died decades before he was born. Of the nineteenth-century writers who captured his attention, only Tolstoy's life overlapped with his own by a year, but that did not keep Berlin from imagining himself in their midst, a well-informed friend who found their manners, values, and ideas sympathetic and attractive. Berlin's tone of utter conviction and easy familiarity, especially in the Herzen-centered essays, has made it a challenge for subsequent scholars to imagine Herzen in any other "clothes" than the ones that Berlin provides.[17] One can argue over whether Berlin put too much of himself into his descriptions of Belinsky, Herzen, Turgenev, and others, but he certainly found himself in their writings. For Joseph Brodsky, the attraction was mutual; meeting Berlin soon after arriving in London, Brodsky found much about the man familiar: his face, his old-fashioned Russian, and his ideas, "a cry from the bowels of a monster, a call not so much for help as *of* help."[18]

---

[17] Harris (forthcoming), ch. 1.5.   [18] Brodsky 1991.

In a 1950 letter to the Warden of All Souls, Berlin requested a fellowship at his old college, making official the postwar turn toward Russian history and culture. Convinced that this was where he could make an original contribution, Berlin announced that a projected series of books would begin with the 1830s and Vissarion Belinsky. Succeeding volumes would track other "ideas and movements," and "the concrete social, political and economic changes with which they are interwoven," all the way to 1917. Berlin hoped to collaborate with American Slavists on a project translating prerevolutionary Russian texts and documents.[19]

Two years later, Berlin reported that the volume on Belinsky and other prerevolutionary radicals was well under way. He asked permission to spend several terms in the USA because "it is the only place where there are facilities – books, catalogues, persons" required to complete work on Belinsky and his circle by 1955.[20] Almost as an afterthought, Berlin mentioned the 1952 publication, in *Oxford Slavonic Papers*, of an essay on "the sources of Tolstoy's view of history in Russian and European thought," a modest reference to the first version of what has been known since 1953 as "The Hedgehog and the Fox."

As "Lev Tolstoy's Historical Scepticism," the essay might have had a quiet life as a study of one aspect of *War and Peace*. As "The Hedgehog and the Fox," it achieved what is now called "rock-star" status, something that Berlin later claimed to regret, as "hedgehog and fox" labels were indiscriminately applied to people, living and dead; still, he valued these metaphors because they "concentrated things" (A 551). The change of title and the additional material requested by Lord Weidenfeld made this a very marketable short book, which asks Tolstoy's provocative question about "first causes ... how and why things happen as they do and not otherwise" (RT 32). A key both to *War and Peace* and to Berlin's evolving theory of monism and pluralism, the expanded essay (and its many reviews) brought attention to the novel's epilogues, which are not "tedious interruptions of the story" (E 378–9). With a colorful binary opposition based on a Greek text (suggested by Lord Oxford, a friend of Berlin's in the 1930s, who later served as a British official in Palestine and elsewhere), Berlin set out to explain Tolstoy's philosophy as it had evolved by the 1860s. Andrzej Walicki has pointed out that while Berlin was a lifelong reader of Tolstoy, he did not see the writer as part of a specific intellectual tradition.[21]

The intensity of Berlin's Russian interests can be seen from letters to the Warden of All Souls in 1954, at which point the new edition of Tolstoy was out, "a somewhat lengthy treatise on the political views of Herzen and Bakunin," and eight chapters on Belinsky and his circle.[22] A year later, Berlin could point

---

[19] To Humphrey Sumner, March 14, 1950 (E+).
[20] To John Sparrow, May 2 and December 25, 1952 (E+).   [21] Walicki 2007, 49.
[22] To John Sparrow, May 4, 1954 (E+).

to a variety of writings and lectures on Russian subjects, including for BBC Radio. Asked to contribute an introduction ("A Revolutionary without Fanaticism") to Herzen's 1850 book *From the Other Shore*, Berlin wound up correcting the translation as well. He anticipated that the Belinsky book and another volume on the prerevolutionary period would be completed by 1960.[23] Instead of such full-length, scholarly books, Berin published a series of intense, Russian-themed essays, which remain indispensable resources on their subjects: the four-part "Remarkable Decade" (the birth of the Russian intelligentsia, the influence of German Romanticism, Vissarion Belinsky, and Alexander Herzen; 1955–6); "The Father of Russian Marxism" (on Plekhanov; 1956); "Russian Populism" (1960); and "Tolstoy and the Enlightenment" (1961).

Because "Herzen and Bakunin on Individual Liberty" (1955) falls outside the "Remarkable Decade" quartet, it often receives less attention, but it is an equally innovative essay. Although Bakunin wrote less than Herzen, his outsize personality made him a figure of enduring fascination and controversy, because he used words "not for descriptive but for inflammatory purposes" (RT 125). Berlin's presentation of Herzen includes excerpts from lesser-known works such as "Doctor Krupov," and a passage on the evils of abstractions (a central preoccupation of Berlin's thought), which are an "attempt to evade facts which do not fit into our preconceived schema" (RT 103). He ends with Herzen's "Letters to an Old Comrade," addressed to Bakunin, but not published until after the author's death in January 1870. Calling these "perhaps the most instructive, prophetic, sober and moving essays on the prospects of human freedom written in the nineteenth century," Berlin describes the gap between the two men as unbridgeable because of Herzen's solid commitment to personal liberty, in contrast to Bakunin, whose apocalyptic vision encompassed larger and vaguer units than real people (RT 116–18, 129).

In "Artistic Commitment. A Russian Legacy" (a 1960s lecture, revised and published in SR, 246–93), Berlin illustrates what he calls the "boomerang effect," by which abstract ideas entered Russia, only to return to Europe as tenets of a fiery faith. To illustrate the idea of artistic commitment, Berlin produced a meticulously argued paper, with citations from an impressive variety of European and Russian sources, about the conflicts caused between and within individual writers by the question and challenge of commitment. It is a scholarly masterpiece that reinforces – if reinforcement was required – Berlin's standing as an authority on prerevolutionary Russia. His review of *The Prose of Osip Mandelstam* exposes the dilemma of pure poets who still feel the responsibility to be witnesses to their age, and calls Mandelstam a shy man with "a fund of mad heroic courage" (SM 42).

By the early 1960s, as Chichele Professor of Social and Political Theory at Oxford, Berlin returned to political philosophy writ large, albeit with the benefit

---

[23] To John Sparrow, February 17, 1955 (E+).

of all he had learned about the impact of Western ideas on Russia and Russian ideas on the world. Essays followed on the two concepts of liberty, Enlightenment thinkers and their enemies, nationalism, utopias, Israel, and "personal impressions" of people he had encountered; there are Russian tonalities and references, but the focus lies elsewhere. The passing years saw Berlin's energies also expended on opera, the British Academy, and Wolfson College, of which he was founder and first president. The continuing gathering, editing, and publication of his Russian scholarship during these years masked to some extent the fact that he was no longer leading the intense Russia-saturated life of the past.

In the late 1960s and early 1970s, it was concern over the present, as much as a fascination with the past, that led to a lengthy essay on *Fathers and Children*, based on his Romanes Lecture. The "liberal predicament" at its core was as much Western, contemporary, and personal, a reaction to radical student movements in the USA and Europe, as it is Russian, past, and intellectual, although it is eloquent on Belinsky's posthumous influence on Turgenev. In this, Berlin mimics Herzen, who had written his own series of "Letters" to Turgenev in 1862–3 and 1868, using the controversial novel to discuss a wide range of issues, including the collapse of liberalism in tsarist Russia. Both authors saw Turgenev as "not terribly brave," and discussed *Fathers and Sons* out of a concern for the possible consequences of the political turbulence around them (CIB 168–9).

The last two decades of Berlin's life saw a return to Russian themes, albeit often in briefer, or more autobiographical and retrospective, forms. In 1981, Berlin wrote a review essay on two books by Andrei Walicki, a Polish scholar with whom he corresponded for several decades.[24] He also finally recorded his impressions of his "Meetings with Russian Writers in 1945 and 1956." Sections of this lengthy piece overlap with his earlier accounts, but the meetings with Pasternak and Akhmatova are described in greater and more vivid detail, and convey a keener sense of how fortunate Berlin had been to see for himself the vanishing world these two figures represented. The locations in which he met them resonated with the past: Pasternak's dacha was on the former estate of the Slavophile Yuri Samarin, active in mid-nineteenth-century Moscow circles, while Akhmatova's room was in the Sheremetevs' once-elegant Baroque palace (PI 386, 400–1). Berlin played his own role in the writers' lives, by transporting a manuscript copy of Pasternak's novel to England, and by, unknowingly, inspiring Akhmatova's highly imaginative version of their meeting in the poetic cycle "Cinque" and her belief that their encounter started the Cold War. In a 1973 letter to Max Hayward, Berlin describes himself as mere "raw material" in the poem "The Guest from the Future" (B 532–3). Berlin ends "Meetings" with the deeply emotional observation that

---

[24] Berlin 1981.

with both poets now dead, he cannot see their names or read their texts without remembering their voices (PI 413, 419, 428).

Berlin strikes a personal note when describing the return to a city he was seeing for the first time since 1920, childhood memories intersecting with the reality of 1945; it was a "legendary city," and he was simultaneously inscribed in the legend and "viewing it from some outside vantage-point," much like the city's beloved writers had done (PI 399). The essay Berlin wrote on receiving the Jerusalem Prize for 1979 (republished as "The Three Strands of My Life" in PI 433–9) begins with the Russian influences on his understanding of the "vast and sometimes sinister power" of ideas, and on his rejection (à la Herzen) of the sacrifice of the present to a utopian future. During the last decade of his life, he sat for interviews with Ramin Jahanbegloo, and with his biographer, Michael Ignatieff, and the books that followed these sessions revisited many of his Russian experiences.

The changes that came to Russia during the last decade of Berlin's life left him unconvinced; for Akhmatova's "Requiem" (with its unforgettable account of the purge years) to appear in Russia was a happy surprise, but more as a reminder of the past than a guarantee of political reform (A 323). His final visit to Russia, in 1988, when he was nearly eighty, was less intense than previous trips, and, three years later, he was rather low-key about the fall of the Soviet Union. When reminded of the revival of liberalism, he pointed out that Russia had many liberals in the professions before 1917, "but there was a singular lack of leaders" and no tradition of civic life (A 484–9). He admitted a strong preference for Andrei Sakharov, who reminded him of Herzen, over Alexander Solzhenitsyn, who looked and acted like an Old Believer (an ultra-conservative adherent of a seventeenth-century religious schism).[25] Were the positive changes now irreversible? Would Russian nationalism and anti-Semitism run rampant? Berlin's lifelong empathy made him unwilling to have the essay collection *The Soviet Mind* published during his lifetime, when it might "add to the works which dance upon [the Soviet Union's] grave" (A 429), echoing Herzen once more in a sensitivity about the nation of his birth, and in a rejection of Russophobia.[26]

Russian specialists and commentators generally use the thousand-year-old "Russian Idea" to gauge the depth of Russianness. This "Idea" includes a reverential attitude toward the Russian land and its people, authoritarianism, the nation's special role in the history of mankind, mysticism, sacred images, spiritual collectivity, suffering, wandering, solitude, and self-denial – all things absent in Berlin. He was, as we have seen, powerfully drawn to a set of "Russian ideas" from the 1830s onward; these can be seen as

---

[25] In correspondence with Beata Polanowska-Sygulska, Berlin praised Adam Michnic's writing about the path of Sakharov versus the path of Solzhenitsyn, calling Michnic the contemporary voice of Sakharov and Herzen (UD 69, 118; A 387).

[26] Cherniss 2013, 87.

a narrow slice of Russian identity, but Berlin convincingly linked them to historical and political issues of great consequence. In Russian philosophy, Berlin was attracted to Lev Shestov, but rejected Berdyaev and seems only slightly familiar with Ivan Ilin, whose essays from the late Stalinist period make a fascinating contrast to what Berlin wrote during those years.[27] Berlin admitted to being "hopelessly secular" (CIB 173), and Walicki claimed that for Berlin, "'religious intelligentsia' was a contradiction in terms."[28] Like Herzen, Berlin rejected the Russian love of miracles in favor of a more modern – if less reassuring – sense of chance (*sluchainost'*) and personal responsibility. Berlin's respect for members of the intelligentsia was anchored in their courageous truth-telling, which in Russian culture is an essential element of *righteousness*.[29]

There is, of course, Berlin's well-documented love for the Russian language. Like many who left the country as children, his written Russian was never native, but he read it avidly and spoke it fluently at every opportunity, with poets, dinner partners, members of the Politburo, or passersby on the streets of Moscow and Leningrad. Speaking Russian transformed him, "as if everything becomes easier to express, & the world brighter and more charming in every way" (E 191, 366), and his "elegant St. Petersburg Russian" delighted interlocutors such as Andrei Sakharov and the cultural historian Dmitri Likhachev.[30] When looking for the *mot juste* in letters to his parents, Berlin generally found it in Russian. More seriously, it was a question of access to what people were thinking, whether in Russia or among Russians in Washington or Israel: "if one knows the language, one sees what goes on" (A 509). In Jahanbegloo's *Conversations*, Berlin says that as much as he loves English poetry, he loves Russian poets more, "because it is my first language and I think that poetry has to be in the language one spoke as a child" (CIB 197).

For those who did not know Russian, translations were essential; Berlin translated a novella, a story, and a play by Turgenev, but more often wrote introductions to translations and advocated for more and better renderings into English of works that got to the heart of Russia. When asked why Herzen remained a largely unknown thinker, Berlin said that it was primarily a question of not having been translated (CIB 175). The Herzen memoirs were available (although he thought the Garnett version not very good) and a few others texts, but much remained locked away from a potential audience. He would, it is hoped, have been happy to see some of his hero's most significant political journalism published in 2012 in *A Herzen Reader* (Herzen 2012).

Did Berlin read enough to be fully inscribed in Russia's "textual community"? Are there gaps or anomalies in Berlin's writing, things with

---

[27] Lesley Chamberlain called Berlin a Russian philosopher, or, at least, "a Russian philosophical anarchist and a defender of souls": Chamberlain 2004, 282–4. Berlin himself said that Russia had produced no real professional philosophers (Berlin 1981, 575).
[28] Walicki 2007, 66–7; and Walicki 2011, 173.   [29] Parthé 2004, 102–59.
[30] From a tribute by James Billington, BI 31–3.

which he should be familiar, but seems not to be? From the 1840s until the end of the twentieth century, one text often dominated Russian society at a given time, and members of the intelligentsia commanded a substantial knowledge of writers and works.[31] In any discussion, a participant need only mention a fictional character's name, the first lines of a song or poem, or the beginning of an anecdote for it to be clear to everyone present which people, ideas, texts, and attitudes were being brought to the debate. For all that Berlin read, and despite his innovative work on Tolstoy and others, there are missing connections in his work, some of them significant, and the depth and detail seen in Berlin's work on the nineteenth century is, on the whole, missing from his comments on twentieth-century writers, with the exception of Akhmatova and Pasternak. He mentions the anti-utopian writer Yevgeny Zamyatin (1884–1937) in passing, but never discusses in detail the brilliant novel *We* or essays such as "On Revolution, Entropy, and other Matters," although kindred insights appear in Berlin's fascinating comments on the "artificial dialectic." Having experienced the absurdities of postrevolutionary life, one would have welcomed greater attention by Berlin to stories from the 1920s and early 1930s by Bulgakov, Zoshchenko (whom he met), and Ilf and Petrov.

Andrei Sinyavsky (1925–97) shows up in Berlin's correspondence at the time of his trial for anti-Soviet propaganda in 1966, when the case garnered support from British intellectuals; Berlin was hesitant to sign petitions because he feared doing more harm than good. In the decades that followed, Sinyavsky's stories, novels, and the transcript of his trial were available in English and Russian, but one finds few references in Berlin's writing – unfortunate, because Berlin would have found strong support for his own analysis of the intelligentsia. There is an enigmatic remark in "Artistic Commitment" to "the published, and perhaps unpublished and, it may be, unwritten, works of Sinyavsky and his companions" (SR 284). Sinyavsky, like Berlin, described an artificially militant atmosphere, manufactured deficits, and the all-around bizarreness of Soviet society. A tantalizing, but unrealized, point of contact lies between Berlin's 1951 essay "Jewish Slavery and Emancipation" with its image of assimilating Jews as hunchbacks, and Sinyavsky's 1965 story "Pkhentz," whose space-alien protagonist is stranded in the USSR and disguises himself as a hunchback in order to survive. Sinyavsky chose the name Abram Tertz (a legendary Jewish gangster from Odessa), as a pseudonym for the fiction he sent abroad. With his combination of imagination, honesty, and dignity, Sinyavsky-Tertz seems a natural addition to Berlin's intelligentsia pantheon.

It is not that Isaiah Berlin read too little; it is simply that his cultural Russianness was in some areas incomplete. There were missed connections because there were writers whose work he did not know in sufficient detail; Russian identity was one of three strands in his life, and he would have needed three lifetimes to give each his complete attention. One can credit him with

---

[31] Billington and Parthé 2003.

having followed Herzen's advice to "activate all possibilities and live in all directions."[32] An "accent" of his birthplace can be detected in his essays on many topics, although some would say that the Russianness "is overemphasized ... at the expense of the Jewish dimension," as though an amalgamated Russian Jewish identity was something imposed on Berlin by his status as an immigrant.[33] Walicki thought that "Berlin's Russian side was not so much an organic feature but rather a conscious construct,"[34] but Berlin himself felt that his best writing was that set in a Russian context, and that the rest was contrived (B 437).

Much has been said about work left undone, such as the Romanticism project, but Berlin seemed satisfied with what he had written and said about Russia, which includes many essays that have become required reading for anyone interested in the nation's rich culture and turbulent politics. By tracing – back to the sources and forward to their consequences – ideas that fascinated and tormented the Russian intelligentsia, by contributing highly original treatments of Tolstoy, Herzen, and other writers, by finding a novel explanation for Stalin's leadership style, and by leaving behind unique memories of Pasternak and Akhmatova, Berlin's "Russian thoughts" are both necessary reading, and sufficient to ensure his legacy.

---

[32] Gertsen 1954–66, xxii, 218.   [33] Dubnov 2012, 11, 34–5.   [34] Walicki 2011, 20.

8

Isaiah Berlin on the Enlightenment and Counter-Enlightenment

Steven B. Smith

No period of modern history has come under more intense intellectual scrutiny than the Enlightenment.[1] What is – or was – the Enlightenment? We have not ceased asking this question, and the answer or answers are far from settled. The question was most famously stated by the greatest of the *Aufklärer*, Immanuel Kant, at the start of his 1784 essay "What is Enlightenment?" "Enlightenment is man's emergence from his self-incurred immaturity," Kant wrote. "Immaturity is the inability to use one's own understanding without the guidance of another... The motto of Enlightenment is therefore: *Sapere aude!* Have courage to use your own understanding."[2] All the rest, as they say, is commentary.

Nevertheless, this has not stopped a host of later authors from adding their own two cents. The twentieth century reopened the debate over the Enlightenment with peculiar intensity. Ernst Cassirer's *The Philosophy of the Enlightenment*, written on the eve of Hitler's revolution, attempted to rehabilitate the eighteenth century as an age of unprecedented intellectual exploration and discovery.[3] Having only recently done battle with Heidegger at Davos, Cassirer's book can be read as a rearguard attempt to defend the tradition of Enlightenment rationalism from the onset of the new *Existenzphilosophie* expounded in Heidegger's *Being and Time*.[4] Following in the footsteps of Cassirer, the German émigré historian Peter Gay wrote the two-volume *The Enlightenment: An Interpretation* to vindicate the Enlightenment as a family – an often fractious and dysfunctional family, to be sure—but one dedicated to advancing the rights of humanity.[5] More recently, in his magisterial *The Radical Enlightenment*, Jonathan Israel has identified the

---

[1] For an excellent anthology on the topics, see Schmidt 1996.   [2] Kant 1970 [1784], 54.
[3] Cassirer 1952.
[4] For an overview of the debate, see Gordon 2012; see also Wokler 2012, 233–43.
[5] Gay 1966, 1969, 1971.

unity of the Enlightenment as providing the backbone of the modern secular democratic state.⁶

To be sure, not everyone has agreed. The most famous dissenters were two German philosophers – Theodor Adorno and Max Horkheimer – writing during World War II, who regarded the Enlightenment as culminating in the death camps of Auschwitz. In *Dialectic of Enlightenment*, they presented the Enlightenment as responsible for the "disenchantment of the world" and as preparing for the unfettered rule of technology. The humane dream of achieving mastery and control over nature for the relief of the human estate had instead created new forms of technological domination and control. They regarded the Holocaust not as the negation but as the fulfillment of the Enlightenment's dream of a perfectly controlled and rationalized social environment. "Enlightenment is totalitarian," they wrote.⁷

Few have subscribed to this radical negation of Enlightenment principles – although Zygmunt Bauman's *Modernity and the Holocaust* (1989) comes close – but in recent years the concept of the Enlightenment has become an object of frequent attack, from Richard Rorty's gentle claim that the Enlightenment rests on a faulty theory of knowledge (even if we must continue to embrace its hope for human emancipation) to John Gray's more aggressive assertion that we are now living at "Enlightenment's wake."⁸ The "Enlightenment Project," as it has been derisively called by Alasdair MacIntyre, has been held responsible for a multitude of sins, ranging from an atomistic conception of human nature that emphasizes the separateness of individuals, to an aggressive secularism that seeks to replace the traditional sources of moral value by an artificially constructed idea of "public reason," to an overweening, not to say hubristic, desire to master and dominate the natural environment.⁹ At the same time, historians have maintained that the Enlightenment – preceded by the definite article – is a fiction that never existed. There was never such a thing as "the Enlightenment" in the singular, only a variety of regional and national enlightenments (all lower case) based in Berlin, Paris, Edinburgh, Naples, Boston, and Philadelphia.¹⁰ In *Modernity and its Discontents*, I have argued that the Enlightenment and its pillars of progress, science, and commerce have given rise to a range of cultural "discontents": from Hegel's "unhappy consciousness," to Marx's world of "commodity fetishism," to Nietzsche's fears of the "last man," to Heidegger's reign of the anonymous *das Man*.¹¹

To be sure, the Enlightenment still has its staunch advocates. In *The Anti-Enlightenment Tradition*, the Israeli political theorist Zeev Sternhell has seen

---

⁶ Israel 2001; Israel has recently turned to Leo Strauss as an important source of the term "Radical Enlightenment" *(radikalen Aufklärung)*; see Israel 2015, 9–28.
⁷ Adorno and Horkheimer 1972, 6.   ⁸ Bauman 1989; see also Rorty 2001, 19–36; Gray 1995.
⁹ MacIntyre 1981, 49–59.   ¹⁰ For a defense of this approach, see Pocock 2008, 83–96.
¹¹ Smith 2016.

any falling away from the Enlightenment as leading down the slippery path to antirationalism and twentieth-century fascism.[12] For Sternhell, the anti-Enlightenment that covers thinkers from Herder and Burke to Carlyle, Nietzsche, Maurras, and Spengler offered a second model of modernity based not on the unity of reason, but on the separation of groups and nations arrayed in a condition of unremitting hostility. Similarly, in *The Enlightenment: And Why It Still Matters*, Anthony Pagden has made the case that the Enlightenment opened up a new era of cosmopolitanism intent on breaking down national barriers and issuing in a new kind of universalist humanity.[13] The debate goes on.

No one has done more to put the Enlightenment and its critics front and center than Isaiah Berlin. Berlin's contribution to Enlightenment studies has been unique because he is neither clearly a champion nor a critic, but both. Although there is much to the Enlightenment that Berlin admired and respected, he is perhaps even better known for resurrecting the ideas of what he called the Counter-Enlightenment. The concept of the Counter-Enlightenment was not of Berlin's coinage, but the term has come to be most widely associated with him. He used the term in a way that was more or less synonymous with German romanticism and historicism as developed by pre-Enlightenment thinkers such as Vico, and then later by Herder, Hamann, and Jacobi. The Enlightenment and Counter-Enlightenment were doppelgangers. They are not so much historical categories but competing and contradictory mentalities. These remain the main dialectical impulses that shape the broad contours of modern history.

I

Berlin's interest in the Enlightenment was given initial expression as early as his 1939 biography of Karl Marx.[14] Berlin himself was no Marxist – his family were refugees from the Bolshevik Revolution – and the work can be read as an exercise in the "know your enemies" genre. Nevertheless, in the course of writing the book, Berlin came to express a grudging respect for Marx, whose ideas, he wrote in the work's penultimate paragraph, have had "a greater and more lasting influence both on opinion and on action than any other system of ideas put forward in modern times" (KM 265). Perhaps anticipating the trajectory of his own later life's work, he acknowledged that historians, social scientists, and creative artists – he did not actually include philosophers – insofar as they try to grasp the changing texture of social life, "owe the form of their ideas in large part to the work of Karl Marx" (KM 265).

In researching the intellectual background of Marx's ideas, Berlin turned to the materialist philosophers of eighteenth-century France. For these thinkers –

---

[12] Sternhell 2010.   [13] Pagden 2013.
[14] For an interesting account of how Berlin came to write his book on Marx, see Ignatieff 1998, 69–72; see also Cherniss 2013, 39–42.

Diderot, Condillac, Helvétius, d'Holbach – "all men are rational and all rational beings have equal rights before the natural tribunal of reason" (KM 36). It is this boundless faith in human reason that is the core of the Enlightenment as Berlin understands it. Yet this optimistic and rationalistic conception of human nature was confronted by an equally powerful influence – namely, the collective resistance of kings, priests, and nobles working in collusion to prevent the spread of reason and therewith the ability of the people to assert their rights. From the beginning, therefore, the Enlightenment regarded itself as a program of educational reform bent on eliminating error, ignorance, and superstition.

There was much in the Enlightenment that Berlin admired even though he was quick to identify a tendency toward authoritarianism and an antiliberal paternalism. He characterized this position as follows: "Reason is always right. To every question there is only one true answer which with sufficient assiduity can be infallibly discovered, and this applies no less to questions of ethics or politics, of personal and social life, than the problems of physics or mathematics" (KM 37). It was this belief in the priority, indeed the primacy, of scientific method in arriving at a single correct answer to all human problems that was at the core of Berlin's skepticism about the Enlightenment and his later engagement with the "Counter-Enlightenment."

The "central tenet" of Enlightenment rationalism was a "boundless faith in the power of reason to explain and improve the world" (KM 35). Within the Enlightenment was a tendency to regard human beings as material objects who can be used and manipulated for their own good. The problems of moral and political life were in principle susceptible to the same forms of proof as were problems in chemistry or physics. The difference between the human and the natural world was one of degree rather than of kind. It is simply a matter of discovering the right method for putting into practice the plans for the creation of a fully rational world organized on scientific lines. It is not difficult to see how these rationalistic aspirations tied into the utopianism of the French and later the socialist revolutionaries. "Once this has been achieved," Berlin notes, "the path is clear to the millennium" (KM 37).

Berlin's conception of the Enlightenment remained more or less constant throughout his long career, although it received is fullest articulation in the introduction to his 1956 anthology *The Age of Enlightenment*.[15] For Berlin, the Enlightenment was first and foremost an epistemological project based on a claim about the scope and limits of knowledge. "The eighteenth century," he wrote, "is perhaps the last period in the history of Western Europe when human omniscience was thought to be an attainable goal" (POI 47). This term "omniscience" has both an epistemic and an ethical connotation, suggesting at once intellectual and moral control over nature and our social environment.

---

[15] Berlin 1956; reprinted in POI 43–62.

The goal in question was dependent on the application of scientific techniques to all branches of human inquiry.

The inspiration for this idea emerged in the seventeenth century with the great rationalists such as Descartes, Spinoza, and Hobbes, but this "mood" persisted and shaped the Enlightenment of the eighteenth century. To be sure, it was not actual scientists such as Newton or Leibniz who propagated these views, but rather propagandists and popularizers, especially Voltaire, who turned reason and science into instruments of social and political reform. "A science of nature had been created," Berlin remarks, "a science of mind had yet to be made" (POI 48). Here again Berlin noted a disjunction between the Enlightenment's belief in intellectual freedom and toleration and a spirit of dogmatism arising from its belief in the omnipotence of the new scientific method: "To every genuine question there were many false answers, and only one that was true; all that was needed was a reliable method of discovery" (POI 48). The great question that remained to be answered is: what was to count as a "genuine question."

This optimism permeated Berlin's idea of the Enlightenment. Marx himself – an heir to this tradition – later boasted that society sets itself only such problems as can be answered.[16] The Enlightenment was a "heroic attempt" to achieve for moral and political matters the same kind of certainty that one could find in mathematics and chemistry (POI 57). The "dominant trend" of this thinking was to reduce everything into ultimate, irreducible atomic components, whether physical or psychological. By regarding human wants and desires in the same manner as lines, planes, and solids (to use Spinoza's apt metaphor), it would be possible to conceive a science of society that would eliminate cruelty, ignorance, and need. The link between this intellectual program and twentieth-century experiments in social engineering is evident. Like his Israeli contemporary Jacob Talmon, Berlin found in the Enlightenment's core values the germ of later "totalitarian democracy."[17]

Like his contemporaries Michael Oakeshott and Frederick Hayek, Berlin believed the Enlightenment was deformed from the beginning by a domineering rationalism.[18] Berlin's view can be expressed in almost syllogistic fashion:

1. All genuine questions can be answered and if a question cannot be answered then it is not a real question;
2. A method exists for the discovery of the correct answers to our questions which can be learned and taught to others;
3. The answers to all questions are compatible with one another and form parts or aspects of a single system of truth.

---

[16] Marx 1973, 504.
[17] See Talmon 1979; for some useful comments on Berlin's connection to Talmon, see Cherniss 2013, 171–4.
[18] For a comparison between Berlin, Oakeshott, and Hayek, see Smith (forthcoming).

This rationalism is not simply a product of the eighteenth century, but can be found in many diverse societies going back to Plato and the Greeks. Berlin sometimes writes as if the entire history of moral and political philosophy rests on a mistake – the "Ionian fallacy" – according to which moral problems are like scientific ones that can be solved by acquiring more complete factual knowledge about nature and history.[19] Lurking behind this rationalism is always the danger of paternalism, the belief that society should be governed by experts – sociologists, psychologists, economists – who can help people harmonize their desires with the needs of society. There is a direct link between the rationalist view that there are discoverable moral truths and the desire to educate or coerce other persons to accept them.

Although Berlin came to have grave doubts about the epistemological monism that he attributed to the Enlightenment, he refused to disavow what he believed were the Enlightenment's key moral and political values, such as rationality, toleration, equality before the law, and freedom of thought. Despite its faulty theory of knowledge, the Enlightenment did "a very great deal of good" (POI 62). Even if "the central dream" of the Enlightenment – namely, "the demonstration that everything in the world moved by mechanical means" and that "all evils could be cured by appropriate technological steps" – proved to be "delusive," it was nevertheless responsible for mitigating human suffering, preventing injustice, and refuting various dogmas and superstitions. All in all, he claimed the eighteenth century remained "one of the best and most hopeful episodes in the life of mankind" (POI 62). As Berlin would admit in an intellectual autobiography written much later in life: "Although I came in due course to oppose some of the bases of their common beliefs, I have never lost my admiration for and sense of solidary with the Enlightenment of that period" (POI 5).

Despite Berlin's qualified defense of the Enlightenment, his understanding of that movement took on some of the very monism that he had accused the Enlightenment itself of creating. To claim that the Enlightenment was premised on the belief that "the truth was one single, harmonious body of knowledge" and that "the final true philosophy ... could solve all theoretical and practical problems, for all men, everywhere, for all time" would seem to omit a great deal of the skepticism and pluralism that is equally a legacy of the Enlightenment (POI 61). Berlin admits as much when attempting to shoehorn such quintessentially eighteenth-century figures as Hume and Montesquieu into his formulation for the Enlightenment.[20]

Hume seems to express none of the faith in the power of reason that Berlin attributes to the Enlightenment. Reason, Hume famously declared, is "the slave of the passions." Civilizations are largely contingent artifacts based upon

---

[19] For the term "Ionian Fallacy," see Berlin, CC 99–100; this sweeping judgment obviously owes something to Prichard 1968, 1–17.
[20] For a useful critique along these lines, see Yack 2013, 49–60.

common rules, standards, and discriminations. History remains a perpetual oscillation between periods of freedom and periods of despotism, but there was no guarantee that there was some method of ensuring perpetual progress. What progress there is in history will always be dependent upon statecraft and the exercise of political judgment. Similarly, Montesquieu introduced the idea of an *esprit générale d'une nation* precisely to account for vast differences in national character. Human nature cannot be deduced from certain common variables, but displays a degree of variety and complexity that defies efforts to construct a uniform science of society. Montesquieu's attention to distinct national cultures was no doubt compatible with a comparative sociology, but this remains opposed to the kind of universalizing project Berlin associated with the Enlightenment.[21]

At the same time, Berlin often paints with so broad a brush that it is difficult to see who would be excluded from his extraordinarily capacious definition of the Enlightenment. Consider the following passage:

This noble faith [in the unity of knowledge] animated Lessing, who believed in reason, and Turgot, who believed in the sciences, Moses Mendelssohn, who believed in God, and Condorcet, who did not. Despite great differences of temperament and outlook and belief, this was the common ground. Theists and atheists, believers in automatic progress and sceptical pessimists, hard-boiled French materialists and sentimental German poets and thinkers seemed united in the conviction that all problems were soluble by objective answers which, once found – and why should they not be? – would be clear for all to see and valid eternally (POI 61–2).

Given such a broad area of agreement, covering theists and atheists, rationalists and sentimentalists, progressives and skeptics, Berlin's Enlightenment seems to be the proverbial night in which all cows are black. It would be tempting to say of this conception what Berlin once said in a caustic review of Cassirer's *The Philosophy of the Enlightenment*: "In this even and gentle evening light, all shapes are slightly hazy and melt into each other too easily. There are few frontiers and no collisions; his clarity is that of a careful impressionist, not a photographer or critical analyst, an attitude of mind which suites the eighteenth century less well perhaps than any other age."[22]

II

Berlin's discovery of the Counter-Enlightenment came relatively late in his career, although his interest in the subject had been gestating as early as his 1952 Bryn Mawr lectures published posthumously as *Political Ideas in the Romantic Age*.[23] Throughout the 1960s and '70s, his reputation rested principally on his defense of individual liberty in his famous "Two Concepts

---

[21] Berlin dealt with Montesquieu in his essay "Montesquieu" in AC 164–203.
[22] Berlin 1953, 617–18. [23] See Berlin, "The March of History," PIRA 261–323.

of Liberty." For most readers, Berlin's fame derived from his attempt to rehabilitate the liberal tradition of Benjamin Constant and John Stuart Mill at a time when liberal political theory was in a period of decay.[24] As Robert Wokler humorously noted, Berlin's occasional forays into the works of such thinkers as Vico and Herder met with the same enthusiasm that greeted the publication of Hume's *Treatise of Human Nature* when its author complained that "It fell dead born from the press."[25] "One might have thought," Wokler continued, "that Berlin's political philosophy would have ripened sufficiently to begin its natural course of decay," yet it is precisely his work on the Counter-Enlightenment that has not only kept it alive, but has also made Berlin appear less a defender of liberalism than a voice for the new multicultural era with its emphasis on pluralism and cultural diversity.[26]

Berlin's appreciation for the Counter-Enlightenment was set out most famously in his 1976 study on Vico and Herder.[27] He used the term more or less synonymously with the romantic revolt against the Enlightenment that found expression in the discovery – actually a recovery – of the idea of national character: that is, the idea that Spartans and Athenians, Greeks and Persians, Germans and Italians, act on different understandings of the world and that their actions cannot be reduced to the same uniform laws of behavior. If the Enlightenment tradition of monism can be traced all the way back to Plato, the appreciation of cultural diversity and the idea of a clash of civilizations can be found in Herodotus and the Greek tragedians. There is on this view a pluralism or diversity of cultures according to which not only our secondary characteristics but also our fundamental human attributes – our heart, soul, and mind – are shaped by the inescapably complex texture of history and social life that we inhabit. The Counter-Enlightenment was inseparable from the rise of this new "historical consciousness."

It is arguable that Berlin's Counter-Enlightenment was intended largely as a counterfoil to his understanding of the monism of the Enlightenment. If the besetting sin of the French *philosophes* was to conceive of human nature as fundamentally the same across time and place, the Counter-Enlightenment – best expressed by the German romantics – posited that there are different, but still rational and coherent, ways of being human, that cultures and nations differ from one another just as people do, and that the only way to understand this diversity is through a form of historical interpretation that regards all human institutions and activities as forms of self-expression. These insights can also be reduced to three propositions:

---

[24] For Berlin's evaluation of the state of political philosophy during the heyday of the analytical movement, see "Does Political Theory Still Exist?," CC 187–225.
[25] Wokler 2003, 14.
[26] Wokler 2003, 14; see Crowder (Chapter 13) and Galston (Chapter 14) in this volume.
[27] Isaiah Berlin, *Vico and Herder: Two Studies in the History of Ideas* (1976); reprinted in a revised edition in TCE.

1 The Enlightenment's belief in the uniformity and permanence of a common human nature is false or superficial; only what is unique, individual, or particular is really authentic or true.
2 The individual is what resists rules, uniformity, and reduction to "cases" or "instances" of some general law. To be individual is to be self-creating, a shaper of ends as well as means; it is to turn life into art. Human life is *expressive* and is most fully revealed through such media as poetry, myth, and literature.
3 What is true of individuals is also true of nations and cultures – they follow no overall pattern of development, whether cyclical or progressive; they constitute distinct and irreducible ways of life for their members. Cultures are characterized by diversity. Each culture has its own special path to happiness that can only be studied and appreciated from "within" – that is, through an act of imaginative sympathy, which Vico called *fantasia* and Herder called *Einfühlung*.

If the Enlightenment had pictured a single science covering both the natural and the human worlds, the Counter-Enlightenment was premised on the idea that the study of the human world differs not only in degree of complexity, but also in kind from the study of nature. The *Naturwissenschaften* and the *Geisteswissenschaften* rest on incommensurable premises (TCE 39). This insight into the specificity of the human sciences – history, anthropology, sociology – has taken many forms, although Berlin finds its finest expression in Vico's *New Science*. Vico's principle of *verum et factum convertuntur* suggests that we understand history in a very different way from understanding the natural world because we make the one but merely observe the other (TCE 43, 175–6). The principle that we know only what we make suggests a fundamental identity between the subject or knower and the object or maker of history. This unity of subject and object, as it was later called, became central to the Counter-Enlightenment's critique of the "dualism" of naturalistic modes of thought.

Berlin acquired his appreciation of Vico from R. G. Collingwood, who had translated Croce's book on Vico and made Vico a prominent figure in his posthumously published *The Idea of History* (CTH 8–9). For Collingwood, historical subjects differ from the natural world in having both an inside and an outside. To study a historical action – a battle, an election, a coup d'état – is something entirely different from studying a physical phenomenon – a weather pattern, a solar eclipse, a volcanic eruption. To understand a historical subject, it is not enough to view it externally as a series of happenings or events in the world. It is also necessary to grasp it internally as the expression of certain ideas, reasons, and beliefs. It is not enough to know what happened; one also needs to know what people thought they were doing and why. Collingwood believed that the study of historical subjects therefore required its own unique method, which he described as a "re-enactment" of the past or a rethinking of the thoughts which give historical events their unique meaning.[28]

Berlin found a precedent for Collingwood's theory of re-enactment in Vico's method of *fantasia* or imaginative insight, which enables the historian to reconstruct the past, to try and understand what it means to be a participant in a form of life very different from our own (see TCE 15, 58, 64 n80, 95, 162–3, 167–8, 199, 349, 390, 399). The same idea was also present in Herder's idea of historical empathy, the attempt to try to feel what it is like to be from another culture or to live in a different age (TCE 244, 261–3, 288–90). Critics have been quick to pounce on the charge that these methods substitute irrationalist intuition and subjectivism for clarity and analytical thinking, but the Counter-Enlightenment still maintained, not without grounds, that the capacity to imagine and reconstruct another culture required a skill set different from that employed in the natural sciences.

What fundamentally distinguishes the Counter-Enlightenment is its appreciation of the centrality of language for understanding culture (TCE 233–43). To be sure, Enlightenment figures such as Hobbes and Locke put great emphasis on our capacity for naming objects as a medium for the expression of thought. For them, words were simply the external vocalizations of ideas, but for Herder language was more than an instrument of communication: it was primarily a medium of self-expression. By expression the romantics meant the view that language is not simply used for designating objects in the world, but is something that unfolds and develops, shaping both cultures and the individuals who inhabit them. Human life is less like a struggle for existence than the creation of a work of art. It is not something that can be reduced to a set of interlocking parts, but is more like an artistic creation in which every part or aspect finds its meaning in relation to every other (TCE 218, 233–53). This helps to account for the romantic fascination with music and poetry as expressing the *Ursprache* of a people. It is not the science and economics, but the mythology, poetry, and religion that shapes the *Geist* or spirit of a people. Berlin summarizes the Herderian view of language as follows:

The only identification that Herder never abandons is that of thought and action, language and activity. Poetry, particularly early epic poetry, is for him pure activity. He was taken in by Ossian, like many of his contemporaries. It is probably from these poems rather than from Homer – although he speaks of the Homeric poems as improvisations, not a dead artefact – that he derives his notion of poetry as activity. Poetry, particularly among early peoples, is, he maintains, magical in character; it is not cool description of nature or of anything else; it is a spur to action for heroes, hunters, lovers; it stimulates and directs. It is not to be savoured by the scholar in his armchair, but is intelligible only to those who have placed themselves in situations similar to the conditions in which such words sprang into existence (TCE 241).

---

[28] Collingwood 1970, 215–16, 282–302; for Collingwood's influence on Berlin, see Ignatieff 1998, 58; Cherniss 2013, 155–6.

This insight into the expressive quality of language formed the basis for the romantic theory of pluralism and nationalism (TCE 224–33).[29] Languages are irrevocably plural. From the idea of linguistic heterogeneity arose the idea of history as the development of a pleasing variety of national spirits each with its own unique culture and taste. Pluralism meant in the first instance a rejection of the progressive or teleological view of history favored by Enlightenment historians. The idea that history is tending in one direction or converging on a single end that will bring about a final consummation ("the end of history") was not only false to the varieties of human experience, but also carried with it the germ of coercion, the desire to "force the end" or to bring about through violence, intimidation, or propaganda the realization of only one form of civilization claiming for itself the status of universality.

From Herder's emphasis on human plurality, Berlin inferred a "need to belong" to a distinct people, group, or nation. These groupings formed the natural units for his distinctive vision of a cultural nationalism. Cultural nationalism, as Herder understood it – and as Berlin seems to agree – is not a doctrine of power and empire, but of the appreciation of human diversity, what makes one people different from but not superior to another. He treated the Hebrew Bible not as a source of divine revelation, but as the basis of a national culture with its distinctive laws, customs, and institutions. This was simply the way that individualism most fully and freely expressed itself at a collective level. Herder was certainly interested in what connected one national grouping to another to form a common vision of *Humanität*, but what was most important was what was unique and special to a people (TCE 270, 289–90, 291–3).

Berlin wrote sympathetically about the appeal of nationalism as the expression of a legitimate human need for a culture. This is especially evident in his writings on Zionism, which he regarded as a humane and liberal expression of the nationalist sentiment.[30] Berlin was not a religious thinker by any means, and even admits to a certain tone-deafness to the music of religious belief, but he believed in the justice of Zionism and regarded the establishment of the state of Israel as a legitimate response to the European persecution of the Jews. While assimilation may be possible in individual cases, it has proven to be unworkable as a collective response to the problem of anti-Semitism. The nineteenth century – the great age of assimilationism – also produced the emergence of anti-Semitism on a hitherto unprecedented scale. Though he could be critical of particular aspects of Israeli policy, Berlin never doubted the

---

[29] For Berlin's most developed statements on nationalism, see "The Bent Twig: On the Rise of Nationalism," CTH 253–78; and "Nationalism: Past Neglect and Present Power," AC 420–48. See also Oz-Salzberger, Chapter 10 in this volume.

[30] For Berlin's views on Zionism and Israel, see especially "The Origins of Israel" and "Jewish Slavery and Emancipation," POI 173–96 and 197–226. See also Oz-Salzberger, Chapter 10 in this volume.

essential justice of the case for Israel to take its place among the nations of the world. There is a wonderful story that Berlin told about a conversation with the Russo–French philosopher Alexandre Kojève, who had his own doubts about Zionism. "You're a Jew," Kojève said to him. "The Jewish people probably have the most interesting history of any people that ever lived. And now you want to be Albania?" "Yes, we do," was Berlin's reply. "For our purposes, for Jews, Albania is a step forward" (CIB 86).

Berlin's defense of Zionism was not just theoretical but personal. A Russian Jew from Riga, he saw the founding of the state of Israel as creating a world historical opportunity. It provided a safety valve from both the excesses of European anti-Semitism and from the delusions of assimilation. The Jewish state – "the last child of the European Risorgimento" – would at last provide for the normalization of the Jewish condition (POI 183). Finally the Jews would have a genuine choice before them: either to make *Aliyah*, or to remain in their home countries in the Diaspora. Berlin's heroes were secular Jews who also embraced their Jewishness, such as Moses Hess, Theodor Herzl, and Chaim Weizmann, and not romantically assimilating Jews, such as Karl Marx and Benjamin Disraeli (AC 252–86). "The creation of the State of Israel has rendered the greatest service that any human institution can perform," he declared; it "has restored to Jews not merely their personal dignity and status as human beings but what is vastly more important, their right to choose as individuals how they shall live" (POI 182).

III

One difficulty in assessing the work of Berlin stems from the question of voice. Like Leo Strauss, Berlin generally presents his own ideas through the medium of the history of thought. It often becomes difficult to tell who is speaking: when Berlin is acting as an interpreter or a critic, and when he is expounding or embracing the ideas under discussion. This is especially true in his treatment of the Counter-Enlightenment.

Berlin appears to embrace the Counter-Enlightenment as the source of the recognition of diversity, individuality, resistance to uniformity, and a love of freedom where this means not just freedom to choose means, but also to create ends. An example is the epigraph he appends to the beginning of his essay on "Herder and the Enlightenment": "We live in a world we ourselves create" – a sentiment of Herder's, but one Berlin clearly endorses (TCE 208). But this is not the whole of the matter. Just as Berlin posits a kind of "dialectic of Enlightenment" in which the ideas of reason become the basis of the tutelary and administrative state, so the Counter-Enlightenment threatens to dissolve into forms of collectivism and group tyranny. The Counter-Enlightenment is not only the source of our ideas of moral pluralism, it is also at the root of modern irrationalism, a resistance to, even a hatred of, science, reason, and "enlightened" morality. It is often associated with the supremacy of faith over intellect and, even worse, the power of the group over the individual.

If Herder's pluralism and liberal nationalism represented the positive side of the Counter-Enlightenment, Joseph de Maistre's irrationalism and pessimism represented its evil twin.[31] To be sure, there is something in Maistre's thought that Berlin found fascinating. Words such as "genius," "bold," "penetrating," and "acute" pepper his analysis.[32] Like Burke, Maistre saw the Enlightenment's doctrine of universal human rights as not only destabilizing of political order, but also as false to human experience. "In the course of my life I have seen Frenchmen, Italians, Russians, etc.; I know, too, thanks to Montesquieu, *that one can be a Persian*," he wrote in the *Considerations on France*; "But as for *man*, I declare that have never in my life; if he exists, he is unknown to me."[33] Yet Maistre's critique of the Enlightenment and the French Revolution went far beyond Burke's Whiggish constitutionalism. The Revolution for Maistre was not the overturning of a legitimate political order but a drama played out against the background of providential history. It was God's judgment on a society that he deemed horribly corrupt and that required nothing less than radical purgation. Maistre would adopt the same apocalyptic language as had the revolutionaries, but he put it in the service of the counter-revolutionary movement of reaction.[34]

Most important, Berlin saw Maistre not as a backward-looking reactionary, but as a "modernist" who foretold some of the most dangerous tendencies of the twentieth century. For Maistre, individualism or "political Protestantism" had eroded the true source of political authority, which is fear. Like Hobbes, Maistre made fear of violent death the basis of society, but, unlike Hobbes, he insisted that authority always needs to be shrouded in a sense of mystery and awe. We obey authority not because of rational consent but from a deep need to believe, a will to believe. This need to believe is the source of Maistre's deep irrationalism and puts him far away from Hobbes and the tradition of enlightened despotism. Maistre pioneered the idea explored later by thinkers such as Bakunin, Sorel, and Schmitt that the foundations of society are not to be found in liberal contractualism, but in force, blood, and violence. It is this that in Berlin's view made Maistre the profound source of fascism.

If one danger of the Counter-Enlightenment was its tendency toward antiliberal forms of irrationalism, another is rejection of science and the use of empirical methods to which Berlin always paid tribute. This goes back to Vico's method of *fantasia* or the imaginative reconstruction of an institution or activity. To understand a way of life, it is necessary to see it from the

---

[31] See Berlin's "Joseph de Maistre and the Origins of Fascism," CTH 95–185.
[32] Garrard 2003, 118.
[33] Joseph de Maistre, cited in Berlin, "Joseph de Maistre and the Origins of Fascism," CTH 104; see also "Montesquieu," AC 176.
[34] Smith 2016, 243–6.

"inside," to see what it means to the lives of those most affected, and to do this requires a special sort of historical empathy that Berlin himself sometimes called judgment.[35] Berlin insisted on a strong distinction between the methods of the natural and the human sciences and rejected the Enlightenment belief in a unified scientific method equally applicable to nature and society – a fallacy known as positivism. The danger comes when the rejection of positivism becomes an opposition to scientific knowledge and empiricism tout court.

A key and surprising source for the rise of this hostility to science was the Scottish philosopher David Hume (AC 204–35). Hume's skepticism about all things, including religion, would seem temperamentally close to Berlin, but Berlin had a way of showing how even the best ideas may have unintended consequences. In *A Treatise of Human Nature*, Hume famously demonstrated how reason alone was inadequate to account for causality or the necessary connections between things. From the observation that one thing seems to follow from another, Hume argued that we can never conclude that there is an actual causal connection between them. Rather, we are at most entitled to infer that they are connected, a feeling that arises from the custom or habit of seeing two things so associated. His goal was to show that instead of necessity governing the world, there was only chance reduced to order by custom and habit. Hume had no intention of denying the importance of science, but his corrosive skepticism had this effect, especially on those who came later.

It was the German romantics – Hamann and Jacobi – who extended Hume's critique of the category of causality to apply to the whole of knowledge. For these thinkers, our knowledge of reality, including our scientific knowledge, is based on a prior act of faith (*Glaube*) (TCE 354, 368–9). By "faith" they did not mean religious belief in any doctrinal sense, but rather a direct, intuitive insight into the way things are that precedes our rational concepts and categories. What the philosophers vainly called "the principle of sufficient reason" – the belief that everything must have a reason or cause – is simply a castle built on sand. The belief that everything has a cause is just that – namely, a belief or an act of faith that precedes reason. Reason is not so much a slave to custom and habit as Hume argued, but it is dependent on certain irrational "givens" that underlie all knowledge claims. From pointing out the irrationalist core of all knowledge – that reason itself presupposes a faith or belief in reason – it was but a further step to see all knowledge, including science, as but a form of "ideology" (Marx), "myth" (Sorel), or "*Weltanschauung*" (Jaspers).

The idea that all knowledge, all science and philosophy, is nothing more than an expression of a particular nation, class, race, or historical epoch is also an extreme outgrowth of the Counter-Enlightenment. The Leninist slogan that all theory is an expression of the class struggle is functionally no different from the execrable fascist injunction to think with the blood. In each case the role of

---

[35] See Berlin, "Political Judgement," SR 50–66. See also Cherniss (Chapter 4) and Hanley (Chapter 5) in this volume.

critical judgment is subordinated to a movement or cause. Indeed, it is the collectivization of thought to which Berlin seems most strenuously to object. This occurred when the Counter-Enlightenment turned the liberal Herderian doctrine of expressive freedom into a theory not only about individual flourishing and self-creation, but also into a doctrine of cultures and nations. When the nation becomes the locus of self-expression, it frequently becomes a cause of chauvinism and imperialism. It subordinates the individual to collective acts of self-expression to which the individual is said to "belong." In its extreme form the Counter-Enlightenment has been associated with the rise of irrationalist movements, even twentieth-century fascism and totalitarianism.[36]

To be sure, Berlin's idea of the Counter-Enlightenment has proved controversial. Just as some historians have cast doubt on the existence of a unitary Enlightenment, so the idea of a Counter-Enlightenment has come under recent attack. The distinction between Enlightenment and Counter-Enlightenment is said to be too neat to make sense of complex historical figures such as Rousseau or Burke, who often straddle both sides of the divide. As if this were not enough, the very idea of the Counter-Enlightenment stands accused of engaging in a piece of "unintended Cold War propaganda" as a means of resisting a political utopianism that had become compromised with its leftist associations. The term made its debut in the English-speaking world in a debate between William Barrett – the author of *Irrational Man* – and Lionel Trilling in the pages of *Partisan Review* in 1949. The Counter-Enlightenment was used by some mid-century liberals as a way of locating the source of resistance to liberalism, while it was used by others, such as Berlin, as a means of resisting communism and fascism. The very term "Counter-Enlightenment" has been called unusable for historical purposes.[37]

One aspect of the legacy of the Counter-Enlightenment over which Berlin seems genuinely ambivalent is its tendency toward cultural relativism. Here is a case where Berlin's sympathetic reconstruction of certain Counter-Enlightenment doctrines has created controversy. Leo Strauss had already found in Berlin's "Two Concepts of Liberty" the germ of a nascent relativism.[38] What Strauss noted was Berlin's belief that the defense of personal liberty needed an "absolute" foundation if it was to defend itself, and his simultaneous admission that no such foundation was any longer possible. Strauss found Berlin's essay valuable as a statement of liberal anticommunism – he called it an "anti-communist manifesto" – in the midst of the Cold War, but found it wanting as a theoretical defense of liberalism. Strauss characterized Berlin's work as "a characteristic document of the crisis of

---

[36] See Sternhell 2010.
[37] See Caradonna 2015, 51–69; the entire issue is devoted to the debate over the Counter-Enlightenment.
[38] Strauss 1989, 13–26.

liberalism." This crisis was due to the fact that "liberalism has abandoned its absolutist basis and is trying to become entirely relativistic."[39]

The charge of relativism was set out most clearly in Arnaldo Momigliano's review of *Vico and Herder* in the *New York Review of Books*.[40] Momigliano was a learned classicist and a friend of both Berlin and Strauss, and his review obviously stung. He charged Berlin first with conflating Vico and Herder who, Momigliano argued, were in fact quite different. Berlin lumped where he should have split ("Between Vico and Herder there was a revolution in historical research"). Vico regarded history along classical lines as cyclical, a perpetual series of *corsi* and *ricorsi* between periods of civilization and barbarism, while Herder was far more committed to the plurality of cultures. Vico focused largely on classical and Christian civilizations, with a focus on law and property rights, while Herder was a kind of "orientalist" avant la lettre with interests in Hebrew, Persian, and Indian poetry and mythology.

More to the point, Momigliano accused Berlin of imposing his own questions on his subjects. "How are we going to avoid moral relativism," he asked, "if we accept with Vico and Herder that societies are at their best when they succeed in expressing themselves most individually in language, custom, institutions, and religion?"[41] Momigliano wondered if at times Herder's *volkish* nationalism bordered on racism – a point that Collingwood had already made in *The Idea of History*.[42] Herder, he concluded, seems more contemporary than Vico, but Momigliano's message is: be careful what you wish for. "Before we celebrate the vitality of Vico and Herder," Momigliano concluded his review, "let us be certain where they are leading us."[43]

Berlin later admitted that he had given the misleading impression that figures such as Vico and Herder, Montesquieu and Hume, were relativists, but claimed that this was false. He spoke of the "alleged relativism" of eighteenth-century thought, suggesting that the term itself was a misnomer (CTH 73–94). None of the eighteenth-century critics of the Enlightenment were relativists in our sense of the term, since what they denied was not the rationality of human values but only our ability to prioritize them in some universally valid order of rank. Relativism was a product of a later age that held that cultures, and hence values, were not only incommensurable but fundamentally unintelligible to one another, that differences between them were so vast as to make mutual understanding virtually impossible. Relativism is the view that our deepest and most precious moral commitments are simply expressions of taste, "emotional attitudes" unsusceptible to judgments of truth or falsehood. "I prefer coffee, you prefer champagne. We have different tastes. There is no more to be said" (CTH 11): this is Berlin's description of relativism. Relativism is the belief that moral principles, like matters of taste, are not subject to rational arbitration or

---

[39] Strauss 1989, 17.   [40] Momigliano 1976.   [41] Momigliano 1976.
[42] Collingwood 1970, 92.   [43] Momigliano 1976.

debate. They are acts of will, the products of pure decision, for which no reasons can be given.

Berlin's response to Momigliano's charge was to draw a distinction between relativism on the one hand and moral pluralism or "objective pluralism," as his disciple John Gray has called it, on the other.[44] Pluralism is the doctrine that though there are many human ends often in conflict with one another and pursued by different peoples at different times, these are all equally ways of being human and stand within a common "human horizon" (CTH 12). Accepting the incommensurability of different values does not entail the suspension of critical judgment. Truth on one side of the Pyrenees does not mean falsehood on the other. Pluralism does not deny – it even assumes – the possibility of communication or translation between different moral languages and ways of life, in part because these can all be identified as moral languages and specifically human ways of life. "Incompatible these ends may be," Berlin writes, "but their variety cannot be unlimited, for the nature of men, however various and subject to change, must possess some generic character if it is to be called human at all" (CTH 83). This idea of a human horizon – the "generic character" of humanity – is invoked in order to set limits to what can count as an authentically valid way of life, but in the end this idea is left underdeveloped in Berlin's writings. He speaks of a "derangement" of the human condition and of "incomplete humanity," but does not indicate where this line between the human and the nonhuman, the normal and the deranged, is to be drawn. An older tradition would have called the rules circumscribing the general character of human life by the term "natural law."

IV

Berlin's work was an effort – a heroic effort – to hold together two ends of a chain: the Enlightenment and the Counter-Enlightenment, an appreciation of national and cultural variety and the recognition of certain universal human values. This is a variant of the ancient problem of distinguishing the good citizen and the good human being, the person whose virtues are relative to a particular regime and the person whose virtues would be acknowledged everywhere. This tension between the one and the many, the universal and the particular, cosmopolitanism and nationalism – or whatever other names one chooses to give it – is not a condition to be deplored. To the contrary, Berlin believed it important to keep this tension alive. It is precisely this conflict – this unresolved and fruitful conflict – that has been the core or nerve of Western civilization. It is this conflict between the Enlightenment and Counter-Enlightenment that has given the West its peculiar vitality. To explore the roots of this conflict has been the indelible legacy of Isaiah Berlin.

[44] Gray 1996, 46–7.

9

Berlin's Romantics and Their Ambiguous Legacy

Gina Gustavsson

Judging from contemporary debates in political theory, romanticism and liberalism are not the most likely of bedfellows. On the contrary, the romantic heritage is often invoked by communitarian or multiculturalist critics of the liberal commitment to liberty, universal human rights, and a state that separates politics from morality. In this account, romanticism stresses particularity over universalism, authenticity over autonomy, nature over reason, and community over individualism – the opposite of the values to which the typical liberal is committed.[1]

Berlin's writings on romanticism, by contrast, bring to life an important side of romanticism that this typical picture obscures. In their youth, many leading thinkers of the romantic movement were radical libertines with clearly anti-authoritarian ideals; only later did they come to sympathise with conservatism and nationalism. Berlin's scintillating, often slightly vertiginous, portrait of these thinkers thus uncovers a surprisingly individualistic and freedom-oriented romanticism, which resists all attempts to place any bonds on the individual will.

This is not to say that romanticism sits comfortably with Berlin's own liberalism. As so often with Berlin, there is a twist. One of his most recurrent arguments is that the romantic movement contained not only the seed of value pluralism, and thus indirectly of liberalism as he envisioned it, but also, ominously, of the sacrifice of the individual 'philistine' for the sake of the self-creation of the genius and the superhuman, and ultimately of fascist tyranny. Romanticism for Berlin is thus both a source of inspiration for liberals and

---

[1] Cf. Taylor 1991. Romanticism and liberalism are also typically seen as two forces that pulled thinkers such as J. S. Mill in opposite directions, so that in his more romantic moments, he is understood to be less liberal, and vice versa, as exemplified by Capaldi 2004, 88–93, and Appiah 2005, 17. It is no coincidence that Berlin, given his insights into the liberal moments in the romantic movement, by contrast recognises that Mill's liberalism itself was also inspired by his reading of romantic thought (L 218–51).

a warning example of how certain ideals of freedom – as he famously argued in *Two Concepts of Liberty* – could go terribly wrong and turn against themselves, ultimately threatening the humane and respectful kind of liberalism that he himself espoused (L 166–217).

Few other liberal thinkers have, to my knowledge, paid much attention to this side of romantic thought. Charles Larmore has offered a helpful and succinct analysis of the most important themes in romanticism from a liberal perspective.[2] Nancy Rosenblum, moreover, has sought to defend what she calls 'another', implicitly romantic, liberalism based largely on the heritage of American thinkers such as Thoreau and Emerson.[3] Yet the most original and captivating account of this liberal side of romanticism, as well as its illiberal dangers, remains the one provided by Berlin. This is not to deny that it includes characteristically Berlinian exaggerations. At times it also suffers from his habit of sweeping generalisations, repetition, and a torrent of synonyms that is more poetic than analytically helpful. Yet Berlin's reconstruction of romanticism is at the same time strikingly elegant, insightful, and complex.

It is thus somewhat surprising that Berlin's analysis of the romantic movement has not, to my knowledge, been given much attention as a topic in its own right.[4] Instead, Berlin's relationship to romanticism has typically been approached through discussions regarding two related yet different topics. The first of these is his defence of value pluralism and its much-debated links to liberalism.[5] This is a mistake, I believe, since although Berlin certainly attributed a revolutionary attack on monism to romanticism, as we shall see in what follows, on his account these meta-ethical assumptions capture only one half of its legacy.

The second theme through which Berlin's relationship to romanticism has often been approached is his analysis of the Counter-Enlightenment. However, I believe it is a mistake to conclude, as Crowder for example does, that for Berlin, romanticism was essentially a 'branch of the Counter-Enlightenment', because he supposedly had in mind 'a process of change which began with the Counter-Enlightenment thinkers and continued with romanticism, a movement very much under their influence'.[6]

This neglects that, with the exception of his essay on the Counter-Enlightenment, Berlin tends to separate this movement from the romantic one, both in terms of substantive themes and of leading thinkers. The recurrent themes in his analysis of the Counter-Enlightenment are belonging, language, tradition, and historical memory (cf. TCE). In his

---

[2] Larmore 1996b.   [3] Rosenblum 1987.
[4] Part of the reason for this is perhaps practical: many of his essays on romanticism, such as 'The Apotheosis of the Romantic Will', 'The Romantic Revolution', and 'European Unity and Its Vicissitudes', were not published until the 1990s. The printed versions of his lectures on romanticism in fact date back only to 1999 (*The Roots of Romanticism*) and 2006 (*Political Ideas in the Romantic Age*), respectively.
[5] Cf. Galipeau 1994, 55–8, and Riley 2001, 285–6.   [6] Crowder 2004, 201.

writings on romanticism, these topics are instead overshadowed by two others, which I shall elaborate in the following: the denial of a given order, and the celebration of a new ethics of sincerity, dedication, and, above all, will.

Berlin also identifies the two movements with different thinkers. Some, such as Herder and to some extent Hamann, admittedly turn up in his writings about both the Counter-Enlightenment and romanticism. But the main cast of the Counter-Enlightenment in his view clearly includes not only Hamann and Herder, but also Vico and de Maistre, neither of whom plays an important role in his writings on romanticism, as well as Möser and Jacobi, who are in fact altogether absent from his Mellon lectures on romanticism, for example (AC 1–32; TCE 208–300). The main cast of romanticism on Berlin's account is instead represented by Schiller, Fichte, Schelling, and the Schlegel brothers, as well as Chateaubriand, Byron, and Baudelaire, to mention but a few (POI 246; RR, chapters 4 and 5). To the extent that the latter are mentioned at all in his writings on the Counter-Enlightenment, they are typically referred to only in passing, as having been influenced by this earlier current of thought (cf. AC 11, 21–4, 26).

Berlin thus seems to have been well aware that, with some notable exceptions, such as Coleridge and Novalis, most romantics saw themselves as taking the Enlightenment in a new direction, rather than fully turning away from it. In this, Berlin – perhaps somewhat unexpectedly, since we often hear that he liked to paint the history of ideas with somewhat broad and generalising brushstrokes – comes across as more intellectually rigorous than some of his later commentators, who jump rather cavalierly from what he said in his writings on the Counter-Enlightenment to concluding that he was in many ways a late romantic.[7]

There is nevertheless no shortage of sources for approaching Berlin's understanding of romanticism specifically. Romantic ideas of both benign and dangerous kinds take a central place already in the lectures gathered in *Political Ideas in the Romantic Age* – the 'torso', as Berlin himself put it, for most of his later writings (PIRA xxv). These themes are also present in the essays 'The Apotheosis of the Romantic Will' (CTH 219–52), 'The Romantic Revolution: A Crisis in the History of Modern Thought' (SR 213–45), 'European Unity and Its Vicissitudes' (CTH 186–218), and his (posthumously published) lecture on Fichte (FIB 53–79), as well as in his short preface to *The Mind of the European Romantics* by H. G. Schenk: 'The Essence of European Romanticism' (POI 243–8). Finally, although he never finished the book on romanticism that he planned, his Mellon lectures from 1965, published posthumously under the title *The Roots of Romanticism*, offer his fullest account of the different aspects of romanticism, and their lasting effects – as reflected in the title of his last lecture.

---

[7] Cf. Gray 1995, ch. 5; Hausheer 2003; Garrard 2007.

By revisiting these writings, this chapter seeks to settle where and why, more precisely, Berlin drew the line between romantic ideas that he saw as inspirational, and those that he deemed as dangerous for liberalism. In the course of this endeavour, we will see that the typical picture of Berlin as an heir of the romantics – a hesitant heir, admittedly, but an heir nonetheless – hides a considerably more complex position.

A GREAT REVOLUTION IN CONSCIOUSNESS

Arthur Lovejoy once famously concluded that 'the word "romantic" has come to mean so many things that by itself, it means nothing'.[8] For Berlin, however, this very elusiveness seems to be one of the attractions with romanticism. In his first Mellon lecture, he does not set out any kind of definition or approximation of what he will argue constitutes the core of this current of ideas. Instead, with an unmistakable tinge of relish, he provides a two page list of the phenomena that have been typically presented as manifestations of romanticism:

> Romanticism is the primitive, the untutored, it is youth, the exuberant sense of life of the natural man, but it is also pallor, fever, disease, decadence, the *maladie du siècle*, La Belle Dame Sans Merci, the Dance of Death, indeed Death itself. . . . It is the strange, the exotic, the grotesque, the mysterious, the supernatural, ruins, moonlight, enchanted castles, hunting horns, elves, giants, griffins, falling water, the old mill on the Floss, darkness and the powers of darkness, phantoms, vampires, nameless terror, the irrational, the unutterable. Also it is the familiar, the sense of one's unique tradition, joy in the smiling aspect of everyday nature, and the accustomed sights and sounds of contented, simple, rural folk – the sane and happy wisdom of rosy-cheeked sons of the soil.

The list continues in the same breathless manner, including the mists of antiquity alongside the pursuit of novelty and revolutionary change; cow-bells and infinite blue skies followed by dandyism, green wigs, blue hair; and finally diabolical laughter and black heroes, together with the eternal order and the great Christian society, to mention but a few of the most poetic examples. This inventory is summed up by the observation that romanticism, in short, is 'strength and weakness, individualism and collectivism, purity and corruption, revolution and reaction, peace and war, love of life and love of death' (RR 20–3).

It was perhaps no wonder, Berlin thus concludes, that Lovejoy would have been driven close to despair in searching for a definition that could unearth the common element in all these wildly contradictory examples. And yet, to give up this quest is a mistake: 'There *was* a Romantic movement; it did have something that was central to it; it did create a great revolution in consciousness; and it is important to discover what this is' (RR 24).

---

[8] Lovejoy 1948, 235.

That which Berlin sets out to discover is thus not so much the romantic movement as such, but 'the largest shift in European consciousness since the Reformation', which romanticism brought about (CTH 221). It would therefore be mistaken to look to Berlin for a systematic account of this movement, one that does justice to all its main turns and nuances, or even only those of its early phase. If that is what we seek, then we would do better to study the careful reconstruction of early romanticism by Frederick Beiser or Nicholas Riasanovsky.[9]

Berlin's portrait of romanticism is something quite different. In line with his unorthodox, and often justly criticised, approach to the history of ideas in general, he never aimed to provide a full interpretation of romanticism as such, in its own historical context:

> It is not my purpose to define Romanticism, only to deal with the revolution of which Romanticism, at any rate in some of its guises, is the strongest expression and symptom. No more than this: but this is a great deal, for I hope to show that this revolution is the deepest and most lasting of all changes in the life of the West. (RR xxiv)[10]

Rather than a well-rounded representation of this movement as a whole, Berlin thus offers us an arresting, if at times dizzying, story of its most dramatic and enthralling aspect, i.e. the 'gigantic and radical transformation' that this movement set in motion in our attitudes to virtue, human nature and morality, 'after which nothing was ever the same' (RR 6).

THE MAIN CAST

From the very outset, Berlin's focus is both geographically and historically confined. The romantic revolution, he tells us, was the result of ideas propounded in Germany during the second third of the eighteenth century (RR 6). This is not to deny that he also quotes English romantics, such as Byron or Wordsworth, and their French counterparts, such as Chateaubriand and Hugo (RR 139, 152–5). In passing, he also draws parallels to later thinkers and writers who were directly or indirectly inspired by the early romantics. Schopenhauer, Baudelaire, Stirner, and Nietszche, for example, make brief but repeated appearances in his writings on romanticism (CTH 248, 251; RR 123, 164, 166–7).

The main cast, however, is consistently limited to the romantic Germans who belonged to the Jena circle at the turn of the nineteenth century. These consist of Fichte, whom Berlin refers to as 'the true father of romanticism' (CTH 239);[11]

---

[9] Riasanovsky 1992; Beiser 1996 and 2003. For an enlightening analysis of romantic thought as a whole, including its later stages, see for example Furst 1966 and 1979.
[10] For a helpful discussion of how Berlin's approach to the history of ideas goes against that of, for example, Quentin Skinner, see Crowder 2004, 193–4.
[11] In his Mellon lectures, however, he also calls Kant and Herder the true fathers of romanticism (RR 57).

Schiller; Schelling; the Schlegel brothers, who were not as clear-cut philosophers but better described as thinkers and literary critics; the poet Novalis; the theologian Schleiermacher; and the playwright Tieck (RR 91, 101–6, 107, 112–17, 131, 132).

Berlin also spends considerable space in his analyses of romanticism on Hamann, Herder, and Schiller – all of whom he treats as early but not full-fledged romantics. Hamann belongs in this camp because he exalted the particular over the universal in human affairs; Herder because he celebrated the expressive element in man, and because he took joy in cultural diversity; and Schiller because he saw art as the free play of the imagination, and because in his plays we see the emergence of the romantic hero, best exemplified by Karl Moor, who murders and destroys but is nevertheless to be admired, because he remains faithful to his own inner principles, and refuses to succumb to the world around him in any way (RR 49, 67–78, 97–101).

Kant, finally, inspired romanticism, because he was 'virtually intoxicated by the idea of human freedom' (RR 80). While Berlin is quick to acknowledge that Kant detested any romantic '*Schwärmerei*' (AC 19–20; CTH 229; RR 79), he insists that Kant influenced the romantics – mainly through Fichte and Schiller – not so much by his sober political theory as by his revolutionary moral philosophy, according to which the characteristic that defines us as human beings is our capacity to rise above nature by imposing on it and ourselves our own free will (CTH 229–33; RR 79–90). This meant that for Kant, famously, it is only our will, our intentions, that can be virtuous, since only these are entirely under our own control; our inclinations, and the consequences of our actions, by contrast, remain governed by the laws of nature and are therefore neither here nor there for morality. 'The only thing worth possessing is the unfettered will – this is the central proposition which Kant put on the map', concludes Berlin (RR 90).

Where, one might ask, is Rousseau in all this; the Swiss *enfant terrible* of the eighteenth century, who attacked the glittering academies and the witty salons for distorting our authenticity, and who enchanted the state of nature into something pure and uncorrupted, in which natural man is moved by a natural sympathy for his fellow man?

Berlin himself rhetorically asks this question, and admits that Rousseau is 'quite correctly assigned to the romantic movement as, in a sense, one of its fathers'. Yet he clearly believes that Rousseau's place in this movement has been exaggerated (RR 8, 62–3; cf. CTH 235). I think this says less about Berlin's notorious bias against Rousseau, whom he has justly been criticised for misrepresenting, than about his specific understanding of romanticism. Indeed, this brings our attention to a central part in Berlin's thesis on romanticism: that the romantic revolution did not, after all, consist in the replacement of reason and rational inquiry with emotion and introspection.

A FATAL BLOW TO MONISM

The clash between dry reason and vibrating feeling, Berlin admits, is certainly a part of the romantic story. Yet, as a summary of its most important contributions, he believes it to be misleading. First of all, sentiments played a significant part in our culture long before the romantics came on to the stage – in the Bible, the works of Virgil, and the tragedies of French classicism, Berlin tells us. Second, and more importantly, the conflict that he sets out to describe goes much deeper than the one between the faculty of reason – the one that 'murder[s] to dissect', in Wordsworth's words[12] – versus that of the passions (CTH 226–7; SR 232–3).

In Berlin's account, romanticism challenges not just the specific Enlightenment idea of knowledge as the result of exercising our reason, but rather the very assumption that knowledge as such – whether acquired by rational inquiry, introspection, intuition, or otherwise – is what we seek in moral and political matters to begin with. Berlin's thesis is thus that the romantics did something much more radical than replace Enlightenment's celebration of reason with a cult of feeling; instead, they replaced the very equation of knowledge and virtue that had dominated Western thought for centuries, and out of which the Enlightenment is but one version, with something entirely different (RR 137–8). In Berlin's – admittedly oversimplified – story, the following three propositions summarised not only the intellectual underpinnings of the Enlightenment, but in fact the attitude to the world of ideas that had dominated the West since Plato. First, there was the assumption that there is one correct solution to all normative problems – one single answer to questions such as 'How am I to live?', or 'How should a state be ruled?' Second, the answers to these questions were all assumed to be knowable in principle; reaching them is simply a matter of finding and employing the right technique. Third, and finally, it was assumed that these answers are all compatible with one another; there is no such thing as any irrevocable conflict between different values or the goals of different agents, since all true answers must fit harmoniously together like the pieces of a giant jigsaw puzzle (CTH 225–6; RR 26–8).[13]

Romanticism, Berlin tells us, shattered this orderly, smooth understanding of the world of values, replacing it with a darker and more chaotic vision of the ultimate goals of men as invented and created rather than found, and of conflict and loss as the inevitable condition in human affairs. The 'backbone of the main Western tradition' that Berlin held was 'cracked' by the romantics, in other words, was nothing less than the very monism he himself relentlessly attacked

---

[12] In 'The Tables Turned' (1798): SR 60; RR 139; TCE 515.
[13] Robert Wokler shows that Berlin's description of these three tenets amounts to a rather embarrassing historical oversimplification (Wokler 2003, 18–19). George Crowder has furthermore argued that Berlin not only distorts history by lumping these three beliefs together, he also neglects that these three ideas are not logically implied by one another (Crowder 2004, 127).

(RR 27). This, then, is why Berlin placed Herder with the romantics while playing down the romanticism of Rousseau. Despite sympathising with the Enlightenment, Herder rejoiced in the diversity and particularity of cultures and value systems. Rousseau, by contrast, was certainly against the particular order that the Enlightenment *philosophes* envisioned, but not against the very idea of an order as such, and in his writings clearly agrees with the monistic assumption that there can be such a thing as a harmonious solution that solves all social and political problems once and for all (RR 62–3).[14]

Sometimes Berlin makes the romantic attack on monism sound as brutal and concrete as if the Jena romantics essentially broke in to a classical garden, uprooted its straight lines of trees cut into pollards, and demolished its symmetrical statues, fountains and palaces, turning them instead into exciting ruins of the kind that can be glimpsed between the unruly scenery of typical romantic gardens. Berlin's thesis is formulated with *forza*, sometimes almost *furore*. But if it is sometimes repeated and exaggerated in almost poetic ways, its content is all the more clear and compelling. He unmistakably believed that the romantics challenged monism by insisting that values are not found but made:

> Whatever the differences between the leading romantic thinkers – the early Schiller and the later Fichte, Schelling and Jacobi, Tieck and the Schlegels when they were young, Chateaubriand and Byron, Coleridge and Carlyle, Kierkegaard. Stirner, Nietzsche, Baudelaire – there runs through their writings a common notion, held with varying degrees of consciousness and depth, that truth is not an objective structure, independent of those who seek it, the hidden treasure waiting to be found, but is itself in all its guises created by the seeker ... the common assumption of the Romantics that runs counter to the *philosophia perennis* is that the answers to the great questions are not to be discovered as much as to be invented. They are not something found, they are something literally made. (POI 246)

As has been noted by Joshua Cherniss, Berlin eventually moved from this description of how values come about through human creation towards a greater emphasis on their plurality and incompatibility.[15] In contrast to the voluntarism he attributed to the romantics, his own pluralism assumed, or at least eventually came to assume, that human values, although many and incommensurable, are after all objective in their nature. Yet even though this is true for Berlin's writings on pluralism, if we separate these from his writings on romanticism specifically, we see that the latter in fact continue to give centre stage to the romantic denial of values as existing outside of our choices. Indeed, if we look closely, we see that the romantic opposition to monism on Berlin's description is not primarily a matter of vindicating diversity over unity or conflict over harmony in the realm of values – although the romantics certainly celebrated both diversity and conflict more generally – but rather

---

[14] For the view that Herder sympathised more with the Enlightenment than Berlin acknowledged, see Wokler 2003, 20.
[15] Cherniss 2014b, lxxii.

one of stressing perpetual motion, change, and flow against any static and hence suffocating model for human existence (RR 121, 132–3, 138–40).

In sum, we can say that in Berlin's view, romanticism challenged the predominant monistic attitude that virtue consists in knowledge of some sort of frictionless order in which all true values fit together perfectly. The romantics instead claimed that there is no pattern to look for, no rational solution; on their view, the individual is left without such answers, radically alone and free in inventing her values, rather than finding them in some pre-existing form. Despite the seemingly abstract nature of such a meta-ethical challenge, Berlin held that it shook the entire civilisation of the West so fiercely that we in fact continue to feel the tremors to this day.

THE RISE OF THE INDOMITABLE WILL

We have seen that Berlin tended to identify the heart of romanticism as its refusal to accept the monistic order that he believed had until then dominated Western thought. Yet this captures but one half of the romantic legacy. In 'The Lasting Effects', his concluding Mellon lecture, Berlin tells us several times that his argument is that at 'the heart of romanticism' lie two values or two principles. The second of these is the one we are familiar with by now: 'that there is no structure of things', no given order to which we must succumb. The first of these, however, is what Berlin calls 'the notion of the indomitable will' (RR 119; also see RR 138; cf. 136, 147, 154–5).

The indomitable – sometimes 'untrammelled' – will refers to the romantic conviction that it is up to the individual to create his own life, his own goals, and ultimately his own universe, and that to do so is the epitome of virtue (RR 136). Just like an artist – or, to be more precise, since this view of the artist itself to a great extent changed with romanticism: just like an artist on the romantic view – creates art and in a way ignites life by moulding dead matter in accordance with his own will, so too we are called upon by the romantics to create ourselves by imposing our own supreme will on the world that surrounds us (RR 98, 113). This is why Berlin also equates the 'essence' of romanticism with 'a kind of tyranny of art over life'. Romanticism unleashes the model of art, and the artist as the ultimate hero, from their previous confinement to the realm of aesthetics, and lets them loose in both ethics and politics (RR xxii–xxiii, 168; CTH 46, 245; SR 233).

The romantic insistence on the will goes back to Kant's disciple Fichte, 'the true father of romanticism, above all in his celebration of will over calm, discursive thought' (CTH 239). Although Fichte does not stray so far from his Kantian roots as to leave reason out of the picture, it was rather his theory of knowledge that was to influence his romantic followers the most, and here we find the idea that the 'I' is not something that exists before it is created, but rather a constant activity of self-creation.[16]

According to Fichte, the only way to know oneself is to come into collision with something else, and to define oneself against it. All other knowledge starts with this freely willed 'positing' of the self. With this, the emphasis starts shifting from the first to the last aspect of the Kantian dictum that we must submit to the moral law of which we ourselves are ultimately the sovereign creators. For, although he remains a Kantian, what Fichte underlines is not primarily our duties of obedience, but our status as sovereign creators. His theory of knowledge thus inspires the romantic idea that, as Berlin puts it, 'the sacred vocation of man is to transform himself and his world by his indomitable will' (CTH 241).

In almost all of his essays and lectures on romanticism, Berlin's analysis of the untrammelled will leads up to an account of the romantic hero. In his evocative story, the Fichtean exaltation of the will inspired the romantic idea that outcasts and exiles in society are admirable, because they have refused to sell out. What the romantics want us to avoid at all costs is to compromise our own integrity in any way, to fail to stand up for ourselves and our principles – whatever their content, and whatever the consequences. This would be to give in to corruption, impurity, insincerity; to yield one's soul to the philistines. The romantic hero may thus be criminal, cruel, even satanic; but he is nevertheless a hero if he remains free, unshackled by anything other than his commitment to following his inner light. What matters on this view is to be true to oneself and to stand up for it no matter what – not the actual nature of this self, its principles, or its success in worldly affairs. For Berlin, this is the committed and idealistic artist elevated to the ultimate role model in social and political affairs (CTH 241–3; SR 232–7; RR 161–3; FIB 67; PIRA 242–6).[17]

AN IMPERFECT EQUILIBRIUM

In the secondary literature, we are often told that while Berlin sympathised with romanticism, he remained hesitant about adopting it 'fully' in its more 'unbridled' forms.[18] It is true that Berlin often defines the parts of romantic thought that he abhors as 'hysterical' or 'extreme' (POI 248; RR 168). Yet I shall now argue that Berlin's doubts about romanticism were not just a matter of degree, or about what ideas are dangerous when put into practice. When Berlin distinguishes, as in his Mellon lectures, between the 'restrained' and the

---

[16] Indeed, Friedrich Schlegel, the leading spokesperson of the romantic movement himself, claimed that the most important sources of inspiration behind romantic thought were the French revolution, Fichte's theory of knowledge, and Goethe's *Meister*. See Schlegel 1991, x.

[17] Note that it has recently been argued that Berlin's claim that the indomitable will is central to romanticism must only be accepted with 'severe qualification'; see Richards 2002, 6.

[18] Cf. Riley 2001, 285.

'unbridled' romantics, or when he issues warnings about romanticism taken to its 'full form', his reason is not so much that some romantics went dangerously far with the ultimately valid ideas of other, more careful ones, but rather that they added new ideas that he believes to be fallacious even in their mildest form (RR 79, 107, 166–8).

Berlin clearly sympathised with the romantic attack on monism by the denial of any given order. *The Apotheosis of the Romantic Will*, for example, ends by concluding that, even if there are good reasons to condemn romanticism – reasons that we shall soon return to – then 'this at least can be set to its credit: that it has permanently shaken the faith in universal, objective truth in matters of conduct, in the possibility of a perfect and harmonious society, wholly free from conflict or injustice or oppression' (CTH 252). As he also tells us in his concluding Mellon lecture, Berlin believed that in this respect, the romantics in fact paved the way for liberalism, albeit unintentionally:

> The result of romanticism, then, is liberalism, toleration, decency and the appreciation of the imperfections of life; some degree of increased rational self-understanding. This was very far from the intentions of the romantic. But at the same time – and to this extent the romantic doctrine is true – they are the persons who most strongly emphasised the unpredictability of all human activities ... Aiming at one thing, they produced, fortunately for us all, almost the exact opposite. (RR 170)

This brings us to one of the most influential and much-debated aspects of Berlin's thought today: the connection he draws between the meta-ethical beliefs of value pluralism and the politics of a liberal society.

As has been argued by George Crowder, Berlin's writings suggest two pluralistic arguments for liberalism. The first of these, and indeed the one most typically discussed, claims that a pluralism of values implies the primacy of choice, or negative liberty, which Berlin places at the centre of liberalism. However, as has been pointed out by several critics, the assumption that the mere necessity of choice would somehow further entail that choice must also be desirable is a case of the naturalistic fallacy, i.e. an unwarranted move from a claim about how things are to a claim about how things should be.[19] Nor is it entirely clear that Berlin really believed that liberalism must necessarily give pride of place to negative liberty. In the later introduction to his essays on liberty, Berlin suggests that his main purpose was to warn against positive liberty taken to its extreme, rather than to defend negative liberty (L 39).

Instead, the more interesting trail from pluralism to liberalism is the one found in the second of Berlin's two arguments, which holds that pluralism supports liberalism by way of anti-perfectionism. This argument assumes that a society that could satisfy all our different wishes and goals is a logical impossibility. An inevitable fact of social life is thus deep moral disagreement and collision, concerning both which values to prioritise over others (such as

---

[19] Gaus 2003, 43; Crowder 2004, 144.

social justice over individual liberty, for example), and which methods to use when solving these conflicts. This in turn suggests that the best and most humane political order is one which is able to harbour and manage these conflicts, instead of striving to dissolve them altogether for the sake of some frictionless utopia. This argument for anti-perfectionism is typically traced back to one of the later passages in *Two Concepts of Liberty*, where Berlin suggests that pluralism supports liberalism not so much by providing a positively formulated argument for a liberal order as by undermining a powerful monistic argument for authoritarianism – the argument that by abolishing freedom we can reach some perfect, final state where we can do away with the agony of choice (L 214).[20]

This argument from pluralism to liberalism by way of anti-perfectionism plays an even more central role in Berlin's later writings on romanticism, however, where this is clearly presented as the reason why liberalism owes a great deal to the romantics. In the concluding discussion of *The Apotheosis of the Romantic Will*, for example, Berlin tells us that from the insight that painful choices between incompatible goods is an inescapable part of human life,

> it would follow that the creation of a social structure that would, at the least, avoid morally intolerable alternatives, and at the most promote active solidarity in the pursuit of common objectives, may be the best that human beings can be expected to achieve, if too many varieties of positive action are not to be repressed, too many equally valid human goals are not to be frustrated.

The hope of such a course, he continues, 'would be no more than a better world, dependent on the maintenance of what is bound to be an unstable equilibrium in need of constant attention and repair' (CTH 250).

On the last page of his concluding Mellon lectures, he traces a similar path from romantic pluralism to the defence of an 'imperfect equilibrium' in politics:

> Here are the Romantics, whose chief burden is to destroy ordinary tolerant life, to destroy philistinism, to destroy common sense, to destroy the peaceful avocations of men, to raise everybody to some passionate level of self-expressive experience . . . and yet, as a result of making clear the existence of a plurality of values . . . they have given prominence to and laid emphasis upon the incompatibility of human ideals. But if these ideals are incompatible, then human beings sooner or later realise that they must make do, they must make compromises, because if they seek to destroy others, others will seek to destroy them; and so, as a result of this passionate, fanatical, half-mad doctrine, we arrive at an appreciation of the necessity of tolerating others, the necessity of preserving an imperfect equilibrium in human affairs. (RR 169–70)

This of course raises a corollary of questions. Why would pluralism give rise to an anti-perfectionism that is specifically liberal, as Berlin goes on to tell us, as opposed to, for example, a conservative one?[21] Is the insight that there are many

---

[20] Cf. Crowder 2004, 146.   [21] Crowder 2004, 146–7.

incommensurable values even compatible with the universalistic claims upon which any kind of liberalism, however anti-perfectionist, nevertheless must rely? In other words, if pluralism is true, how can we hold that a liberal society outranks an illiberal one, with the presumably incommensurable values that this society in turn expresses?[22] Or is it mistaken to assume that Berlin is tracing a logical link between pluralism and liberalism at all? Perhaps the steps from pluralism to liberalism are not a matter of logical implications but of psychological affinities? If so, is this more psychological version of the argument successful – i.e. is it really the case that those with a pluralistic mentality tend to be more inclined to support anti-perfectionist politics?[23]

George Crowder (Chapter 13 in this volume) offers an overview and discussion of the longstanding debates around these questions. In this chapter, however, our specific concern is Berlin's relation to romanticism, not pluralism. I should therefore like to leave pluralism aside for now, and instead consider the more neglected issue of how Berlin viewed the romantic ideal of the indomitable will.

THE FASCIST DANGERS OF SELF-REALISATION

Together with his conclusions regarding the liberal heritage of value pluralism, Berlin consistently argues that the other side of romanticism – the one that emphasises the will and the artistic ideal as a role model for moral and political life – is both invalid and politically dangerous. The very same sentence with which Berlin concludes in *The Apotheosis of the Romantic Will* that the romantic challenge to monism can be 'set to its credit', for example, begins with the following observation:

this movement is justly condemned for the monstrous fallacy that life is, or can be made, a work of art, that the aesthetic model of life applies to politics, that the political leader is, at his highest, a sublime artist who shapes men according to his creative design – a fallacy that leads to dangerous nonsense in theory and savage brutality in practice. (CTH 252)

Similarly, the concluding section in his Mellon lectures tells us that to say, as the romantics did, that everything must be created by my unbridled imagination, that there are no common values at all but only the creations of my own free will, is a 'kind of lunacy'. Thus, while the aesthetic model may hold a great deal of validity for the artist, to impose it on moral and social life is, again, 'fallacious' (RR 167–8).

What truth, then, is it that Berlin believes the artistic ideal as a model for life denies? First, by treating human beings as material for the creative superman to mould in line with his supreme will, it clearly goes against Berlin's agreement

---

[22] Cf. Gray 1995; Galston 1999; Riley 2001; Gaus 2003, ch. 2; Myers 2010.
[23] Crowder 2013a; Zakaras 2013a, b. And, vice versa, does monism have a psychological connection with tyranny, as I have myself argued elsewhere? See Gustavsson 2014 and Allen 2009.

with Kant that all individuals are ends in themselves, itself an insight that Berlin connects, somewhat questionably, to romanticism (PIRA 259). Secondly, the cult of the sovereign artistic will denies that there are certain common values and truths which make it possible for human beings to communicate with one another (RR 167–8). Thus, although Berlin certainly values self-expression and creation, the romantic voluntarism that assumes it is entirely up to our own free will to create our own reality clearly goes against his empiricist attitude to life. Contrary to the romantics, to whom he repeatedly attributes the idea that the world inhabited by the artist is for example a completely different world than that inhabited by the banker or the nun (CTH 239–40), Berlin famously believed in a shared reality and a universally valid 'human horizon' of values which place undeniable restrictions on the individual will (CTH 83, 87).[24]

Finally, Berlin finds the romantic emphasis on the unfettered will not only invalid, but politically lethal. This is why in *Two Concepts of Freedom*, the forerunner to *Two Concepts of Liberty*, he identifies positive liberty – 'the precise opposite of the *liberal* notion of [freedom]' – with this romantic notion, and spends a considerable part of this essay on Schiller and Fichte, the latter of whom eventually took the step from this notion to nationalism and the beginnings of fascism (PIRA 225).[25] In *Two Concepts of Liberty*, Berlin admittedly broadens his notion of positive liberty. Yet, even here, his target includes the romantic identification of freedom with the realisation of our true will (L 197).

The specific steps through which Berlin believed positive liberty leads to tyranny are notoriously difficult to specify.[26] Are they logical, historical, psychological, or a mix of all of the above?[27] What is clear, however, is that Berlin warns against the division of the self into one ideal, metaphysical part, which is identified with our 'true self', and another, empirical, lower part, which tends to be seen as a plaything for external forces and thus an obstacle to be overcome. This division of the self is also an important aspect of Berlin's account of the romantic, typically Fichtean, notion of freedom as the realisation of the indomitable will:

Fichte begins to move towards a theological conception of the self; he says that the true, free self is not the empirical self which is clothed in a body and has a date and a place, it is a self which is common to all bodies, it is a super-self, it is a larger, divine self which he gradually begins to identify now with nature, now with God, now with history, now with a nation. (FIB 71–2)[28]

---

[24] Sometimes Berlin describes the belief in these universal values and indeed a certain shared human nature as one of the few welcome results of the atrocities of the twentieth century; see, for example, CTH 214–18. For Berlin's account of how the romantics shunned ordinary life, science, and communication, see CTH 245–7.
[25] Also, these two notions of liberty and the sinister consequences of one of them are discussed in his lecture on Fichte, also from the early '50s (FIB 73).
[26] Crowder 2004, 84.   [27] For a brief overview, see Gustavsson 2014, 268–9.
[28] Also see CTH 240; PIRA 223, 227.

This is the beginning, according to Berlin, of the ominous identification of the self with the state or the nation, and with my true freedom as a matter of realising not my empirical, individual desires, but the greater purpose of this larger self of which I am but a part. Applied to this type of reasoning, the inner division has fatal consequences, for 'if I can suppress that which is lower in me, then the leader or the race can suppress that which is lower in it, as the spirit does the sinning flesh' (FIB 75). When this step has been reached we have in fact arrived at the insidious conclusion that freedom is nothing but submission; in the romantic case specifically the conclusion that freedom for ordinary man is to submit to the godlike artist, genius or superman, who alone can 'liberate' the philistines from their trivial everyday concerns, and instead lift them up to their one true purpose, which they themselves are too simple to see (CTH 240, 241, 245; RR 104–6; FIB 75–6; PIRA 252–4).

Whether Berlin's allegations are ultimately warranted or not is a topic discussed by Alan Ryan (Chapter 12 in this volume). What is important to note here is that Berlin's writings on the romantic will, and the notion of liberty as the realisation of this will, most typically found in Fichte, remind us of something that tends to be obscured by Berlin's more well-known writings. Contrary to what is sometimes assumed, Berlin was namely just as fearful of romantic irrationalism as of enlightenment rationalism. In his mind, the risks he saw with positive liberty were not exhausted by the association he drew between Enlightenment reason and communistic tyranny. Importantly, he was also anxious to point out the risks with the positive liberty that he associated with the romantic will, and which he believed had eventually given rise to another form of tyranny, in the form of extreme nationalism and fascism.[29]

A LIBERALISM THAT RECOGNISES THE BEAUTY OF IMPERFECTION

Berlin, we have seen, believed that the romantic revolution could be summarised in terms of two main movements. One is the first important step from a monistic to a pluralistic understanding of values and human existence: the belief that values are created rather than found, and that human existence is constantly in motion, an endless flow, as opposed to anything that could ever be contained or fixed in one final order or structure. The other shift that romanticism sets in motion consists in the ascent of a 'new set of values' in the realms of moral and political life: the unbounded expression of the will, self-realisation, sincerity, and dedication (SR 222–3).

These two aspects of romanticism may at times seem to be variations on what is essentially the same idea. The exaltation of the will, and the concomitant

---

[29] For an elaboration of this, see Gustavsson 2014, 282–3, 285–6. For an application to the contemporary debates on banning the full Muslim veil in the name of liberty, see Gustavsson 2015b. For examples of those who neglect this side of Berlin's critique, cf. Christman 1991, 354–5; Galipeau 1994, 101; Gray 1995, 21.

stress on self-expression and integrity, would make little sense without the meta-ethical assumption that there is no point in searching for any given model to emulate, for there is no pre-existing knowledge of who we are or should be that could ever be acquired, no solution able to unburden the individual from the task of self-creation. Yet, in contrast to this assumption about the nature of our ideals, the idea of the indomitable will is itself an ideal, or a set of ideals – even if, in the words of contemporary political theorists, they mainly apply at a second-order level, since they are ideals about how to hold our other more substantial ideals.

This means that it is quite possible to accept only what has here been discussed as the first half of the romantic creed: to agree that there is indeed no given order of values without, however, supporting the ideal of the indomitable will.[30] I have argued that Berlin took something close to this position himself. As we have seen, he clearly considered the romantic exaltation of the unbounded will as both mistaken and lethal. He also condemned one of the most 'typical' features of romanticism: 'the insane, egomaniacal self-prostration before one's true inner essence, one's private feelings ... as against that which one shares with other people' (CTH 209). Thus, although he certainly did not consider the romantic ideals of sincerity and integrity as being without value, in contrast to the romantics he believed they should be weighed against the value of compromise, tactfulness, sensitivity to context and the ability to consider, and on occasion adapt oneself to, the needs of others.

Berlin's analysis of romanticism shaped his own liberalism in three crucial ways. As we saw in the previous section, he associated the inversion of liberty into tyranny not only with positive liberty in the shape of rational self-direction, but also with its romantic version, according to which liberty consists in the triumph not of reason but of the unbounded will over everything that resists it, be it our own fears and habits, or those of other, supposedly philistine, human beings or cultures. The first link between romanticism and liberalism for Berlin is thus a prudential one: liberals, the romantic example reminded him, must avoid not only the Scylla of rationalist monism, but also the Charybdis of the indomitable will.

At the same time, one of the most recurrent conclusions Berlin draws from his writings on romanticism is that the romantics inadvertently gave rise to liberal tolerance. The reason for this is that their attack on monism rules out all forms of utopia, and instead suggests that an unstable equilibrium is the best we can hope for in human affairs. The second link between romanticism and liberalism, for Berlin, then, consists in pluralism: his own defence of tolerance draws heavily on the pluralistic insights brought to us by the romantics. His

---

[30] Indeed, Crowder has pointed to a potential conflict between these two ideas. The cult of the untrammelled will may lead to a fascist form of monism, with the *Volksgeist* as the supreme value. See Crowder 2004, 129.

particular understanding of value pluralism, however, developed into a more tempered and objectivist kind than that espoused by the romantics. Clearly, he did not condone 'the extravagances of romantic irrationalism' (CTH 251).

Finally, Berlin treats perfection as not only dangerous, but also, much as the romantics did, as a bleak and bloodless ideal when compared to the splendid spectacle of human diversity, both within and between human beings. This brings us to 'romantic humanism', the third and final path between romanticism and Berlinian liberalism. The core of romantic humanism is the insight that man himself is infinitely higher than anything else, and hence that to manipulate or sacrifice human beings for the sake of any ideas or values or institutions is the most heinous of sins, for this is to trample on the one thing that remains sacred: the human will (CTH 210–11).

As Berlin is well aware, the origins of this command to treat man as an end in himself go back to Kant and his understanding of man as capable of willingly imposing upon himself the universal law of reason. With the romantics, however, the emphasis shifted from the latter part of this notion – submission to the law of reason – to the former – the act of freely willing or indeed even creating our values. In addition, the romantics also insisted, in direct opposition to Kant, that individual personality, the very characteristic which makes us different from rather than similar to others, is itself something to be encouraged and indeed revered. While Berlin also believed we shared a great deal with other human beings, his own defence of individual rights and liberal tolerance was clearly inspired by this romantic understanding of human choice as infinitely valuable, independently of its consequences, and of individual personality as worthy of our deepest respect, perhaps especially when it goes against the grain (PIRA 258).

It has even been suggested that the heart of Berlin's discussion of liberty is better captured not by his distinction between positive and negative liberty, but by the less famous distinction he originally drew in *Two Concepts of Liberty* between ideals of liberty that are humanistic in the above sense, and those that are anti-humanistic in that they identify liberty with submission of the individual self to some impersonal system or order.[31] What is certain is that Berlin was anxious for liberalism to make room for imperfection, both for the reason that he believed the search for perfection to be the path to tyranny, and, importantly, because he agreed with the romantics that any humane society must recognise the true beauty of human diversity, choice, and personality, for 'the glory and dignity of man consist in the fact that it is he who chooses, and is not chosen for' (CTH 214).

Berlin's writings on romanticism thus show another side of him than the realist 'Cold War liberal', the pessimist about human nature, inspired in the inverted sense by all the atrocities he wants liberalism to avoid – essentially a champion of what Judith Shklar has termed 'the liberalism of fear'.[32] For all

---

[31] Cherniss 2014b, lviii–lvix. [32] Shklar 1998; Crowder 2004, 172–3; Müller 2008.

his anti-utopianism, and his commitment to avoiding the fascist catastrophes to which he believed that romantic thought had eventually led, Berlin here comes across as virtually intoxicated – to use the striking expression he himself applied to Kant's relationship with the free will (RR 80) – by the diversity and richness of human experience revealed by the romantics. With barely contained enthusiasm, Berlin agrees with the romantics that the crooked timber of humanity is not something to be lamented, as Kant believed. In all its painful imperfection, this unruly characteristic of humanity is, on the contrary, both our most tantalising and awe-inspiring feature.

PART IV

BERLIN AND POLITICS: LIBERALISM, NATIONALISM, AND PLURALISM

10

Isaiah Berlin on Nationalism, the Modern Jewish Condition, and Zionism

Fania Oz-Salzberger

POSING THE QUESTIONS

In a televised conversation in 1972, Isaiah Berlin made the following opening point:

I'd like to distinguish between nationalism and national consciousness or national feeling. National feeling seems to me a perfectly normal phenomenon of human beings brought together by whatever it may be, unity of tradition, living on the same soil, possessing common memories, having gone through common experiences, and needn't take a particular aggressive form. But if it's in some way insulted or humiliated, or some kind of pressure is brought against it, then I think it becomes inflamed, and this is what is called nationalism.[1]

This statement encapsulates a crucial distinction made in several of Berlin's published works. It usefully sets the term "nationalism" at the extreme of Berlin's vocabulary of national self-awareness, denoting an "inflamed" variant ("aggressive," "fervid," and "pathological" were three of the adjectives he used for it elsewhere) of the normal, and indeed normative, "national feeling" or "national consciousness."

During the same year, Berlin published his essay "The Bent Twig: A Note on Nationalism" (CTH 253–78.), which evolved seven years later into his seminal essay titled "Nationalism: Past Neglect and Present Power" (AC 420–48). The basic distinction laid out in these major sources represents, *grosso modo*, Berlin's enduring grasp of the vicissitudes of national self-awareness.[2] Although in a very few instances he used "nationalism" to denote the whole spectrum, it

---

I am grateful to the editors and to Henry Hardy, Avishai Margalit, Amos Oz, and my doctoral student Gal Amir, for helpful comments.

[1] Berlin and Hampshire, "The Problems of Nationalism" (1972).
[2] I take issue with David Miller's claim that Berlin's attitude to nationalism is a "puzzle ... that no-one ... has yet been able to resolve," because (1) his liberalism was incommensurable with his "apparent nationalism," and (2) his disparate accounts of nationalism are mutually inconsistent (Miller 2005, esp. 100–2). Only rarely did Berlin confound "nationalism," which he deemed

was far more common for Berlin to employ it uniquely for the fanatical upshot, not the general form.

A decade earlier, in the little-known "A Note on Nationalism" published obscurely in 1964, Berlin had already defined his subject matter as "the most powerful of all influences upon the public life of the West; and today of the entire world" (POI 302). He also spelled out a clear distinction between what we might call "non-pathological" and "pathological" nationalism or national feeling (POI 310).

The distinction is not only semantic. Russian and Hebrew, the languages imprinted (albeit unequally) on Berlin in his childhood, both offer differentiated terminology for neutral and negative national phenomena. Native English speakers may find it difficult to intuit the distance between the deep, intuitive sense of Russian peoplehood expressed by the term *narod* and the westernized *nazion*, which in turn allowed morally neutral usage in *nationalnost* (nationhood) and *nazionalni* (national) and pejorative usage in *nazionalizm* and *nazionalisticheskiy*. In Hebrew, the Biblical *uma* and *leom* are neutral, while the modern *leumiut* and *leumanut* fit Berlin's "national consciousness (or feeling, or sentiment)" and "nationalism," respectively.[3] Thus, speakers of Russian or Hebrew, unlike speakers of English, can deem Berlin's philosophical distinction a "natural" one, rooted in language.

The present chapter outlines Berlin's chief prototype of nationalism, set in motion by German thinkers in the late eighteenth century and – in modified political form – during the nineteenth century. At roughly the same time, gentler forms of national consciousness were developed by liberal West Europeans, and, briefly, by liberal Russians. The nonextremist varieties were an essentially modern, European-born but globally applicable, reframing in national context of the "perfectly normal phenomenon of human beings brought together by whatever it may be." Berlin took mainstream Zionism, the Jewish variant of this movement of ideas, to be largely "normal"; it was close to his heart, but his attention to it was emotive rather than intellectual. By contrast, nationalism – notably German and Italian – veered into pathology, and it was this "inflamed condition" (POI 15) that Berlin found philosophically spellbinding.

How relevant, and how affective, was Berlin's own Jewish birth, upbringing, and sense of national belonging? This chapter offers a brief account of his Jewishness and his lifelong and adamant, albeit critical, adherence to Zionism. The task of bringing his own national self-awareness to bear on his theory of national feeling and nationalism is a tricky one: the Jewish case was

---

morally appalling, with ordinary national consciousness. He would certainly not regard himself as a nationalist. See also Avineri 2007, 73–94.

[3] I am grateful to Alexander Yakobson for illuminating information and insights about the Russian terms, conveyed in personal conversation and correspondence. The Hebrew *leumiut* and *leumanut* are both twentieth-century neologisms, the latter injected with Modern Hebrew's "pejorative n-suffix." Berlin was probably aware of this clear-cut and useful dichotomy available to speakers of Modern Hebrew.

hardly mentioned in his major essays on nationalism, but his writings on Zionism and on Israel employ vocabulary and bank on ideas gleaned from his general engagement with the concept. I will dwell on one main question: how does Berlin's account of Jewish national awareness fit into his understanding of the general phenomenon? Is the Jewish case an ordinary instance of "human beings brought together," unique only in being Berlin's own national group? Is it an exception, or perhaps a gauge for all others?[4]

Two caveats are in order. First, Berlin dealt with the history of ideas, not with political and social history as such. Of course he acknowledged the enormous impact of what he often called "sociology" on ideas, but effective intellectuals were his specialty. Therefore, while Nazi Germany and Fascist Italy were an obvious part of his life experience and mental horizon, they did not figure prominently in his writings on nationalism. He was far more interested in the intellectual ancestors of these barbaric outgrowths of European political cultures. Thus, his source material and origins of philosophical inspiration hail from the eighteenth and nineteenth centuries, petering out in the early twentieth. In the same vein, individual thinkers outweighed ideological movements, political leadership, diplomacy, and warfare in Berlin's mind. Whenever he tackled a historic political figure at a depth that surpassed the mere vignette, as in the cases of Benjamin Disraeli and Chaim Weizmann, it was because he took them for intellectuals as well as statesmen.

Second, it is crucial to note that Berlin offered neither an analytic taxonomy nor a tidy historical genealogy of every form of national consciousness and nationalism.[5] Even though he claimed not to be a historian (protesting this twice in his seminal essay on nationalism), Berlin aligned the pivotal forms of national consciousness or nationalism with particular cultures in specific historical eras, peopled by the thinkers he found fascinating. There was more intellectual excitement for him in epoch-making instances than in running the conceptual gamut. This bias derives from his choice of European Enlightenment and post- (or counter-) Enlightenment thought as the mainstay of his work. It also reflects his belief in the historical importance of individuals, including – perhaps especially – of individual thinkers.

But in a world inhabited by Hamann and Fichte, Burke and Michelet, Maistre and Bonald and the Fascists, nationalism itself represents a spectrum,

---

[4] Cf. Miller's claim that "we can extract a general account of the roots of nationalism from Berlin's reflections on Zionism": Miller 2005, 111. However, Miller employs the term "nationalism" for both major forms of national consciousness, while Zionism does not appear in Berlin's account of the roots of nationalism in the "inflamed" sense of the concept.

[5] Yael Tamir and David Miller have extracted sharper taxonomies from Berlin's premises. Tamir's *Liberal Nationalism* (Tamir 1995) suggests a philosophical–political cohesiveness of moderate national belonging and liberalism, while Miller, "Berlin's Nationalism," distinguishes between political/cultural, unified/pluralist, and morally limited/unlimited nationalisms and proceeds to propose a coherent model of his own. Berlin's toolkit, however, was historical, and not aimed at filling all possible categorical slots.

alongside its milder counterpart or "normal" national feeling. Thus, some scholars who have recently deduced a dichotomy of "benign" and "malign" types of national consciousness are downplaying the variety of individual minds at work. Berlin's nationalist thinkers are not a uniform cadre but a garden of colorful, sometimes alluring monstrosities. There were shades of gray in his outlook, apparent in his view of the temporal growth of nationalism: Herder, Fichte, and Nazi ideologues, pivotal markers in the nationalist genealogy, differ remarkably in contents and moral significance.[6]

National and nationalist theories may pretend to be strictly homegrown, but at crucial moments in their development, national movements were fed, in Berlin's account, by external sources. They could absorb cultural legacies unique to a particular people, such as the Jewish communal ethos of the *shtetl* merging with European ideas to form Zionist thought. In a different sort of twist, philosophers who were very remote from nationalism – notably Kant, as we shall see – unintentionally helped its rise to prominence. National theories were never stand-alones.

Even while implying that forms of national self-awareness inhabit a range rather than a dichotomy, Berlin focused only on some parts of that range, in particular the "inflamed" form, which he most often called nationalism, mapping its historical trajectory and ascending scale. His treatment of nationalism was evocative and often episodic, but it was always fed by a deep fascination. Conversely, the "perfectly normal" sense of belonging in its modern guise as harmless "national feeling" is not particularly variegated in Berlin's writings, with the possible exception of Jewish nationalism. One might argue that for Berlin, to adapt Tolstoy, all moderate national sentiments look alike, but each fervid nationalism is nationalist in its own way.

NATIONALISM: BERLIN'S DEFINITION

In the beginning was Germany (POI 307). German by birth, German too in its earliest and most crucial mutation, Berlin's concept of nationalism is firmly anchored in one nation's backlash, triggered by a handful of seminal thinkers, against political and intellectual humiliation. Neither "pride of ancestry," nor "passionate patriotism," dating back to antiquity or the early modern era, can count as nationalism. It has a moment of birth and a homeland in the late eighteenth-century Holy Roman Empire.[7]

---

[6] Alongside the references quoted in footnotes 2–4, see also Berlin 1991.
[7] This premise, while largely borne out by Berlin's two major essays on our theme, is somewhat compromised by his view of Edmund Burke as a co-founder of nationalism. However, Berlin's Burke did not breed a lineage of nationalist thinkers, and he did not take part in the crucial transition between Herder and Fichte. German culture was by no means the only "bent twig" in late eighteenth-century Europe, but its backlash proved momentous.

This historical branding may not be obvious at first sight to a reader of Berlin's best-known definition of nationalism – or, rather, "European nationalism as a state of mind":

> By nationalism I mean something more definite, ideologically important and dangerous [than mere national sentiment]: namely the conviction, in the first place, that men belong to a particular human group, and that the way of life of the group differs from that of others; that the characters of the individuals who compose the group are shaped by, and cannot be understood apart from, that of the group, defined in terms of common territory, customs, laws, memories, beliefs, language, artistic and religious expression, social institutions, ways of life, to which some add heredity, kinship, racial characteristics; and that it is these factors which shape human beings, their purposes and their values. (AC 431)

National uniqueness is only the preliminary factor defining an ideology as nationalist rather than just national. More will follow. At this level, what we may call "first-order nationalism" focuses on the particularity, the essential disparity (but not superiority) and the self-sufficient integrity of a human group or culture. This incipient notion, as we shall later observe, is tailored to fit Herder (POI 308). However, the image of a world accommodating "different but equal" cultures is less benign than it might look at first blush. There is no exit clause. An individual is fermented, formed, and formatted by his or her native culture, and can only escape it at the risk of losing self, identity, and meaning.

The second element in Berlin's definition introduces the organism metaphor, which Fichte and others circulated in the wake of a politicized national movement in the Napoleon-era German lands:

> Secondly, that the pattern of life of a society is similar to that of a biological organism; that what this organism needs for its proper development, which those most sensitive to its nature articulate in words or images or other forms of human expression, constitutes its common goals; that these goals are supreme; in cases of conflict with other values which do not derive from the specific ends of a specific "organism" – intellectual or religious or moral, personal or universal – these supreme values should prevail, since only so will the decadence and ruin of the nation be averted. (AC 431)

The organism metaphor does not allow the invention of national consciousness ex nihilo. We cannot "artificially forge" it. In fact, neither "we" nor "I" are of relevance. Individual preference or interference is always for naught. Nationalism harbors no free will (unless we ascribe it to the organic whole), and personal free choice is out of the question: "the essential human unit in which man's nature is fully realised is not the individual or a voluntary association which can be dissolved or altered or abandoned at will, but the nation" (AC 432). Moreover, rational analysis of human society, the Enlightenment's crowning ambition, is a delusion. No French materialist can dissect "the indissoluble and unanalysable organic whole which Burke identified with society, Hegel with the state, but which for nationalists is, and can only be, the nation" (AC 432).

Individual freedom – as Rousseau taught the German nationalists – has no meaning beyond its partaking in collective reason. In their hands, collective reason became the nation and/or the state.

This part of Berlin's definition of nationalism sheds necessary light on his understanding of moderate forms of national awareness. In the nonorganic, nondeterminist modes of nationhood, individual freedom is relevant. It is most deeply relevant – as we shall see – in the Jewish case. If nationalism denies personal freedom by rendering it subordinate to the "essential human unit," milder forms of nationhood can expand personal freedom by enriching the intellectual, aesthetic, and emotional experiences of human beings, and ultimately by giving them more choice.

The third element in Berlin's definition of nationalism can be summed up by two nineteenth-century dicta: "My country, right or wrong" (with a lineage winding from Stephen Decatur to G. K. Chesterton); and Henrik Ibsen's chief troll, the Dovre Master in *Peer Gynt*: "Don't ask if the taste is sweet or sour; / The main thing is, and don't you forget it, / It's all home-made."[8] Our goals, beliefs, policies, and lifestyles are good simply because they are ours. Universal values of any kind, religious or lay, are nonexistent, and so are universal laws, standards, and sanctions. Each nation hails the goodness of its own values and acts for the sole reason – the superb reason, "perhaps the most compelling" (AC 432) reason – that they are its own.

Significantly, after listing three characteristics of nationalism in an abstract manner – the fourth and last element is yet to follow – Berlin digressed to a historical discussion of the chief players in the early history of the idea. I argued earlier that Herder's presence is immanent within Berlin's discussion of cultural particularism, and that Fichte is the thinker implied in his dealing with the organic metaphor; at this point Berlin moves from concepts to personalities:

> Florid and emotive prose of this kind was used by Herder, Burke, Fichte, Michelet and after them by sundry awakeners of the national souls of their dormant peoples in the Slav provinces of the Austrian or Turkish empires, or the oppressed nationalities (as well as the dominant majority population) ruled by the Tsar; and then throughout the world. (AC 433)

However, these mainstays of the nationalist traditions were not made of one skin. Herder and Burke were the immediate forebears of nationalism, but Fichte was its torchbearer.[9] "There is a distance between Burke's assertion that the individual may be foolish but the species is wise, and Fichte's declaration,

---

[8] Mackenzie 1848, 295; Ibsen 1998, 42. Ibsen's trolls, sardonically basking in "Our simple, homely way of living" (ibid.), are a likely stab at nationalism.
[9] Though included here for his "florid prose," Berlin did not see Jules Michelet as a student of Herder but as a fervent, albeit selective, disciple of Vico. Cf. TCE; Mali 2012.

a dozen or so years later, that the individual must vanish, must be absorbed, sublimated, into the species" (AC 433); this and similar distinctions pepper Berlin's genealogies of nationalist thought. As we shall see, Herder's role as a father of both moderate and aggressive national consciousness reflects a certain ambiguity in Berlin's narrative of their evolution.

The fourth feature of "full blown" nationalism – now that its origin in Fichte's writings has been established in a revealing historical aside – is built-in aggression. So far this has not been a necessary corollary of cultural uniqueness, or organic wholeness, or even the sense of superiority ascribed by nationalists to all "home-made" accomplishments. None of these three elements would immediately place nations on the warpath. But if nations' goals are incommensurable – an evil mirror image of Berlin's celebrated pluralism of individual and cultural values – violence must follow.

> Finally, by a development which need cause no surprise, full-blown nationalism has arrived at the position that, if the satisfaction of the needs of the organism to which I belong turns out to be incompatible with the fulfillment of the goals of other groups, I, or the society to which I indissolubly belong, have no choice but to compel them to yield, if need be by force. If my group – let us call it nation – is freely to realize its true nature, this entails the need to remove obstacles in its path. Nothing that obstructs that which I recognize as my – that is, my nation's – supreme goal, can be allowed to have equal value with it. (AC 433)

Thus, nationalism holds a burning match to the dry haystack of international conflicts. Negotiation and compromise would be futile in a world of unmitigated self-interest, where no general standards are allowed to override each nation's inner *telos*. The three elements of Berlin's definition of nationalism – a sense of uniqueness, organic belonging, and supremacism – jointly produce its fourth element: aggression.

There is one possible exception: if a nation's core values are in themselves humanely universalist, if its "supreme goal," for example, is peace on earth, would it still develop belligerent nationalism? After all, many nations measure their grandeur by their perceived contribution to mankind. One could argue that certain cultural values, including some professed by Jews, ancient Greeks, Romans, and Indians, rose above national interest and sought universal standards. Berlin was well aware that his own Jewish legacy, for one, harbored run-of-the-mill chauvinism alongside lofty universal principles. Could it be that humanist ingredients tend to diminish the danger of aggressive nationalist eruption? Such a stance could perhaps fit Berlin's view, but he did not directly discuss it.

NATIONALISM: THE HISTORICAL TRAJECTORY

As we have seen, Berlin's attempt to present a conceptual, seemingly ahistorical taxonomy of the basic components of nationalism was interrupted – Berlin often interrupted his own chain of thought – by an impatient wish to introduce some of the major thinkers. In the ensuing digression, and in most other treatments of the genealogy of national ideas, Berlin shunned "Whig" unilinear progressivism. As with socialism and liberalism, Berlin's trajectories of ideologies resemble a forking river, with clashing currents and countercurrents. Thus some harbingers of nationalism, such as Vico and Burke, did not directly affect the first generation proper. Although Vico and Burke chimed earlier bells on collective sentiment, they did not launch nationalism proper: this was done by Herder, who modernized the perennial human group feeling into a concept of nationhood, and by Fichte, who politicized and at the same time distorted "normal" national sentiment. It was left to later thinkers, notably Michelet, to rediscover Vico, to harness his insights and adapt them to their own national theory.

This is a storyline, not a taxonomy. Berlin needed the thinkers themselves, the human agency of intellectual change, to explain nationalism's rampant rise. Germany's pioneering nationalism, in particular, was interlinked with the Germans' unmatched bedazzlement with their own great philosophers. "[T]he most conspicuous case of the tyranny of ideas," Berlin wrote, "is that of Germany, the modern history of which is scarcely intelligible apart from the great ideological spell-binders."[10] Hence, his analysis of nationalism is most fittingly displayed as a history, twisting and turning its way along the two recent centuries.

Many scholars have posited Herder as the originator and epitome of Berlin's concept of "normal" national consciousness. Berlin's Herder is more complex than that; he was "the father of cultural (and ultimately every kind of) nationalism in Europe" (SR 295), and may have invented the term *nationalismus*. Although "he is not a political nationalist (that kind of nationalism had not developed in his time)," Herder "believed in the independence of cultures and the need to preserve each in its uniqueness" (POI 11). This description satisfies the first criterion in Berlin's four-phase definition of nationalism we explored earlier: a worldview of mutually exclusive national cultures, which individuals can never exit or swap, which obey no universal norms, and whose distinctive features must never be allowed to blend.

In the same place, however – the essay "My Intellectual Path" – Berlin proceeds to describe Herder's view in the softer terms of communal belonging, befitting the harmless and perennial nature of nations, alongside other groups.

[Herder] believed that the desire to belong to a culture, something that united a group or a province or a nation, was a very basic human need, as deep as the desire for food or

---

[10] Among these spell-binders were "Herder and Kant, Schiller and Goethe, Hegel and Fichte, Arndt and Jahn, Treitschke and Droysen, Wagner and Nietzsche"; Berlin 1962b.

drink or liberty; and that this need to belong to a community where you understood what others said, where you could move freely, where you had emotional as well as economic, social and political bonds, was the basis of developed, mature human life. (POI 11)

Was Herder, then, the prophet of national consciousness in general, or the founder of first-order nationalism?[11] Berlin neither recognized this as a problem nor resolved it. His ambiguity about Herder, parallel to his occasionally confusing usage of the term "nationalism," requires some clarification: Berlin was a Herderian in his theory of group belonging, not in an adherence to cultural exclusivism.[12]

A possible answer points to Fichte's role in the genealogy of pathological national thought. If Herder's idea of cultural uniqueness is the first factor in Berlin's definition of nationalism, as explored earlier, Fichte and German romantic nationalists such as Görres, Müller, and Arndt provided the second factor, the organic nature of nationhood, and the third factor, national supremacism. It was these two factors that "inflamed" Herderian nationalism. As Berlin put it elsewhere,

in its inflamed condition – my nation is better than yours ... you are inferior to me, because my nation is top and yours is far, far below mine and must offer itself as material to mine, which is the only nation entitled to create the best possible world – it is a form of pathological extremism which can lead, and has led, to unimaginable horrors. (POI 13)

Note, however, that these two ideas do not *constitute* Fichte's politicization of nationalism: both the organic metaphor and the sense of superiority could have remained within the cultural realm alone. It would be more accurate to say that Fichte, drawing on the post-Revolutionary and Napoleonic-era experiences that Herder did not have, was in a position to demand national liberty for the German states, and thus to invent political nationalism on his podium in Berlin.

The nation (or state) as organism, the sense of its own pre-eminence, and the new call for national statehood enabled Fichte and the romantic nationalists of his generation to step decisively away from Herder. The state took over culture as the nation's hearth. Herder, a near-anarchist in Berlin's view, would not have cared for this transition (TCE 254). Furthermore, for Fichte individuals ceased to matter beyond their national belonging. Third, Fichte overrode the equality

---

[11] As a doctoral student I argued with Berlin about Herder's alleged apoliticality; the *Volk* and the *Reich* sometimes crept into *Ideas of a Philosophy of History of Mankind*, signifying Herder's interest in the political nation, though not in modern statehood. Berlin remained unmoved. But see Patten 2010, 657–89.

[12] Steven B. Smith, like Miller and other Anglophone scholars, takes the term "nationalism" in Berlin's opus to denote "not simply a pathology." He therefore deems Herder's theory "One of the earliest and finest expressions of the kind of nationalism that Berlin seems to endorse." But while "nationalism" is arguably the right term here, "endorsement" is not. Berlin admired Herder's idea of cultural diversity but would obviously not accept Herder's mutually exclusive uniqueness of all cultures. See Smith 2016, 282.

Herder conceded to all cultures, raising the German nation above all others in a way Herder would probably loathe.

Still, the ensuing doctrine of full-blown nationalism drew on Herder's world of inward-looking, wholly incommensurable cultures, each adhering only to its *Schwerpunkt*, its own realm of values and creativity. A sad irony lurks here: had Herder's cultural emphasis prevailed, lethal nationalism would not have been born. Without Fichte, Herder would have sired no pathology. By politicizing Herder's cultural theory, Fichte retroactively put Herder on nationalism's founding pedestal.

During the romantic era, the nationalist current received fresh reinforcement from an unexpected source. In what is perhaps the most surprising twist in Berlin's crooked saga of nationalist theory, Immanuel Kant and his "impeccably enlightened rationalism" were intercepted by Fichte and the romantics to serve pathological nationalism. Like "Frankenstein's monster," Kant's Pietist notion of "the immense stress on independence, inner-directedness, self-determination," his "austere self-insulation," took two sinister turns. First, Fichte converted Kantian reason, the pillar of our moral self-sufficiency, into irrational individual will, which succumbs to inner truth and not to universal rationality. Then Fichte and his allies turned selfhood from individual to national, a "quasi-metaphysical super-personality" that is an end in itself. Armed with their highjacked version of Kant's autonomous will, the nationalists were now ready for their full-blown historical appearance (SR 307, 297, 306, 312). In the decades leading to the First World War, German theorists and politicians pushed forward with the Fichte-poisoned, Kant-misreading warp of the Herderian legacy. No great theoretical changes were introduced; all four elements of Berlin's definition of nationalism were already in place.

Elsewhere in Europe, intellectuals oscillated along the spectrum of national theory. In Italy the gentler national sentiment of Verdi, Mazzini and Cavour eventually lost the battle to Fascism. Other thinkers, such as Moses Hess, and statesmen, notably Clemenceau, Roosevelt, and Weizmann, successfully kept their nations on the moderate side in an age of rampant nationalism. Political sociology made a difference, of course: "In the case of the relatively independent, socially developed, culturally progressive societies" such as England, Holland, or Scandinavia, "this sense of the nation as a central source of moral authority took a relatively mild form" (SR 313). By the late nineteenth century, nationalism emerged as a mainstream movement in Germany and Italy, and as an extremist but vibrant fringe of national sentiment in France and elsewhere.

Russia was a different case. As the core of a multination empire, the Russian state had no use for rampant particularism. Its few liberal thinkers, engaged with social issues or with shades of religious mystique, did not concoct a Western-style moderate model of national consciousness. Extremist thinkers of the Slavophil mindset were too pan-Slavic, or else too inward-looking, to develop the comparative outlook requisite for fanning a sense of Russian nationalist supremacy.

The twentieth century – at least its first half – was a vicious arena of lethal nationalism, but it did not add much to the evolution of the nationalist idea. On Nazism as an end-case of nationalism, Berlin had curiously little of theoretical interest to say. He did not deem the Nazi notions of racist cleansing and "scientific" anti-Semitism, for example, to be substantial additions to nationalist theory. As for the Soviet Union, it went through a phase of rampant Russian nationalism during the Second World War (POI 305).[13] Deep-set Russian and Ukrainian anti-Semitism raised its head again. To be sure, some Soviet Jews held important roles, but calamity befell the Jewish intelligentsia, as well as other Soviet cultural groups seeking Herderian identity. Nevertheless, for Berlin, as in the case of Nazism, Stalinist nationalism offered little new by way of theory. Political cataclysms did not amount to philosophical breakthroughs.

Other nations, including the British and the Jews, experienced snippets of hardcore nationalism, but it did not take over their politics and culture. In his historical account of nationalism's onward march, Berlin was therefore far more interested in the nineteenth century than in the twentieth.

Jewish nationalism, one topic of this chapter, was a special case, but only up to a point. It presented Berlin with sociological and historical anomalies, and blended a unique *shtetl*-legacy into the national brew. The founders of Zionism were part of the European genealogy, drawing mainly from its moderate versions. Thinkers such as Hess and Herzl imbibed the Western European legacy, while the practical Zionist pioneers of Eastern Europe were obviously indebted to Russian liberalism and socialism, as well as Tolstoyan romanticism and *narodnik* utopianism. The ensuing national model was mostly of the mild sort, despite some extremist and even quasi-fascist elements in the far right of the Revisionist current.

Three singularities pertain to the Jewish national consciousness. First, it happened to be Berlin's own. Second, it stemmed intellectually from both sides of the European continent – as did Isaiah Berlin himself. No other national movement and very few individual thinkers could claim such latitude. Third, Zionism had a special interface with liberty. I will discuss these claims to uniqueness later. It is nevertheless important to note here that the Jewish case is part and parcel of the general European trajectory of national theory. Unique in some ways, it was neither a chimera nor a hybrid.

CROOKED TIMBER AND BENT TWIG

Berlin's two "arboreal metaphors,"[14] the crooked timber and the bent twig, are not mutually exclusive. They pertain to his account of national feeling on two

---

[13] See also Parthé, Chapter 7 in this volume.   [14] Miller 2005, 100.

different levels and in two different ways. One stands for unregimented normality, the other helps explain pathology. It may be helpful to stress the difference, and also to point out a third tree-related image that Berlin briefly used.

"The Crooked Timber of Humanity," gleaned from Kant's general observation on the incorrigible untidiness of human existence, served Berlin to depict the irreparable, but fortuitous, plurality of our personalities and preferences. Our very humanity is kinked and oblique, unfit for rationalist *philosophes*, abstract social reformers, and simplistic levelers. The diversity of modern national cultures at best reflects our human crookedness, our intrinsic timber-hood. Which is all well and good, as long as the snake of nationalism is not warped around the tree of national variety.

The need to belong to a society or, in modern times, to a nation, is for Berlin a corollary of mankind's crooked timber. Both resist philosophical reductionism and theoretical straightening-out. In the interview quoted at the beginning of this chapter, Berlin took "the desire to belong to a community or to some kind of unit ... [which] has been national for the last 400 years" to be "a basic human need or desire," misunderstood by would-be straighteners and polishers; "[t]herefore socialist and, I suppose, liberal theories have gravely underestimated the force of this."[15] Thus, the metaphor of crooked timber serves Berlin on two of his favorite fronts: celebrating the untamable hodgepodge of human values, and lambasting modern political rationalists for their futile attempt at smoothing it out.

The bent twig metaphor is deployed very differently. Human beings are crooked timber by nature, but they may or may not become a bent twig due to historical circumstances. The bent twig – unlike the crooked timber – denotes an anomaly, the sudden whiplash of a downtrodden group pouncing on its real or imagined oppressors. A "wound," a term Berlin used often, preceded the detonation of powerful group anger, which can in turn become revolutionary violence or nationalist extremism. But a wound is not a sufficient condition: some maltreated groups did not respond with a totalitarian contortion, others did.

The Germans were history's most interesting bent twig. Their nationalism "is perhaps a consequence of the accumulating resentment ... against, as it seemed to them, the contemptuous domination of French culture and French power," and their initial backlash response was cultural and intellectual: their "true inner life" will prevail (SR 304–5). German nationalism then fell into the misfortune of translating spiritual ascendancy into military aggression. It never struck Berlin, as far as I know, to ask whether the Jews acted as a "bent twig" when constructing their own modern nationhood. One can find some nationalist backlash both among early Zionists and latter-day Israelis, especially on the political right and extreme right; but Berlin did not ascribe

---

[15] Berlin and Hampshire, "The Problems of Nationalism."

such tendencies to the mainstream Zionism of Weizmann and Ben Gurion, even though their people had suffered more carnage, oppression, and indignity than the Germans, Italians, or Russians.

A subtle Jewish context may apply to Berlin's overlooked *third* arboreal metaphor, tucked away in his essay on nationalism: the *broken* twig. In nationalist theory, he says, an individual excluding himself or herself from the nation is "a leaf, a twig, broken off from the tree which alone can give it life":

> If I am separated from [my group] by circumstance or my own willfulness, I shall become aimless, I shall wither away, being left, at best, with nostalgic memories of what it once was to have been truly alive and active and performing that function in the pattern of the national life understanding of which alone gave meaning and value to all I was and did. (AC 433)

This sad fable parallels the attempt of modern Jews to assimilate into their Gentile surroundings, a move which Berlin deemed tragically impossible and harmful. Admittedly, the broken twig and the dead leaf are not part of Berlin's liberal-national language, but an image from the supremacist vocabulary of nationalism. Still, they resonate with a typical modern Jewish predicament.[16]

BERLIN AND THE TWENTIETH-CENTURY JEWISH CONDITION

Isaiah Berlin's Jewishness was a deeply intuitive, apolitical, familial sense of belonging. "I suppose I do owe my Judaeocentricity," he wrote to his friend Stuart Hampshire after the death of his mother, Marie (Mussa) Berlin, "to her & her world & Russian-Jewish cultural roots." A few months later, in another letter, he wrote: "my mother's death has broken a vital link."[17] Berlin's attitude to his Jewish identity was not, at rock level, intellectual. He too, like numerous other Europeans of his era, was an heir and keeper of a national sentiment fed to him by his closest and earliest providers of human affection.[18]

In public, rather than in intimate correspondence, Berlin famously declared himself to be "formed by three traditions – Russian, British and Jewish" (PI 433). This is a drier, more cerebral statement, mapping his intellectual origins and explaining his penchant for cultural pluralism. But the trio was not made equal. In his conversations, Berlin referred to both "English" and "Jewish" as

---

[16] This one-of-a-kind image of a broken twig is suggestively similar to the main metaphor of Chaim Nachman Bialik's famous Hebrew poem "A Twig Alighted," of 1911, which Berlin may have known, or known of. The context of Bialik's poem is the opening of new horizons for young Jews in his time, including Zionism, with the poetic narrator left behind in the old synagogue like a fallen twig dormant on a fence.

[17] Letter to Stuart Hampshire, February 23, 1974, and letter to Walter Eytan of April 1974, B 564, 565. On Berlin's childhood in Riga and in Petrograd, see Dubnov 2012.

[18] On Berlin sense of Jewish belonging see, first and foremost, Dubnov 2012 and – with a stronger "Russian" emphasis – Cherniss 2017.

ethnic groups, while "British" was more of a civic construction.[19] Yet Berlin never hyphenated "British" and "Jewish." He was both, of course, but he did not care to place himself in their intersection. By contrast, his hyphenated reference to Mussa Berlin's "Russian-Jewish" roots made sense to Berlin. While the British part of his identity was not a mother's milk belonging to him, the Russian-Jewish amalgam clearly was.

Berlin's emotional attachment to Herder's thought may have something to do with the closeness of his own formative memories to Herder's philosophy. Not to the cultural exclusivism, but to the tender delineation of linguistic belonging. When Berlin feelingly quoted Herder on language – "Has a nation ... anything more precious than the language of its fathers? In it dwells its entire world of tradition, history, religion, principles of existence; its whole heart and soul"[20] – this is not a mere exercise in *Einfühlung*; his identification with this sort of national sentiment is palpable.

But Berlin was also a child of turn-of-the-century East European Jewry, a crowded, textual, talkative, brutally self-conscious minority in a dramatic age of renewal, transition, and dispersion. Although his parents were well off and their lifestyle bourgeois, his mother (less so his father) and relatives conveyed older traditions. His grandparents and cousins, Chassids of the Schneersohn clan, belonged to a major current of Jewish religious practice, resplendent with unique theological, literary, and musical offerings. Modern Jewish intellectuals, observant and lay, were also part of the Berlins' circle in Riga. Here was the Eastern European Jewish *Mishpoche*, a family close-knit but broadly defined, blending emotional intimacy with bookish legacies, in which texts served as intergenerational arteries and tools of family-table education. The penchant for scholarly parenting, in the Berlin family and their contemporaries, survived the crossing into modernity and even secularism. This was not a *völkisch* culture in the sense purveyed by Herder or the German romantics, but it shared the peasant-like virtues associated with storytelling, musicality, folklore, and warmth.[21]

A British school and university education, following the family's migration to Britain in 1921, overlaid Berlin's "Russian-Jewish" childhood but did not erase it. He remained a proud and low-key Jew. He also became British, and in this case no qualifying adjective seems to be required. Michael Ignatieff's biography touchingly pinpoints this humble miracle, "the uncanny ability of a plump, unprepossessing Jewish child in a Gentile school, a bookish boy with a foreign accent and a limp left arm, to win people over," first at Arundel House School, then in Oxford.[22]

---

[19] Avishai Margalit, letter to the author, May 1, 2017.
[20] RT 165; TCE 234, quoting *Herder's sämmtliche Werke*, ed. Bernhard Suphan and others (Berlin, 1877–1913), xvii, 58.
[21] On the familial nature of Berlin's view of Jewishness, see Margalit 1998. On Jewish literacy as a classless family practice, see Oz and Oz-Salzberger 2012.
[22] Ignatieff 1998, 34.

Berlin seemed to have exempted himself from the Jewish habit of perpetual unease. Of course, he was aware of and affected by the Jewish predicaments encountered in his lifetime – the holocaust, anti-Semitism old and new, the Jewish sensitivities sometimes dubbed "Jewish self-hatred" – but these were fodder for analysis or conversational sparkle, not crosses to bear. Ultimately, Berlin's scholarship helped him to set both Jewishness and Zionism in satisfactory intellectual context, but this double legacy of Mussa-Masha Berlin was in place long before her son became interested in Disraeli, Hess, and Weizmann. He was endowed with an exceptionally secure sense of identity from a relatively early age.

Thus, the compliment Berlin paid Weizmann for his lack of Jewish neuroses could well be applied to Berlin himself. A sly reader might suspect that perhaps it was:

> He was a complete and unbroken personality of immense strength, dignity and political wisdom, he did not suffer from the usual Jewish disabilities, the "ambivalences," the lack of social balance, the uncertainty about what one is and where one belongs, the self-conscious vacillations and doubts and hesitations in the matter of one's proper class or outlook or profession or status. (POI 233)

British playfulness (rather than sportsmanship) and a certain love of mischief, coupled with Russian-Jewish irony, often breezes through Berlin's writings on Jewish themes and persons. This was rare. Twentieth-century Jewish intellectuals of East European origin were often stern and oracular, sardonic rather than ironic. A quintessential case is Berlin's Riga-born contemporary and classmate, "the other Isaiah": Israeli philosopher Yeshayahu Leibowitz. Berlin admired Leibowitz's great mind and ethical depth, and called him "the conscience of Israel," but a certain smile hovers above his truly admiring tribute.[23] Was it Berlin's character or upbringing that allowed him to *enjoy* observing and studying personalities and events of the twentieth century?

His attitude, I suggest, stood him in good stead for one of the two greatest Jewish experiences of the twentieth century: Zionism and the foundation of Israel. It did not serve him well in his dealings with the other pivotal event, the Holocaust. Michael Ignatieff ponders a retrospectively deplorable document that Berlin penned for the Foreign Office in 1944 responding to allegations that the Allies ignored the extermination of Europe's Jews: "Words like 'massacre' suggest that the magnitude of what was happening escaped Berlin's milieu entirely. It was as if his usual sense of reality, the capacity to infer the larger

---

[23] A Hebrew translation of Sir Isaiah's tribute to Professor Leibowitz, on the occasion of his eightieth birthday, appeared in *Ha'aretz*, March 4, 1983. "It is not so much his intellectual attainments and achievements as a thinker and teacher that have made so profound an impression on me ... as the unshakable moral and political stand which he took up for so many years in the face of so much pressure to be sensible, to be realistic, not to let down the side, not to give comfort to the enemy, not to fight against conventional current wisdom," he wrote. Quoted in Goldman 1992, vii. Cf. Dubnov 2012, 43. A Hedgehog, then.

picture from a host of details, deserted him. One wonders, for example, to what extent he thought of his relatives left in Riga."[24] Many of those relatives, including both his grandfathers, had been shot by German and Latvian troops at the edge of mass graves in Rumbula forest on the outskirts of Riga three years earlier.

In a conversation with Ramin Jahanbegloo Berlin opened up on the topic.

R. J. – How did you experience the Second World War as a Jew?

I. B. – I do not think that my reactions were different from those of the vast majority of Jews outside the area controlled by the Germans and Italians. Horror about what was happening was appalling and continuous ... There is something in this connection which I must confess with a degree of shame. I assumed from the very beginning that Hitler meant to inflict terrible sufferings on the Jews – he was a fiend and implacable, that was obvious ... Before 1944 I knew nothing of systematic extermination – the gas chambers. Nobody told me, in England or America; there was nothing about it in anything I read – perhaps that was my own fault ...

R. J. – Were any members of your family killed by the Nazis?

I. B. – Yes. Both my grandfathers, an uncle, an aunt, three cousins,[25] were killed in Riga in 1941.

R. J. – What was your reaction once you knew about the extermination of the Jews? I ask you this question because you haven't written on the subject.

I. B. – I felt exactly like everybody else. I thought that it was the greatest disaster that had ever happened to the Jews, worse than the destruction of the second Temple. What can one possibly say about so great a horror? I didn't change my opinions. I thought that the one thing it proved historically is that Marx and Hegel proved false prophets – that and the hopelessness of assimilation.

(CIB 19–21)

Many would view this rare on-record statement as a very disappointing synopsis of Berlin's personal Holocaust experience.[26] His service in the British embassy in Washington, and his hobnobbing with the Jewish cultural elite of New York, shed dubious light on his confessed blindness to horrors he should have seen, at latest by 1944. His hasty attempt at intellectualization, his fallback on Marx and Hegel, his disconcerting use of the Holocaust as proof for the failure of Jewish–European assimilation, and the smugness of "I didn't change my opinions" can make painful reading.

These maneuvers could also spell a sad tacit admission that Nazism was beyond philosophical analysis. Berlin gave Jahanbegloo an Adorno-like response, seeking refuge in silence. Perhaps Nazism remained outside his historical scope due to its dismal intellectual output. Herder, Kant, Hegel, Fichte, and nineteenth-century ultra-nationalists were players in the genealogy

---

[24] Ignatieff 1998, 122–3.
[25] Henry Hardy deems this "an understatement." By his count, Berlin lost both grandfathers (though one probably died from natural causes), a great-uncle and great-aunt, and five cousins.
[26] Cf. Ignatieff 1998, 122–3; and Dubnov 2012, 172.

of an idea, but Hitler's henchmen were not. The Nazis abandoned the genealogy by storming out of the history of ideas itself. Berlin was unable to follow them.

BERLIN ON ZIONISM AND ISRAEL

In 1934, returning from his tour of Mandate Palestine aboard a ship bound to Italy, Berlin met Abraham Stern, the future Jewish terrorist and founder of the extreme-right (but also somewhat Stalinist, somewhat anarchist) *Lehi* underground.

When they got talking, Isaiah asked him what Stern thought of the recent British move to create a legislative council in Palestine. We shall fight that, Stern said. Why? Because it would give the Arabs representation in proportion to their demographic superiority. But, Isaiah countered, the council was merely advisory. It does not matter, Stern replied. "We will fight and fight, and if blood has to be shed ... " He shrugged expressively ... Both in what he wrote home, and in whom he chanced to meet in return, Isaiah saw the future coming and was already defining his liberal Zionism in response.[27]

The "Stern Gang," it is important to note, was a tiny splinter faction with certain Fascist leanings, more extreme than the Revisionist underground known as the Irgun, and far removed from Weizmann's and Ben Gurion's mainstream Zionist establishment. It is with that establishment that Berlin aligned himself, and against what he called "some Zionist hotheads" (E 9). He was not the only liberal Zionist, of course, but his experience of 1934 urged him to pull his weight in that direction. Still, his Zionism was not (and never became) anchored in liberalism only. He was also a moderate national Zionist, recognizing the value and magic of communal memory and culture – a Herderian Zionist minus the Herderian *Schwerpunkt*-inwardness and cultural incommensurability.[28]

Ben Gurion's mainstream movement was of course labor Zionism – there were differing strands in it, and Berlin adhered to none of them. His aversion to Hegel and Marx kept him away from that stretch in the spectrum. Yet socialist Zionism was never only socialist: it created blends of Hess and Tolstoy, Herzl and Marx. It also soaked up some tenets of the pre-modern Jewish communality of the East European Pale of Settlement.

Here sat the crowded, troubled, self-conscious, multi-ideological mass, the critical mass of *Ostjuden* that – as Berlin deftly argued – made Zionism possible. "[I]t is a truism," he wrote, "that if the Russian Government had not concentrated the Jews in its Western provinces there would not have been this closely packed mass of people of the same tradition, religion, nationality, outlook and ethnic composition ... This was the demographic origin of the Zionist movement."[29]

---

[27] Ignatieff 1998, 80.   [28] See also Morgenbesser and Lieberson 1991, esp. 18–19.
[29] Berlin, "The Achievement of Zionism," 5–6.

This was Mussa Berlin's territory as well as Ben Gurion's and Jabotinsky's. What kept this ideological array of socialists and revisionists, ultra-orthodox and secular, conservative and liberal, Yiddishists and Zionists, together, with remarkably little physical violence within it, was the *shtetl* ethos of a familial, noisy, argumentative, long-winding culture. Far from turning its back on the world and embracing its own uniqueness, the Jewish national movement took up Western liberalism, moderate nationalism (with a minority nationalist strain, which is presently threatening to become a majority in Israel as in other democracies), several types of socialism, and the full gamut of European arts and letters. In its array of Jewish–European confluences, Zionism could play the fox to German nationalism's hedgehog. It remained a fairly successful fox, too, while the Russian whirlwind of social theories that inspired some of its founding fathers receded into totalitarian monism.

Berlin was and remained a follower of the "temperate" Chaim Weizmann, a political pragmatist, evolutionist, and liberal believer in wholesome national restructuring of the Jews in the Land of Israel. No automatic Zionist, evidently able to entertain doubts and opposing views, he was nevertheless a staunch one.[30] Like other liberal Zionists he supported peaceful coexistence with the Arab neighbors, whose own right to national self-definition was fully acknowledged, and full civil equality to Israel's Arab minority. In the 1970s he agreed with the Israeli Left that Palestinian claims for sovereign statehood alongside Israel should be met. During the last two decades of his life he was a strong supporter and fundraiser for the Israeli organization Peace Now. This fell in line with his humanist creed as well as his concept of national belonging.

He was not destined to become an Israeli. Weizmann's cautious, liberal, diplomatic leadership declined after 1944, and became merely symbolic, as the first President of Israel, after 1948. After rejecting an invitation to become President Weizmann's chief of staff, Berlin settled comfortably into the role of an involved diaspora Zionist. In his frequent visits to Israel he became a bemused but fond observer of its young generation, the suntanned sabra Jews whom he (mistakenly) took for a new breed. He felt totally remote from them and oddly proud of them, a stooped bookish grandfather marveling at the young athletes his family had suddenly produced.[31]

At least until the Likud's rise to power in the late 1970s, and perhaps even thereafter, Berlin retained his faith in Israel's moderate majority. This could amount to embarrassing romanticism tinged with Hegelian dialectic: "as a result of this violent clash and collision of various cultures a common denominator is emerging, something identifiable and fascinating, namely a politically liberal, egalitarian human being with a mentality not unlike that of the Italian Risorgimento: on the whole, left of centre, of a kind rightly

---

[30] On Berlin's "paradoxical" support of a vocal anti-Zionist, see Albert 2013, 103–30.
[31] Ignatieff 1998, 123–4, 179; Dubnov 2012, 187f.

admired by English liberals and radicals in the nineteenth century" (POI 173, 194).

Berlin was not blind to the Abraham Sterns of Zionist history. Long before Israeli independence he understood the potential threat of Jewish nationalism. Berlin consistently regarded the majority of the Zionist movement as a proper case of moderate nationalism. Israel's military conflict with Arab states, and the increasingly violent occupation of the Palestinian territories, were an unfortunate reality but not the result of Jewish extremism. Despite the muddy waters of war and conflict, and the relative paucity of gifted public intellectuals (the few exceptions included historian Jacob Talmon) he considered first-generation Israel to be steered with reasonable safety by liberals such as Weizmann and democrats such as Ben Gurion.

Younger Israeli thinkers whom he met in Oxford also struck Berlin as good navigators between the Scylla of Marxism and the Charybdis of nationalism. They also steered clear of imperialist delusions and of the one-state solution, which Berlin opposed.[32] It may have been those young intellectuals who stood for Israel in his assessment of the 1970s, "on the whole left of centre" and solidly liberal-national.

How colonialist was the Zionist vision? Berlin did not ascribe colonial, let alone imperial, aspirations to Eastern European Zionism, coming as it did from the huddled masses of downtrodden Jews. Unlike Western colonialism, not a single early Zionist came to the ancestral land in order to get rich by exploiting the natives. Somewhat different was "the small group of English Jews who accepted Herzl's ideas," and were "to some degree affected by the liberal imperialism of their surroundings," seeking spiritual enlightenment or "a Western outpost in the East, a body of missionaries for Western culture, with peculiar duties and responsibilities towards the undeveloped communities of the east, both Jews and Arabs." But these British purveyors of "the most idealistic liberal conception of the white man's burden" (B 146) were a tiny segment, an ironic episode at the British–Zionist fault-line.

Berlin was uneasy with the conquest ensuing from the 1967 war, which he deemed a just war, and like many Israelis he expected the occupation to end with a tenable peace agreement. But during the last two decades of his life he became more critical of the ongoing occupation and right-wing nationalist radicalization, as did many liberal Israelis and friends of Israel, and more skeptical about the prospects of Israeli–Palestinian peace. A few days before his death, he penned his last text, an appeal for a two-state solution in Israel and Palestine, "for supporting which [Prime Minister Yitzchak] Rabin was

---

[32] In a telling passage in a letter to Noam Chomsky of 1969, Berlin wrote: "I shall introduce Bob [Silvers] to [Amos] Oz and two other Israeli philosophers at Oxford who share his views – one of them belongs to some kind of revolutionary organisation of Israeli students which nevertheless does not favour bi-Nationalism, is anti-Stalinist-Brezhnevist and is ultimately, and very decently, patriotic, without being nationalist"; B 406.

assassinated by a Jewish bigot" (A 568). There was nothing novel in Berlin's endorsement of this solution except for its new and pressing urgency. His rejection of a one state, binational solution, and his insistence that Jerusalem remains the capital of (only) Israel, are in line with his Herderian Zionism, politicized along the moderate branch, still insisting on the need for Jews (and Palestinians) to inhabit their own national territory. His final words on the topic, despite the reference to Rabin's extremist assassin, do not reflect any concern about the path Israelis may be taking from temperate nationhood to inflamed nationalism. He still considered the nationalists among them a minority.[33]

ZIONISM: THEORETICAL ASPECTS

"Unless a creature can determine itself," wrote Berlin of Kantian moral autonomy, "it is not a moral being: whether it is casually determined, or floats about at random, or is subject to statistical laws, it is not a moral agent" (SR 299). In the Jewish case, national emancipation did not endow a hitherto subjugated group with political self-rule; more profoundly, it afforded its individual members a liberty – and hence a dignity – they had never had before.

For Berlin, the Jewish national movement was unique not because it was pioneering; just as the Haskalah was born of the German Enlightenment, Zionism was a child of European national ideas, rising as it did, mainly in the East, among other newly self-conscious nations. But the Jews were a deterritorialized and dispersed minority, endowed with powerful collective memory, soiled by the momentous mythology of Christian and lay anti-Semitism. Their categorization was a confusing chore to modern social science, and a bane to its populist disciples:

> Perpetual discussions went on, particularly during the nineteenth century – the most historically conscious of all ages – about whether the Jews were a race, or solely a religion; a people, a community, or merely an economic category ... But there was one persistent fact about this problem, which was in some respects more clearly perceived by Gentiles than by the Jews themselves: namely, that if they were only a religion, this would not have needed quite so much argument and insistence; while if they were nothing but a race, this would not have been denied quite as vehemently as it has been by persons who nevertheless professed to denote a unique group of human beings by the term "Jew." (POI 143)

The national self-assertion of the Jews was thus a tidying force in Jewish history and also in European political theory. Being a moderate type of national consciousness, Zionism did not compel Jews to join the new project for a nation state, but coaxed them instead. For the first time in many centuries, individual Jews were able to face a political choice: country of birth or ancestral homeland;

---

[33] Cf. CIB 103.

Jewish nationhood or French, British, American; and, for Berlin himself, Oxford or Jerusalem. It was the choice itself that mattered. Zionism had freed all Jews by becoming an available alternative.

This Israel, the positive image that Berlin kept almost intact into the last years of his life, beautifully illustrated two great theoretical themes in his opus. First, it epitomized the role of human choice in history, the capacity of individual thinkers and actors to change the course of events, the triumphal response to Hegelianism, Marxism, nationalism, Fascism – all versions of the intellectual travesty that Berlin called historical inevitability. The Jewish national awakening, borne on the shoulders of visionary individuals, was for Berlin a fine case against the scientization of history, against all manner of determinist creed.[34]

Secondly, Zionism granted the Jews the dignity of political choice. "Before the present situation the tragedy of the Jews was that no real choice was open to them" (POI 219). This new political freedom aligned with the religious and cultural variety offered by modern reformers of Judaism. Regardless of what each Jew might choose, they were no longer Kant's dismal creatures deprived of self-determination:

The creation of the State of Israel has rendered the greatest service that any human institution can perform for individuals – has restored to Jews not merely their personal dignity and status as human beings, but what is vastly more important, their right to choose as individuals how they shall live – the basic freedom of choice, the right to live or perish, go to the good or the bad in one's own way, without which life is a form of slavery, as it has been, indeed, for the Jewish community for almost two thousand years. (POI 222)

In "Jewish Slavery and Emancipation" (1951), still unsure of the young country's liberal instincts, Berlin warned that "a new slavery" may emerge if "the notion [is] hammered into the heads of the ignorant and the confused that as Jews they have virtually no right to live beyond the borders of Israel, and that ... their lives are not their own, but belong to their race and nation and State." Zionism would then become nationalist, "a narrow and fatal and wholly indefensible chauvinism" (POI 223).

By the 1990s, Berlin understood that Zionism's nationalist distortion was not likely to stem from a new enslavement of the Jews, but from the continuing occupation of the Palestinians. "Today Zionism has unfortunately developed a nationalistic phase. The origins of Zionism were very civilized and Herderian," he told Jahanbegloo (CIB 102). What Berlin would have had to say of Israel's public atmosphere today must, alas, be left to the reader's imagination.

CONCLUSION

This chapter has argued that Isaiah Berlin's idea of national belonging is best understood in terms of history and genealogy, which are complex and not

---

[34] See Hanley 2007, 159–80; "Introduction," Crowder and Hardy 2007, 24.

unilinear. The "pathology" of nationalism interested Berlin most, and his story of its growth is a tale of twists and turns in the German history of ideas.

Berlin fully embraced his own belonging to the Jewish nation first and foremost because this was his family. A lifelong Zionist, he felt until the last decade of his life that mainstream Zionism belonged to the moderate flock of civilized modern nations; only in the 1990s did events begin to crack his optimism.

It is hardly surprising that Berlin, like most other political philosophers, worked his biographical experience and emotional commitment into his theory of nationalism. His thoughtful espousal of Zionism dovetailed with his private national belonging. But Berlin's theory did not simply support or confirm national feeling (as long as it is benign); it also showed that feeling itself, the irrational sense of communality, cannot be replaced by rational projections. Not only political values matter; human psychology is no less real or less worthy of respect. The attention to emotional needs, in particular to the yearning to belong, also underlies Berlin's appreciation of Montesquieu, a great precursor of political psychology. The "Counter-Enlightenment" thinkers too, notably Hamann and Herder, understood something deep about human nature that the flat rationalism of liberals ignored at its peril.[35]

This was a risky road to take: isn't group sentiment a mainstay of the evils of nationalism? Berlin was able to avert this slippery slope using a handcrafted tool, a semi-Herderian concept of cultural nationhood, which in his hand remains devoid of exclusivism, and politicized only up to a moderate liberal pitch. Berlin hoped that by rescuing Herder from Fichte's clutch, all national aspirations could blossom peacefully. Some version of this Berlinite Herderism was always present in his philosophical support of all moderate nationhood, including the Jewish quest for liberty.

In Berlin's analysis, however, the Jews differed from other European nations not in the solution, but in the problem. Their plight was no ordinary national minority oppression, because it was also burdened by their dispersion, their exile from ancestral territory, the dormant state of their original language, their religious seclusion, and the constant bane of anti-Semitism. However, these predicaments also made them scholarly, and in modern times cosmopolitan and pluralist. This was the reason that Zionism would never become a sole option; it was only – and wonderfully – an enabler of choice. Here was an unusual and exciting interface of liberty and nationhood: the very optionality of nationhood makes individuals free. Thus, for Berlin, the Jewish national emancipation was perhaps the grandest of all European national emancipations, as well as a valuable historical prop for his own philosophy of liberty.

In other words, whereas all national movements offered their members positive liberty, Zionism and the State of Israel singularly also gave the Jews negative liberty: more doors are now open to me, and because one of them offers

---

[35] See especially Margalit 1997, 74–87; also O'Brien 2016, 79–88.

self-government of Jews by Jews, my scope of political choices has expanded from zero to several. This is perhaps the most interesting uniqueness that Berlin ascribed to the Jewish national case (POI 223–4).[36]

Finally, of all the ideas and images discussed in this chapter, global current affairs at the time of writing reveal the comeback of one crucial force: the bent twig. Berlin (who thought he borrowed it from Schiller) invented this profound metaphor for the violent backlash of wounded nations or social classes. Today it can apply to new groups of disenfranchised citizens in digital-age democracies, men and women who have the vote but lack a voice. Nationalism is reawakened, populism never slept; Berlin's analytic powers and bold metaphors are utterly timely.

---

[36] Cf. POI 179–80; CIB 40–1. See also Dubnov 2007, 320.

11

Negative Liberty and the Cold War

Ian Shapiro and Alicia Steinmetz

Isaiah Berlin's "Two Concepts of Liberty," delivered as his inaugural lecture for the Chichele professorship at Oxford on October 31, 1958, remains his most influential contribution to political philosophy. Published shortly thereafter as a pamphlet by the Clarendon Press, "Two Concepts" established him as one of the leading theorists – if not *the* leading theorist – of the subject writing in English in the twentieth century. Citation indexes stand as emphatic testimony of that status, but perhaps even more so is the reality that the terms *negative liberty* and *negative freedom*, which Berlin – like many successors – used interchangeably, have become commonplace in ordinary usage. They are widely deployed to depict the freedom that is created and preserved when the state acts, if at all, principally to stop people from interfering with one another. "Two Concepts" was presented as an analytical treatment of the differences between it and *positive* liberty, conceived as the freedom *to do* something that might be more or less fully specified, but Berlin was a manifest champion of the negative idea that has become so widely associated with his name.

Berlin was not, as he would be the first to say, negative liberty's original advocate.[1] Hobbes's discussion of "liberty by pretermission" in chapter 21 of *Leviathan* is a close relative at least. So are the robust zones for liberty of conscience and private action carved out in Locke's third *Letter Concerning Toleration* and Mill's *On Liberty*, and – if more ambiguously, as we will see – in Kant's insistence that people should always be recognized as ends in themselves, not mere instruments for the use of others. Berlin was keen to establish that negative liberty has a substantial pedigree and provenance among these and other canonical thinkers as part of his case for its enduring appeal. He stood firm for it, but he did not stand alone.

Even negative liberty's critics affirm its importance. The revival of civic humanism since the 1970s rests, for instance, on self-conscious repudiation of a Berlinian construction of the alternatives. J. G. A. Pocock embraces a version

---

[1] On the antecedents of Belin's political theory, see Cherniss 2013, 144–88.

of the dichotomy by counterposing his virtue-based paradigm to the characteristic liberal focus on legal protections for individuals.[2] Philip Pettit anchors his choice of a third conception of freedom in what he finds unsatisfying in the choice between the negative and positive alternatives.[3] Sensing, perhaps, negative liberty's enduring appeal, Quentin Skinner takes a different tack. His civic humanism centers on reclaiming negative liberty from Hobbes and his successors in a contest in which battles have been lost but Skinner is as yet unwilling to concede the longer war.[4] For the civic humanists, it seems that negative liberty must be displaced, transcended, or co-opted, but it cannot be ignored. Nor were the civic humanists the first to throw down the gauntlet. In *Natural Right and History*, Leo Strauss took aim at the seventeenth-century shift in focus from natural law to the centrality of natural rights, which he read as heralding the modern fetish with individualism – a cousin if not a precursor of the negative idea.[5] From a different perspective, C. B. Macpherson viewed those same developments as ushering in an ideology supportive of the emerging capitalist market order.[6] In this he echoed Marx's polemical footnotes directed at Mill in *Das Kapital* and elsewhere, where the individual's freedom to transact freely is seen to buttress – while it obscures – an exploitative economic order.[7] In these and related formulations, negative freedom's staying power has more to do with ideological considerations than intellectual ones – or at least the two bleed into one another.

It is the staying power that interests us in this chapter. That endurance is all the more remarkable in view of the fact that the negative/positive dichotomy rests on questionable logical foundations. In 1967, Gerald MacCallum Jr. asserted that liberty is a relational concept that ranges over agents, restraining or enabling conditions, and actions.[8] That is, for any claim about freedom it is always possible to ask: "*Who* is free; *from what* restraint *or because of what* enabling conditions; *to do what*?" When people seem to disagree about the meaning of the term "freedom," they are really disagreeing about how to characterize the relevant agent, the relevant restraining or enabling conditions, or the relevant action. Moreover, the restraining or enabling conditions can easily be re-described as one another: one might characterize a prisoner as unfree because of the presence of chains or the lack of a key. Proponents of negative freedom, he argued, tend to focus attention on the first term in the relation – the agent – while describing the second in terms of impediments and leaving the relevant action implicit. Positive libertarians, by contrast, pay less explicit attention to agents, typically speak in terms of enabling conditions, and focus explicit attention centrally on the actions to be performed.

---

[2] Pocock 1985, 39–40; and Pocock 1981, 357–9.   [3] Pettit 1997, 17–79.
[4] Skinner 2008, 211–16.   [5] Strauss 1953, 323.   [6] Macpherson 1962.   [7] Marx 1976, 492.
[8] MacCallum, Jr. 1967, 312–34. For Berlin's own response to MacCallum, see L 36 n.1.

While much of the philosophic writing on freedom now accepts MacCallum's analysis, the persistence of attacks on negative freedom, old and new, suggest that something more is at stake than analytical clear-headedness. They make it obvious that negative freedom carries substantial ideological freight regardless of philosophical considerations. The standard contention is that this has to do with the logic of individualism that undergirds the market behavior of *homo economicus*.[9] Instead, we advance the different – though perhaps complementary – thesis that Berlin's influential formulation is best understood through the lens of the Cold War. Our evidence for this is taken largely from Berlin's letters, published over the past decade. Fascinating in their own right, the letters illuminate Berlin's experience of the ideological context of the 1950s, his agenda in defending negative liberty, and his contemporaries' reaction to that agenda.

Both in his own mind and in the minds of his audience – including such figures as Karl Popper and Friedrich Hayek, who developed comparable accounts of liberty, and George Kennan, for whom the confrontation between positive and negative freedom was "the greatest contest of the age"[10] – Berlin's negative freedom was a bulwark against communism, and particularly the Stalinist form it had taken by the 1950s. Like Popper's "open society" and Hayek's "constitution of liberty," Berlin's negative liberty was welcomed as a repudiation of the oppressive teleology built into Soviet communism. And like Kennan, Berlin saw negative liberty as an integral component of the bulwark that was needed to face down that threat. But unlike other Cold War liberals, Berlin believed that developing a technically sound philosophical defense of negative freedom and repudiating communism, while important, were not enough. He doubted whether people are naturally inclined to opt for freedom, let alone fight for it. As a result, he thought it necessary to develop a powerfully appealing, even romantic, defense of his favored conception of it that differentiated him from such negative libertarians as Popper and Hayek. This brought him, at times, uncomfortably close to positive libertarians such as Rousseau – with whom he wrestled ambivalently for much of his life.

As we discuss in Section II, Berlin agreed with Kennan that the Soviets took advantage of frailties in human psychology for nefarious ends, but he thought those frailties were a good deal older, and ran a lot deeper, than the Soviets' perverse exploitation of them. They are part of what it means to be human as he thought Rousseau understood and exemplified it, and we discount them at our peril. Exploring Berlin's view of the human psychology that underlies both the need for freedom and its vulnerability leads us to discuss what he saw as Kant's successful modification of Rousseau's treatment of the matter in Section III, and his belief that Kant's account of autonomy is a viable – perhaps even the best – philosophical basis for the view of liberty that might win the high political ground. But, perhaps ironically, Berlin was not confident that removing the

---

[9] See Shapiro 1989, 73–6. [10] Gaddis 2011, 416.

external impediments to the negative liberty he prized would be enough for it to triumph. He saw it as a value that must be argued and even fought for, and, partly because of the reasons that give malevolent forms of positive liberty their powerful psychological pull, he was unsure that this battle could be won.

I THE INTELLECTUAL CONTEXT OF THE COLD WAR

The Cold War had a profound impact on all areas of public life, and academia was far from an exception, particularly in the United States, where Berlin was to take up nearly 25 years of visiting appointments, starting in 1949 with a position at Harvard's Russian Research Center. Toward the end of that year, Berlin gave a speech at Mount Holyoke College on "Democracy, Communism and the Individual." This was a high-profile event which included speakers such as Eleanor Roosevelt, Sir Alexander Cadogan, and Abba Eban. Berlin expressed fears that "very grave"[11] consequences might follow for his various contacts in the USSR if his speech was quoted by the *New York Times* reporter present; he nevertheless delivered a speech which he later described as being "somewhat Fascist Beast in character, on how a modus vivendi wasn't really possible between any democracy and 'them', etc." (E 98, note 3) (though his biographer Michael Ignatieff judged Berlin's remarks a "worthy but hardly incendiary sermon"[12]).

While the body of the speech may critique Marx, it is framed as an attack on eighteenth-century rationalism – and principally Rousseau – of which Marxism is described as a particular instance. Berlin's main argument suggested that "the root of communism ... lay in the eighteenth-century belief – expressed in its most extreme form by Rousseau – that there was one right way for human beings to live,"[13] and that "Communism, Fascism and all other totalitarian orders" were an offshoot of that basic proposition (POI 277). But they were not the only offshoot. In his opening paragraph, Berlin submitted that both democracy and communism issue from this same central idea, and that where Marxism went wrong was in thinking that liberty and equality are completely compatible, even as the lesson of the nineteenth century was that they are not.

One can recognize here the pieces of what would become Berlin's celebrated distinction between positive and negative liberty, and of his contention that the former "[denied] that different ideals of life, not necessarily altogether reconcilable with each other, are equally valid and equally worthy," whereas the latter embraced that idea (POI 277). Yet in this early formulation, with

---

[11] In a note to Elizabeth Green, the Director of the Mount Holyoke College News Bureau, Berlin said "I must again beg you not permit any of this to appear in print under my name as the consequences to various persons in the USSR would be very grave, & I should certainly decline to speak if I thought that there [was] any risk of my words appearing in print anywhere." When Green replied that this would not be possible, Berlin apparently decided to speak anyway and agreed to meet briefly with the *New York Times* correspondent; E 98.
[12] Ignatieff 1998, 192.   [13] Ignatieff 1998, 192.

Rousseau taking a central role, Berlin found that in a world with ears keenly attuned to how one would take a position on Marx, Marxism, and the USSR, his eighteenth-century culprit hardly registered an impact, and instead seemed to make him vulnerable to the appearance of defending Marx and Marxism. Accordingly, the day after the event, a write-up of Berlin's speech appeared in the *New York Times* under the headline "Study of Marxism Backed at Parley," in which Berlin's key purpose in the speech was described as "to impress upon [his] audience the importance of studying Marxism, and specifically of not placing a ban upon such studies" (E 99). Berlin felt he had been interpreted "as backing more and more Marxism in American universities and staunchly defending the Russian Revolution and all the other horrors" (E 101) and (apparently now worrying less for his USSR informants than about the possibility that he might be seen as a pro-Marxist) wrote a frantic letter to the *Times* clarifying his position, which was published under the headline "Attitude on Marxism Stated: Dr. Berlin Amplifies his Remarks Made at Mount Holyoke."

In addition to his letter to the *Times*, Berlin also wrote to the Provost of Harvard to assure him that he was not a secret communist, and to George Kennan at the State Department, asking him "to write a reassuring note to the FBI liaison officer at State."[14] The event clearly rattled Berlin profoundly, and even in his indignation he seems to have taken it to heart as a critique of his work and his way of communicating it, for he wrote shortly afterwards that "I feel that the rest of my life will be spent in démentis to people like the Provost of Harvard that I am an ambiguous snake of some sort" (E 100). Berlin seems nonetheless to have walked away from his first stint in the USA with a heartening lesson. In the same letter, he expressed admiration for Eleanor Roosevelt's speech at the Mount Holyoke event, writing "I feel that she really did, almost single-handedly, make it possible for people here to be critical of the USSR and still not afraid of being condemned as Fascist Beasts – the opportunity for an anti-Soviet but 'progressive' attitude." He saw this accomplishment reflected in her clash with Soviet jurist Andrey Yanuar'evich Vyshinsky over civil liberties in the UN General Assembly, commenting that this clash's impact "really does seem to me to be important and very satisfying" (E 101).

These lessons provide an important orienting framework for understanding Berlin's subsequent intellectual trajectory, as well as the larger fabric of intellectual and social pressures within which Cold War political theory operated. On the one hand, there was powerful pressure to place one's thought in clear relationship to the Marxist East, which for Berlin at times would develop into a fight not just over ideas and the meaning of the history of ideas, but also the task of political philosophy as such. On the other hand, there was a fear, even among liberals, that postwar malaise, social transformation, and a kind of temperate, perhaps unfocused commitment to pluralism were

---

[14] Ignatieff 1998, 193.

breeding the possibility for communism to gain root in Western Europe. People worried that the available arguments against communism were essentially negative and technical, and hardly inspiring.

This anxiety is manifest in an exchange between Berlin and Alan Dudley, head of the Information Policy Department in the Foreign Office, in the spring of 1948. In January of that year, the British Foreign Secretary, Ernest Bevin, had expressed the need "to stem the further encroachment of the Soviet tide ... by creating some form of union in Western Europe."[15] But in distinguishing the West from the Soviet encroachment in the East, Bevin remarked on the importance of not just economic and political union, but also of a spiritual component: "if we are to have an organism in the West, it must be a spiritual union."[16] The Working Party on Spiritual Aspects of Western Union was set up in 1948 to explore what this unity would consist of, and apparently ran into immediate difficulties in identifying, as Dudley wrote to Berlin, "common factors in terms of attitudes towards a great variety of things (and ideas) ranging from art to social services." Dudley thought these must ultimately lie in "what philosophical ideas there are which are common to the West" – which he sought Berlin's help in identifying.

Berlin at first responds that he cannot identify any ideas in "technical philosophy" which belong specifically to the West more than the East. "But you do not, of course, mean that. You mean to refer to general ideas, attitudes to this or that activity or form of life etc.," Berlin writes, and then quickly rules out some unwise avenues of approach to the question. First, he says that Hegel, being key to both Marxism and "dominant English philosophy from, say, 1870 to say 1920," is a bad avenue of criticism. He also suggests that pointing to the West as standing for "scientific objectivity [and] pursuit of truth by disinterested means" is a poor strategy since Marxist thought makes the same claims. Finally, Berlin suggests that any meaningful differences "seem to me to boil down to ... conflicting views of social life" (E 45). But even here he suggests that things are not clear-cut: at most, "the West" affirms the protection of civil liberties as a public ideal, believing that without them, justice and liberty are not possible, while "Marxists" believe that the meaningful enjoyment of liberty requires a certain level of economic wellbeing. Ultimately, Berlin recommends that Dudley dispense with the attempt to distinguish "Western" from "Eastern" ideas, and suggests that it would be better to write "a clear & unwooly" liberal manifesto.

---

[15] "Summary of a Memorandum Representing Mr. Bevin's Views of the Formation of a Western Union," in "Foreign Relations of the United States, 1948, Western Europe, Volume III," at https://history.state.gov/historicaldocuments/frus1948v03/d3.

[16] "Address given by Ernest Bevin to the House of Commons (22 January 1948)." Parliamentary Debates. House of Commons. Official Report. Third session of the Thirty-Eight[h] Parliament of the United Kingdom of Great Britain and Northern Ireland. www.cvce.eu/content/publication/2002/9/9/7bc0ecbd-c50e-4035-8e36-ed70bfbd204c/publishable_en.pdf

The pressure to provide intellectual ammunition against communism continued to appear in the impetus for and reception of Berlin's developing work. This is evident from the correspondence which followed the airing of Berlin's BBC 1952 lecture series (*Freedom and Its Betrayal*). The lectures took the form of discussions of six thinkers – Helvétius, Rousseau, Fichte, Hegel, Saint-Simon, and Maistre – who all wrote around the time of the French Revolution, and shared two central things in common. The first was that while they all seemed to Berlin to be concerned with human liberty, "in the end their doctrines are inimical to what is normally meant, at any rate, by individual liberty, or political liberty" (FIB 5). Second, Berlin thought they were all affected by the Newtonian revolution in establishing order in the realm of the sciences in such a way that they sought to find "some simple single principle" (FIB 9) which could establish a similar degree of order within political life. The broadcasts created something of a sensation, inspiring an unprecedented leader column published in *The Times* on December 6, 1952, called "The Fate of Liberty," whose topic was then taken up in the correspondence columns of the paper, to which Berlin himself contributed.

In a letter to Herbert Elliston referencing the *Times* leader, Berlin reacts to the characterization of the purpose of his lectures by journalist Thomas Utley. Utley had described Berlin's argument as that "The need of the twentieth century is not so much for a new political faith (it has had too many) as for a firm foundation for political doubt" (E 343). Berlin agrees that he indeed meant to suggest that there had been too many political faiths, but disagrees with the conclusion that this meant he was calling for systematic doubt. Instead, he suggests that he is calling for "a kind of cautious empiricism" and mentions Popper and Hayek (although the latter with reservations)[17] as writers with kindred projects, although he specifies that this implies

a society in which the largest number of persons are allowed to pursue the largest number of ends as freely as possible, in which these ends are themselves criticised as little as possible and the fervor with which such ends are held is not required to be bolstered up by some bogus rational or supernatural argument to prove the universal validity of ends. (E 350)

Here again, Berlin struggles to articulate this in a way that is not just clear and distinct from (and critical of) the Communist alternative, but also involves some emotional and moral force of its own, i.e. one that is not merely skeptical or hangs mainly on doubt and empirical uncertainty. To some extent, he denied the problem: "I do not see why it is not possible to believe in the various ends in which we do believe with as much fervor and self-dedication as Communists believe theirs" (E 350). But he also expresses a double-edged anxiety: that

---

[17] "I even find myself in some sympathy with the wicked Hayek, although I think he is quite wrong in assuming that political liberty is indissolubly tied to economic private enterprise": Isaiah Berlin to Herbert Elliston, December 30, 1952; E 350.

defenders of the West will not be able to find some (inspiring) way to describe their own moral commitments in contrast to the Soviets; but also that in the process, the West might manifest the very same tendency that it seeks to combat in the enemy – "as people here think is happening in America, what with McCarran Acts etc., although I keep trying to persuade them that this is not so" (E 351).

Here Berlin voiced an anxiety that was pressed in the political domain by George Kennan, someone who greatly admired Berlin and who seems later to have had considerable influence on Berlin's understanding of his own project.[18] Both men were appalled by Joseph McCarthy, whom Kennan saw as meriting at least as much opprobrium as the Marxism he was allegedly rooting out, and whom Berlin deplored as "a sadist who enjoys tormenting the egg-heads who give him a sense of inferiority" (E 435).[19] Indeed, Berlin himself was not immune to the threat. In March of 1953 he worried that he might become the target of a probe at Harvard, and, a few months later, that he might be denied a US visa (E 162, 378). Nor did he think McCarthy was a transient menace who could safely be ignored. As he wrote to Alice James in June of 1953, "I do not for a moment believe in the doctrine of giving him enough rope – enough rope and he will hang everybody else" (E 37). Apart from McCarthy's deleterious effect on American foreign policy and diplomacy, both men worried about his assault on the USA as an appealing alternative to the USSR, one whose allure depended on its embodying the negative freedom that McCarthy was undermining. In Kennan's case this was rooted in his view of what today is called the battle for hearts and minds. Rather than engage in hopeless ideological debates with Soviet leaders, the way to prevail was to build manifestly flourishing democratic capitalist systems that the populations behind the iron curtain would envy. This meant resisting pressures to erode the quality of Western institutions, lest they start resembling those whom they sought to contain.[20]

Berlin's letter to Elliston is frequently cited by others with a different interpretation in view – that Berlin was not an anxious but willing participant in the ideological battles of the Cold War, but rather a proud champion of a version of liberalism free from the fervency which grows out of ideological fault lines, a liberalism which could celebrate moderation and pluralism. Aurelian Craiutu argues, for instance, that "Berlin's anticommunism lacked the fervent zeal of those who saw themselves in an all-or-nothing crusade against communism and thirsted for absolute moral clarity and purity."[21] Similarly, Joshua Cherniss claims that Berlin should be read as principled and

---

[18] Kennan's long standing admiration for Berlin dates to their meeting in the Soviet Union in December of 1945 when Berlin, who Kennan quickly identified as "undoubtedly the best informed and most intelligent foreigner in Moscow," was working for the Foreign Office and Kennan was the State Department's Deputy Chief of Mission: Kennan 2014, 191. On Berlin's relationship with and view of Kennan, see Cherniss 2013, 76.
[19] See also Gaddis 2011, 417.   [20] See Shapiro 2016, 139.   [21] Craiutu 2016, 87.

not just hand-wringing in his resistance to pressures to offer a clearer and more inspiring account of liberalism, asserting that "opposition to crusading was central to his outlook."[22] Our view is not incompatible with these readings. But we contend that Berlin was not merely arguing against passionate, simplistic, or ideological political views. His underlying claim was that those views are compelling to people for a reason, and that they cannot be discounted, no matter how destructive they seem or how much one feels themselves to be immune to their pull. For even in Berlin's rejection of "monolithic ... establishments," his language of choosing between a certain loss in "energy" or "drive" and being "hypnotised by the blood-curdling threats of the enemy into a frame of mind similar to his own" (E 351) reflects his conviction that people commit themselves to such causes for reasons that lie outside the measured logic of trade-offs. Berlin's spirited insistence that we *must* choose operates alongside his darker acknowledgment that in reality people often embrace monolithic conceptions of politics because the mere possibility of choice does not inspire them.

This reading is supported by Berlin's letter to Denis Paul in December of 1952, written in response to Paul's comment that Berlin's lectures might breed complacency among those already opposed to communism and fascism, while doing little to affect those in the West who were sympathetic to socialist ideas. Berlin agreed that he should say more, but struggled to offer any clear prescriptions: "I did try and make it clear that the notion of freedom which I approved of was what the English and French Liberals and Radicals were preaching in the early 19th century as opposed to the German brand, that it was a negative concept, that it was what you call elbow-room freedom, that it largely meant non-interference." But in the end, when that preferred brand of freedom conflicts with other social purposes, "there is no clear solution." As a result, he concluded that "it is all a matter for compromise and balance and adjustment and empirical Popperism etc., and, in short, that the truth, when found, is not dramatic but possibly rather dreary" (E 352). Here Berlin appears both frustrated with Paul's critique and simultaneously troubled by it, and even in defending his approach, he says "I daresay I really avoided crucial issues and should have said something else. I wish you would tell me what" (E 353).

Similarly, in his article on "The Intellectual Life of American Universities" (1949), Berlin does not conclude with a resolute and straightforward rejection of outlooks that promote protection "from the intellectual and moral burden of facing problems that may be too deep or complex to be dealt with by any patented method" (E760), but, rather, a question which evinces genuine grappling with the complex forces that foster such mindsets: "what is to become of us?" Even if Berlin thought anxiety might be necessary in a world of complex and contradictory moral and political institutions and commitments, and we might do well to reject those who promise easy cures to

---

[22] Cherniss 2013, 67.

it (as if it is simply a disease to be treated), the fact of the matter is that anxiety is not a pleasant experience. Indeed, in the closing paragraphs of "Political Ideas in the Twentieth Century" (1950), Berlin explained that "[t]he progress of technological skill makes it rational and indeed imperative to plan, and anxiety for the success of a particular planned society naturally inclines the planners to seek insulation from dangerous, because incalculable, forces which may jeopardize the plan" (L 91).

After "Political Ideas in the Twentieth Century" was published in *Foreign Affairs* in April of 1950, Berlin wrote a letter to the editor, Hamilton Fish Armstrong, in which he remarked on the reception of the article, and particularly the reaction he had received from Charles Bohlen, a US diplomat and an expert on the Soviet Union: "he said he had talked most seriously with George Kennan about it, and they thought it was unfinished (!) and there should have been a long piece explaining why communism cannot last and is contrary to human nature etc., and in effect formally refuting it and its claim to survive" (E 179). Berlin responds that he feels that this might move his exercise in analysis closer to propaganda, and in any case would have required a separate article likely taking the form of "a long coda full of exorcisms against the devil" (E179). Berlin's resistance, in both principled and personal ways, to the ideological pressures issuing from Cold War politics does not mean he was not deeply affected by them. After all, even if he did not give in to pressures to create propaganda, his understanding of the predicament was nonetheless informed by the evident existence of voices he admired that were actively calling for it. And yet, Berlin's response was not simply to combat Soviet communism by championing a notion of freedom at variance with theirs, but also to seek to do so in a way that could account for what made this brand of communism, and other outlooks like it, attractive to its adherents.

II THE PSYCHOLOGY OF FREEDOM

In 1935, while working on what would become his celebrated book on Karl Marx, a 26-year-old Berlin wrote to his undergraduate classmate John Hilton complaining of his troubles: "I am trying desperately to write a book on Marx: & find myself (a) unable to write at all for at least an hour after settling to, (b) when I begin I suddenly let loose a flood of words about Rousseau's influence on the romantic style, & then remember that the relevance needs proving" (F 137). From the first, Rousseau held a deep connection to Marx in Berlin's mind, albeit an uncertain one, and it was a connection that would continue to trouble Berlin throughout his career.[23] But whereas Berlin's Russian would offer him a perspective on Marx denied to many of his English contemporaries, and through it lead him to both his hero Herzen and his perspective on Marx's place in Enlightenment thought via Plekhanov, his position on Rousseau would

---

[23] On the early influences on Berlin's reading of Rousseau, see Cherniss 2013, 161–2.

remain uncertain (and increasingly disdainful).[24] Nearly twenty years later, he would write to Jacob Talmon, speaking again of the connection between Marx and Rousseau, and the troublesome position of the latter in his thought: "Now I must sit down to the hideous task of writing a book. God knows, the awful shadow of Marx broods over the entire thing, and I do not know whether to put him in or keep him out, and I still feel terribly obscure and muddled about Rousseau" (E 354).

All of Berlin's major substantive treatments of Rousseau were in lecture form and remained unpublished, including what would become *Political Ideas in the Romantic Age*, *Freedom and Its Betrayal*, and *The Roots of Romanticism*. Yet even as Berlin would exhibit great reticence in committing his engagement with Rousseau to publication, Rousseau would serve as an influential foundation and point of reference for his most famous insights. And while positive and negative freedom would permeate the language and structure of debates within political theory for the second half of the twentieth century, the debates that would play out concerning his interpretation and use of Rousseau seem to have been comparatively more heated even as they were less influential. Berlin often explained the fervency with which people reacted to Rousseau as a sign of some special, powerful, and enduring insight even as he insisted that Rousseau was not all that innovative or unique at the level of "technical" philosophical ideas. What, then, made Rousseau such a crucial figure in Berlin's understanding of the history of political thought?

Berlin's fullest treatment of the relevant intellectual history was developed as a series of lectures for Bryn Mawr College, prepared and delivered between 1951 and 1952 during his second extended visit to the USA. These lectures, only four of which survived, were drawn from writings that would later become *Political Ideas in the Romantic Age*. In Henry Hardy's preface to the volume, he suggests that it "may be seen as Isaiah Berlin's *Grundrisse*, the ur-text or 'torso', as Berlin called it, from which a great deal of his subsequent work derived" (PIRA ix). Others have agreed that in *Political Ideas in the Romantic Age* one can see the development of arguments central to what, in 1958, would become "Two Concepts."

The opportunity to present the Flexner lectures at Bryn Mawr was fortuitous, arriving as it did at an important moment of transition in Berlin's intellectual trajectory. He was about to return to All Souls as a researcher in the history of ideas rather than in philosophy, which had previously been his appointment. When he accepted the offer to deliver the lectures, Berlin wrote Katherine McBride, the President of Bryn Mawr College, to propose a topic, which he provisionally described as "Six (or however many) Types of Political Theory." He said his reason for choosing this project was that "these seem to me

---

[24] It has often been noted that Berlin's interpretation of Rousseau appears to be one of his weakest treatments of a figure in the history of political thought. For some speculation on where Berlin may have gotten his peculiar reading of Rousseau, see Brooke 2016.

to be the prototypes from which our modern views in their great and colliding variety have developed" (E 182–3), and in a later letter, in which he shifted the proposed title to "Political Ideas in the Romantic Age," he clarified that he wanted to avoid the term "origins" in the title because he felt that would force him to talk about thinkers "like Machiavelli, Hobbes, Locke, etc., who may be the fathers of all these things, but are definitely felt to be predecessors and precursors and, certainly as far as mode of expression is concerned, altogether obsolete" (E 257–8).

This description certainly accords with Berlin's understanding of many of the authors he discusses, and Rousseau in particular. Throughout his writings and letters, Berlin would emphasize that, whatever might have been unique or original about Rousseau's view of liberty, his impact ultimately was a result not of his innovation in ideas, but rather of his "words and imagery" (PIRA 2). What seemed to have grabbed and troubled Berlin about Rousseau was the impact of his language on the moral imagination of Western civilization. He writes years later: "[Rousseau] obviously said things, and said them in a fashion which, for the first time, touched chords, and brought into the open feelings and self-images which have, no doubt, in some sense always been there, but which no one had articulated so vividly and passionately" (B 512). Berlin thought Rousseau hit on something that both exposed and exploited a feature of human psychology with which liberalism had to contend. For this reason, perhaps the most revealing context for understanding how Rousseau would shape Berlin's famous division of liberty appears in a letter in which Berlin does not mention Rousseau at all.

In May of 1950, Kennan wrote to Berlin, commenting on the latter's "Political Ideas in the Twentieth Century." Kennan offered a more psychological analysis of totalitarianism than Berlin had put forward, to which he added this emotional appeal against what he took to be the heart of the phenomenon:

I really believe that this that the totalitarians have done – this taking advantage of the helpless corner of man's psychic structure – is the original sin. It is this knowledge which men were not supposed to develop and exploit... For when a man's ultimate dignity is destroyed, he is killed, of course, as a man. This exploitation of his weakness is therefore only another form of taking human life arbitrarily and in cold blood, as a result of calculation and not of passions... The success of civilization seems somehow to depend on the willingness of men to realise that by taking advantage of this Achilles' heel in man's moral composition, they shame themselves as well as others; on their readiness to refrain from doing so; and on their sticking to the rational appeal which assumes – perhaps in defiance of the evident – that in the long run each man can be taught to rise above himself. (E 212–13)

When Berlin at last responded in February of 1951, he began by saying that he had many times attempted to write back but had felt that he had not been capable of a worthy response, and even now felt that what he had to offer was chaotic and scattered. This sentiment might be chalked up to Berlin's tendency to self-deprecate, except for the intensity and length of the letter that followed, in which Berlin ranged over many topics, including the Holocaust, the Soviets, Hegel, and Marx, grouping them together under a common, central problem. "I must begin by saying that you have put in words something which I believe not only to be the centre of the subject," Berlin writes,

> but something which, perhaps because of a certain reluctance to face the fundamental moral issue on which everything turns, I failed to say; but once forced to face it, I realise now that it is craven to sail round it as I have done, and moreover that it is, in fact, what I myself believe, and deeply believe, to be true. (E 213–14)

Moreover, Berlin suggests that it is likely that a person's attitude on this question determines the entirety of their moral outlook.

The question that Berlin identifies at the heart of Kennan's observation comes down to nothing less than what it means to be a human being, and, therefore, the true "evil" involved in denying a person that status. For Berlin, this turns on a specific interpretation of the Kantian imperative to treat people as "ends in themselves" based on the consciousness of choice, however narrowly constrained or tortuous that choice may be; and "that all the categories, the concepts, in terms of which we think about and act towards one another ... all this becomes meaningless unless we think of human beings as capable of pursuing ends for their own sakes by deliberate acts of choice – which alone makes nobility noble and sacrifices sacrifices" (E 214). In this view, what made the Nazi (and Soviet) practices so horrifying was not just the deeds themselves, but, more importantly, the deception that accompanied them:

> Why does this deception, which may in fact have diminished the anguish of the victims, arouse a really unutterable kind of horror in us? The spectacle, I mean, of the victims, marching off in happy ignorance of their doom amid the smiling faces of their tormentors? Surely because we cannot bear the thought of human beings denied their last rights – of knowing the truth, of acting with at least the freedom of the condemned, of being able to face their destruction with fear or courage, according to their temperaments, but at least as human beings, armed with the power of choice. (E 216)

Berlin thought even in desperate circumstances, even facing degrading, certain death, a human being could still make choices about how to respond to his or her fate, and what mattered was not that one's deeds would be witnessed or remembered by others (as it would for Hannah Arendt), but rather that, from one's own perspective, "the possibility of goodness ... is still open" (E 217). Without this ability and willingness to choose, Berlin suggested, "there are no worthwhile motives left: nothing is worth doing or avoiding, the reasons for existing are gone," and there remained no framework for moral evaluation of self or other – and therefore, no moral identity as such. This conviction motivated Berlin's rejection of Hegel and Marx. For Marx and Hegel, Berlin argues, the moral question "what is good?" has a correct answer, and therefore being irrational coincides with being immoral. In this view, success comes to define the good and failure comes to define the wicked. In contrast to the Hegelian/Marxist view, the morality of the nineteenth century, and "in particular in the romantic period," suggests that a person's motive to serve an idea or "bear witness to something which he believes to be true," separate from whether one agrees with the aims or how one evaluates the consequences, is something always to be admired. Berlin uses Don Quixote to bring out the contrast. From a Hegelian or Marxist perspective on morality, Quixote is both absurd and immoral, whereas for the liberal, Quixote can be admired even when he is somewhat ridiculous.

While Berlin thought this moral outlook lay "at the heart of all that is most horrifying both in utilitarianism and in 'historicism' of the Hegelian, Marxist type" (E 217), he hardly thought it was limited to that. He agreed with Kennan that the phenomenon was psychological in origin, but he resisted Kennan's view that it was some perversion or manipulation specific to the Soviets. Instead he saw it "as an extreme and distorted but only too typical form of some general attitude of mind from which our own countries are not exempt" (E 219). For this reason, Berlin also doubted that the West would win this ideological war through moral purity and commitment to its principles and institutions alone; or that it could triumph absolutely, or without turning into "inverted Marxists" in the process of triumphing. The battle for the modern soul was larger, deeper, and older than the conflict between the West and the Soviets.

III FREEDOM'S INSECURITY

Berlin's exchange with Kennan provides a useful framework for viewing what Berlin's concern with freedom really was – and why its division into positive and negative varieties would have seemed so illuminating and useful to both him and his contemporaries. He saw positive freedom, or at least the variants of it that were likely to gain traction in real politics, as posing dangerous threats to the freedom of choice that he prized. The danger was not merely that proponents of positive freedom typically traffic in monistic conceptions of the good life. In politics, the more serious danger was that these monistic conceptions would be imposed on others in the name of making them "genuinely" free.[25]

But a simple blanket condemnation of freedom's positive varieties would not be a viable avenue of attack. Berlin was convinced that the vision of freedom at

---

[25] Commentators have noted that Berlin tended to slip from the plausible claim that positive libertarianism permits the endorsement of monistic conceptions of the good to the more debatable one that positive libertarianism requires such a commitment. On this subject, see Gustavsson 2014, 276–91; Crowder 2015b, 271–8; and Gustavsson 2015a, 279–84. We are inclined to think that Berlin might have conceded that positive liberty need not require a commitment to a monistic conception of the good, yet still have insisted that the variants of positive liberty that are likely to gain purchase in politics would involve monistic conceptions.

the heart of liberalism had both positive and negative aspects, and thus could not be meaningfully reduced into its fully negative form without losing a considerable part of its moral force. Indeed, what Berlin found so puzzling and enchanting about the romantics, and Rousseau in particular, was that they seemed, through exactly the same central moral insight, to be the inspiration of both liberal–democratic moral sensibilities and the moral justification driving the Soviet political project. Berlin sees both tendencies as admiring individuals' self-sacrifice to ideals higher and greater than themselves; but for the former, this can only happen on the individual level through conscious choice, whereas for the latter, it can be enacted and justified through – if it does not positively require – a collective political project.[26]

In Rousseau, Berlin finds this tension over the moral identity of the human being – and the logic that serves both strands – at its muddled apex. Rousseau saw liberty as an absolute value – and, like Berlin himself, as what made human beings human:

human freedom was to him what the possession of an immortal soul was for orthodox Christians, and indeed it had an almost identical meaning for him ... To rob a man of his freedom was to refuse him the right to say his word: to be human at all; it was to depersonalise him, to degrade or destroy his humanity, in other words those characteristics to maintain and promote which was the sole justification of any action; justice, virtue, duty, truth, the morally good and bad, could not exist unless man was a free being capable of choosing freely between right and wrong, and therefore accountable for his acts. (PIRA 144)

It was this passion, intensity, and absoluteness that made Rousseau unwilling to limit or curtail the freedom of the individual in any way for the sake of social existence. Therefore, Berlin argued, Rousseau required that any solution to the difficulties of social and political organization must necessarily include "the total preservation of absolute human freedom – the freedom from invasion of one human personality by another, the prohibition of all coercion and violence, of the crushing of one human will by another or the maiming of one will to make it serve another's egoistic purposes" (PIRA 115).

The flip side of embracing such an absolute conception of freedom is that any political authority, if it is to be compatible with protecting that freedom, must also be absolute. Rousseau's solution was, for Berlin, "the mysterious, the unique point of intersection of the two scales of value. Men must freely want that which alone is right for them to want, which must be one and the same for all right-minded men" (PIRA 116). Rousseau thus evinced two failings that ultimately led liberty's most avid defender to become its worst enemy: on one hand, the intensity of desire for freedom, and on the other hand, the idea that in

---

[26] Joshua Cherniss remarks that this distinction, which (following Berlin in *Political Ideas in the Romantic Age*) he describes as "humanistic and non-humanistic conceptions of liberty," may have been the more crucial distinction for Berlin than the positive and negative conceptual divide which is more commonly and enduringly associated with his name. See Cherniss 2013, 201–3.

being truly free we must necessarily arrive at the same, universal answer. But to attack intensity of commitment to freedom threatened to undermine Western liberalism in the context of the Cold War. Intensity of commitment to liberty had to be both protected and checked. Berlin thus made Rousseau's second failing – his monism and faith in ultimate consensus – the main target of his critique, while continuing to assent to Rousseau's view of freedom as basic to the human condition.

This presents a paradox: Berlin seems to have wanted to defend the absolute value of human liberty, at the same time that he thought the only way this liberty could be defended required viewing it as a choice among others. But how can liberty both be an absolute value and also be available for the logic of political trade-offs?[27]

This paradox might have been resolvable as a philosophical matter for Berlin; indeed, his engagement with Kant's legacy shows how he might have thought this possible. Berlin contends that Kant's vital innovation was to sharpen Rousseau's distinction between humanity's "rational and 'animal' nature" by granting us some metaphysical distance from nature, such that our moral identity cannot be reduced entirely to whatever unity is believed to exist in our empirical nature. This was "Kant's specific contribution and the basis of the romantic doctrine of man, who stands, in Herder's words, intermediate between nature and God, beasts and angels, touching at one extremity the mechanical world of the sciences, and at the other the spiritual realm revealed only in moments of the special illumination peculiar to spiritual beings" (PIRA 148). In other words, our spiritual nature (and the domain of our freedom) could be revealed only in the act of choice, which could never be dictated to us without infringing on the specifically human quality of our action (A 89).[28] Indeed, Berlin's conception of what it means to treat others as "ends in themselves" emphasizes the respect for choice over self-actualization: "that every human being is assumed to possess the capacity to choose what to do, and what to be, however narrow the limits within which his choice may lie, however hemmed in by circumstances beyond his control" (E 214). Respect for

---

[27] For discussion of Berlin's attempt to blunt the tension that gives rise to this paradox by distinguishing pluralism from relativism, see Smith, Chapter 8 in this volume.

[28] The rational universalism of Kant's thought and the ease with which it translated into the logic that propelled romantic nationalism made Berlin wary about wholeheartedly endorsing him. For instance, responding to Noel Annan's drafted introductory essay to *Personal Impressions*, Berlin clarified his views on Kant as follows: "I am deeply pro-Kantian on certain issues, e.g. his obscure but epoch-making doctrine of freedom of the will, his concept of the moral autonomy of the individual, his doctrine of human beings as ends in themselves, and of moral values as constituted by human commitment to them ... So I am not to be taken as an opponent of Kantian morality *tout court* ... I think that if I am described as wanting to throw doubt on any moral or political system which is founded on, or includes, an unalterable hierarchy of values binding on all men at all times in all places, capable of providing an objective and unalterable solution to every moral and political (and aesthetic) problem, this would be true. But not much more than this." Berlin to Annan, October 2, 1978; A 89.

choice certainly does not promise self-mastery, but it also does not preclude this possibility.

But the psychological problem remained. For Berlin, the danger regarding freedom was the tendency to equate freedom with the realization or pursuit of some political goal, even if in the process of realizing that goal it might seem necessary or expedient to sacrifice one's capacity for individual choice. Freedom rallies us, but choice often confronts us as a burden. This is not simply because choices usually appear to us only in uncertain light, where information is incomplete, and the impact of our action as yet unknown. It is also because choices are often tragic, and their tragic nature issues specifically from the fact that not all good things go together. The great challenge and importance of freedom for Berlin "is that it is involved in the necessity for these hideous choices, the making of which liberals should certainly regard as an end in itself" (E 656). Some varieties of positive liberty, particularly in the Marxist form, offer emancipation from having to make such tragic choices. Berlin believed that this could be particularly attractive and powerful in a world caught in the frequently inefficient and often unromantic demands of pluralism.

This raises the question whether Berlin was concerned with the nature of freedom as such, or with our psychological vulnerability. Writing to Karl Popper in 1959, several months after "Two Concepts" first appeared, Berlin insisted that

> the whole of my lecture, in a sense, is an attempt at a brief study ... of the way in which innocent or virtuous or truly liberating ideas ([know yourself] or sapere aude or the man who is free although he is a slave, in prison, etc.) tend (not inevitably!) to become authoritarian & despotic and lead to enslavement and slaughter when they are isolated & driven ahead by themselves. (E 682)

Did Berlin think this phenomenon was unique and limited to freedom, or did he think freedom merely constituted a clear, identifiable example of a larger feature of human psychology? The answer seems to fall between these options: Berlin thought the psychological vulnerability was larger than freedom, but (positive) freedom was a particularly dangerous and malleable trigger of that vulnerability.

In the midst of the Cold War, to claim that Anglo-American democracy and Soviet communism were, philosophically speaking, two sides of the same coin would have been a difficult proposition, even if some of what Berlin said might seem to imply this. Western Europe seemed to be under political, economic, but also *spiritual* threat as the Soviets encroached on Eastern Europe. On a more personal level, Berlin perhaps (as he himself often confessed) was excessively anxious to please others. In any case, the lasting impact of "Two Concepts" suggests that it touched a nerve in the broader intellectual culture. When Karl Popper first read the work, he wrote to Berlin: "I am delighted by your clear distinction between what you call negative and positive freedom; in your own confession of faith – even though it is only implicit, it is no less open and forceful – for negative freedom; by your exposition of the dangers of the ideology of positive freedom" (E 680). Yet Berlin appears to have been, or to have become, conscious that the distinction between positive and negative liberty was flawed. Two years before his death, Berlin wrote to Michael Walzer that he believed that there was a way of distinguishing types of liberty other than the positive/negative dichotomy. This was to distinguish between liberty (including both positive and negative varieties) that exists as a value among other possible values that a society might choose to promote or curtail. "But," he clarifies, "there is another more basic sense of liberty, which is ability to choose *telle quelle* – as such" (A 517–18 and UD 287–9).[29]

In the same letter to Walzer, Berlin returned to his anxieties about the vulnerability of liberty. Following his hero Herzen, Berlin suggests that

> men do not really all seek liberty – security, yes, but liberty? ... all men seek security, only some seek liberty. And even if Rousseau denounces the former as a disgraceful choice of slavery, they still are as they are. I cannot pretend that human beings as such (even if I do) put liberty as a primary value, with a special status. I think that simply as a fact that is not the case. (A 518)

Berlin feared not so much any particular political or material condition, as the psychological vulnerability to manipulation, the tendency to submit to some grand planner or inspiring vision of political order. This threat could appear at any time, but in particular during those times when it was easiest to feel lost, displaced, or torn by conflicting impulses. Writing to a friend shortly after the publication of *Four Essays on Liberty* in 1969, Berlin remarks that he doubts his message will register with the students of the present, lamenting:

> I have a feeling that the Gods of yesterday have failed the young, that just as the Soviet Union can no longer be believed in with that utter and guileless faith which so many found so easy to hold in the 1930s, so the Welfare State, prosperity, security, increasing efficiency etc. do not attract those young who feel the need to sacrifice themselves for some worthy ideal ... and that they are desperately searching for some form of self-expression which will cause them to swim against some sort of stream and not simply drift in a harmless way, too comfortably, with it. (EB 392)

Negative liberty was, for Berlin, a rare and precious human accomplishment, which humanity might prove incapable of sustaining. Berlin worried that the lack of concrete prospects, of figures and projects to rally around and adversaries to fear, was perhaps an even more dangerous breeding ground than the threat of Soviet encroachment. Between the ills of fear and ennui in the surrounding political landscape as he perceived it, Berlin concluded that fear may be the better option. After all, fear can be tempered, met with calls for moderation and skepticism; but ennui only stirs the longing to find a cause for which to sacrifice oneself.

---

[29] On this distinction between "basic" and political liberty, see Cherniss 2013, 193–9.

IV CONCLUSION

We suggested at the outset that negative liberty's staying power was buttressed by the Cold War, both for Berlin and for those who attended to his arguments in the 1950s and '60s. Evidence adduced from his correspondence, forays into the media, and other ancillary writings support this contention. Berlin was acutely sensitive to being perceived or portrayed as soft on Marxism in any of its forms, and he was gratified when voices on the left began criticizing the USSR. He shared the antipathy of Cold War liberals such as Popper, Hayek, and especially Kennan for the Soviet Union's virulent oppression, and he welcomed the elective affinities that they and others discerned between his views and theirs.

Yet Berlin's account was distinctive nonetheless. Ironically, perhaps, in view of Kennan's reputation as a hardboiled political realist, Berlin found his outlook too sanguine. Kennan believed that the Soviet experiment was bound to fail because its economic model was unsustainable and its imperial ambitions would lead it to become overextended. All the West had to do was contain it behind the iron curtain, rebuild visibly prospering Western democracies, resist the McCarthyite temptation to emulate authoritarian practices in the ostensible defense of freedom, and wait.[30] Patience and resolution would be enough for the West to prevail.

Berlin was not convinced. Despite sharing Kennan's attitude toward the Soviets and his hostility to McCarthyite impulses in the West, Berlin was doubtful that Kennan's recipe was a sufficient guarantor of the kind of freedom – geared to protecting pluralism – that they both prized. He agreed that fear and insecurity made people all too easily manipulated by the Soviets, but, because he saw that fear and insecurity as deeply rooted features of the human condition rather than artifacts of the Cold War confrontation, Berlin saw no reason to believe that malevolent variants of positive freedom would cease to be threats in the future. By the same token, Berlin could never have endorsed Hayek's view that "spontaneous order" would be the blossoming byproduct of human interaction if government simply got out of the way.[31] Indeed, one helpful byproduct of bringing the Cold War lens to bear on Berlin's account of negative liberty is to dispatch the distortions that result from reducing it to a possessive individualist ideological creed. In this respect, Berlin is a useful ally in Skinner's quest to rescue negative freedom from Hobbes and his successors, if not in a civic humanist idiom.

Berlin saw people's instinct for freedom as halting and fragile, not a coiled spring that would regain its natural form if only the compressing impediments were removed. Commentators such as Gina Gustavsson emphasize Berlin's worry that people who see freedom as self-mastery can become dangerous partisans of positive liberty, committed to obliterating freedom in the name of preserving it.[32] Here we have sought to illuminate the corollary of this concern

---

[30] Shapiro 2007, 32–6, 42–6.   [31] Hayek 1960, 160.   [32] Gustavsson 2014, 276–91.

that worried Berlin just as much: that champions of negative freedom would continue to find it difficult, and perhaps even impossible, to get traction for their view because it lacked positive liberty's mesmerizing potential. Monistic conceptions of human purposes threaten human freedom, but when push comes to shove people might not care – particularly when their sense of security is in doubt. Berlin believed that we have to take that possibility seriously, revealing a Hobbesian streak in his view of the human psyche. The Hobbesian solution was no more available to Berlin than was Rousseau's oxymoronic dictum that people should be forced to be free. What appealed to Berlin about Rousseau was his passion for freedom, but Berlin doubted that it could be pressed into the service of sustaining negative freedom through the temptations and vicissitudes of real politics.

The Cold War was an incubator for Berlin's defense of negative freedom, but he discerned threats to it that ran deeper than the particular malevolent brand of positive freedom at the heart of Soviet communism. They are rooted in human insecurity, and he feared that they would likely become more serious in circumstances where that insecurity increases. From our post–Cold War vantage point it seems obvious that Berlin's concerns were prescient and well-founded. Since the collapse of Soviet communism, fundamentalisms that submerge the human agency Berlin valued in totalizing ideologies have flourished to a degree that would likely have surprised even him. And insecure voters in Western democracies have been all too willing to throw their support to leaders who show open contempt for negative liberty and the institutions on which it depends. A Berlinian moral of this story is that unless the champions of negative liberty find ways to diminish the insecurity that feeds people's susceptibility to such appeals, all bets are off.

12

Isaiah Berlin: Contested Conceptions of Liberty and Liberalism

Alan Ryan

Isaiah Berlin was such an engaging writer – and even more engaging *viva voce* – that writing about his work presents unusual difficulties. One is that it can seem pointless. He wrote both engagingly and transparently; the task of explaining what he meant by what he wrote appears to have been made otiose by the person best placed to undertake it. In much the same way, the commentator's task of situating Berlin in the intellectual landscape is one that Berlin was better able to perform on his own behalf than anyone writing about him, both for obvious reasons, and because 'figures in a landscape' was his preferred mode of writing the history of ideas. His essays on historical figures from Machiavelli to Mill give the impression that he not only knows all there is to be known about them, but has been discussing their views with them within the past half-hour. This talent for ventriloquism yielded impressive results when he wrote about figures who were little known to Anglophone readers at the time, such as Vissarion Belinsky and Alexander Herzen in the 1950s,[1] or J. G. Hamann[2] in the 1960s; and it served his talent for revealing better-known writers in a new light, as in perhaps the best known of all his work, the long essay on Tolstoy's philosophy of history that made 'The Hedgehog and the Fox' one of the best known and most exploited antitheses in Anglophone intellectual life.[3]

I have written a good deal about Berlin elsewhere.[4] Here, I try to avoid more than the inescapable minimum of repetition, but some of what follows will inevitably be familiar to anyone who has read my previous work. After a sketch of the argument of *Two Concepts*, I summarise my own views on the concept of liberty and positive and negative conceptions of liberty, to avoid a running

---

[1] 'A Remarkable Decade', first published as four essays in *Encounter*, 1955–6, republished in RT.
[2] *The Magus of the North: J. G. Hamann and the Origins of Modern Irrationalism*, republished in TCE.
[3] *The Hedgehog and the Fox: An Essay on Tolstoy's View of History*, Weidenfeld & Nicolson, London, 1953, republished in RT.
[4] Most of it is collected in Ryan 2012.

commentary on every twist and turn of Berlin's argument in *Two Concepts*. I then turn to the question of what kind of liberalism Berlin espoused; again, I discuss Berlin's conception of value pluralism – the *idée maîtresse* of *Two Concepts* and much else – only briefly, in order to focus on the political implications of the lecture.[5] I set my discussion against, and in the context of, another famous discussion of two concepts of liberty, namely Benjamin Constant's essay on *The Liberty of the Ancients Compared with that of the Moderns*.

Berlin's liberalism closely resembles the liberalism that Constant defends in the work he wrote some years before his lecture on the liberty of the ancients and the moderns, *The Spirit of Conquest and Usurpation*, in which Constant's focus, like Berlin's, was on the dangers posed to liberty both by tutelary projects of instilling virtue, and attempts to impose uniformity.[6] A sentence from *The Spirit of Conquest* provided the epigraph for the introduction that Berlin wrote for *Four Essays on Liberty*: 'l'on immole à l'être abstrait les êtres réels; l'on offre aux peuple en masse l'holocauste du peuple en détail' ['Real beings are sacrificed to an abstraction; individual people are offered up in a holocaust to the people as a collectivity'] (L 3).[7] Constant is (or, at any rate, was when Berlin wrote) better known as the author of the romantic novel *Adolphe* than as a political thinker, but Berlin cites Constant along with Mill as an influential theorist of modern liberalism early in *Two Concepts* and picks up the theme of *The Liberty of the Ancients* a few pages from the end of the lecture when he denies that popular sovereignty is a form of freedom at all (L 168, 208–12). But there are some interesting differences between *The Liberty of the Ancients* and Constant's earlier discussion, as well as between Constant and Berlin, that illuminate both the strengths of *Two Concepts* and what some critics see as *lacunae*. It need hardly be said that the object of the exercise is not to add to recent scholarship on Constant,[8] but to shine whatever light one discussion of 'two concepts of liberty' may shed on its successor almost a century and a half later.

I TWO CONCEPTS

One question that this chapter sets out to answer is whether Berlin's liberalism was in interesting ways apolitical, or even anti-political. One recent occupant of Berlin's chair has argued that it was: that Berlin ignored one of the central questions for political theorists, that of the constitutional arrangements that would secure citizens' human rights.[9] My reason for invoking the shade of Benjamin Constant is that he held something very like Berlin's views on

---

[5] Discussed at book length by Crowder 2004. [6] Constant 1988, 51–167.
[7] L 3, quoting *De l'esprit de conquête et de l'usurpation dans leur rapports avec la civilisation européenne*, part 1, ch. 13, 'De l'uniformité' Constant 1997, 169. Cf. Constant 1988, 77.
[8] Holmes 1984; Rosenblatt 2014. [9] Waldron 2013.

liberty, but devoted a great deal of attention to constitutional issues.[10] Moreover, Constant's best-known contribution to political theory, so far as Anglophone readers are concerned, was itself a lecture on 'two concepts of liberty', *La liberté des anciens comparée à celle des modernes*.[11] Although he does not say so in *Two Concepts,* Berlin's defence of a negative conception of liberty was a defence of an essentially 'modern' conception of liberty, something other and more than the conception of liberty defended by Pericles. Berlin acknowledged a debt to Constant in two subsequent essays on liberty, written in 1962 but not published until some forty years after *Two Concepts* (L 283–6 and 287–321).[12]

Two Concepts of Liberty was Berlin's inaugural lecture as the Chichele Professor of Social and Political Thought Theory in 1958. The chair was a recent creation, and Berlin only its second occupant. His predecessor was G. D. H. Cole, author of a six-volume history of socialism, and an enthusiast for guild socialism. Guild socialism is a forgotten taste, to the regret of many of us. The point of mentioning it here, however, is that anyone writing about guild socialism was inescapably obliged to give an account of what political and economic arrangements guild socialism implied. It was a form of corporatism; the term has ugly connotations, but need not have. Corporatism was tainted by its association with Fascism, but in its liberal or socialist forms corporatism is anti-statist, since it holds that power should be devolved to institutions that occupy a salient role in individual lives and which help to order those lives and represent their members' needs to more all-embracing and, in the usual sense, 'political' bodies.

The state is a residual mechanism, coordinating the 'guilds' that deal with our everyday lives, and maintaining the institutions of the criminal law. Bertrand Russell's little book on *Roads to Freedom* saw guild socialism as the solution to the problems of an unloved capitalist economy; socialist anarchism was attractive but impractical; proletarian dictatorship of the Soviet variety was practicable but tyrannical; guild socialism could free workers from the tyranny of capitalist employers, without subjecting them to the tyranny of a Lenin or a Trotsky. Cole was no admirer of Russell, who, he thought, suffered from delusions of grandeur and wished to set up as a philosopher king. Nonetheless, he saw that Russell was engaged in a perfectly rational exercise in political analysis, spelling out the way a society that took individual liberty seriously should organise its political and economic life.

The relevance of all this to the discussion at hand is that G. D. H. Cole took the remit of 'social and political thought' to include the discussion of all and any social and political institutions about which thinkers of his own and earlier times had interesting ideas. Berlin was strikingly uninterested in social and political institutions. I share the sense that this unconcern is a lacuna in

---

[10] Constant 1988, 171–305. [11] Constant 1988, 309–28.
[12] "Liberty" and 'The Birth of Greek Individualism', L 283–6 and 287–321.

Berlin's work, and want to explore the reasons for its absence a little further. One possible reason is local, personal, and perhaps of biographical interest only. There were two chairs of politics when Berlin became Chichele Professor in 1957; the other, the Gladstone Professorship of Government, was occupied by Max Beloff. Both carried fellowships at All Souls. There was also a chair of International Relations attached to Balliol. The study of political institutions or 'government' at the time was, by the standards of any serious American department of politics, government, or political science, seriously underdeveloped. The 'political institutions' paper in Politics, Philosophy, and Economics (PPE) was not a paper in comparative politics, but as was often said, a paper in 'consecutive politics'; students spent a couple of weeks mugging up on the formal institutions of Britain, France, the United States, and Russia, one after the other.

The tyranny of the final examination meant that examiners had to be cautious about asking for much in the way of comparison between one political system and another, because a student was required to 'display knowledge' of only three of the four countries, and was vulnerable to questions requiring a comparison involving the country they hadn't studied. 'Empirical' politics was thus historical, descriptive, and – not inevitably, but in fact – atheoretical. None of this was likely to interest Berlin. Personalities came into it. Berlin described Max Beloff to me as 'a swot', to Jenifer Hart as 'perfectly decent' but 'silly and strident' (A 216); he thought he was intellectually second-rate (A 227). Beloff in turn seemed to dislike philosophers both on principle and in person. He could be very amusing, and he was an accomplished public speaker; but his jokes usually carried a sneer, as though he was working off a grudge. He must have found Berlin hard work; he certainly found the disparity in esteem between philosophy and his own discipline galling. However, personal antipathies, to the extent that they existed, would not have deterred someone who was more curious about social, economic, and political institutions than Berlin was. Moreover, Berlin had many friends who were more institutionally minded than he. The more plausible view is that Berlin simply followed his own instincts as a philosopher and intellectual biographer.

This is not the place to analyse his strengths and weaknesses in that field, beyond observing that if ideas for Berlin came attached to the personalities whose ideas they were, his account of those personalities was shaped by the ideas that he thought of as their particular contribution, for good or ill. Thus, Rousseau was conscripted to the discussion of what Jacob Talmon characterised as 'totalitarian democracy'; he was the begetter of dangerous doctrines, among them the identification of the General Will with Reason, and that with the *moi commun*, and the doctrine that my true or real self is identical with the majority will of my political community (when it is confronted with the right question). Berlin never displayed the curiosity that might lead a reader of Rousseau to wonder how his explanation of the conditions of legitimate authority in the first few chapters of *The Social Contract* relates to the later discussions of republican government, or what the twentieth-century implications for representative democracy might be of Rousseau's insistence that elective aristocracy was the best practicable form of government. It is perhaps nit-picking to wish that Berlin had not assigned Rousseau to the 'wrong' side of the debate between the two concepts of liberty and that he never allowed himself to be unsettled by the fact that Kant regarded Rousseau as the Newton of the moral sciences. Kant's insistence that 'out of the crooked timber of humanity, no straight thing was ever made' was very much to Berlin's taste. Berlin's assault on theorists whom he describes as *grands simplificateurs* or the inspiration of *grands simplificateurs* gained in rhetorical force by engaging in a certain amount of simplification itself.

The basic mechanism of *Two Concepts* is simple. Negative liberty answers the question 'within what range of activities may I act as I choose without anyone else saying me nay?', while positive liberty answers the question 'who or what is the source of control of my actions?' (L 168–9). The motivation for drawing the distinction in this way is not complicated. On the one hand, Berlin was anxious to insist as a measure of what we might call mental hygiene that freedom is one thing, and other values something else. This was anything but a matter of simple intellectual tidiness. Passing off other values as if they were all aspects of freedom was the route to political disaster. In the context of the defence of liberalism, the two competing values to be distinguished from liberty uppermost in Berlin's mind were democracy and economic equality. He was not opposed to either, but was actively opposed to their conflation with liberty. There is no evidence that Berlin tried to come to terms with Ronald Dworkin's claim that equality rather than liberty was the fundamental value of liberalism,[13] or that he paid much attention to John Rawls's delicate balancing act in his explication of the way in which justice as fairness implied a regime of maximum equal liberty.[14]

Of course, there was an egalitarian element in Berlin's insistence that nobody was to be treated as a mere means to ends they had no part in determining. Each person had a life of their own to live as they chose. But this did not entail economic egalitarianism; Berlin would not subscribe to the view that freedom for an Oxford don was 'a very different thing from' freedom for an Egyptian peasant (L 171–2). The insistence that liberty was what it was and not some other thing was not identical to his ethical pluralism, but it was hospitable to it. Liberty, or freedom – terms he used interchangeably – was far from the only value that a society should pursue. His much-discussed pluralism entailed that values were numerous, frequently in conflict, and not susceptible of being amalgamated in the way a monistic moral theory such as utilitarianism supposes. Although many moral decisions are simple enough, there is no uniquely rational solution to every moral problem. Freedom is

---

[13] Dworkin 1978.   [14] Rawls 1999, 171–221.

overwhelmingly important, both in itself and as a precondition for much else; but many restrictions of our liberty are essential to protect other values; and restrictions on the liberty of some are essential to protect the liberty of others (A 423–8).

Two Concepts of Liberty is a somewhat misleading title for a lecture that discusses positive and negative liberty quite briefly early on (and by way of recapitulation in conclusion), and then takes the listener on a whirlwind tour of topics ranging from the Stoics' 'retreat to the inner citadel', to the dangers of both rationalism and romanticism, the multiplicity of human values, and more. Berlin was well aware, as the introduction to *Four Essays on Liberty* attested, that critics would – indeed, long before the collected essays appeared ten years after the publication of *Two Concepts*, they had already done so – accuse him of defending the negative libertarianism that was the stock in trade of American neo-liberalism, or neo-conservatism. He insisted that he was not doing so. His attitude to property rights was the key. American libertarians held property rights to be absolute; Berlin thought that some human rights were absolute, but property rights were not among them. Moreover, he had no time for, and no interest in, the view that all rights are best analysed as property rights.

Berlin's view was not unlike the view Mill briefly defended in *Liberty*: property rights were a socially useful device, amenable in principle to whatever degree of regulation a society chose to implement, although *laissez-faire* was a good rule of thumb. The interpretive problem presented by 'Two Concepts' does not lie there. The problem is that Berlin seems to say *both* that there really are two concepts of liberty *and* that there is only one. Both views leave room for Berlin's defence of pluralism, but by different routes. On the first view, both negative and positive liberty are forms of liberty, and both are valuable, but both would produce problems if their advocates made them the only value a society pursued – the poorly resourced would starve in a society devoted only to negative liberty, and philosopher-kings might well enslave us in the pursuit of positive liberty. That is, if we were lucky, since the overwhelming likelihood is that the tyranny of the virtuous would turn into simple tyranny, as both the French Revolution of 1789 and the Russian Revolution of 1917 suggest.

The second view is that liberty is negative as a matter of conceptual truth. The pursuit of liberty does not rule out the pursuit of other goods, but liberty as such is in essence negative; to talk of liberty is to talk of obstructions that might be present but are not. This is Hobbes's doctrine of 'hindrances'. On this reading, many of the things that the proponents of positive liberty have advocated are good things, but what they are not is freedom. Freedom is a matter of non-obstruction. Both ways of tackling the contrast between positive and negative liberty are wholly defensible, but it is argumentatively confusing to be unclear which view one is pursuing.

II

My view is far from incontestable. It is that there is only one concept of liberty, and it is what Berlin saw as the positive concept. 'Who (or what) dictates what I must do?' is the right question to ask; 'am I my own master?' asks the same question in different words. Moreover, it matters that the concept of liberty is in origin political or legal-political. If we set store by genealogy, it matters that these are the questions that Greeks and Romans were asking when talking about freedom. The Athenians thought they were free because 'we have no master here' – no *despotes* whose slaves they were.[15] A free Roman was an adult whose word could bind him, commercially, matrimonially, and as a citizen interacting with other citizens. Children and slaves shared a similar incapacity; they were not their own masters, and their status was not that of free persons. Slaves in law were permanent children. The complications of Roman law vis-à-vis adult women are another, and fascinating, issue, as is the entire body of the Roman law of slavery; the only point being made here is that freedom is in its origin and essence a legal and political concept, defined by the mirror-image of slavery. The exiled Spartan king Demaratus made the point when explaining to Xerxes how it was that the Spartans would fight to the death against the overwhelming forces ranged against them. They were free men, not slaves; but not, he said, wholly free, since they had a master whose name was law, whom they feared more than Xerxes' slaves feared him.[16]

All else is analogical, although an analogical redefinition may in time displace what was formerly the paradigm. One might, for instance, think that with the rise of Christianity a new paradigm came into being. The focus moved to the inner life, and the slavery from which we seek to be emancipated is slavery to sin. The logic of freedom still dictated that the opposition is the opposition of slavery and freedom. What of negative liberty? On my reading, it is the claim that the conditions of liberty are largely negative. There is little or nothing that we must be or do in order to be free. We are our own masters if nobody else is; we are free in the absence of coercion or obligation. Hobbes disliked republicans prattling about liberty, but both Hobbes's conception of liberty and the republicans' more 'political' conception fit well enough within the framework suggested here. A free man, said Hobbes, is one who is not hindered in doing what he has a mind to do and the means to do it. The absence of means is not a hindrance, but something that renders discussion of hindrances otiose. Hobbes observes that we distinguish between a want of power and a lack of freedom. This is the distinction Berlin makes in a footnote, paraphrasing a quotation he much enjoyed: 'It is not lack of freedom not to fly like an eagle or swim like a whale' (L 169 n2).[17] 'Hindrances' are

---

[15] Euripides, in Gagarin and Woodruff 1995, 64–5.   [16] Herodotus 2005, 449–50.
[17] The original quote, from Helvetius, reads: 'to consider as a lack of liberty our inability to soar through the clouds like an eagle, or to live under the waters like a whale ... would be ridiculous'. Helvétius 1909 [1759], first discourse, ch. 4, 36.

external obstacles, although Hobbes tied himself in knots in explaining how threats on the one hand and promises on the other reduced our liberty.

Not everything in Hobbes's account is plausible. Notoriously, Hobbes argued that a sovereign by acquisition – one whom we agreed to obey when he had his sword at our throat – was the beneficiary of a freely made and therefore binding promise: we had been free to refuse to promise obedience and so bring down death upon ourselves. The crucial element in Hobbes's conception of liberty, as in Berlin's negative conception, is that there is nothing special that anyone must do, or must be, to be free, and in particular no moral or (beyond the minimum conditions of responsibility) cognitive conditions; the conditions of what we may term 'natural' liberty are negative and external. We may choose perversely or foolishly or ignorantly, and so on; we may worship false gods. As long as we are not 'hindered' in what we have a mind to do, we are free.

Matters become complicated when we scrutinise the idea of hindrances more carefully; here, however, I content myself with the simple point that a hindrance is relative to the action we are free to perform or not. A rich man is not free to marry if he is already married, but a poor man is, if he is not. The beggar whose freedom to dine at the Ritz has been much discussed is not hindered by laws specifically aimed at preventing him from dining there, as would be the case if he were African-American in a state with Jim Crow laws on the book, but he is certainly going to be hindered in any attempt to get his dinner for nothing. A point to which I will return is that civil liberty, in a sense other than Berlin's, presupposes the existence of political and legal institutions; one cannot be a Roman citizen in the state of nature. A woman may be free to marry inasmuch as she is not already married, but she can be neither free nor unfree in that respect in a society where the institution of marriage is unknown. Nor do all freedoms naturally reinforce one another, or mutually imply each other; a lack of civil or political freedom may be consistent with a good deal of social freedom, and vice versa. It is sometimes argued that the Turkish *millet* system achieved something of the sort; the subjects of the Ottoman Empire had no political rights but enjoyed a lot of freedom to conduct their domestic affairs as they liked. Mill thought much of Europe less socially constrained than middle-class English society, though more widely subject to political oppression.[18]

I have already said that Berlin disposes of the basic analytical task, separating positive and negative liberty from one another, swiftly and early on in *Two Concepts of Liberty*. It is worth noting that Berlin also performed early on in the lecture one of the tasks incumbent on whoever is delivering an inaugural lecture. In 1958, it was widely held that political theory was dead. It was thought that analytical philosophy had cut the ground from under its feet; if moral claims were neither true nor false but either expressive of emotion – the so-called 'boo-hooray' theory of ethics – or disguised imperatives, there might be interesting

---

[18] Mill to Pasquale Villari, March 9, 1858, in Mill 1972, 550.

things to be said about the techniques of persuasion that allowed us to get others to share our emotions or to obey the imperatives we are uttering, but nothing about their truth or falsity strictly speaking. Berlin's response owed little or nothing to a concern to rebut the scepticism of contemporary analytical philosophers on their own terms. He was, for all that, unmoved by their arguments.

On the one hand, he thought that philosophical issues were inescapable; when all the factual questions had been answered, there would be others with no reliable answers, and philosophers would struggle with them as best they could. On the other hand, he thought, more defensively, that in a world where political disasters were the predictable outcome of the adherence of leaders and followers to destructive ideologies of one sort and another, it was essential to maintain a critical engagement with such doctrines. Berlin seemed to hold a version of Keynes's view that political leaders were too often the slaves of defunct economists, or in this case political theorists, philosophers of history, intellectuals more generally. Political theory might, on the lowest estimate, serve a therapeutic purpose by unmasking logical incoherence, factual error, and perhaps the sheer implausibility of the view of human nature which many theories presuppose. He made the case with a good deal of passion (L 167–8).

The cruelty of too many twentieth-century tyrants was anything but 'mindless'; it stemmed from a fanatical attachment to theories whose implementation brought disaster in their train. In correspondence, Berlin suggested that he thought that the only justification for what he worked on was its human interest, contrasting his own scepticism with what he thought to be the confidence of H. L. A. Hart and John Plamenatz about the possibility of reaching the truth about issues in political theory (E 411–12). What he says in the lecture suggests a much more powerful case for the political theorist's importance. Nonetheless, one might think that an emphasis on the human interest of the subject was closely allied to Berlin's well-known concern to preserve a sense of reality in thinking about politics.[19] An obvious contrast is with John Rawls, who devoted a great deal of time and energy to the question of method in political theory, and who had more time than Berlin for the exploration of so-called 'ideal theory'.[20] Berlin's lack of interest in exploring further the nature of political theory is striking. He wrote a good deal about the philosophy of history, but almost nothing about the conceptual underpinnings of political theory. He was content to think of political theory as a matter of bringing moral considerations to bear on political practice, and to leave it at that. Political theory was, he said, a branch of moral philosophy, the branch dealing with intractable social and political conflicts. It was to be distinguished from those aspects of politics that were merely technical (L 165–6). Whether

---

[19] See the first two essays collected in SR; and Cherniss, Chapter 4 in this volume.
[20] Rawls 1999, 7–8, 212–16.

questions of constitutional design are merely technical is something on which he never pronounced.

III

Pluralism was the *idée maîtresse* of Berlin's political theory, and it has been endlessly discussed. Its conceptual elusiveness, however, means that knowing what its essence was for Berlin is not easy. Different commentators have seized on different aspects of Berlin's many and varied statements of his position, what they seize on often seeming to reflect their own temperaments rather than any particular conceptual position. It is, it must be said, tempting to take Berlin's depiction of Tolstoy all but driving himself mad in the search for the one great truth about how he should live – trying to turn himself from a fox into a hedgehog – and see pluralism as deeply anguishing. It is a temptation that should be resisted. The sceptic could observe that there are innumerable different but legitimate claims on our time and attention, and the choice between them is for the most part anything but agonising; items on a menu come to mind as an obvious example. Certainly, as Hobbes insisted, the absence of a 'natural' consensus on such matters as the existence or non-existence of a deity, or the nature of a deity's wishes for our conduct, or on more mundane matters such as how to show respect to one another, might all too easily lead to bloodshed. Hobbes, not unlike Berlin, thought that allowing people to think what they liked in private was the only rational policy; unlike Berlin, he was hesitant about allowing such liberty to the public profession of our opinions. An imposed consensus about *doctrine* kept the peace. The respect in which he was wholly unlike Berlin was that he had no time for the assertion of rights against the state; political authority must be absolute.

The role of pluralism in Berlin's political theory, and in the discussion of liberty and liberalism, is too complicated to be more than summarised here.[21] Beginning with what one might call the foundations of the doctrine, we have the indeterminacy of both individual goals and moral conceptions. Wants and wishes, and goals more generally, are infinitely various, and no moral theory offers a uniquely compelling answer to the question of how we should choose between them. Attempts such as were made by utilitarians from Bentham to Sidgwick to corral this variety by means of some version of a felicific calculus are transparently implausible. Berlin did not engage in a detailed, point-by-point refutation of such efforts, but seems rather to have thought it simply not true to the reality of experience to think that the value of any number of passionately pursued goals was best understood in terms of their contribution to an abstract entity called the sum of human happiness. He sometimes struck a cautious note, turning the claim that values were incommensurable into the modest claim that there was no calculus to tell us by how much one outcome was preferable to

---

[21] But see Crowder (Chapter 13) and Galston (Chapter 14) in this volume.

another. This was not only a matter of there being no way of saying just how much better or worse an outcome was in which people were more prosperous but less free than one in which they were more free but less prosperous; even when it seemed on the face of it to be a matter of only one value, there was no way of saying exactly how free people were overall when the freedom of some was sacrificed to the freedom of others.

Berlin did not explore the question whether our usual rough-and-ready evaluations might be made more exact, and if so, how. We do, after all, decide that some deprivations of freedom are worth accepting for the sake of a greater good, as when we renounce the freedom to decide for ourselves which side of the road to drive on for the sake of everyone's safety and convenience; it is, we tend to say, a small sacrifice, or none, in return for a large benefit. Supposing someone with truly eccentric tastes were to fixate on being able to decide for themselves whenever they took their car out: we might say that because of their strange tastes they suffer a large individual loss of liberty, or that they suffer a very small loss of liberty which they take absurdly hard. It is easy enough to see why we might say either; in the one case, we focus on how obstructed in the pursuit of a goal they are, in the other, on what a vast range of more interesting and important activities they are free to pursue unhindered. For whatever reason, Berlin was not interested, as his life-long friend Stuart Hampshire was, in distinguishing public and private morality.[22] Hampshire thought that states but not individual human beings should be guided by utilitarian considerations; a traffic engineer may aim to reduce overall casualties from traffic accidents by rerouting traffic in a way that will predictably kill or injure some people who would not have been at risk before and save those who would have been at risk. In such cases, the desired outcome can be and is calculated: so many lives lost versus so many lives saved. Public officials solve the famous 'trolley problem' in the obvious way; the fact that the solution is not obvious for us as private individuals highlights the contrast between the morality of states and the morality of individuals.[23]

The connection between pluralism and liberalism is not simple, either in principle or in Berlin's discussion in *Two Concepts*. One simple but important point is clear: pluralism is not scepticism. The multiple values between which choices must be made, and which cannot be ranked in a way that enables us to say that a given choice is uniquely correct, are genuine values. That said, everything is left to play for. Does pluralism support a modus vivendi liberalism rather than a principled liberalism? Indeed, is *modus vivendi* liberalism at all? The Turkish *millet* system allowed different ethnic and religious communities to run their own affairs much as they liked, but under the Ottoman autocracy. It was hardly a liberal system; its great virtue was that it kept the peace. Must a principled liberalism, then, rest on the claim that liberty trumps all other values, and, if so, what becomes of the pluralist claim that there

---

[22] Hampshire 1978.   [23] See Kamm 1993, 1996.

is no uniquely rational ranking of values? It is manifestly incoherent to begin from the claim that values are multiple and incommensurable and conclude that therefore liberty is the most important of all values. What varieties of liberalism are worth distinguishing? I have elsewhere written, somewhat awkwardly, of 'adjectival liberalism'.[24] Tocqueville, to take one example, was certainly a political liberal, attached to the rule of law, the sanctity of property, and the liberty of the individual. On the other hand, he was not entirely a social liberal or a liberal about the private realm. He insisted that politics was a masculine preserve; the place of a woman was in the home, not on the hustings, and her political role was to exercise a disciplining effect on her husband and her sons. Enthusiasts for votes for women, or for opening the professions to women, he dismissed as wanting to blur the differences between the sexes and defeminise women. In general, he seemed persuaded that liberty in the political sphere rested on discipline in the domestic sphere. Mill may have learned to fear 'soft despotism' from Tocqueville, but he conceded nothing to Tocqueville's views on women.

It is an old observation that life under an idle or good-natured despot might allow a great deal of private freedom while not offering any guarantees of the sort that political liberalism provides. In the twenty-first century, one might think that American social conservatives are political liberals insofar as they cherish the rule of law and limited government, but not 'private' liberals insofar as they want non-political institutions such as families, or churches, to exercise a great deal of informal discipline, and do not want the law to protect individuals from that informal discipline. The sociologist Daniel Bell used to describe himself as a political liberal, an economic socialist, and a cultural conservative. No doubt there is some 'leakage' from one form of liberalism to another, but not so much that being a liberal in one sphere simply entails that one must be a liberal in others. Bell argued in *The Cultural Contradictions of Capitalism* that market freedom tended to erode the moral constraints that made capitalism possible in the first place; Puritans made good capitalists because they saw hard work, honesty, and straight dealing as moral demands, not just 'good for business'. The prosperity that resulted then sapped the foundations on which it was built by elevating consumer choice to an absolute.[25]

The plausibility of Bell's account is neither here nor there; its intelligibility is sufficient. It is, perhaps, worth labouring the point that the erosion of a sense of obligation, visible in the public's disengagement from politics, may operate either by a kind of distraction – the rise of easily accessible television entertainment distracts us from engaging with politics – or by a direct intellectual process – we think political engagement is a waste of time because we think a modern state can be run only as a bureaucratically organised system of welfare delivery. Voting does not convey the kind of information that

[24] See Ryan 2015, 62. [25] Bell 1976.

a benign administrator needs, so doggedly turning out to vote is a waste of time. We could imagine something of the sort happening to change our view of the conceptual landscape vis-à-vis liberty; we might either be 'distracted' by consumer freedoms or come to think that the freedom to vote for one benign manager over another was not worth exercising.

Neither view can get much purchase in Berlin's writings, because he did not pay much attention to political engagement. It is time to turn directly to the question of the kind of liberalism that Berlin's *Two Concepts* supports. I am not here concerned with the question whether Berlin was a 'cold war liberal', since I take it for granted that he was; it would have been surprising if he had not been, and 'cold war liberal' is not, to my mind, a term of abuse, rather a simple descriptive term indicating which sorts of tyranny were salient when Berlin was writing. Here, however, I am concerned with the question whether, and it what sense, he was an apolitical or even an anti-political liberal. Berlin's Oxford Chair was the Chichele Professorship of Social and Political Theory. I have already mentioned the fact that Berlin's election to the chair occurred at a time when it was widely thought that political theory was dead, and that Berlin's response was not so much to declare it alive and thriving as to declare it inescapable. Given his preference for writing about particular thinkers and their thoughts rather than engaging in meta-theoretical discussions about just what political theory was *about*, it may seem to be pointless nit-picking to question Berlin's view that political theory is a matter of bringing moral judgement to bear on political action. Nonetheless, it is what I am about to do – not to deny it outright, which would be absurd, but to suggest that it omits a great deal of what political thinkers traditionally have concerned themselves with. In particular it slights the central question for liberals: 'How can we govern ourselves as free and equal citizens?'

Where does this leave the question of Berlin's liberalism? To find an answer, we may invoke Benjamin Constant on the one hand and Judith Shklar on the other. The latter's discussion of what she called 'the liberalism of fear' catches much of the essence of Berlin's liberalism, although her discussion is, unsurprisingly, indebted to John Rawls's *A Theory of Justice* and his later *Political Liberalism*.[26] It also reveals the ambiguity inherent in describing liberalism as a political or apolitical doctrine; when Shklar follows Rawls in describing liberalism as a political doctrine and nothing else, she is making the point that liberalism is not what Rawls called a 'comprehensive' moral doctrine concerned with the ends of life, and providing a blueprint for the individual life. Political liberalism is primarily concerned to set out the limits of what a state may do to the citizens over whom it claims authority. The underlying thought is that individuals should be free to do as many things as possible consistent with everyone having the same freedom. This is a version of Rawls's claim that 'maximum equal liberty' is one of the dictates of justice as fairness.

---

[26] Shklar 1998, 3–20.

The emphasis on individuals having the widest possible range of options is also very much in line with Berlin's argument against the Stoic 'retreat to the inner citadel'. The Stoic insistence that we can retain the power to choose what happens to us under absolutely all conditions, and thus remain our own masters even if we are legally speaking slaves, falls foul of the fact that our only 'choice' is a choice of evils.

Shklar thought the most defensible liberalism was a 'liberalism of fear', not as a conceptual matter, but because Shklar, like Berlin and many others, including myself, held that the worst of the vices to which human beings are vulnerable, both as perpetrators and as victims, is cruelty. The overriding point of the usual liberal safeguards summed up as human rights is therefore to protect us against cruelty perpetrated by the agents of the state. One sense in which liberalism is plausibly thought of as a 'political' doctrine is therefore that the cruelty most to be feared is that exercised actually or potentially by the state. Certainly, individual acts of cruelty should be suppressed, either by law or by the informal pressure of opinion, but what one might call ordinary criminality is not the specific focus of liberalism. The state is another matter. Its *raison d'être* is the exercise of force, and its agents can call on resources unmatched by individual miscreants. Moreover, it can permeate an entire society with its threats to our lives and liberty.

We might pause to observe that the liberalism of fear is both like and unlike the liberalism defended by John Stuart Mill in his essay *On Liberty*. It is like in the sense that it is a negative doctrine: we are not presumed to require liberty to pursue any particular course of action, but to have the opportunity to choose from as wide a range of possibilities as possible. It is unlike in the sense that Mill, thinking that he was addressing an English audience above all others, took the view that the great threat to liberty was social rather than political, and the evil to be feared was not cruelty but blanket conformity. This is not to say that Mill would have dissented from Shklar's view of the horrors of states ruled by kleptocrat despots or totalitarian dictators, but, unlike her, he focused his attention – in *Liberty* – on a society where these were not the threats to attend to. Moreover, he thought – and here he comes closer to Berlin – that democracy, or popular government, could check traditional forms of despotism, but might bring a new form of despotism in its wake.

Narrowing our focus, then, we can consider the ways in which *Two Concepts* espouses an apolitical or anti-political liberalism. The senses in which Berlin's *Two Concepts* is anti-political are easy enough to spell out; the sense in which the essay is apolitical perhaps less so. The value of Constant as an interlocutor is that his version of 'two concepts of liberty' picks up these themes with some clarity. Constant worked with a contrast between the liberty of the moderns and the liberty of the ancients that is implicit in Berlin's essay, but is far from explicit. Simply put, the liberty of the ancients was the individual citizen's share of 'the sovereignty of the people'. Berlin, but not Constant, took the view that the citizen's membership of a sovereign people was not liberty at all;

popular sovereignty might or might not be a good thing, but being part of a sovereign people was not 'liberty.' This illuminates Berlin's explanation of why Pericles was wrong about the liberty of the Athenians.

Pericles claimed that the ability of almost all free-born adult males to speak and vote in the *ecclesia* on the same terms as anyone else was a crucial element in their freedom. Berlin, however, argued that civil freedom was freedom *from* politics. Pericles had been scathing about the man who took no interest in public affairs: 'We do not say he minds his own business, but that he has no business here'.[27] This was the doctrine that left Berlin cold. He held that Pericles, and perhaps the Greeks of his day more generally, had no conception of political liberty – in the sense in which Berlin meant the phrase, which was the sense in which he meant it in *Two Concepts*. Constant provided comfort for both Pericles and Berlin. A share of the sovereignty was what ancient liberty consisted in. But, it was a distinctively political form of freedom, and not the 'civil' liberty of the modern world. In particular, ancient liberty had no room for freedom of conscience. Constant insisted that freedom of religion was central to modern liberty. Berlin said that he was tone-deaf to the claims of religion, and in the nature of the case he was unlikely to engage with it in the way the Swiss-born protestant Constant did. But if religious liberty, or freedom of conscience more generally, is allowed to stand for the claim that each of us must be allowed to find our own path to salvation in whatever way we conceive of it, Berlin and Constant are clearly as one.

We must return to Berlin's insistence on the importance of freedom from the claims of politics in due course, but before we do, we should pause on the contrast between ancient and modern liberty. Constant usefully muddied the waters by claiming that Athens discovered (or simply practised) 'modern' liberty; and it is perfectly true that one of the features of Athenian life that Pericles praised was the ability of Athenians to live with the fact that their fellow citizens might live very differently from themselves and hold very different opinions on many matters. They felt no need to bully one another into conformity to a uniform plan of life: 'We do not get into a state with our next-door neighbour if he enjoys himself in his own way, nor do we give him the kind of black looks which, though they do no real harm, still do hurt people's feelings. We are free and tolerant in our private lives; but in public affairs we keep to the law'.[28] The contrast, of course, was with Sparta. What one might call *pure* ancient liberty according to Constant was what Demaratus claimed the Spartans possessed, and it was vulnerable to Hobbes's dismissive insistence that although Lucca had inscribed *LIBERTAS* in great letters on its walls, nobody could infer that a citizen had more liberty – 'that is, immunity to the service of the commonwealth' – at Lucca than at Constantinople.[29] Constant's target was the attempt to turn modern Frenchmen into Spartans, but he was far from

[27] Thucydides 1972, 147.   [28] Thucydides 1972, 145.   [29] Hobbes 1996, 149.

sharing Hobbes's view that being left alone was liberty enough, and that trying to shackle the sovereign was a suicidal error.

Constant's liberalism was in some respects anti-political, in its rejection of the ancient identification of liberty as such with active citizenship; but it was not apolitical. He insisted that modern liberty required constitutional guarantees of a kind unknown to the ancient world. There was nothing to restrain an idle despot's urge to dictate what his subjects might do beyond idleness; but an American president and congress get their authority from a constitution that also sets strict limits on what they may lawfully do. This is the point at which the complaint that Berlin's *Two Concepts* is excessively apolitical begins to bite, and where Berlin and Constant diverge. Like Constant (particularly in *The Spirit of Conquest*), Berlin takes the variety of human desires, beliefs, and moral and religious attachments as a deeply morally significant fact; it is what his pluralism rests on. Because human beings are made of 'crooked timber', individual men and women cannot be made into something straight without violence or manipulation. That, in essence, is the negative libertarian argument for negative liberty. Attached to a doctrine of the sanctity of the individual conscience, it becomes a powerful argument against besotted utopians and their scheme.[30] In *Two Concepts*, Berlin makes little of the thought that this conception of human inviolability is essentially modern, and provides no positive account of the political framework that it implies; it is in this regard that his, unlike Constant's, is an apolitical liberalism. Berlin seems in fact to have thought of negative liberty as a distinctively modern ideal, but he does not dwell on the point.

Constant takes our concern for our inner lives as a distinctively modern fact; modern liberty does not merely accept the existence of a plurality of views of the good life, but regards individual conscience as sacred. But modern liberty must be assured, and it can only be assured politically and constitutionally. This is not an argument for democracy in the sense of 'one person, one vote', but for a liberal representative regime in which sufficient numbers of ordinary citizens participate and hold government to account. It certainly implies that representative government is most likely to assure a rights-respecting regime, and hence it comes as no surprise that Constant frequently praises the United States and Britain. Between *The Spirit of Conquest* and *The Liberty of the Ancients*, however, Constant seemed to change his mind about the extent to which the liberty of the ancients should simply be jettisoned as an ideal for the modern world. In the later work he argued that a share of the sovereignty is not the same as constitutional guarantees of the civic freedoms – freedom of religion, marriage, work, place of residence, and so indefinitely on – that modern man must have; but unless enough of us participate in politics these freedoms are precarious. Modern liberty needs ancient liberty as its complement.

[30] Berlin to Frederick Rosen, A 423–8.

What accounts for the affection in which innumerable readers hold *Two Concepts* and Berlin's subsequent explications of what he was concerned with is implicit in the text, and throughout almost all of his work, rather than explicit. It is the emphasis on preserving a maximum of variety. The engaging quality of Berlin's work that I referred to earlier reflects his obvious enjoyment of the sheer variousness of individuals and their achievements. Politically, that is one of many reasons why his liberalism is essentially unaggressive; trying to turn everyone into good liberals by force or manipulation would be absurd. Negatively (as for Shklar and Constant) keeping the state off our backs is a defence against tyranny in its most obvious forms, against official cruelty and brutality. Positively, there is implicit a vision of what we can do with our liberty and why we cherish it. There is no one best life, but, as Berlin's opposition to the Stoic 'retreat to the inner citadel' attests, for freedom to be a reality, we must have as wide a range of options as possible to choose among. The sheer variousness of individual temperaments and of the cultures in which they flourish means that we need a wide range of options if we are to find those that suit us. This emphasis on the preservation of variety is one of the things that set limits to Berlin's enthusiasm for social and economic reform, although the need for resources to make use of our opportunities meant that he was friendly to the welfare state. That friendliness had limits, too. Like Mill and Tocqueville, Berlin feared the 'soft despotism' of a benign, but omnipresent, bureaucratic state (L 87).[31] Whether they were right to be as afraid as they were is a question for further study.

---

[31] See his criticism of 'the great philanthropic foundations of the West' in 'Political Ideas in the Twentieth Century', L 87ff.

13

Pluralism, Relativism, and Liberalism

George Crowder

In Isaiah Berlin's moral and political thought no set of issues has attracted more attention in recent years than that concerning his concept of 'value pluralism'.[1] What should we understand by this idea? What are its sources? What is its relation with liberalism and other political views? Berlin throws out various responses to these questions, not all of them consistent with one another, and none of them systematically developed. Consequently, vigorous controversies have arisen as to what Berlin intends, whether he is right, and how these questions might be answered independently of Berlin's views.[2]

There is general agreement on some matters. It is clear that Berlin's pluralism emerges from his opposition to moral 'monism', the idea that ethical questions can be answered by a single formula that is correct for all cases. That idea, Berlin believes, is the most fundamental source of authoritarian thinking in the Western tradition. The possibility of a single monist formula in ethics suggests a single correct moral formula for every individual life and for social and political organisation. The prospect of such perfection justifies any sacrifice necessary to achieve it. The tyranny of the Soviet Union is merely the latest, scientific form taken by this old idea.

To moral monism Berlin opposes the idea of value pluralism: human values do not fit neatly within a single monist structure, but are deeply plural – multiple and 'incommensurable' – and often in conflict with one another. Berlin does not claim to have invented the concept of value pluralism; he traces its basic insights

---

For their helpful comments I am grateful to the audience at the conference on 'The Life and Legacy of Isaiah Berlin', at the Yale Center for the Study of Representative Institutions', 2–3 February 2017, where I presented an earlier version of this chapter. My special thanks for more extensive comments go to the editors, and to Henry Hardy and Gina Gustavsson.

[1] Berlin usually calls this 'pluralism'. The term 'value pluralism' has been popularised by others, John Gray in particular: see Gray 1993, 1995, 2000a, b, 2013. I shall use the two terms interchangeably.

[2] For general surveys of the field see Müller 2012; Crowder 2013b; Crowder 2016.

to Machiavelli, Vico, and Herder in particular.³ It is Berlin, however, who is the most influential pluralist in contemporary political thought, certainly in the Anglo-American literature. He is able to link the idea of pluralism with both deep philosophical trends and current political issues, a writer capable of inspiring readers with his vision of the plurality of values. Although it is often said that Berlin is not a careful or precise philosopher, it is just as often added that he has the ability, not universal among philosophers, to bring his subject alive.

This chapter sets out the idea of value pluralism as it is found in Berlin, and discusses some of the issues the idea raises.⁴ In particular I shall be concerned with the crucial relation between Berlin's pluralism and his liberalism. On the face of things, these two aspects of his thought seem to be in serious tension: the idea that basic values are plural and incommensurable apparently points to a multiplicity of legitimate political choices of which liberalism is at best only one, with no convincing claims to superiority over the alternatives. Berlin responds to this difficulty in various ways – I shall highlight contextual, universalist, conceptual, and psychological approaches. However, I shall also argue that none of these, as presented by Berlin, entirely solves the problem. It has been left to his successors to connect pluralism and liberalism more securely. I conclude by sketching two ways by which this might be done: arguments from diversity, and from personal autonomy.

BERLIN'S IDEA OF VALUE PLURALISM

Value pluralism permeates Berlin's work but in a scattered, diffuse way. There is no single, extended discussion that can be regarded as the definitive statement. The closest Berlin gets to such a statement is in three texts: the classic 'Two Concepts of Liberty' (1958: see L), especially the last section, and two retrospective pieces, 'The Pursuit of the Ideal' (1988: see CTH), and 'My Intellectual Path' (1998: see POI).

As is well known, Berlin's immediate purpose in 'Two Concepts' is to define and contrast two conceptions of liberty, negative and positive – respectively, liberty as non-interference and liberty as self-mastery. The immediate political context is the Cold War, and negative liberty is presented by Berlin as the liberty of the liberal-democratic West in conflict with the positive liberty of the

---

³ There are other pluralist sources that he does not seem to have been aware of when he formulated his own view. Among the modern sources, Berlin's most obvious omission is Weber (1948a, b̲). In an interview Berlin says, 'People often ask me, but surely Weber was the first person to say this. I answer that I am sure he is, but I had no idea of it': Lukes 1998, 102. Other modern pre-Berlinian formulations of value pluralism, unknown to Berlin when he wrote, can be found in Lamprecht 1920, 1921; and Brogan 1931.
⁴ I shall not attempt to discuss the question of the truth of Berlin's value pluralism. On that issue see Stocker 1990; Kekes 1993; Dworkin 2001, 2011; Crowder 2002, 64–73; Galston 2002, 6–7; Talisse 2012, ch. 5.

Communist world. On the whole, Berlin defends the negative liberty of the liberals and is critical of the positive idea. Historically, if not logically, he argues, positive liberty has too often been used to support authoritarian forms of politics, since its defining notion of the 'true' or 'authentic' self is vulnerable to manipulation by those claiming authority.

Some readers of 'Two Concepts' have the impression that Berlin rejects positive liberty completely, but things are not so simple. It is true that for much of his discussion he is saying that, in the political realm at least, negative liberty is the safer and perhaps the more coherent ideal. Sometimes, indeed, he hints at the thought that the negative idea is the 'fundamental' or 'normal' form of liberty or 'the essence of the notion of liberty', and that the positive variations are metaphorical extensions or departures from it (L 48, 169, 204). Nevertheless, Berlin never condemns the positive idea entirely. Moreover, towards the end of the essay, he is inclined to see the two ideas as moral equals: 'the satisfaction that each of them seeks is an ultimate value which, both historically and morally, has an equal right to be classed among the deepest interests of mankind' (L 212).

This theme of the ultimate equality of the two liberties is deepened in the final section of the essay, 'The One and the Many', where Berlin sets it in the context of his underlying idea of value pluralism. He begins by defining the monist target. 'One belief, more than any other, is responsible for the slaughter of individuals on the altars of the great historical ideals' (L 212). This is the idea of a 'final solution', a single formula that will answer all moral – and, by extension, political – questions correctly. A range of thinkers 'from Plato to the last disciples of Hegel or Marx' have embraced this ideal 'of a final harmony in which all riddles are solved, all contradictions reconciled' (L 213). These are the great authoritarians, thinkers who have argued that there is only one right way to live and that those who disagree must be brought into line by force if necessary.

It may be objected that the link between monism and authoritarianism is not obvious. Certainly it is not a matter of logical necessity. Someone could be a monist but believe that the final solution involves a stress on the importance of individual liberty, or that, whatever the ultimate truth may be, we should be wary that we can ever be sure we possess it or have a right to enforce it. Indeed, some monist thinkers have used precisely these considerations to turn monism in a liberal direction – for example, Locke, Kant, John Stuart Mill, T. H. Green, and Ronald Dworkin. Berlin might reply that the connection is, at least in part, empirical or historical, on the model of his explanation of the danger of positive liberty. On this account monism, while not necessarily leading to authoritarianism, offers a temptation in that direction by holding up the notion of moral and political perfection as an ideal. Some thinkers, armed with additional ideas and motivations, have taken up that notion and run with it in undesirable directions.[5]

---

[5] This account of the problem of monism is developed in Crowder 2004: 129–30; Allen 2009; Gustavsson 2014; Crowder 2015b.

In any case, Berlin has another reason for rejecting moral monism, namely that it is false. Human values do not form a unity; they are multiple and conflicting. 'The world that we encounter in ordinary experience is one in which we are faced with choices between ends equally ultimate, and claims equally absolute, the realisation of some of which must inevitably involve the sacrifice of others' (L 213–14). Value conflict is not merely an appearance that a more refined reason can show to be an illusion, but a deep reality from which we cannot escape. It is monism that is delusional.

In this light negative and positive liberty are now revealed to be irreducibly plural and incommensurable values on a level with other basic goods such as equality, justice, and security. 'Incommensurable' here means that there is no common measure by which we can weigh one value against the other. In cases of conflict we must make hard choices between the two liberties, and between liberty and other goods.

The choices we make between such conflicting values reflect our cultural and historical situation rather than an eternal law grounded in metaphysics. To seek greater certainty and permanence for our values is understandable and may be inevitable, but it is a wish that is bound to be disappointed, and is 'perhaps only a craving for the certainties of childhood or the absolute values of our primitive past' (L 217). Nevertheless, our choices are our own. 'Principles are not less sacred because their duration cannot be guaranteed' (L 217).

Where did Berlin's pluralism come from? He goes some way towards answering that question in two essays he wrote later in life. In 'The Pursuit of the Ideal' and 'My Intellectual Path' he looks back on his intellectual development and sees it as centrally shaped by an emerging sense of the plurality of values in opposition to what he sees as the dominant monism of Western moral and political theory.[6] The two essays tell much the same story, but there are some odd differences. I shall focus primarily on 'Pursuit', taking note of 'Path' mainly at the points where it diverges.

In 'Pursuit' Berlin paints himself as initially an idealist, indeed a monist.[7] The turbulence of the twentieth century shows us that ideas matter, and that political ideas are extensions of moral values. The Russian novelists of the nineteenth century, such as Tolstoy, 'did much to shape my outlook', Berlin reports, and theirs was an 'essentially moral' approach (CTH 3). The world is an arena of contending goods and evils: truth, love, honesty, and so forth, are confronted by injustice, oppression, falsity. The goal of moral and political thought is to find a general solution to all these problems, although there is widespread disagreement over what the solution may be. Is it, for example,

---

[6] Care should be taken with these later sources, in which Berlin rationalises his own development retrospectively. For alternative and perhaps more objective accounts of Berlin's formative intellectual development, see Dubnov 2012; Cherniss 2013.
[7] Compare 'My Intellectual Path', where he says he 'always felt sceptical' about the idealism he describes there: POI 8.

religion, or scientific progress, or liberal-democracy, or nationalism, or the simple life commended by Rousseau?

The idea of the final solution is what Berlin comes to understand as ethical or moral monism, and he sees this as 'a Platonic ideal' resting on three assumptions: that every moral question has a single correct answer; that 'a dependable path' to that answer can be discovered; and that all correct answers are compatible, fitting together like a 'cosmic jigsaw puzzle' (CTH 6). In principle, the goal is a 'perfect life'.

Monism has taken various forms in Western thought, Berlin observes. Socrates, Plato, Jews, Christians, Muslims – all have subscribed to different conceptions of the optimal good life. In the seventeenth and eighteenth centuries the rationalists and the empiricists differed over the method by which the final truth is to be found, but did not question that there is such a truth. Although he does not do so explicitly, Berlin might have added that in the modern world the leading monists in moral theory are Kant, with his categorical imperative, and the utilitarians (Bentham, the Mills, and their followers), who see utility as a common denominator in terms of which all other values can be cashed out – in a particular situation, freedom will generate X amount of utility, equality Y amount, and so on. The right action will simply be that which produces the most utility.

Berlin also points to differences among monists as to how far and by what means monist goals can be achieved in practice. Hegel and Marx, for example, believe that even though the shape of human history assures us that we shall achieve human perfection eventually, progress towards it will be fraught with conflict – it is 'dialectical' rather than smoothly linear. Still, the historicist monists share the faith that history has a purpose and that this is underpinned by the notion of the uniquely correct general solution to all problems. In whatever form, monism, Berlin believes, is the dominant outlook of Western ethical thought, the *philosophia perennis* (CTH 9; POI 6).

According to Berlin's recollection in 'Pursuit', his own early monist view is challenged in his reading by three writers in particular. First, Machiavelli 'shook my earlier faith' (CTH 8).[8] Here was a writer who did not seem to believe in a single ideal. In his advice to the prince on how to retain political power, Machiavelli notoriously rejects the conventional Christian morality of honesty, love, and compassion in favour of the values of pagan civilisation (more precisely, pre-imperial Rome): strength, courage, ethical flexibility, ruthlessness. On the other hand, Machiavelli does not reject Christian values outside the context of politics, so he does not oppose them entirely. For Berlin,

---

[8] 'My Intellectual Path' is again different on this point because Machiavelli does not feature. There Berlin says that it was reading Vico that 'first shook me', and that 'my political pluralism is a product of reading Vico and Herder, and of understanding the roots of romanticism': POI 8, 15. On the link between pluralism and romanticism see RR 158–9, 169; see also Gustavsson, Chapter 9 in this volume.

Machiavelli sees the two sets of values as those of incompatible civilisations with incommensurably distinct merits. Each announces its own ethical standard, and there is no 'overarching criterion whereby we are enabled to decide the right life for men' (CTH 8). In the end there is no uniquely right answer to the question of how to live.[9]

Similarly, Berlin finds in Giambattista Vico and J. G. Herder an understanding of human cultures as 'incommensurable' with one another – they are so deeply distinct as to be incomparable. For Vico, this occurs when cultures are separated by history. There is 'no ladder of ascent from the ancients to the moderns', but rather 'a plurality of civilisations ... each with its own unique pattern' (CTH 9, 10). Instead of progress towards a single universal ideal, we should be aware of multiple ideals expressed by multiple civilisations. Although these are not different in every respect, since they share a common humanity, they differ 'in some profound, irreconcilable ways, not combinable in any final synthesis' (CTH 10). In Herder, Berlin sees the same idea extended from civilisations to 'national cultures' (CTH 10). Each possesses its own 'centre of gravity', profoundly different from that of others.

The insights from Machiavelli, Vico, and Herder enable Berlin to elaborate his idea of value pluralism: 'the conception that there are many different ends that men may seek and still be fully rational, fully men, capable of understanding each other and sympathising and deriving light from each other, as we derive it from reading Plato or the novels of medieval Japan – worlds, outlooks, very remote from our own' (CTH 11). People pursue a range of different goods, and different combinations of these constitute different ways of life. These ways of life must have something in common, a universally human element, or we would not understand each other at all. But there is no single correct ideal to which all should conform. If ways of life are diverse, that is not in itself a sign of some failure of rationality or conduct in some of them, but a natural variation that is only to be expected – indeed, valued.

QUESTIONS OF INTERPRETATION

To understand Berlin's value pluralism in greater detail it may help to divide it into four main claims: there are at least some fundamental values that are objective and universal; there is a plurality of these fundamental values; such values are liable to come into conflict with one another; and such conflicts are often hard to resolve because fundamental human values are incommensurable. Each of these claims raises questions of interpretation.

First, Berlin's treatment of values, including the most fundamental, is ambiguous between seeing values as subjective and local – values are whatever particular individuals or groups happen to value – and seeing them as objective and universal – values are truths about the world, independent of

---

[9] For Berlin's more detailed discussion of Machiavelli, see 'The Originality of Machiavelli' in AC.

any particular human judgement or recognition. On the one hand, Berlin is attracted to the idea that values in general are 'not found, but made', an idea he attributes to the German romantics; on the other, he regards certain 'human' values as having an 'objective' status independent 'of men's subjective fancies' (POI 11, 14).

To some extent the subjective–objective ambiguity in Berlin can be accounted for by a distinction between values that are more basic or fundamental (objective and universal) and those that are less so (subjective and local).[10] However, even within the ostensibly objective and universal category of 'human' values, Berlin's account is less than completely univocal. Sometimes he seems to identify the human values with 'the essence of humanity' (POI 14). In 'Two Concepts' he refers to values that are 'bound up with our conception of man, and of the basic demands of his nature' (L 215). By contrast there are passages in which Berlin insists on his credentials as an empiricist, relying solely on the evidence of experience and avoiding any kind of metaphysical speculation, which would include, apparently, speculation on the essential nature of man (e.g. POI 13).

Different again, and perhaps most characteristic, are those passages where Berlin strikes a compromise, describing the fundamental human values as 'quasi-empirical', or ends 'that dominate life and thought over a very large portion (even if not the whole) of recorded history' (L 45; see similarly CTH 12, 19). Neither unchangingly essential nor the mere inventions of individuals or even single societies, the basic human goods answer to fundamental human needs but in historically contingent ways.

What is the content of these basic values? Again, Berlin is more suggestive than definitive. In various places he gives the following examples: 'truth, love, honesty, justice, security, personal relations based on the possibility of human dignity, decency, independence, freedom, spiritual fulfilment' (CTH 3); liberty and equality, justice and mercy (CTH 12); 'justice, or happiness, or culture, or security, or varying degrees of equality' (L 171); courage (CIB 37). These remain suggestions, without any attempt to systematise them.[11] All Berlin will say of their overall shape is that 'the number of human values, of values which I can pursue while maintaining my human semblance, my human character, is finite – let us say 74, or perhaps 122, or 26, but finite, whatever it may be' (POI 14). This cannot be literally true, since there is no theoretical limit to the subdivision of value.[12] Presumably, Berlin means just that there is some limit to the

---

[10] See, in a pluralist context, John Kekes's distinction between 'primary' and 'secondary' values: Kekes 1993, 18–19, 38–44.

[11] For more systematic accounts of fundamental human values as part of a pluralist outlook, see Kekes 1993, 17–21, ch. 3; Nussbaum 2000, 2011.

[12] I owe this point to Henry Hardy.

range of values recognisable as human. I take up this theme later in relation to Berlin's idea of the 'human horizon'.

A second element of Berlin's pluralism is, of course, plurality: the world of value is fragmented rather than unitary. But what exactly is it that is plural? Berlin gives two broadly different answers.[13] Sometimes, as we have seen, he refers to the plurality of individual values or goods such as liberty, equality, justice, and so on – as in his argument that 'liberty is not the only goal of men' (L 172). Call this the 'analytical' interpretation of value pluralism. At other times he sees whole systems or packages of values as incommensurable: pagan versus Christian civilisations in Machiavelli's *Prince*, historical civilisations in the work of Vico, national cultures in Herder. Call this the 'holistic' interpretation. I shall return to this analytical–holistic distinction when I discuss the boundary between pluralism and relativism.

Third, Berlin emphasises the potential for conflict among the plural values. A standard theme in his work is that to choose one value is often to forego another, or at least to call for a compromise where one value is partially traded off so that another can be partially realised. The general insight is that no single individual life, social order, or conception of the good can accommodate, or at any rate maximise, all genuine values. But there are different kinds of value conflict, and Berlin is not careful to distinguish these. A useful typology is presented by Thomas Nagel. To begin with, value conflict may be merely contingent, the result of subjective or historical views that could be otherwise, or of other practical circumstances such as lack of time or resources. Alternatively it may be 'noncontingent', arising 'essentially', or from the nature of the values themselves (Nagel 2001: 105, 106). For example, the values involved in living a city life exclude those intrinsic to living in the country.

Further, noncontingent conflict may itself take weaker and stronger forms. In its weaker sense it may be a matter of 'incompatibility', meaning 'the impossibility in principle of realising one value while realising the other, or without frustrating the other' – as in the city versus country example: both kinds of life may be valuable, but their respective natures prevent them from being lived simultaneously (Nagel 2001: 106). In its stronger form, noncontingent conflict becomes 'opposition', where 'each value actually condemns the other, rather than merely interfering with it' (Nagel 2001: 106–7). An example is Machiavelli's opposition 'between the virtues of Christian humility and the pagan virtues of assertion and power'.

Although Berlin sometimes speaks in more contingent terms, Nagel argues that it is noncontingent conflict that is his more distinctive concern, since it is this that points more decisively towards the kind of pluralism that interests him, namely a deep plurality in the structure of value. Pluralism in Berlin's sense involves a meta-ethical thesis about the nature of value, not just the uncontroversial empirical observation that opinions about value differ.

---

[13] A similar distinction has been drawn by Charles Taylor 2001, 113–14.

If value conflict were merely a matter of different opinions, or of contingent circumstances such as time constraints, that would be consistent with monism: there could still be a 'final solution' or overriding formula, it is just that time or ignorance get in the way of its realisation. Stronger forms of conflict are a stronger indication of value pluralism.

The noncontingent view of value conflict connects with the final element of Berlin's pluralism, its most distinctive and controversial component, namely the idea that fundamental human values are 'incommensurable' with one another. If we ask why it is that basic values can conflict with one another at these more profound levels, Berlin's answer is that each basic value stakes a completely distinct claim. No matter how deeply we look into the nature of these fundamental goods, we will find that there is no basis on which they can be commensurated – either cashed out according to a single measure (e.g. utility) or ranked within a single hierarchy subject to a super-good (e.g. Plato's philosophical contemplation). Basic human values are fundamentally too different to be brought within a single formula that solves all conflicts in the same way.

Here again there are divergent interpretations: most importantly, a distinction can be drawn between strong and moderate accounts of incommensurability.[14] The strong interpretation insists that there can be no reasoned ranking of incommensurable values *in any circumstances*. On this view, liberty and equality, say, are such distinct considerations that we never, in any case, have any decisive reason to rank either ahead of the other. Of course, each generates its own reason for action, namely the intrinsic good of liberty or equality. But each of those reasons speaks with such a unique voice that there can under no conditions be any overarching or independent rationale for preferring either option. When we have to choose among such values in cases of conflict, our choice is always ultimately non-rational.[15]

By contrast, the moderate interpretation holds that although ranking for decisive reason may be impossible in the abstract, or in accordance with a final solution or single formula that applies in every case, that is compatible with allowing that there may be a decisive reason for ranking incommensurable values *in a particular case*. This view is advanced by Berlin in an article co-written with Bernard Williams, where they use the example of justice and loyalty (CC 326). Neither justice nor loyalty always outranks the other in every situation; considered in the abstract, each is an independent and

---

[14] A weak interpretation might also be identified, which rules out only measurable rankings: see Crowder 2002, 50–2.
[15] See, for example, Raz 1986, ch. 13; Moore 2009; Mulligan 2015. Gray seems sometimes to hold this view, as when he refers to choice among incommensurables as 'radical choice – choice without criteria, grounds or principles': Gray 2013, 97. But elsewhere he appears to agree with the more moderate interpretation of incommensurability discussed next: 'Value-pluralism does not imply that there are not in particular circumstances good reasons for favouring one value, or constellation of values, over others': Gray 2013, 188.

fundamental good with its own claim to respect. But there may be good reason to rank one above the other in a particular context. For example, impartial justice should come first for the judge presiding over a trial, while impartiality will legitimately bow to personal loyalty for the parent at her child's netball game. As Berlin writes in 'Pursuit of the Ideal', 'the concrete situation is almost everything' (CTH 19). Often the circumstances will suggest not an absolute ranking of values, but trade-offs or compromises. 'Claims can be balanced, compromises can be reached: in concrete situations not every claim is of equal force – so much liberty and so much equality'; 'rules, values, principles must yield to each other in varying degrees in specific situations' (CTH 18).

The moderate interpretation of incommensurability has two points to recommend it against the strong interpretation. First, it accords more closely with ethical experience. It captures the widely held sense that even when fundamental values are conceived as incommensurable, and therefore unrankable in the abstract, people are nevertheless capable of choosing between them for good reason in concrete circumstances. William Galston recounts his experience as a White House official faced with the 'irreducibly heterogeneous' views of the various government departments arguing their case before his interagency task force:

> I found it remarkable how often we could reach deliberative closure in the face of this heterogeneity. Many practitioners (and not a few philosophers) shy away from value pluralism out of fear that it leads to deliberative anarchy. Experience suggests that this is not necessarily so. There can be right answers, widely recognised as such, even in the absence of general rules for ordering or aggregating diverse goods. (Galston 2002, 7)

Second, the moderate view has a very respectable philosophical pedigree stretching back to Aristotle. Berlin sometimes thinks of Aristotle, along with Plato, as a monist theorist of the 'contemplative life as the highest that a man can lead' (L 295).[16] But Aristotelian thought has another feature that fits well with the pluralist outlook, namely the notion of practical wisdom (*phronesis*). This is the idea that moral decisions are typically made not by the application of abstract rules but by intuitive perceptions, grounded in experience, of the action called for by a particular set of circumstances. As Charles Taylor puts it, conflicting incommensurable goods can be combined or balanced or traded off

> if we approach value pluralism in an Aristotelian framework. That is, in any given situation we can weigh the relative importance of the goods that concern us, in some cases upholding one more strongly, and in others another ... And it's quite possible that in any given circumstance the overwhelming weight of one good will clearly take precedence against the lesser weight of another. (Taylor 2001: 118)

---

[16] See also CIB 32 and 56 (where Aristotle is explicitly described by Berlin as a representative of 'monism'). On the other hand, Aristotle is listed among the pluralist 'foxes' in Berlin's famous essay 'The Hedgehog and the Fox': see RT.

Taylor's metaphor of 'weighing' competing goods is not quite right because it suggests a common measure, but he correctly emphasises the central role of the 'given situation'. The Aristotelian model is one of situated judgement rather than abstract commensuration, so even when, strictly, there can be no commensuration – no reduction to a common measure, whether common denominator or super-value – there can still be judgement in context.

There are, of course, different kinds of context in which incommensurable values can conflict – personal, cultural, and historical, for example (although these interconnect). The first of these, the context of an individual life – its dominant or constitutive goods and overall shape – is not much discussed by Berlin, although it has been examined by thinkers influenced by his value pluralism, such as Taylor.[17] Usually Berlin is concerned with political judgement, whether that of individual leaders or of whole societies faced by conflicts among fundamental values. In the former case he refers to the 'sense of reality' that enables the successful statesman to 'grasp the unique combination of characteristics that constitute this situation – this and no other' (SR 56).[18] When it comes to the judgement of whole societies he appeals rather more narrowly to the authority of culture. Responding to pluralist conflict among public goods is 'not a matter of purely subjective judgement: it is dictated by the forms of life of the society to which one belongs' (CTH 19). 'To decide rationally in such situations is to decide in the light of general ideals, the overall pattern of life pursued by a man or a group or a society' (L 42).[19] By implication a similar role is accorded to historical context, the 'centre of gravity' of a period or age, when Berlin is discussing Vico and Herder in particular.[20]

This is not to say that context always points to a painless answer or a clear one. It does not rule out the possibility of tragedy – a frequent theme in Berlin – where any decision results in severe loss. That is possible even when the best decision has been made overall (Williams 2001). In other cases the best decision will be hard to identify because there will be more than one relevant context and these will conflict – as, for example, in the conflict between private and public identities (family and city) dramatised in *Antigone*. Even wholly within the context of public culture there may be conflict between rival cultural traditions.[21] Again, there may sometimes be genuine dilemmas in which all

---

[17] For discussions of pluralist practical reasoning in the context of an individual life, see, e.g., Hampshire 1983, ch. 5; Nussbaum 1992, ch. 2; Kekes 1993, ch. 5; Richardson 1994; Taylor 1997; Nussbaum 2001, ch. 10.

[18] Berlin's discussions of the political judgement of individual leaders are examined in this volume by Cherniss, Chapter 4.

[19] See, similarly, L 47; also Walzer 1983; Kekes 1993, 1997, 1998; Gray 2000b, 2013, 189; Taylor 2001; Parekh 2006.

[20] Another pluralist who emphasises the role of historical context in ethical and political thought is Berlin's close friend Bernard Williams (2005, 2006). See also Gray 2013, 188–9.

[21] The issue of how pluralists should respond to tensions between and within cultural traditions is discussed, in the context of multiculturalism, in Raz 1995; Parekh 2006; Crowder 2013c, chs 7 and 9.

the contending options are as bad as each other. The possibility of tragedy, uncertainty, and dilemma cannot be discounted, nor should it be. Value pluralism is not a view that seeks neat and tidy formulas in ethics and politics; on the contrary, it is explicitly anti-formulaic. On the other hand, neither does pluralism imply blankly non-rational choice in all instances. It is consistent with more routine cases in which basic values are ranked for good reason generated by given circumstances.

PLURALISM, RELATIVISM, AND LIBERALISM

The moderate or contextual interpretation of choice among incommensurable values saves Berlin's position from irrationalism, but does it open up another difficulty? The fundamental practical question for the pluralist is always: why rank one set of basic values ahead of another? As Berlin writes, 'If we allow that Great Goods can collide', then 'how do we choose between possibilities? What and how much must we sacrifice to what?' (CTH 17–18). When it comes to politics why should we choose the distinctively liberal package of values – with its emphasis on certain interpretations of individual liberty, equality, and justice – supported by Berlin? Why should pluralists not endorse some other political value-package: the equality, social justice, and solidarity that define the socialist view, or the caution and fidelity to tradition characteristic of conservatives, or even the extreme nationalism and aggression of fascism?

Berlin's contextual approach to such choices may be rational, some critics would say, but it is relativist and consequently his liberalism is still undermined.[22] At its broadest, relativism in ethics is the idea that moral claims have no universal or objective validity but express some particular point of view, which may be that of a person or culture or some other perspective (Wong 1993; Lukes 2008). Cultural relativists, for example, may see the standard liberal list of 'human rights' – including freedom of speech and religion – not as truly universal or objective, but as reflecting a characteristically Western cultural outlook.[23] The practical consequence is that relativists resist the universal application of any ethical norms, including those of liberalism. According to the relativist, all ethical claims are made from within some local or personal perspective, and none has any critical purchase on beliefs or practices endorsed from within some other perspective. If Berlin's pluralism turns out, after all, to be a species of relativism, then the implication is that he cannot justify his liberal political preferences, such as his emphasis on negative liberty, in the universal or cross-cultural terms that liberalism traditionally requires.

---

[22] See Anderson 1992; Kateb 1999; Sandall 2001; Strauss 1989 [1961]; Sternhell 2010. Berlin's pluralism is distinguished from relativism by Lukes 2003; Ferrell 2008.
[23] See, e.g., Pollis and Schwab 1980; cf. Donnelly 2003: chs 4–6.

A wedge is apparently driven between his ethics and his politics, between his pluralism and his liberalism.[24]

Is Berlin's value pluralism really a kind of relativism? It certainly is if it is interpreted on the holistic model, introduced earlier, that ascribes plurality and incommensurability to whole systems of values such as national cultures. If whole cultures are incommensurable, then they have nothing in common and there is no overarching measure or standard according to which one can be ranked above another in any respect. Therefore, there is no basis from which any culture can be criticised on terms other than its own. The result is a world of deeply separate and indefeasible ethical perspectives – a world, essentially, of cultural relativism. Berlin sometimes seems to endorse this picture, especially when he is discussing Machiavelli, Vico, and Herder.[25] If so, the values of liberalism offer only one ethical perspective among others and the critics are right about the tension at the heart of Berlin's thought. It follows that in order to separate pluralism from relativism, Berlin needs to abandon the holistic notion that whole systems of value are incommensurable.

But even if we are clear that Berlinian pluralism concerns incommensurability in the analytical sense – that is, incommensurability of values or goods rather than of whole systems of value – the problem of relativism remains. There is still a question of how to rank or trade off incommensurable values when they conflict. If the answer is to appeal to a personal, local or historical context, then we seem still to be in the realm of moral relativity. How far, for example, will we be able to make a case for freedom of speech and religion in societies where the local form of life happens not to accept such freedoms as norms?

This leads Berlin to a second approach to choice under pluralism, in which he qualifies his contextualism with an account of a universal level of values. In 'Alleged Relativism in Eighteenth Century European Thought' (1980: see CTH) he responds to criticism that his previous treatment of Vico and Herder, which presents their accounts of civilisations and cultures as discrete and holistic, effectively paints them as relativists. Berlin admits that this was a mistake (CTH 79–80). Rather, they are pluralists who urge us 'to look upon life as affording a plurality of values, equally genuine, equally ultimate, above all equally objective' (CTH 82). The key distinction between pluralist and relativist is that the pluralist acknowledges a framework of objective and universal human values, while the relativist denies this.

---

[24] This is Gray's view of Berlin's political position. Gray sees Berlin's value pluralism as implying either non-rational or contextual choice but in either case as undermining any ranking of values that purports to be universally valid. This, he believes, rules out most forms of liberal political theory. He does allow that pluralism is consistent with an 'agonistic' form of liberalism, according to which liberal values apply only locally where they are culturally appropriate: Gray 1995, 2000a, b, 2013, ch. 6. However, few liberals would be happy to see human rights as applying only where a pre-existing liberal culture already endorses them.
[25] For criticism of Berlin's interpretation of Vico and Herder as relativists, see Momigliano 1976.

Berlin refers in this connection to the notion of a 'human horizon'. 'Forms of life differ. Ends, moral principles, are many. But not infinitely many: they must be within the human horizon. If they are not, then they are outside the human sphere' (CTH 12). There is a (wide) limit to the range of values that are recognisable as human. It is this human limit that makes cross-cultural and trans-historical understanding possible, since human beings, even those distantly separated by space or time, share the same fundamental purposes. Although 'the world of the Greeks is not that of the Jews nor of the eighteenth-century Germans or Italians', nevertheless the 'values and ultimate ends' that constitute those different worlds are all 'open to human pursuit' (CTH 88). All human ends are comprehensible because 'all respond to the real needs and aspirations of normal human beings', so that 'members of one culture can understand and enter the minds of, and sympathise with, those of another' (CTH 87).

So, Berlin's view is that the 'many worlds' he speaks of 'overlap': all are worlds in which the ends pursued are interpretations of ends common to humanity (CTH 88). In principle such universal ends could provide standards against which the performance of particular persons, institutions, cultures, and societies can be evaluated. This is not to say that human societies can be easily ranged in a single, fixed hierarchy of worth, since it would seem that strengths in respect of one basic value are likely to be mirrored by weaknesses in another — more freedom, for example, may result in less equality or solidarity. But it will not be true on the pluralist view, as it is on the relativist, that cultures or societies are 'windowless boxes' immune to external criticism (CTH 88). On the contrary, the pluralist outlook demands that we take seriously the full range of fundamental human goods present in the human horizon, acknowledging the extent to which they are present or absent in particular social and cultural systems.

Unfortunately, while the idea of the human horizon shows that Berlin's value pluralism is not just the same thing as relativism, the problem of relativism persists in practice. The human horizon is so wide that it excludes hardly anything. By definition it includes all recognisably human purposes, so every identifiably human norm or practice or institution falls within it. It includes even the values of Nazi Germany, since Berlin is explicit that these, although grossly misguided and repulsive to most people, are not inhuman or insane (CIB 38). Consequently, the human horizon offers only the weakest basis for critical judgement. Someone might appeal to the horizon to make the point, for example, that society A is rich in individual liberty while society B is weak in liberty but, say, stronger in equality. But the human horizon itself tells us nothing about what priorities or balances should be decided between competing basic values, such as liberty and equality, in particular circumstances. That question remains open, and so on the face of it the problem of how to defend specifically liberal values and institutions remains.

If the horizon is not much help in this respect, what about Berlin's different idea of the 'core' human values?[26] While the human horizon primarily identifies those actions and institutions that are recognisably human and therefore comprehensible to others, the core is the narrower notion of those values that are not only universally comprehensible but actually endorsed by all or most human societies. So, for example, while the practice of human sacrifice falls (like almost all practices) within the human horizon, it is arguably outside the human core and potentially open to objection on that ground.

What, however, is the content of the core? We saw earlier that this is a question that Berlin answers only in an ad hoc way. Further, whatever the precise content of the core, if this is to be genuinely universal in Berlin's sense – that is, values actually held by all or most human societies – that content is likely to be highly generic. The core, by being more specific than the horizon, may get us further away from relativism, but it is unlikely to be a sufficient basis for liberalism.[27]

On a different tack, might it be possible to adjudicate between clashing incommensurables by finding norms implicit in the concept of value pluralism itself? The basic idea is that features of the concept of pluralism themselves suggest the importance of values such as individual liberty that are in turn best promoted by liberalism. This third approach may be called 'conceptual'. It faces an immediate objection, invoking 'Hume's Law' against deriving values from facts, or ought from is. Value pluralism, the objection runs, is a set of meta-ethical claims about the factual nature of value. How can such a factual thesis give rise to conclusions about how people ought to behave and organise their political institutions?[28]

This objection is debatable. To begin with, it assumes that the pluralist thesis is wholly factual or descriptive rather than normative. But the foundational elements of pluralism include the idea of objective and universal values. Once the content of these values is specified – to include liberty, equality, justice, for example – pluralism can then be seen to have a normative component written into its definition. To this it might be further objected that giving content to the basic values is going beyond the definition of pluralism by adding a distinct claim about the human good. But must a pluralist position be defined in strictly meta-ethical, factual terms, or might it admit an ethical component at the point where its foundational values are specified? Moreover, even if pluralists agree to the narrower definition, that means only that the conceptual approach is not freestanding but needs to be supplemented by additional normative assumptions or claims.[29]

---

[26] On the relation between horizon and core, which is controversial, see Crowder and Hardy 2007b.
[27] For a different view see Jonathan Riley 2000, 2001, 2002, 2013.
[28] See Berlin and Polanowska-Sygulksa 2006: 295–6; Talisse 2012: ch. 4.
[29] The latter course is taken by William Galston, for example, who supplements the concept of pluralism with the value of 'expressive liberty': Galston 2002, 2004, 2005.

Berlin offers a hint of the conceptual approach in 'Two Concepts', where he writes that if basic values are plural and incommensurable, 'the necessity of choosing between absolute claims is then an inescapable characteristic of the human condition. This gives its value to freedom' (L 214). We can know that individual freedom is an objective and permanent human value by reflecting on the nature of pluralism. If pluralism is true, then choice among fundamental goods is unavoidable. If so, then the freedom with which to make such choices must itself be a fundamental good.

However, Berlin's conceptual argument does not succeed as he presents it. The necessity of choice does not demonstrate that either choice or the freedom to choose is a value. Berlin himself describes tragic choices as painful human experiences – the 'agony of choice' (L 214) – so it would be open to someone to argue that we should be relieved of that pain by a dictator who makes our choices for us.

There is also a conceptual argument for liberalism implicit in Berlin's linking of pluralism with anti-utopianism, but this, too, is not wholly convincing or complete. To appreciate the plurality and incommensurability of basic values, Berlin teaches, is to accept that there is no final, perfect system of politics that maximises all such values simultaneously and harmoniously. All political forms are imperfect in the sense that they carry costs as well as benefits. Consequently, pluralism rules out political utopianism – the visions of Plato, Hegel, and Marx, Berlin would argue – and commends those forms of politics that seek only to manage human imperfection and conflict rather than trying to transcend it. The trouble is that although liberalism would meet this bill, so would conservatism, as Berlin implicitly concedes when he refers to the contextual authority of 'the forms of life of the society to which one belongs' (CTH 18). Pluralism does imply anti-utopianism, but anti-utopianism is not sufficient to single out liberalism as a uniquely desirable form of politics.

Finally, some recent commentators have claimed to find in Berlin a 'psychological' link between pluralism and liberalism.[30] There is some evidence of Berlin's holding such a view, but its best-known expression comes from Michael Walzer: 'I don't know anyone who believes in value pluralism who isn't a liberal, in sensibility as well as conviction' (Walzer 1995: 31). To be a pluralist requires personal qualities of 'receptivity, generosity, and scepticism', which are also qualities supportive of liberalism.

The immediate difficulty here is that several prominent pluralists, explicitly influenced by Berlin, are not liberals. John Kekes is a conservative; John Gray has passed through various stages of postmodernism, traditionalism, and modus vivendi politics, all of which he distances from orthodox liberalism; Walzer himself is better described as a communitarian or social democrat than a liberal.[31] So, a pluralist temperament does not guarantee a liberal sensibility

---

[30] Berlin and Polonowska-Sygulska 2006: 290–1; Zakaras 2013a, Zakaras 2013b.
[31] See Kekes 1993, 1997, 1998; Gray 1993, 1995, 2000a, 2000b, 2013; Walzer 1983.

and conviction. Even the more qualified claim that *most* pluralists are liberals is not obviously true either, since it is not clear which ideological tendency is the rule and which is the exception for pluralists. If Berlinians want to link pluralism to liberalism they cannot rely on empirical claims of this kind; rather, they need normative arguments to show why pluralists *ought* to be liberals.[32]

BEYOND BERLIN

If Berlin's value pluralism is to be linked to liberalism, or more generally if we are to find practical guidance to the making of choices among competing incommensurables, then we must go beyond the arguments that Berlin himself provides. Although his suggestions are valuable starting points they are never sufficiently developed to be convincing. However, a considerable literature has been devoted to building on Berlin's hints and clues in this connection. Among several lines of argument I shall outline three.[33]

First, it may be argued that pluralism connects with liberalism by way of value diversity. As Bernard Williams writes, 'if there are many and competing genuine values, then the greater the extent to which a society tends to be single-valued, the more genuine values it neglects or suppresses' (Williams 2013, xxxvii). This is an instance of the conceptual approach. To take pluralism seriously is to respect, and so far as possible promote, the full range of genuine human values. The best society will therefore be one in which it is open to people to pursue as great a range of genuine human values as possible – a society of diversity, in that sense. Compared with the alternatives, liberal societies are more likely to meet this standard of diversity because of their emphasis on personal liberty, which frees people to pursue different goods. Of course, this stress on liberty will have costs in terms of other values that liberty diminishes, but all societies promote some values at the expense of others. From a pluralist perspective the question is, what kind of society will maximise value diversity? Liberalism has a good claim to meeting that standard.

Second, a diversity of values will suggest a diversity of cultures. As argued earlier, pluralists should not see cultures as incommensurable. But the denial of cultural incommensurability does not entail a denial of the value, from a pluralist point of view, of cultural diversity; on the contrary, cultural diversity is, *prima facie*, itself a pluralist value. A Berlinian pluralist will see cultures as vehicles for the pursuit of multiple values, again understood as

---

[32] See the exchange between Zakaras 2013a, Galston 2013, and Crowder 2013a.
[33] These are developed in greater detail elsewhere: see Crowder 2002, 2004, 2015a. Other attempts to connect pluralism with liberalism include William Galston's argument by way of expressive liberty (note 29); Jonathan Riley's case based on minimal universals (note 27); Bernard Williams's historical thesis (note 20); and Alex Zakaras's development of the psychological proposal (note 30).

multiple combinations and interpretations of legitimate and valuable human purposes. Different understandings of those purposes will be embodied, in different ways, in different cultures. Prima facie – I shall qualify this in a moment – the greater the variety of cultures present in the world, or within a single society, the better. Pluralists are natural multiculturalists.[34]

Note that this point indicates the step needed to complete Berlin's implicit argument from pluralism to liberalism by way of anti-utopianism. That argument stalled when it was realised that the requirement of anti-utopianism is satisfied not only by liberalism but also by conservatism. The question here is: what might commend liberalism against conservatism from a pluralist point of view? One answer is that liberalism accommodates, as conservatism does not, the cultural diversity endorsed by pluralism. The classic conservative response to the problem of conflict among incommensurable values within a given society is to assert the authority of a single dominant way of life. But the logic of pluralism is that more than one such way of life may have a reasonable claim to authority. To put it another way, under pluralism the claims of any one way of life may be reasonably contested by alternative views of which values to prioritise and how to interpret them. This connects with the notion of 'reasonable disagreement' made prominent by John Rawls as part of the foundation of modern liberalism.[35] Berlinian pluralism points to the legitimacy and value of multiple ways of life, and these are better accommodated by liberal toleration or recognition of multiple cultures than by conservative insistence on a single tradition.

Two qualifications are in order, however. For one thing, there is an issue of the compatibility of cultures, indeed of the values embodied in cultures. As Williams notes, we should 'grant the important qualification that not all values *can* be pluralistically combined, and that some become very pale in too much pluralistic company' (Williams 2013, xxxvii). Not all cultures, or all values, can be combined comfortably – or even logically, given Nagel's point about the possibility of noncontingent opposition. The internal coherence of a society's values and of its constituent cultures is one of its legitimate concerns.[36]

Moreover, not all cultures are uniformly admirable from a pluralist point of view, since not all are equally hospitable to the multiplicity of goods that is upheld as desirable by pluralists. At first sight Gray may seem correct to say that

---

[34] For the relation between value pluralism and multiculturalism, see the references in note 21. Note, however, that Berlin is not himself a multiculturalist: Berlin 1991, 21.

[35] Indeed, Rawls explicitly cites Berlin's value pluralism as a source for the 'burdens of judgement' that he says account for the reasonableness of modern disagreement about the good life: Rawls 1993, 57. Note, however, the contrary view that Berlinian pluralism is distinct from Rawlsian pluralism, and too controversial a basis for modern liberalism: Larmore 1996a, ch. 7. For replies to Larmore, see Crowder 2002, ch. 7; Galston 2002, ch. 4; Crowder 2004, 159–61.

[36] See my account of the pluralist goal of value 'diversity' as combining considerations of multiplicity and coherence: Crowder 2002, 136–45; Crowder 2015a.

the best world for pluralists will be one containing the greatest variety of cultures, whether liberal or illiberal (Gray 2013: 186). But on reflection this has to be questioned if some of those cultures have authoritarian structures that prevent people from pursuing a variety of goods. For value pluralists, cultural diversity is desirable, but only so far as it serves *value* diversity.

A third post-Berlinian line of argument from pluralism to liberalism focuses on personal autonomy, or a person's capacity for individual self-direction in accordance with critical reflection rather than uncritical conformity with rules or customs. This is the ideal celebrated as 'individuality' by John Stuart Mill (1974 [1859]: ch. 3). From a pluralist point of view, people need to be autonomous in this strong sense in order to navigate the decisions thrust upon them by a pluralist world. Pluralist choices among competing incommensurables cannot be settled adequately by standard rules like utilitarianism, since these tend to depend on a monist account of some or other value being overriding.[37] Nor can such choices be wholly guided by cultural traditions, in part for the same reason and also because, as noted before, traditions are multiple and conflicting. Rather, to choose well under pluralism requires people to look behind such rules and traditions and think for themselves in a strong sense – that is, to be autonomous. On the assumption that personal autonomy does not emerge automatically but requires education, a good society will be one in which personal autonomy is promoted as a matter of public policy. Again, such a society will be liberal.

This argument is opposed by William Galston's view that personal autonomy is too demanding a value to be the basis for liberalism under modern conditions (Galston 2002, 2005). Galston observes that personal autonomy is not valued highly by some minorities, especially those identifying with a traditional religion, in the contemporary United States. For Galston, the more inclusive ideal is that of toleration, specifically a group toleration that embraces not only internally liberal but also non-liberal cultural groups, such as the Amish. Pluralism points to a 'Reformation' (toleration-based) rather than 'Enlightenment' (autonomy-based) liberalism. As already noted, however, this is debatable, especially if the point is taken that Berlinian pluralism is primarily a pluralism of values and only secondarily of cultures.[38]

Finally, it may be asked whether these arguments from diversity and autonomy do not violate the most basic insight of Berlinian pluralism by setting up monist standards of their own. That will be true only if diversity and autonomy are advanced as overriding, or part of a formula, a final solution, that applies in every situation – and that is not so. Diversity, as employed here, is

---

[37] Mill was, of course, also a utilitarian, but a complex one. For Berlin's account of the tension between Mill's utilitarianism and his background sense of pluralism, see 'John Stuart Mill and the Ends of Life': see L.

[38] See also the criticism of Galston's view by way of the right of exit he allows from non-liberal groups, which will be weak unless combined with personal autonomy: Crowder 2007a, 126–30.

not a single, substantial value on a par with goods such as liberty and equality but a meta-value that represents a whole range of goods that is optimal in the circumstances. To say that a society should promote 'diversity' is to say that it should promote that constellation of liberty, equality, justice, and so on that maximises people's access to plural goods under current conditions. In the case of autonomy, liberals need say only that this is a good that ought to be emphasised in private and public life, not that it must outrank all other goods in every situation. This model is Berlin's own. In his case it is negative liberty that is held up as a value of great importance, especially in a political context, but even there it may make sense to trade it off against other goods, such as equality or social justice, where necessary (L 38–9, 52, 172; CTH 13).

CONCLUSION

The central issue arising from Berlin's account of value pluralism is the relation between pluralism and liberalism. In reviewing Berlin's response to this question, I have emphasised the following points. To begin with, he rejects the view that, for pluralists, the prioritising of liberal values (or any values) must be ultimately non-rational. Rather, he argues that the ranking of incommensurable values may be rational in particular contexts.

This contextual account, however, reinforces the worry that Berlin's pluralism may really be a form of relativism, which would still present problems for his liberalism. In some of his texts, Berlin confuses value pluralism with cultural relativism by identifying the incommensurability of values with the incommensurability of whole systems of value, including cultures. Against this, it is important to be clear that value pluralism is primarily a pluralism of values, not of cultures or other value systems. But even when that matter is clarified, the contextual account of choice under pluralism suggests that value rankings will vary with cultural circumstances, so that liberal values will not have the cross-cultural authority they traditionally claim.

At this point one possible response is to constrain this contextual variation by appealing to universal values, which are an essential feature of the pluralist view. Berlin does conceive, rather loosely, of a set of moral universals, in the form either of a human horizon of comprehensible purposes or of a common core of social values. But although these levels of universality help to distance pluralism from relativism, they are far too generic to possess much critical force, and far too weak to connect pluralism to liberalism.

Alternatively, Berlin's texts sometimes reveal conceptual or psychological approaches. In his conceptual mode, Berlin sees the idea of pluralism itself as implying an emphasis on the role of choice or on anti-utopianism. The psychological link is suggested by comments hinting at a temperamental affinity between pluralism and liberalism. Once more, however, these arguments, at least as presented by Berlin, fail to link pluralism uniquely with liberalism.

In the end, that link must be sought beyond Berlin's own work. I have outlined arguments from diversity and from personal autonomy as two possibilities. To say this, however, is not to deny the crucial significance of Berlin's pioneering thought. It is Berlin, more than any other thinker, who has made us aware of the concept of value pluralism and the issues it raises.

14

Liberalism, Nationalism, Pluralism: The Political Thought of Isaiah Berlin

William A. Galston

INTRODUCTION: BERLIN'S LIBERALISM

Isaiah Berlin was one of the most notable liberal thinkers of the twentieth century, and a continuing influence on political thought in the twenty-first. Yet he was anything but a conventional liberal, at least as this persuasion is currently understood. He rejected both utilitarianism and Kantian-style deontology,[1] the most frequently employed moral bases of liberal politics, espousing instead the innovative value pluralism that George Crowder has analyzed in Chapter 13 of this volume. Although he saw himself as a "liberal rationalist," he spurned both the scientism and the authority of experts to which liberals often resort (CIB 70). Nor was he impressed with what he saw as modern liberalism's thin and unpersuasive account of human motivation. He regarded rational hedonism as a caricature; he insisted that liberalism give due weight to passions, emotions, irrationality, and even the unconscious.[2] Rejecting all forms of historical directionality, teleology, and inevitability, he could not be a "progressive." Although it would be mistaken to attribute to him a tragic view of history, he was anything but a triumphalist: there is no "arc of

---

[1] I should complicate this summary sketch a bit. Berlin was by no means as critical of Kant as readers who have encountered only his "Two Concepts of Liberty" might be led to suppose. Kant's account of human dignity moved and permanently influenced him. In a letter to George Kennan, he wrote that "When, in the famous passage, Ivan Karamazov rejects the worlds upon worlds of happiness that may be bought at the price of the torture to death of one innocent child, what can utilitarians, even the most civilized and humane, say to him?" adding "Ivan Karamazov cannot be totally exorcised; he speaks for us all." See L 338.

[2] In a generally admiring discussion of John Stuart Mill, Berlin remarks that the great liberal thinker "had no inkling of the mounting strength of the irrational forces that ... moulded the history of twentieth century," adding that many thinkers, Freud among them, "saw a good deal more deeply into the springs of individual and social behavior" (L 242). Like Mill, Berlin wanted to fuse rationalism and romanticism into a more adequate account of human life than either by itself could offer. But when it came to human motivation, Berlin thought, Mill did not sufficiently take into account the insights of romanticism. See also Crowder 2004, 174–5.

the moral universe," and it certainly does not bend toward justice. There is no end of history. Most liberals, finally, are inclined toward cosmopolitanism; not Berlin, who embraced a distinctive form of particularism. "I regard cosmopolitanism as empty," he declared, adding that "people can't develop unless they belong to a culture."[3]

Berlin was staunchly anticommunist in times during which elite opinion in the West tilted toward accommodation and in notable cases outright support of communist parties and regimes. But he was not a conservative. Although he gave cultural tradition a central place in his political thought, he was not a Burkean. Nor did his famous account of negative liberty incline him to embrace *laissez-faire*. Because he acknowledged that the effective exercise of liberty required certain basic material conditions, he favored FDR's New Deal and the postwar construction of the British welfare state.

Berlin defended his practical politics in terms with wide implications. As a general proposition, he once remarked, "the case for intervention by the State and other effective agencies, to secure conditions for both positive, and at least a degree of negative, liberty for individuals, is overwhelmingly strong" (L 38). He characterized the New Deal as "certainly the most constructive compromise between individual liberty and economic security which our own time has witnessed" (L 84).

These words contradict two widespread misunderstandings: that Berlin saw no virtue, but only danger, in positive liberty, and that he subordinated all other goods to the claims of negative liberty. His value pluralism, described by George Crowder in Chapter 13, made it theoretically untenable for him to adopt either of these positions, and his practice was consistent with his theory. Whether value pluralism requires not just recognizing in theory the merits of competing values and virtues, but also making an affirmative effort in practice to accommodate and balance them, is another matter.

LIBERAL NATIONALISM

Berlin was a staunch Zionist when many other Jews were not, for reasons that extended well beyond the need for a safe haven for the legions of displaced refugees and threatened Jewish minorities. Not long after the Zionist movement achieved its improbable goal, he declared that "The creation of the state of Israel has liberated *all* Jews, whatever their relation to it" (POI 225, emphasis mine).[4] One might have expected him to justify his stance with reference to collective security and self-determination. Instead, he spoke of gains for liberty. The state of Israel, he asserted, "has restored to Jews not merely their personal

---

[3] Berlin 1991, 22.
[4] In a similar vein, another loyal if unbelieving Jew and lifelong Zionist remarked that the establishment of the state of Israel had "procured a blessing for all Jews everywhere regardless of whether they admit it or not": Strauss 1965, 7.

dignity and status as human beings, but also what is *vastly more important*, their right to choose as individuals how they should live – the basic freedom of choice, the right to live or perish, go to the good or the bad in one's own way" (POI 222).[5]

That said, Berlin's Zionism was far from classic Anglo-American individualism. He was a stinging critic of Jewish attempts to assimilate, which he regarded as humiliating, inauthentic, and doomed to fail. As David Miller summarizes Berlin's argument, asimilationist Jews "try too hard to master and copy the social and cultural norms of their adopted nation, distorting their own lives in various ways, but without convincing the natives that they genuinely belong."[6]

Although each of us makes choices, and in so doing participates in a process of self-creation, Berlin believed, we are not writing on a blank slate. As he said of himself, "My Jewish roots ... are so deep, so native to me, that it is idle for me to try to identify them, let alone analyze them" (PI 438). Each of us inherits a complex weave of tradition that shapes our identity in ways that we may modify but never completely transcend. An identity combines the residue of the past with choices in the present that promote but also restrict future possibilities.

Whether individual Jews like it or not, Berlin argued, Jews form a collectivity, a people constituted by history more than choice. And this shared history shaped and sustained modern Zionism. As he put it,

Two thousand years of Jewish history have been nothing but a single longing to return, to cease being strangers everywhere; morning and evening, the exiles have prayed for a renewal of the days of old, to be one people again, living normal lives on their own soil – the only condition in which individuals can live unbowed and realise their potential fully. (PI 438–9)

For Berlin, Zionism was distinctive but hardly unique. He saw it as the Jewish version of a much broader phenomenon – nationalism – which he regarded as both central to modern politics and grounded in permanent features of the human condition. Human beings, he believed, need to belong to communities united by language, history, custom, and often shared descent or ethnicity. These communities provide the conditions for human development. They meet the need for collective identity and social solidarity. They enable their members to enjoy standing before one another and other communities. And they assist the quest for recognition, which Berlin (like Hegel) viewed as primordially human.

The diversity of communities, Berlin argued, is an enduring fact; we are not and never will be in the process of converging toward a universal culture. (This

---

[5] Italics mine. Compare this to the parallel but distinct view of Leo Strauss: "Political Zionism was the attempt to retain that inner freedom, that simple dignity, of which only people who remember their heritage and are loyal to their fate are capable": Smith 2006, 195.

[6] Miller in Crowder and Hardy 2007a, 191.

view was part of his well-known critique of historical theories premised on teleology and determinism.) Diversity reflects the plasticity of human nature and our capacity for self-creation in response to varying circumstances and path-dependent processes. Self-creation often involves conscious choice, but always against the backdrop of unchosen conditions. Like Herder, who deeply influenced this aspect of Berlin's thought, he viewed communities in partly organic terms. Language, which provides not only solidarity but also the categories through which communities interpret the world, evolves through unending interactions among members of the linguistic group. Efforts to develop new languages such as Esperanto from scratch have never amounted to much because they are not organically related to specific communities. Modern Hebrew was erected on a linguistic foundation that Jews had preserved through two millennia in exile.

So understood, nations are cultural communities. Whether these communities assume political form is a further question, which is why the familiar phrase "nation-state" is not tautological. Throughout history there have been multinational political entities, almost all imperial – the Romans, Ottomans, and Habsburgs, among others. The structures are broadly similar – a substantial measure of communal autonomy within a framework of overarching authority that conducts foreign policy, keeps the peace among communities, and exacts the communal tribute needed to sustain the imperial system. There are always centrifugal forces, which strengthened in the nineteenth century in response to powerful intellectual articulations of national particularity and self-determination. Within a period of less than five years, both the Ottoman and Habsburg empires shattered, replaced by a mix of nation-states and smaller multinational entities that in turn proved unstable, with consequences that are still playing out in the contemporary Middle East.

Considering Berlin's respect for the varieties of cultures, one might have expected him to be sympathetic to multiculturalism as a strategy for dealing with cultural diversity within individual political communities. After all, multiculturalism can help provide minorities within majority cultures with a sense of belonging they might otherwise lack, sometimes but not always a way-station on the road to fuller integration. But Berlin leaned in the other direction: "I believe that the common culture that all societies deeply need can only be disrupted by more than a moderate amount of self-assertion on the part of ethnic or other minorities conscious of a common identity," he said in a 1991 interview.[7]

Given Berlin's rejection of assimilation as an honorable strategy for Jews, he was hardly in a position to recommend it for other national groups. It is more charitable to read his opposition to multiculturalism as the counsel of self-restraint to these groups – to enact their distinctive cultures in ways that do not challenge or disrupt the common culture, which in practice is the culture of

---

[7] Quoted in Miller, cited in Crowder and Hardy 2007, 189 and Berlin 1991, 4–10.

the majority. The difficulty is that majority cultures often act in ways that minorities experience as invading their own cultural space, even as disrespectful and discriminatory. It may not be psychologically healthy for minorities to hold their peace in the face of these affronts, and eventually leaders will emerge who reject this course as dishonorable. Berlin was not wrong to focus on the requisites of social unity. But if he had reflected more deeply on the American experience, he might have arrived at a more nuanced view of how minorities can interact with majority cultures to expand the range of valued goods and choices within these cultures, rendering them more genuinely "common."

Berlin's effort to bring together liberalism and nationalism, which many in both camps regarded as antithetical, proved influential. As David Miller remarks, "Berlin has some claim to be considered the founding father of contemporary liberal nationalism, that strand of liberal thought that tries to combine liberal freedoms with the value of national belonging and national self-determination."[8] The question is whether the elements of this ensemble hold together.

Berlin sought to relax this tension by keeping his distance from nationalism as it came to be understood and practiced in the twentieth century. Otherwise, if too crudely put, he distinguished between good and bad forms of national consciousness. Good nationalism provides individuals with a sense of belonging, standing, and recognition. But nationalism sees the nation as an organic entity whose goals override the preferences of individuals and serve as the principal source of moral justification for its actions. When the nation becomes the highest value, it lapses into a blinkered and destructive monism. The practical challenge is to acknowledge legitimate national aspirations without opening the door to nationalist excesses, especially a belief in the superiority of one's own country as a warrant for dominating others, by force if necessary.

The complex psychological roots of nationalism made it (even) harder to meet this challenge. All human beings want recognition, but some want it as the antidote for a deep sense of humiliation. When entire cultures are treated as inferior, it is hard to separate legitimate national self-assertion from resentment and the desire for revenge. The German response to French domination during the Napoleonic period is often interpreted in this light, as is the recent surge of political Islam.

When it came to the Jewish case, Berlin felt no such qualms. He believed that Jewish identity is a form of national identity. In nearly all nations with non-Jewish majorities, centuries of anti-Jewish denigration and persecution had shown that Jews could live neither safely nor honorably. They could live free and dignified lives only in what the Balfour Declaration had called a national home for the Jewish people. And given the circumstances in mandatory

---

[8] Miller, cited in Crowder and Hardy 2007, 184.

Palestine, this home had to contain a Jewish majority. It was not logic but reality that compelled the move from a home to a sovereign nation-state of the Jewish people.⁹

The more than theoretical question was whether a Jewish state could be a liberal state, as Israel's Declaration of Independence promised. The easy side of this question, at least for Berlin, was external. He understood that the logic of his case for a Jewish national home also supported a homeland for the Palestinians. As Shlomo Avineri reports, just weeks before his death, Berlin wrote a letter to his Israeli friend and colleague Avishai Margalit endorsing the Oslo agreements on the grounds that only a two-state solution would be consistent with the liberal basis of Zionism (L 568).

The harder question was whether Israel could measure up to the minimal standards of liberalism in its domestic affairs. In effect, Judaism is the state's established religion, and traditional Jewish law governs issues of marriage and divorce, at least for Jews. (Minority religions enjoy their own confessional authority in these matters.) Religious Jews press constantly to enshrine more of their practices in public law, and they sometimes get their way. The Jewish calendar determines the rhythm of the week and the year.

Much of this might have been otherwise had David Ben-Gurion, Israel's first prime minister, been less determined to accommodate what he regarded as the dying vestiges of Jewish Orthodoxy. Israeli policy could have done much more to ensure that all citizens, regardless of religion, would be treated fairly in the allocation of public resources. It would even be possible to remove the symbol of Jewish nationhood, the Star of David, from Israel's flag and to replace Hatikvah with a more inclusive national anthem. In short, Israel could have been, and can be, more fully liberal without ceasing to be the national homeland for the Jewish people.

But what about the Jewish state's core commitment to Jews everywhere – the Law of Return? Every Jew (and the law defines the group as capaciously as did the Nuremberg Laws) is entitled to enter the land of Israel and receive citizenship immediately. For Jews, Israel is Robert Frost's famous definition of home as "the place where, when you have to go there, they have to take you in."¹⁰ No other group enjoys such a guarantee.

To be sure, many countries – including the United States, for much of its history – have used their immigration laws to encourage the entrance of some groups while restricting or excluding others. But in few of these countries – certainly not the United States – would a shift toward equal treatment of all groups have required a fundamental revision of its national identity and mission. As has often been noted, America's common ground is supposed to be creedal, not ethnic. When the United States in 1965 opened its doors to immigrants from all continents, it became truer to the founding principles enshrined in its Declaration of Independence. By contrast, treating Jewish and

⁹ See E 671–3, 763–7. ¹⁰ Frost 1995, 43.

non-Jewish immigrants equally would mark a fundamental shift in Israel's identity and mission. The gap between liberalism and ethno-national particularism can be narrowed, but not closed altogether.

Berlin always insisted that the goods we prize do not necessarily cohere, and often do not. To have more of some, we must have less of others. A synthesis is not a mash-up but rather a trade-off. As Berlin understood and insisted, liberalism has an egalitarian component (as does the Jewish tradition). So at some point, national particularism will require some compromise of liberal principles. This is true of Israel, but also of any country that tries to combine preference for its own people and its own ways with basic liberal commitments.

This is not to condemn such countries. Specific trade-offs may meet reasonable moral standards, and Berlin was convinced that Israel's did so. But the fact that the trade-offs are there – and that typically they work to the disadvantage of less favored groups – should always be kept in view. Whether Berlin adequately did so in the case of Israel is a matter of reasonable disagreement and ongoing debate.

LIBERAL PLURALISM

Isaiah Berlin embraced both a somewhat heterodox liberalism in politics and an innovative pluralist account of morality. This raises an unavoidable question: what is the relation between them? One link is tolerably clear: value pluralism applies to collectivities as well as individuals. Among other things, different cultures represent distinctive selections and orderings of basic goods and excellences. Communities organized around war and imperial conquest will prize martial traits of character; commercial societies will value pacific and acquisitive virtues. Christian communities cherish humility, while the Greeks celebrated justified pride as greatness of soul. For value pluralists, cultural diversity is not only a fact, but also a flourishing of different modes of being human. As such, it is to be celebrated, not just acknowledged.

The link between value pluralism and the justification of liberal political orders raises more difficult questions. Berlin did nothing to make his interpreters' job easier. Although he spent his early years working in the English analytic mode, his mature style was poles apart from that of his Oxford contemporary, A. J. Ayer, the author of the astringent *Language, Truth, and Logic*. The capacity for empathic identification that made him such a brilliant expositor of the history of ideas sometimes made it hard to determine where his subject's thoughts left off and his own began. His verbal fecundity and passion for endless distinctions and qualifications, often within single lengthy sentences, make the philosophical proposition on offer difficult to pin down. And when it came to the relation between his liberalism and his value pluralism, Berlin gestured toward a number of contradictory positions.

Still, as Crowder points out, Berlin more than once asserted that value pluralists must be liberals – for example, when he refers to "pluralism, with the measure of negative liberty it entails" and when he writes that "if pluralism is a valid view ... then toleration and liberal consequences follow" (L 216 POI 15). Not surprisingly, this strong thesis became a central topic of debate among thinkers Berlin inspired.

In form if not content, Berlin's argument is on all fours with that of the John Rawls of *A Theory of Justice*: if a specific account of moral theory (in Rawls's case, a Kantian theory that gives priority to the right over the good; in Berlin's, value pluralism), then liberal political conclusions follow. This is not the only way of making the case for liberalism, which can be defended on more straightforward human and political grounds. Indeed, Rawls famously shifted to a "political" theory of liberalism in response to the diversity of moral outlooks.

Writing in a Rawlsian spirit, Charles Larmore offered a strong argument against using Berlinian value pluralism as a basis for liberalism. The aim of political liberalism, he insisted, is to find principles that reasonable people can accept, regardless of their particular comprehensive conception of the good. But value pluralism is far too controversial to be counted among these principles, because reasonable people can and do reject the pluralist account of the good. It is unreasonable, he concludes, to ask individuals to subscribe to binding principles of political association (not to mention coercive legislation) on the basis of claims they can reasonably reject.[11]

Although Berlin's embrace of moral pluralism and cultural diversity ensured that his views would be controversial, he was not willing to broaden the concept of religious tolerance to encompass philosophical truth-claims (as the later Rawls proposed in *Political Liberalism*) because he did not believe that political theory could do without them. The issue for him was the truth of his theory, not its acceptability to diverse audiences or its workability as public philosophy for a liberal state.

That said, can the strong claim that value pluralism *entails* liberal politics be sustained? Is it true? This question has evoked a wide range of responses. John Gray, a scholar who acknowledges Berlin's deep influence on his own thinking, goes farthest in arguing that it is not and cannot be true, that Berlin's two master-ideas do not fit together. Berlin saw a connection between value pluralism and negative liberty, which he regarded as the core of liberal politics. As he memorably declared,

> The world that we encounter in ordinary experience is one in which we are faced with choices between ends equally ultimate, and claims equally absolute, the realisation of some of which must inevitably involve the sacrifice of others. Indeed, it is because this is their situation that men place such immense value upon the freedom to choose. (L 213–14)

Not so, Gray retorts: the more seriously we take value pluralism, the less inclined we will be to give pride of place to negative liberty as a preferred

---

[11] This paragraph is adapted from Galston 2002, 44.

good or value. We will certainly not be able to give it anything like absolute priority. We will accept that lives defined by habit, tradition, or unswerving acceptance of authority can be valid forms of human flourishing, and that forms of political association organized to defend groups practicing these ways of life are legitimate. And maintaining these ways of life may require denying negative liberty to dissenters. If diversity comes into conflict with individual liberty, Gray asks, why should liberty trump diversity? "To claim that it must do so is to say that no form of life deserves to survive if it cannot withstand the force of the exercise of free choice by its members." But this is precisely what Berlinian value pluralists cannot say, Gray insists.[12] We will therefore recognize that liberalism – understood as the doctrine of societies in which negative liberty takes pride of place – enjoys only local authority. If Berlin's account of value pluralism is correct, Gray concludes, liberal democracy cannot sustain its universalist claims and must be viewed as but one form of valid political association.[13]

The eminent political theorist Michael Walzer takes a different tack. The connection between value pluralism and liberalism, he contends, is less logical than psychological. What matters most is the orientation that leads certain kinds of people to embrace them both:

I don't know anyone who believes in value pluralism who isn't a liberal, in sensibility as well as conviction ... You have to look at the world in a receptive and generous way to see a pluralism of Berlin's sort ... And you also have to look at the world in a skeptical way, since the adherents of each of the different values are likely to rank them high on a scale designed for exactly that purpose. And receptivity, generosity, and skepticism are, if not liberal values, then qualities of mind that make it possible to accept liberal values (or better, that make it likely that liberal values will be accepted).[14]

Whatever its empirical validity, Walzer's observation leaves open the truth or falsity of Berlin's thesis. And it opens up another question: Why should we endeavor to be the kind of person – receptive, generous, skeptical – who is likely to embrace both value pluralism and liberalism? It is easy to find examples of individuals – pagan warriors and religious believers, for example – who would reject these traits as disabling, even perverse. As a stand-alone argument, Walzer's thesis positions him at no great distance from Gray's claim that liberalism enjoys only a local authority: liberalism is valuable for liberals, less so for those with different outlooks and temperaments.

Berlin always distinguished between value pluralism and moral relativism, a position he firmly rejected. Although he was not perfectly clear about the basis of the distinction, two relevant *leitmotifs* emerge regularly in his writings. The first is the idea of the *common human horizon* – those basic experiences and responses that mark us as human and enable us to make sense of other cultures. Human groups are not sealed off from and incomprehensible to each other.[15]

---

[12] Gray 1996, 155. [13] Adapted from Galston 2002, 48–9. [14] Walzer 1995, 31.
[15] See Crowder 2007b, 209.

Even if another society's funerary practices horrify us, we can recognize them as an effort to respond to the fact and fear of our shared mortality.

The second is a bedrock understanding of what is good and bad for us as human beings, not as members of particular societies. There is a shared understanding of the great evils of the human condition – such as oppression and tyranny and the Four Horsemen of the Apocalypse – as well as of basic goods. Berlin once remarked that

> The idea of human rights rests on the true belief that there are certain goods – freedom, justice, pursuit of happiness, honesty, love – that are in the interest of all human beings, as such, not as members of this or that nationality, religion, profession, character; and that it is right to meet these claims and to protect people against those who ignore or deny them (CIB 39).

Taken together, these theses suggest Berlin saw the space of moral value as divided by a horizontal line, with the plurality of individual ways of life and cultures above the line and a parsimonious account of universally valid basic goods and evils below it. Against this backdrop, the political theorist Jonathan Riley proposes a link between value pluralism and liberalism based on what lies below the line. What we have in common as human beings is enough to motivate at least a "minimal liberalism."[16]

One may wonder, as Crowder and Gray do, whether the political implications of a shared humanity are so minimal as not to amount to liberalism at all. Illiberal regimes may measure up to this standard without recognizing basic liberal values such as freedom of speech and religion.[17]

Although this objection may be valid in principle, its validity in practice is another matter. As Gray acknowledges, "It may be true that the universal minimum requirements of morality have the best chance of being met under liberal institutions ... *if* that is so, it is a very good argument for liberalism."[18] This move transforms Riley's conceptual thesis into an empirical question. My own reading of the evidence is that liberal regimes are far more likely to avoid the great evils of the human condition and to promote basic goods than are their illiberal counterparts. This does not mean that illiberal regimes cannot be decent, but it does imply a presumption in favor of liberalism that may be rebutted in specific circumstances – for example, when bitter disagreements among groups within a society necessitate a measure of autocracy to prevent a descent to outright civil war.

Crowder agrees with Gray that Berlin's stated reasons for a conceptual link between value pluralism and liberalism are unpersuasive, but he takes the argument in the opposite direction. In positing the conceptual link, Berlin was on the right path, Crowder contends, but he did not go far enough. This is why it is necessary to go "beyond" the letter of his argument while remaining faithful to its spirit.

---

[16] Riley 2000, 120–55. [17] See Crowder 2002, 101 n. 4. [18] Gray 1996, 155.

In an impressively detailed argument, Crowder urges a series of steps, each of which would have the effect of expanding Berlin's core premises. As Martha Nussbaum has shown in her work on human capabilities, it is possible to provide a thicker account of universal human goods without obliterating diversity and individual choice. The plurality of genuine goods implies not only respect for each but also the prima facie desirability of societies that contain more rather than fewer of them, that are capacious rather than narrowly focused. Internal diversity, in turn, implies a preference for societies that recognize and treat the inevitable disagreements among individuals and groups as reasonable. And because individuals in such societies are presented with a wide range (some would say a dizzying array) of options, they cannot avoid the necessity of choice. Each individual, then, has a stake in choosing well, an interest that Crowder expands into a fuller theory of personal autonomy. And the exercise of autonomy in a diverse society requires the practice of distinctively liberal virtues. At the end of this long and winding road, then, we rejoin Walzer's account of the traits of character most compatible with liberal societies.[19]

Crowder's thesis diverges from Berlin's in several respects. Crowder opts for the Enlightenment over Romanticism and the Counter-Enlightenment more decisively than I take Berlin to have done. His quasi-Aristotelian account of the human good differs from Berlin's not only in degree but also in kind. His concept of autonomy puts positive rather than negative liberty at the center of liberal society. And he relaxes Berlin's insistence that the requirement of social unity trumps minority demands for public recognition, opting instead for a carefully qualified multiculturalism.

To say that Crowder parts ways with Berlin is not to say that he is wrong. It is to say that he finds Berlin's case for liberalism radically defective. My own view is that there is more to be said for Berlin's thesis within his own frame of argumentation. Recall Gray's insistence that many worthwhile ways of life reject freedom of choice as a value and cannot coexist with it in practice – and that in some case there is no Berlinian reason to prefer individual choice over communal goods. This argument trades on the ambiguity of "worthwhile." Unless one adopts an organic view of community, to say that a way of life is collectively worthwhile is to say (in part) that it is worthwhile for the people who are actually leading it. It is hard to see how that claim can be sustained for those individuals who cannot accept it.

This leaves regimes that insist on a uniform account of human goods and values on the horns of a dilemma. What can they say to their restive dissenters? They can claim that their singular view of the good life and good society is

---

[19] For all this and much more, see Crowder 2007, 207–30 and Crowder 2002, 135–216.

rationally, demonstrably superior to the rest. But this is simply to deny the truth of value pluralism.

Alternatively, as Gray suggests, they can offer a particularist claim: their way of life is not universally valid, but it is worthwhile, so they are justified in doing what is needed to maintain it – even if this means denying free choice by its members, whether or not they accept the regime's constitutive view.[20] It is easy to see why the regime's leaders and the moral majority of its citizens would find this argument attractive. But what appeal can it have to the dissenting minority? From their point of view, the government is depriving them of the ability to lead their lives in ways they would find valuable – in the name of enabling others to do so. Far from offering a reasonable defense of its policy, the government is simply insisting on it in a manner that the minority is bound to experience as arbitrary and oppressive. Shorn of any reason for obeying the government, the minority finds itself morally separated from its society, constrained from rebelling or exiting only by the threat of force.

Value pluralism provides members of societies (and political theorists) a rational basis – a principle of preclusion – for distinguishing between defensible and indefensible regimes. Once the latter have been removed from the set of acceptable options, the remaining alternatives may not all be liberal, but they will be broadly consistent with at least the minimal requirements for liberal regimes. Combined with the normative force of Berlin's below-the-line universalism, we have most of what we need to mount a defense of the liberal political order. Or so I believe.

CONCLUSION

Isaiah Berlin was a fertile thinker who produced a wide range of striking insights and challenging theses. Although his most basic convictions never wavered, he was not always of one mind about the best way of characterizing and defending what he believed. He is hardly the only figure in the history of political thought of whom this can be said.

The principal task before us is to make sense of the aspects of his legacy that matter most for theory and practice in the twenty-first century. Beyond his accomplishments as an historian of ideas, he has left a fourfold theoretical legacy: an influential account of individual liberty, understood as the unimpeded right to choose and act; an innovative pluralist account of the moral world we inhabit; a celebration of cultural variety as the flowering of different ways of being human; and a robust defense of liberal politics as the best guarantor of liberty and diversity.

Berlin presented his ideas in broad strokes more notable for their fecundity than their precision. He left it to others to replace ambiguity with clarity and to

---

[20] Gray 1996, 152–3.

fit the pieces of the puzzle together into a larger whole. As is always the case when such a figure passes from the scene, this process is bound to generate disagreement among followers who are conscientiously endeavoring to make sense of the master-thinker's legacy. In the long run, we must hope, this contestation will lead us to a fuller and more compelling understanding of political life.

PART V

EPILOGUE

15

The Lessons of History

Isaiah Berlin

In January 1966 Isaiah Berlin gave a talk at one of two Columbia University seminars on technical and social change held that year at the Onchiota Conference Center, Sterling Forest, New York. What is described as 'Summary of Remarks of Sir Isaiah Berlin' was published under the title 'The Hazards of Social Revolution' as part of the seminar proceedings.[1] The identity of the summariser is not revealed, but the flavour of Berlin's speaking voice has been well preserved, and my guess is that the text is based on a recording. There is a typescript of the talk in Berlin's papers that is heavily corrected throughout by Berlin, and the corrections are incorporated in the published text, which gives a lively overview of many of his central preoccupations. For this reason, as well as because of the relative obscurity of its original publication, the editors accepted my suggestion that this text should be included in this Companion as a contribution from its subject. I have compared the typescript with the published text and adopted what seem to me the best readings where there are variations, eliminating superfluous or misguided editorial alterations. Accordingly the text that follows supersedes the one published half a century ago.[2]

Henry Hardy

Everyone wants to know the answers to the great questions that preoccupy human beings: What kind of world do we live in? What is wrong with it? How can we change it for the better? But there is something very peculiar about the fact that although thinkers – both learned men and politicians – have applied all the resources of reason and observation to these questions, history at times fails to turn in the directions they predict or aim for.

Consider the French Revolution. No event was more consciously awaited. Throughout the eighteenth century people expected an overturn, discussed it, wrote books about it, wondered what would make it. By the 1770s and 1780s the atmosphere was charged with impending change. Even though what happened in 1789–91 came suddenly, those who stood to lose most, the

---

[1] Warner and others 1969, 127. [2] MSB 581/162–82.

aristocracy, the Church, the royal bureaucracy, were, some of them, filled long before with the expectation of change, even of doom.

That period marks the rise of science and the rise of faith in technology. People supposed in the eighteenth century, partly under the influence of the unique discoveries of Newton, and the vast prestige and success of the natural sciences, that for the first time a real transformation of the human consciousness had occurred. Newton's work really did change the world and the field of possibilities. It was thought that if Newton was able in principle to determine the position and the motion of every particle in the universe by deduction from the relatively few laws that his genius, and the genius of others, had discovered, there was no reason why the whole of human life could not be organised in the same fashion. After all, men were three-dimensional objects in space and time, they were bodies controlled by physical, physiological and psychological laws. If we could learn the laws of physics, chemistry, psychology and physiology, why not the laws governing human society too? As Condorcet suggested, we study the societies of bees and beavers;[3] and if we can discover what causes bees and beavers to be and behave as they do, there is no reason why we should not be able to do the same for human beings.

The conviction that we should study human society scientifically led to a simple view: the main problems of human life resulted from various human errors made in the past. These errors were a result of stupidity or idleness, or were the fault of a minority of wicked men who had deliberately thrown dust in the eyes of the majority of simple men, in order to acquire power over them – a lot of knaves leading a lot of fools by the nose. Some of these knaves had been taken in by their own propaganda; others knew what they were doing. But in both cases wicked and ruthless kings, commanders and priests had misled humanity for generations. Now all that had to be done was to eliminate the errors, to expose such propositions as that God exists, that the soul is immortal, that the earth is flat. These could be disproved by observation and argument, and once this was done, the task would become relatively simple. First, it had to be discovered what human beings were like, what the laws were under which they operated. Then it would be necessary to discover what human beings wanted. This could be done by careful physiological and sociological enquiry. Men were not so very different from each other; these differences could be noted. It would be necessary to discover what human desires were, and what means were available to realise them. All this could be done by disinterested scientists. What was needed was the verified truth. Since all the evils in the world were caused solely by error, often 'interested error', as Holbach called it,[4] it could be supposed that once the facts were known, once it was discovered what human beings were really like and what

---

[3] Condorcet 1847–9, 392.

[4] Holbach 1817, 26 [where 'recourons à nos sens, que l'on nous a faussement fait regarder comme suspects' (Holbach 1770, vol. 1, ch. 1, §§ 9–10) is somewhat freely translated as 'let us fall back on our senses, which error, interested error, has taught us to suspect'].

they wanted, once means had been found by human genius to provide what they wanted, nothing more would be necessary.

Condorcet expressed this most forcibly when he said that 'nature binds, by an indissoluble chain, truth, happiness and virtue'.[5] This led to all kinds of corollaries in the eighteenth century; for instance, that a good chemist is necessarily a good man. It could not be otherwise, because a good chemist is a man dedicated to truth. The truth is obtainable in human relations too. Once it was found, it was impossible not to live and act in its light. Hence a good chemist or a good physicist or a good anthropologist cannot fail to be a good father, a good citizen, a good man. All human problems could be solved by education, which made men want to search for the truth – and alter nature accordingly.

This was the great principle that animated the French Revolution. The ideal was, of course, to achieve universal justice, universal peace, universal happiness, universal wisdom and universal fraternity. The whole movement of 1789 and 1790 was one of the high moments of human exaltation and enthusiasm. When people called themselves good patriots in France, this was not nationalistic. At that stage, what they meant was, 'How marvellous to live under a constitution which at last is rational as well as human; which at last has destroyed the privilege of caste and class; which is founded on rational principles and truth, objective truth, which any intelligent man, using the proper instruments, can discover for himself; how wonderful that the nation which is achieving this is my own.' The ideal was the scientific organisation of life in accordance with publicly communicable principles.

But how very different were the results of the Revolution from those planned. The assumptions of the revolutionists were that man is capable of rationality and of organisation: that man, if properly taught by qualified experts, could organise his life on true and harmonious principles. The reformers believed in at least three propositions. They believed, first of all, that all serious questions have answers that can be discovered by human reason. If a question cannot be answered, it is not a genuine question. But if a question is so formulated that, in principle, there must be an answer, then men can and will find the answer. One can, in principle, tell what the centre of the moon is like. One can, in principle, tell how various kinds of human beings behave in all conceivable sets of circumstances.

The second proposition was that the truth can be discovered by communicable techniques, not by intuition, revelation, in sacred books, but by techniques that a man of genius can discover and any technician in a laboratory can thenceforth apply.

The third proposition was that all the answers are compatible: they can be put together. This followed from a principle rightly found in books on logic: that one true proposition cannot be incompatible with another true proposition. If all questions could be properly formulated and answered, and

---

[5] Condorcet 1970, 228.

the answers then put together, the jigsaw puzzle would be solved, and we would know how to make humanity happy for ever.

And value judgements? Answers to such questions as what we live for, what is good, what is right, why do it, what is honour, why not betray one's friends, why freedom should be preferred to tyranny, why kindness is better than cruelty, peace better than aggression – the truth on all these matters would be established by the application of techniques very similar to those that worked in physics, biology, psychology, economics. Everything that was called philosophical, theological or psychological could be converted into positive science. That is more or less what Hume believed. That is what the French revolutionaries believed, what Comte believed, what H. G. Wells believed, what quite a lot of people still believe.

What actually happened as a result of the French Revolution? The events that occurred after 1789 drew attention not so much to human wisdom, human virtue, human rationality, human organisation, human order, but to the opposite. They showed the power of mobs, crowds and the masses – the exact opposite of what had been planned. They showed the enormous, astonishing influence of great men, of charismatic leaders such as Danton and Robespierre; and they uncovered the irrational forces to which such leaders appealed. They showed the role of accident and of violence in human affairs. By 1815, when the French Revolution was said to have completed itself, the picture is unlike what was planned. Instead of a rational, well-organised international order governed by sage assemblies, people are in the grip of acute nationalism – irrational and divisive passions which the Revolution was against. There was not much real nationalism in the eighteenth century. It was thought to be an irrational, emotional drive that placed local interests before those of mankind. It was, in particular, much disapproved of by Frederick the Great, by the Emperor Joseph II, by the French *philosophes*, by Condorcet, by Robespierre. But the French Revolution led to the invasion of Germany, Italy, the Low Countries, and to an extremely violent nationalistic reaction against the French invaders. The result was an outburst of wounded national feeling that is really the source of European nationalism in the nineteenth century. In fact, the word 'chauvinism' dates from the French Revolution.

The fate of the French Revolution made a number of people ask why it had gone wrong. The liberals held that this was because mobs and demagogues had not been sufficiently controlled. The socialists maintained that the economic and social factors lying beneath the surface had not been taken into consideration, and that too much attention had been paid to purely political organisation. Historicists – Burke, Herder, Hegel – supposed that the factor of historical growth – unquantifiable, qualitative change of individuals and groups, of thought and action – had been ignored or grossly oversimplified. Catholic ultramontanes took the line that the whole rationalist approach was a mistake, that human beings were weak, sinful and cruel, and that only by throwing oneself upon the mercy of God, and trusting oneself to the authorised interpreters of his inscrutable will, could humanity survive at all.

Later came the more complex doctrine of Karl Marx. He certainly supposed that he was a truly scientific observer of human affairs. Marx's critique of the French Revolution was that the class struggle had not been taken into consideration. So long as there was such a thing as class war, and its existence was not recognised, the judgements of excellent scientists, rationalists and ardent improvers of mankind, especially those who did not take enough notice of historical change, would be perverted by class interests, usually because these good people came from a class that stood to win by preserving the status quo in certain ways.

This was still an exceedingly rationalist answer. Marx in effect said, 'These people have taken only factors A, B, C, D into consideration; we scientific socialists recognise factors E, F, G and H. And if we take *them* into consideration, we will comprehend reality: this will do the job; the trick will be done.' The form of the argument was still the same: perfection is possible, humanity can be saved, a stable and decent free society can be created – if only we take into account certain important but hitherto overlooked factors: the economic 'base', the class struggle, and so on.

I cannot dwell long on Marx, only note this time-worn fact: that even in his case history did not proceed according to his prophecies. Marx supposed – with good reason, according to his own premisses – that in the most highly industrialised countries, in the course of the sheer growth of productive forces, a proletariat would grow, organised and disciplined by the capitalists themselves. But, once organised, the proletariat would, if they understood their own interests and power, be capable of shaking off the capitalists, who would become progressively fewer because they were compelled to cut each other's throats in savage competition. Because the capitalists would do so much to eliminate themselves, Marx warned against premature rebellions, terrorism or disorganised activity of any kind. He recommended that his followers form solid political parties, which would make the Revolution by gradually squeezing the bourgeoisie to death.

As we know, very nearly the opposite occurred. The only country in which the programme was followed faithfully was Germany. There, a splendid organised socialist party came into existence. Industrialism increased in all parts of Germany, particularly in Prussia and the Rhineland. The workers grew in number. Their party grew more and more powerful. It built its own world of schools, hospitals, insurance schemes, theatres, playgrounds, concerts; the party looked after its members very humanely; it won more and more seats in the Reichstag. And after the defeat of 1918, the socialist party became the most powerful single party in Germany, and ended by being easily and utterly eliminated by the Nazis. This happened, in part at least, because the socialists were so beautifully organised, so respectable, so integrated into German society, because they had created so many stable institutions, enjoyed so much security. When it came to the point, they were peace-loving, security-minded, with no revolutionary zeal, no aggressive feelings.

The only countries in which Marxist revolutions of a serious kind broke out, at least before the Second World War, were the two in which industrialism was least advanced, and in which, according to Marx's principles, there should not have existed an adequate base for political activities by the workers: Russia and Spain. In Russia, where there was continuing oppression that was both corrupt and inefficient, one could operate only by the method of putsches, small revolts – in the end, organised revolution. This worked. But it worked against the programme Marx enunciated. The German Social Democrats obeyed the precepts of the Master blindly, and were crushed by the Nazis; the Russians deviated from them and, by doing so, won.

Let us look at the Russian Revolution of 1917. In theory, this revolution was to bring about a rational organisation of society. It was supposed to permit the gradual application of scientific method to the whole of society by means of a proletariat enlightened enough to support it. But again the results were the opposite. The effect of the Revolution was to draw attention to the existence of the forces that had been ignored; it showed that terrorism paid, that charismatic leaders were obeyed, that democratic methods could be ignored, that minorities could sit on top of majorities and dominate – and oppress – them in their own name, without effective opposition.

The results of the last two great wars are not dissimilar. The 1914–18 war was fought, among other reasons, for the principle of self-determination. Empires were crushed. Small nations were established and given their proper frontiers. Again the old dogma was applied: here is the disease, and, if the doctor is well enough informed, he has the cure. This is exactly what Woodrow Wilson thought. But instead of the result anticipated, an appalling degree of economic instability, violence and general chaos resulted. As Trotsky said, the Treaty of Versailles converted Europe into a lunatic asylum but failed to provide the inmates with straitjackets. The Second World War was intended to produce some kind of democratic system once Nazism and Fascism were crushed. But, again, its results were paradoxical. Instead of ushering in victory by the forces of democracy over totalitarianism, irrationalism, and anti-humanism, it ushered in a reign of military dictatorships. There are probably more military dictators and more charismatic leaders in the world today than there have ever been before in human history.

But perhaps the most significant unforeseen result of the Second World War was to show the power of National Socialism and Fascism to organise human irrationality, to play on other people's nerves and aggressive instincts, to utilise everything the rationalists had always denounced. The use of this power by manipulators such as Goebbels was one thing not predicted by any of the prophets in the nineteenth century.

In fact, the experience of the twentieth century showed that an alliance could exist between science and irrationality. This, indeed, was something new. The general assumption had been that a scientist was a rational man, and would surely not have anything to do with somebody who was the opposite. But we have recently seen the emergence of politically irrational systems (Fascism and Nazism) that used the latest technological devices. And the scientists who submitted to the requirements of these governments felt that they could not simply opt out of the social system. They would do a good job on lines which the state commanded; they would be as loyal to the irrational state as they had been to any other. The combination of extreme competence among scientists with the violent irrationality of the leaders of the state was something that had never been foreseen. This was a new combination, and struck humanity with amazement and horror. And this is again something we learned from experience and not through scientific prediction, or analysis of human character.

This terrifying alliance caused people to wonder whether it was enough to say that more knowledge would of itself make our lives more charitable, more humane, richer in aesthetic and ethical experience. No people had produced more erudite and brilliant scholars or more magnificent achievements in natural science than the German universities in the late nineteenth century and the early twentieth. No country had a better system of public education, or had more distinguished historians and philosophers, than Germany in the 1920s. By ordinary criteria, it was one of the most civilised nations in the world. Yet this did not prevent that happening which did happen.

And now, twenty years after Germany's fall, there are still people with ready explanations of our problems. They tend to say: If only we could get rid of one more obstacle, we really would be on the way to progress. If only we could get rid of the fanatical Chinese Communists (let us say), who hate the Western world or are possessed by some kind of intolerant Marxism, that would rid us of the last obstacle. Or: If we could only get some kind of permanent agreement with Russia, *that* would do it; only the absence of this obstructs our path.

It is the ancient fallacy again. Men say: We know what the true ideal is, we know exactly where we want to arrive, but the enemy simply cannot be reasoned with; somehow our opponents have been brainwashed. For God's sake, can't this last obstacle be removed? Can't we have a peaceful world at last? If only we could overcome X or Y or Z – Communists, nationalists, imperialists, Americans, Chinese. There are a great many of them; well, that makes the task bigger ...

The temptation is obvious. There are many people who are convinced that they know what is right and good. They know that there seems to be only one final appalling obstacle. If it could only be shoved out of the way, even at the cost of a certain number of human lives, then at last mankind could progress.

By now it should be apparent that there is something wrong with this approach. Whenever it has been used, it has produced not what was anticipated, but the opposite. This is not to say that the approach is ineffective. On the contrary, it has at times had a considerable effect. The wars of religion, the French Revolution certainly changed things radically. So did Marxism, so did the Russian Revolution, so did the First World War and the Second World War. Man is not weak or ineffective in the face of forces of nature and history: he is strong, exceedingly strong. When people really do get together and make a revolution or a war, they do alter history, and they alter it in very violent ways, but often not in the ways they anticipate.

These facts suggest two central propositions. The first is that there may be something wrong with the belief that all political questions can be answered in definitive ways. In physics and mathematics and physiology we have no doubt made progress: we do know more than our predecessors, and can prove it. But in human affairs this is more doubtful. We do our best to perform rational analysis. But lessons of experience induce a certain modesty in claiming definite advance.

The second point is that it may not be true that all the answers – if we can find them – are necessarily compatible. This has been the premiss of the proposition that final, single solutions to the great social problems can be discovered.

To the French revolutionary, for instance, all moral and political issues – for example, questions involving choice between peace and honour, liberty and efficiency, equality and liberty – must in fact have final and mutually compatible answers. The end is given – we know, said Saint-Simon, the oasis towards which we are all marching. The only problem is how to get the human caravan there. Thus all moral problems become questions of the correct technical means. One good end cannot (it is thought) conflict with any other good end. The jigsaw puzzle can be solved.

But if we consider some of these propositions, we will see that certain human values are not so evidently compatible with certain other human values. For example, when we say that we want the truth at all costs (if we really mean at all costs), we find that the costs are at times very high indeed. If we say we want to establish and proclaim the truth in all human matters at all times, we will have to tell the truth to some people who will be deeply wounded by it: how much good will it do to tell the stupid, the ugly, the unattractive, the incurably sick that they are so? It is not self-evident that truth and happiness are always compatible – although this seemed so to the people of the eighteenth century. Neither is it self-evident that the highest efficiency and the widest liberty are necessarily compatible. Obviously, to allow unimpeded technological advance, human beings have to be organised in all kinds of ways which they may not understand, may dislike even if they do understand them, and may often resist. The questions are: How far can one justifiably go in trying to break their resistance? What about human rights? If we really believe in the supreme importance of technological organisation (as Saint-Simon did), then we must (as he did) deny the existence of human rights; it would be argued that no man should be allowed to resist the rational organisation of mankind, without which there can be no human progress, creativity, happiness. The people who refuse to obey well-laid plans for their happiness, and to move to their new houses (jobs, countries), are enemies of progress; we may be sorry for them, but they must be made to move. Rational organisation is guaranteed to make humanity happy; we cannot stop and consider the prejudices or the sensibilities of a few individuals who happen to cling in a sentimental fashion to some irrational or traditional form of life. Where the reward is so vast, all obstacles must be swept away: the price must be paid.

This leads some people to feel qualms. In *The Brothers Karamazov*, by Dostoevsky, Ivan Karamazov says that if he is told that human happiness can be obtained only by the torture of an innocent child, his answer would be, 'This is not a price I am prepared to pay. If that is the cost, I have no wish to see the performance. I return the ticket.'[6] How many innocent victims are worth sacrificing for how much human happiness? Hundreds? Some would say yes. Thousands? Some would still say yes. Hundreds of thousands? Millions? Some would stop only at that point; or not even there.

The fact that such figures can be considered by some calculators, while others reject the very notion of such sums with horror, indicates that there is some kind of collision of values here – and that it is not clear how it can be resolved.

The same can be said about liberty. If everybody were really free, the stronger could hit the weaker on the head. So we say, 'Yes, I'm afraid you'll have to forgo some of your freedom, because others are human beings too, and they too have rights. They have the same rights as you: in fact they are your equals. The liberty of the pike is not compatible with that of the carp.'

The general assumption, then, that all values can exist comfortably side by side, that we could have perfect freedom together with perfect equality and perfect efficiency, if only we knew how to achieve this, is not a self-evident truth at all. It would seem, rather, that certain values are not merely de facto incompatible with certain other values because we are ignorant, or because we have only limited resources to be divided between them. There is also, apparently, an inherent conflict; there seems to be an insuperable conceptual incompatibility between perfect justice and perfect mercy, between perfect equality and perfect liberty. All these are human values, and if anyone is ready to die for one of them, we respect him for it. But how do we decide which of these various values to pursue, or how much of which value should be sacrificed to what other value? It is not easy to be sure what guarantees moral progress: what is the unique final goal of men on earth.

Of course, this is not an argument for doing nothing: the fact that choices can be agonising does not entail that it is best not to make any choice at all. But there is a vast difference between saying that some ends are worth pursuing for their own sake, because they are good or right, and saying that we should pursue them because they embody the elimination of the last great obstacles, after which the gates of paradise will open. Evil things must be attacked and good ones promoted. But not because the end of the struggle is at last in sight.

Two further reflections. First, some good things appear to have a darker side. In our own age, for example, we point out that automation has liberated people

---

[6] Dostoevsky 1958, book 5, ch. 4 (vol. 1, 287): 'too high a price has been placed on harmony. We cannot afford to pay so much for admission. And therefore I hasten to return my ticket of admission.'

from all kinds of degrading forms of toil, that as a result there is a much wider and nobler future before them. But when we produce more leisure we also tend to produce the possibility of boredom. There is no doubt, for example, that boredom has affected young people in my own country today. The young men of England do not greatly fear unemployment or poverty. Most of them have jobs, and many have acquired material possessions which their parents could not afford and their grandparents could not even dream of. Having got these things, some among them naturally ask: What next? Having more leisure on their hands, and feeling uncertain about how to use it, they become exceedingly exhibitionistic, and now we have the young men in Carnaby Street suits whose unusual appearance is some sort of protest against society as it is. This is not a form of political indignation against specific evils, as some people try to maintain, but a result of the fact that, somehow, these young men feel stranded – without direction or ends to which they feel committed. This is what some of John Osborne's plays are about. His heroes feel that, idiotic as the old rigid ways of loyalty to king and country, or service in the army and a traditional family life, may have been, nothing has taken their place. The army may have meant fighting a lot of Indians or Africans, and loyalty to the family may have meant oppression by some ghastly head of it, but still these were stable forms of life: there may have been misery and injustice, but the framework was firm. Obviously, we should not refuse to liberate prisoners simply because they do not quite know what to do with their freedom. But we must recognise that a certain kind of liberation creates its own problems.

The second reflection is that good is at times achieved in unexpected ways. When we examine the history of human happiness, toleration, peace, of all those ideals to which we in the Western world are wedded, we realise that they have not often come about as a benefit of the consciously thought-out, rational application of universal plans made by infinitely wise social engineers or technologists. Mostly they have been attained the hard way. If we ask ourselves, for example, how religious toleration came to the Western world, we find that it came only after the Protestants and Catholics had fought bloody wars to the point of exhaustion in the sixteenth and seventeenth centuries. They fought until enough of them realised that if they went on fighting they might be destroyed themselves. And although neither side gave up its principles, and each thought the other damned, they stopped fighting because they were afraid of a Pyrrhic victory. It was not the preaching of wise men like Erasmus or Comenius, or a general trend toward toleration, rationality or peace, that influenced them, but simply the problem of survival. Because they exhausted each other in these battles, they finally stopped fighting, and toleration became a kind of de facto compromise, or armistice, that lasted, fortunately, for quite a long time. And in this way many other human blessings have been achieved. People start with a fanatical belief in the possibility of some monistic solution, some kind of single end which, once achieved, will ensure happiness to mankind. They believe, therefore, that anything is worth sacrificing, because *the* solution – whatever it is – will surely be the *final* solution. Their belief in a monistic solution tends, in the end, to be toned down to a compromise. We should like to hope that this is the result of argument, of looking at the facts of human history, of the advances of psychology or sociology. But in fact compromises are usually reached only after various factions fight and fight until they can no more, and the dreadful cost gradually leads men to the realisation that they must learn to tolerate each other. It is very difficult to get people to tolerate each other unless they have tried intolerance and failed. This is a melancholy reflection on human character.

What should we do? No doubt we need more knowledge of ourselves: individual and collective, psychological and social. No doubt we must admit that we have not studied ourselves enough; there are all kinds of dark and irrational drives in us that have not yet been properly understood. The reactionary French philosophers of the late eighteenth and early nineteenth centuries, influenced perhaps by the loss of life in the Revolution and the wars that followed, claimed that what people really like is not co-operation, but collective self-immolation on a common altar. Armies are told to march, and though they do not know where or why they are marching, they march. Mutiny in an army is comparatively very rare. What people evidently adore, one of these pessimistic reactionaries said, is being slaughtered together for some unintelligible ideal. This is exaggerated – but so is the optimistic opposite. Too many rationalists have not noticed these dark destructive forces, or do not consider them or accept them until they hit their own heads against them. By that time it can be too late. They begin by discovering the solution – the official solution – and this they must embrace: the simpler, the more attractive. That is why the prophecies of the system-builders often come to naught.

Contemplation of modern history alone ought to lead us to the view that there is no simple solution, such as that the answer lies in technological advance, or a return to some ancient faith, or self-determination, or utilitarianism, or Communism, or socialism, or individualism, or capitalism, or any other -ism or single idea. If our generation can learn anything from the past, it ought to contemplate two suppositions about human goals. The first is that not all goals are compatible. The goal is chosen for itself, not in the hope that success in attaining it will guarantee the attainment of other corollary goals, but with the realisation that it may foreclose them. If X is chosen, Y may be irretrievably lost, and nothing can be done about it.

The second supposition is that human beings, in the process of seeking their goals, transform themselves. And by transforming themselves they alter their goals too. We begin by seeking goal A – let us say, economic prosperity or social equality – and the more we improve our own social structure and outlook and behaviour, the more our aims and goals will in turn alter. We cannot therefore predict today what our goal will be tomorrow. Any attempt to put humanity in a straitjacket, no matter how noble the intention, is dangerous. We say that what men really want is A, B and C; so we will provide them with A, B and C, though of course at some cost. One must (we are told) break eggs to make omelettes. Very well, we break the eggs – but the question is whether the omelette has been worth it. After breaking the eggs, even though the omelette is edible, those for whom it is made may no longer want to eat it. Their very success has altered them: they now want quite a different dish. So more eggs have to be broken, and so the egg-breaking process can continue for ever, so long as we insist that a given omelette is the final goal of our – or mankind's – desire. It is better to be more scrupulous about breaking eggs – or lives – once we know that, no matter how many are broken, the dish produced may well not be what, by then, we shall need and idealise.

These two suppositions seem to constitute one of the few dependable lessons of history. We cannot fully predict the future, and we have to realise the necessity for choosing among incompatible ideals; and for living in a society in which different people may seek different, equally valid, ends. We must learn to be satisfied with the maximum effort to preserve some kind of precarious equilibrium between varieties of goals and of men, a system of world order in which necessary change can occur without breaking the delicate crust without which human life cannot exist, and without which no ideals can be properly worked for and preserved.

This is a very difficult and a very undramatic thing to do; it can be tedious, and the tension is not good for the nerves. It is an extreme strain to have to be continuously aware of the fact that all we are trying to do is preserve a social framework or individual health which is constantly threatening to crack and requires to be patched up and propped and protected. It is far more agreeable and exciting to have a shining ideal, to think that we are approaching it because we have already conquered a given number of obstacles, and there are only a finite number more, after which we or our children or grandchildren will enjoy perpetual sunshine. The most noble and moving of democrats, Condorcet, was sure that the day would arrive at last: the day on which mankind will be happy, free and wise. But this is not very likely, because it is an a priori truth that one cannot have everything. Herder said long ago that we cannot recapture that which made the ancient Greeks or Jews or Indians wise or happy or great. That is gone for ever. This truism – that we build for our time, and then we shall see – is the strongest argument for what must be called a rather untidy liberalism. Values are not less sacred because they are not eternal. This is a liberalism in which one is not over-excited by any solution claiming finality or any single answer; where, above all, one is not deluded by the thought that one is called upon to remove the terrible obstacles that are the last great stones that stand before the doors of perfection, and that the destruction of entire societies is not too high a price to pay for victory in the war to end all wars, the overcoming of the last great obstacle, after which prehistory ends and true history begins.

Bibliography

Published works are cited in the text by author's name and year of publication; unpublished works are cited by author's name and title. Frequently cited collections of Berlin's work are cited parenthetically in-text by abbreviations, which are given at the beginning of the volume.

1. UNPUBLISHED WORKS AND ARCHIVES

Copies of Berlin's unpublished works, correspondence, and other papers are housed in the Isaiah Berlin Papers, Department of Special Collections and Western Manuscripts, Bodleian Library, University of Oxford. A catalogue of the papers, by Michael J. Hughes, is available online at www.bodley.ox.ac.uk/dept/scwmss/wmss/online/modern/berlin/berlin.html. Citation is by shelfmarks and folios, e.g. MSB 232/1–3.

Many of Isaiah Berlin's unpublished writings (as well as drafts of published writings, and published writings long out of print) are posted online, as are catalogues of Berlin's works and writings on Berlin, in the Isaiah Berlin Virtual Library (IBVL), curated by Henry Hardy, at http://berlin.wolf.ox.ac.uk/. The catalogues are also available, with smart search options, in Isaiah Berlin Online, the website of the Isaiah Berlin Literary Trust, at https://isaiah-berlin.wolfson.ox.ac.uk/.

The following works hosted at the IBVL are cited in this volume:

"The Achievement of Zionism" (1975), http://berlin.wolf.ox.ac.uk/lists/nachlass/achiezio.pdf.
"Introduction: Induction and Logic" (1937), http://berlin.wolf.ox.ac.uk/lists/nachlass/logic.pdf.
"Matter" (1934), http://berlin.wolf.ox.ac.uk/lists/nachlass/matter.pdf.
Dialogue with Stuart Hampshire, "I'm Going to Tamper with Your Beliefs a Little," http://berlin.wolf.ox.ac.uk/lists/nachlass/imgoing.pdf.
Dialogue with Stuart Hampshire and Bryan Magee, "The Problems of Nationalism," Thames Television, November 6, 1972, http://berlin.wolf.ox.ac.uk/lists/nachlass/probnati.pdf.

Supplement to *Flourishing: Letters 1928–1946*, http://berlin.wolf.ox.ac.uk/published_works/f/l1supp.pdf.
Supplement to *Enlightening: Letters 1946–1960*, http://berlin.wolf.ox.ac.uk/published_works/e/l2supp.pdf.

II PUBLISHED WORKS BY ISAIAH BERLIN

A. Collected Writings and Correspondence

Berlin, Isaiah. 2019 [1996]. *The Sense of Reality: Studies in Ideas and Their History*, 2nd edn., ed. Henry Hardy (Princeton: Princeton University Press).
 1997. *The Proper Study of Mankind: An Anthology of Essays*, ed. Henry Hardy and Roger Hausheer (New York: Farrar, Straus, and Giroux).
 2002. *Liberty*, ed. Henry Hardy (Oxford: Oxford University Press).
 2004. *Flourishing: Letters 1928–1946*, ed. Henry Hardy (London: Chatto & Windus).
 2008 [1978]. *Russian Thinkers*, ed. Henry Hardy and Aileen Kelly, 2nd edn., revised by Henry Hardy (London: Penguin Classics).
 2009. *Enlightening: Letters 1946–1960*, ed. Henry Hardy and Jennifer Holmes (London: Chatto & Windus).
 2013 [1979]. *Against the Current*: Essays in the History of Ideas, ed. Henry Hardy, 2nd edn. (Princeton: Princeton University Press).
 2013. *Building: Letters 1960–1975*, ed. Henry Hardy and Mark Pottle (London: Chatto & Windus).
 2013 [1978]. *Concepts and Categories: Philosophical Essays*, ed. Henry Hardy, 2nd edn. (Princeton: Princeton University Press).
 2013 [1990]. *The Crooked Timber of Humanity*: Chapters in the History of Ideas, ed. Henry Hardy, 2nd edn. (Princeton: Princeton University Press).
 2013 [1953]. The Hedgehog and the Fox: An Essay on Tolstoy's View of History, 2nd edn., ed. Henry Hardy (Princeton: Princeton University Press).
 2013 [1939]. *Karl Marx*, 5th edn., ed. Henry Hardy (Princeton: Princeton University Press).
 2013 [2000]. *The Power of Ideas*, ed. Henry Hardy, 2nd edn. (Princeton: Princeton University Press).
 2013 [1999]. *The Roots of Romanticism*, ed. Henry Hardy, 2nd edn. (Princeton: Princeton University Press).
 2013 [2000]. *Three Critics of the Enlightenment: Vico, Hamann, Herder*, ed. Henry Hardy, 2nd edn. (Princeton: Princeton University Press).
 2014 [2002]. *Freedom and Its Betrayal: Six Enemies of Human Liberty*, ed. Henry Hardy, 2nd edn. (Princeton: Princeton University Press).
 2014 [1980] *Personal Impressions*, ed. Henry Hardy, 3rd edn. (Princeton: Princeton University Press).
 2014 [2006]. *Political Ideas in the Romantic Age: Their Rise and Influence on Modern Thought*, ed. Henry Hardy, 2nd edn. (Princeton: Princeton University Press).
 2015. *Affirming: Letters 1975–1997*, ed. Henry Hardy and Mark Pottle (London: Chatto and Windus).
 2016 [2004]. *The Soviet Mind: Russian Culture under Communism*, ed. Henry Hardy, 2nd edn. (Washington: Brookings Institution Press).
 2017 [1956]. *The Age of Enlightenment: The Eighteenth-Century Philosophers*, 2nd edn, ed. Henry Hardy (Oxford: Isaiah Berlin Literary Trust), http://berlin.wolf.ox.ac.uk/published_works/ae/AE2.pdf.

Bibliography

Berlin, Isaiah, and Polanowska-Sygulska, Beata. 2006. *Unfinished Dialogue* (New York: Prometheus Books).

B. Miscellaneous Publications

1950a. "Soviet Beginnings." *Sunday Times*, December 10, 1950, http://berlin.wolf.ox.ac.uk/published_works/singles/carrrev.pdf.

1950b. "The Year 1949 in Historical Perspective: The Trends of Culture." In *1950 Encyclopedia Britannica Book of the Year* (Chicago: Encyclopedia Britannica).

1951. "Nineteen Fifty: A Survey of Politico-Cultural Trends of the Year." In *Britannica Book of the Year* (Chicago: Encyclopedia Britannica).

1952a. "Nineteen Fifty-One: A Survey of Cultural Trends of the Year." In *1952 Britannica Book of the Year* (Chicago: Encyclopedia Britannica).

1952b. Review of Benedetto Croce, *My Philosophy*, Mind 61, 574–8.

1953. Review of Ernst Cassirer, *The Philosophy of the Enlightenment*, English Historical Review 68, 617–18.

1961. "What is History?" (An Exchange of Letters with E. H. Carr), *Listener* 65, 877, 1048–9.

1962a. "Mr. Carr's Big Battalions," *New Statesman* 63, 15–16.

1962b. "The Road to Catastrophe," *The Times Literary Supplement*, March 30, 216.

1970. "Weizmann as Exilarch," in Berlin, Isaiah, and Kolatt, Israel, *Chaim Weizmann as Leader: Inaugural Lectures of the Israel Goldstein chair of the history of Zionism and the Yishuv at the Institute of Contemporary Jewry, the Hebrew University of Jerusalem* (Jerusalem: Hebrew University).

1972. "The Bent Twig: A Note on Nationalism," *Foreign Affairs* 51, 11–30.

1981. "Russian Thought and the Slavophile Controversy," *Slavonic and East European Review* 59: 4, 572–86.

1991. "Two Concepts of Nationalism: An Interview with Isaiah Berlin," *New York Review of Books*, November 21, 1991, 19–23; Berlin, letter to the editor, ibid. December 5, 1991, 58.

1998. "Isaiah Berlin in Conversation with Steven Lukes," *Salmagundi* 120 (Fall), 52–134.

2001 [1935]. "A Sense of Impending Doom," *The Times Literary Supplement*, July 27, 11–12.

2014. "A Message to the Twenty-first Century," *New York Review of Books*, October 23, www.nybooks.com/articles/archives/2014/oct/23/message-21st-century/.

Berlin, Isaiah, Hampshire, Stuart, Murdoch, Iris, and Quinton, Anthony. 1955. "Philosophy and Beliefs," *Twentieth Century* 157: 940, 495–521.

II. PUBLISHED WORKS BY OTHERS

Aarsbergen-Ligtvoet, Connie. 2006. *Isaiah Berlin: A Value-Pluralist and Humanist Vision of Human Nature and the Meaning of Life* (Amsterdam: Rodopi).

Adcock, Robert and Bevir, Mark. 2007. "The Remaking of Political Theory," in *Modern Political Science: Anglo-American Exchanges since 1880*, ed. R. Adcock, M. Bevir, and S. Stimson (Princeton: Princeton University Press).

Adorno, Theodor and Horkheimer, Max. 1972 [1947]. *The Dialectic of Enlightenment*, trans. John Cummings (New York: Seabury Press).
Akehurst, Thomas L. 2010. *The Cultural Politics of Analytic Philosophy: Britishness and the Spectre of Europe* (London: Continuum Press).
Albert, Simon. 2013. "The Wartime 'Special Relationship', 1941–45: Isaiah Berlin, Freya Stark and Mandate Palestine," *Jewish Historical Studies* 45, 103–30.
Allen, Jonathan 2004. "Isaiah Berlin's Anti-Procrustean Liberalism: Ideas, Circumstances, and the Protean Individual," paper presented at the annual meeting of the American Political Science Association (August 28–31, 2003, Philadelphia), online at http://berlin.wolf.ox.ac.uk/lists/onib/allen2003.pdf.
  1998. Review of Isaiah Berlin's *The Sense of Reality*, *South African Journal of Philosophy* 17: 2, 173–7.
  2009. "What's the Matter with Monism?" *Critical Review of International Social and Political Philosophy* 12: 3, 469–89.
Anderson, Perry. 1992. "The Pluralism of Isaiah Berlin," in *A Zone of Engagement* (London: Verso).
Annan, Noel. 1974. "A Man I Loved," in *Maurice Bowra: A Celebration*, ed. Hugh Lloyd-Jones (London: Duckworth).
  2014. "Afterword," in Isaiah Berlin, *Personal Impressions*, ed. Henry Hardy, 3rd edn (Princeton: Princeton University Press).
Appiah, Kwame Anthony. 2005. *The Ethics of Identity* (Princeton and Oxford: Princeton University Press).
Arendt, Hannah. 1982. *Lectures on Kant's Political Philosophy*, ed. Ronald Beiner (Chicago: University of Chicago Press).
  1993 [1968]. *Between Past and Future* (London: Penguin Books).
  1994. *Essays in Understanding:,1930–1954: Formation, Exile, and Totalitarianism*, ed. Jerome Kohn (New York: Schocken Books).
Arneson, Richard. 2006. "Justice After Rawls," in *The Oxford Handbook of Political Theory*, ed. J. Dryzek, B. Honig, and A. Phillips (Oxford: Oxford University Press).
Aron, Raymond. 2001 [1955]. *The Opium of the Intellectuals*, trans. Terrence Kilmartin, ed. Daniel J. Mahoney and Brian Anderson (New Brunswick: Transaction Publishers).
Austin, J. L. 1958. "Pretending." *Proceedings of the Aristotelian Society*, supplementary vol. 32, 261–78.
  1962. *Sense and Sensibilia* (Oxford: Clarendon Press).
Avineri, Shlomo. 2007. "A Jew and a Gentleman." *The One and the Many: Reading Isaiah Berlin*, ed. George Crowder and Henry Hardy (Amherst: Prometheus Books).
Ayer, A. J. 1977. *Part of My Life* (London: William Collins).
  2001 [1936]. *Language, Truth, and Logic* (London: Gollancz).
Bambach, Charles R. 1995. *Heidegger, Dilthey, and the Crisis of Historicism* (Ithaca: Cornell University Press).
Bauman, Zygmunt. 1989. *Modernity and the Holocaust* (Ithaca: Cornell University Press).
Beiser, Frederick C. 1996. "Early Romanticism and the *Aufklärung*," in *What is Enlightenment? Eighteenth-Century Answers and Twentieth-Century Questions*, ed. James Schmidt (Berkeley: University of California Press).

2003. *The Romantic Imperative: The Concept of Early German Romanticism* (Cambridge, MA: Harvard University Press).
  2011. *The German Historicist Tradition* (Oxford: Oxford University Press).
  2014. *After Hegel: German Philosophy, 1840–1900* (Princeton: Princeton University Press).
Bell, Daniel. 1976. *The Cultural Contradictions of Capitalism* (New York: Basic Books).
Bentley, Michael. 2005. *Modernizing England's Past: English Historiography in the Age of Modernism 1870–1970* (Cambridge: Cambridge University Press).
Bevin, Ernest. 1948. "Address given by Ernest Bevin to the House of Commons (22 January 1948)." Parliamentary Debates. House of Commons. Official Report. Third session of the Thirty-Eight Parliament of the United Kingdom of Great Britain and Northern Ireland. www.cvce.eu/content/publication/2002/9/9/7bc0ecbd-c50e-4035-8e36-ed70bfbd204c/publishable_en.pdf.
Bevir, Mark. 2006. "Political Studies as Narrative and Science, 1880–2000," *Political Studies* 54:3, 583–606.
  2011. "Histories of Analytic Political Philosophy," *History of European Ideas* 23, 243–8.
Bevir, Mark and O'Brien, David. 2003. "From Idealism to Communitarianism: The Inheritance and Legacy of John MacMurray," *History of Political Thought* 24:2, 305–29.
Billington, James and Parthé, Kathleen. 2003. *The Search for a new Russian National Identity: Russian Perspectives*. Washington, DC: Library of Congress, February 2003; available online at www.loc.gov/portals/static/about/about-the-librarian/images/perspectives.pdf
Bowra, C. M. 1966. *Memories* (London: Weidenfeld and Nicolson).
Brodsky, Joseph. 1991. "Isaiah Berlin: A Tribute," in Edna Ullmann-Margalit and Avishai Margalit, eds. *Isaiah Berlin. A Celebration* (Chicago: University of Chicago Press), 205–14.
Brogan, A. P. 1931. "Objective Pluralism in the Theory of Value," *International Journal of Ethics* 41, 287–95.
Brooke, Christopher. 2016. "Isaiah Berlin and the Origins of the 'Totalitarian' Rousseau," in *Isaiah Berlin and the Enlightenment*, ed. Laurence Brockliss and Ritchie Robertson (Oxford: Oxford University Press).
Burnham, James. 1941. *The Managerial Revolution* (New York: John Day).
Capaldi, Nicholas. 2004. *John Stuart Mill: A Biography* (Cambridge: Cambridge University Press).
Caradonna, Jeremy L. 2015. "There Was No Counter-Enlightenment," *Eighteenth Century Studies*, 49:1, 51–69.
Cassirer, Ernst. 1952. *The Philosophy of the Enlightenment*, trans. Fritz C. A. Koelln and James P. Pettegrove (Princeton: Princeton University Press).
Chamberlain, Lesley. 2004. *Motherland. A Philosophical History of Russia* (London: Atlantic Books).
Cherniss, Joshua L. 2013. *A Mind and Its Time: The Development of Isaiah Berlin's Political Thought* (Oxford: Oxford University Press).
  2014a. "Against 'Engineers of Human Souls': Isaiah Berlin's Anti-Managerial Liberalism," *History of Political Thought* 35:3, 565–88.

2014b. "Isaiah Berlin's Political Ideas: From the Twentieth Century to the Romantic Age," in Isaiah Berlin, *Political Ideas in the Romantic Age*, ed. Henry Hardy (Princeton: Princeton University Press).

2017. "Isaiah Berlin: Russo-Jewish Roots, Liberal Commitments, and the Ethos of Pluralism," *International Journal of Politics, Culture and Society* 30:2, 183–99.

Choi, Naomi. 2015. "Liberalism and the Interpretive Turn: Rival Approaches or Cross-Purposes?," *Review of Politics* 77:2, 243–70.

Christman, John. 1991. "Liberalism and Individual Positive Freedom," *Ethics* 101:2, 343–59.

Clive, John. 1981. "Painter of Character," *The New Republic* 184:5, 35–7.

Collingwood, R. G. 1970. *The Idea of History*, ed. T. M. Knox (New York: Oxford University Press).

Condorcet, Marie Jean Antoine Nicolas Caritat, Marquis de. 1847–9 [1782]. "Discours prononcé dans l'Académie française le jeudi 21 février 1782, à la réception de M. le marquis de Condorcet," in *Oeuvres de Condorcet*, ed. A. Condorcet O'Connor and M. F. Arago (Paris: Firmin Didot), vol. 1.

1970 [1795]. *Esquisse d'un tableau historique dès progrès de l'esprit humain*, ed. O. H. Prior and Yvon Belaval (Paris: Vrin).

Constant, Benjamin. 1988. *Political Writings*, ed. Biancamaria Fontana (Cambridge: Cambridge University Press).

1997. *Écrits politiques*, ed. Marcel Gauchet (Paris: Gallimard).

Craiutu, Aurelian. 2016. *Faces of Moderation: The Art of Balance in an Age of Extremes* (Philadelphia: University of Pennsylvania Press).

Crowder, George. 2002. *Liberalism and Value Pluralism* (London and New York: Continuum).

2004. *Isaiah Berlin: Liberty and Pluralism* (Cambridge: Polity Press).

2007a. "Two Concepts of Liberal Pluralism," *Political Theory* 35:2, 121–46.

2007b. "Value Pluralism and Liberalism: Berlin and Beyond," in *The One and the Many: Reading Isaiah Berlin*, ed. George Crowder and Henry Hardy (Amherst: Prometheus Books), 207–30.

2013a. "Justification and Psychology in Liberal Pluralism: A Reply to Zakaras," *Review of Politics* 75:1, 103–10.

2013b. "Pluralism," in G. Gaus and F. D'Agostino, eds, *Routledge Companion to Social and Political Philosophy* (New York and London: Routledge).

2013c. *Theories of Multiculturalism* (Cambridge: Polity).

2015a. "Value Pluralism, Diversity and Liberalism," *Ethical Theory and Moral Practice* 18:3, 549–64.

2015b. "Why We Need Positive Liberty," *Review of Politics* 77:2, 271–8.

2016. "After Berlin: The Literature Since 2002," in The Isaiah Berlin Literary Trust, *The Isaiah Berlin Virtual Library*, http://berlin.wolf.ox.ac.uk/lists/onib/after-berlin.pdf

Crowder, George, and Hardy, Henry, eds. 2007a. *The One and the Many* (Amherst: Prometheus Books).

2007b. "Appendix: Berlin's Universal Vales – Core or Horizon?," in George Crowder and Henry Hardy, eds, *The One and the Many: Reading Isaiah Berlin* (Amherst: Prometheus Books).

Dabney, Lewis. 1998. "The Philosopher and the Critic," *The New York Times Book Review*, Nov. 29, 31.

Donnelly, Jack. 2003. *Universal Human Rights in Theory and Practice* (Ithaca: Cornell University Press).

Dostoyevsky, Fyodor M. 1958 [1879–80]. *The Brothers Karamazov*, trans. David Magarshack (Harmondsworth: Penguin).

Dubnov, Arie M. 2007. "Between Liberalism and Jewish Nationalism: Young Isaiah Berlin on the Road Toward Diaspora Zionism," *Modern Intellectual History* 4, 303–26.

2012. *Isaiah Berlin: The Journey of a Jewish Liberal* (Basingstoke: Palgrave Macmillan).

Dworkin, Ronald M. 1978. "Liberalism," in *Public and Private Morality*, ed. Stuart Hampshire (Cambridge: Cambridge University Press).

2001. "Do Liberal Values Conflict?," in Ronald M. Dworkin, Mark Lilla, and Robert B. Silvers, eds, *The Legacy of Isaiah Berlin* (New York: New York Review Books).

2011. *Justice for Hedgehogs* (Cambridge, MA: Harvard University Press).

Dworkin, Ronald M., Lilla, Mark, and Silvers, Robert B. 2001. *The Legacy of Isaiah Berlin* (New York: New York Review Books).

Erlich, Victor. 2006. *Child of a Turbulent Century* (Evanston: Northwestern University Press).

Ferrell, Jason 2008. "The Alleged Relativism of Isaiah Berlin," *Critical Review of International Social and Political Philosophy* 11:1, 41–56.

Frost, Robert. 1995. "The Death of the Hired Man," in *Collected Poems, Prose, and Plays*, ed. Richard Poirier and Mark Richardson (New York: Library of America).

Furst, Lilian R. 1966. *Romanticism in Perspective* (London: Macmillan Press).

1979. *The Contours of European Romanticism* (London: Macmillan Press).

Gaddis, John Lewis. 2011. *George F. Kennan: An American Life* (London: Penguin).

Gagarin, Michael and Paul Woodruff, eds. 1995, *Early Greek Political Thought From Homer to the Sophists* (Cambridge: Cambridge University Press).

Galipeau, Claude J. 1994. *Isaiah Berlin's Liberalism* (Oxford: Clarendon Press).

Galston, William A. 1999. "Value Pluralism and Liberal Political Theory," *American Political Science Review* 93:4, 769–78.

2002. *Liberal Pluralism: The Implications of Value Pluralism for Political Theory and Practice* (Cambridge: Cambridge University Press).

2004. "Liberal Pluralism: A Reply to Talisse," *Contemporary Political Theory* 3, 140–7.

2005. *The Practice of Liberal Pluralism* (Cambridge: Cambridge University Press).

2013. "Between Logic and Psychology: The Links between Value Pluralism and Liberal Theory," *Review of Politics* 75, 97–101.

Garrard, Graeme. 2003. "Isaiah Berlin's Joseph de Maistre," in *Isaiah Berlin's Counter-Enlightenment*, ed. Joseph Mali and Robert Wokler (Philadelphia: American Philosophical Society).

2007. "Strange Reversals: Berlin on the Enlightenment and the Counter-Enlightenment," in *The One and the Many: Reading Isaiah Berlin*, ed. George Crowder and Henry Hardy (New York: Prometheus Books), 141–57.

Gardels, Nathan. 1991. "The Ingathering Storm of Nationalism: The Return of the *Volksgeist*" (interview with Berlin) *New Perspectives Quarterly* 8:4 (Fall), 4–10. (Reprinted as "Two Concepts of Nationalism." *New York Review of Books*, 21 November 1991, 19–23.)

Gaus, Gerald F. 2003. *Contemporary Theories of Liberalism* (London: Sage Publications).
Gay, Peter. 1966, 1969. *The Enlightenment: An Interpretation*, 2 vols (New York: Random House).
　1971. *The Party of Humanity: Essays in the French Enlightenment* (New York: Norton).
Gellner, Ernest. 1995. "Sauce for the Liberal Goose," *Prospect*, November 1995, 56–61.
Gertsen, Aleksandr. 1954–66 *Sobranie sochinenii v tridtsati tomakh* (Moscow: ANSSSR).
Goldman, Eliezer. 1992. "Introduction," in Yeshayahu Leibowitz, *Judaism, Human Values, and the Jewish State* (Cambridge, MA: Harvard University Press).
Gordon, Peter E. 2012. *Continental Divide: Heidegger, Cassirer, Davos* (Cambridge, MA: Harvard University Press).
Gray, John. 1993. *Post-Liberalism: Studies in Political Thought* (London: Routledge).
　1995. *Enlightenment's Wake: Politics and Culture at the Close of the Modern Age* (London: Routledge).
　1996. *Isaiah Berlin* (Princeton: Princeton University Press).
　2000a. *Two Faces of Liberalism* (Cambridge: Polity).
　2000b. "Where Pluralists and Liberals Part Company," in M. Baghramian and A. Ingram, eds, *Pluralism: The Philosophy and Politics of Diversity* (London: Routledge).
　2013. *Isaiah Berlin: An Interpretation of His Thought*, 2nd edn (Princeton: Princeton University Press).
Grayling, A. C. 1998. "Meditations on a Thinker," *The Financial Times*, Nov. 21–22, 1998.
Gurvich-Lishchiner, S. D., ed. 1987. *Letopis' zhizni i tvorchestva A. I. Gertsena 1864–1867* (Moscow: Nauka).
Gustavsson, Gina. 2014. "The Psychological Dangers of Positive Liberty: Reconstructing a Neglected Undercurrent in Isaiah Berlin's *Two Concepts of Liberty*," *The Review of Politics* 76:2, 267–91.
　2015a. "Reply to Crowder," *Review of Politics* 77:2, 279–84.
　2015b. "A Romantic Reading of the French 'Burqa Ban': Liberty as Self-Expression and the Symbolism of Uncovered Faces in the French Debate on Full Veils," *Confluence* 2, 88–106.
Hacker, P. M. S. 1996. *Wittgenstein's Place in Twentieth-Century Analytic Philosophy* (Oxford: Blackwell).
Hampshire, Stuart. 1978. "Public and Private Morality," in *Public and Private Morality*, ed. Stuart Hampshire (Cambridge: Cambridge University Press).
　1983. *Morality and Conflict* (Cambridge, MA: Harvard University Press).
　1989. *Innocence and Experience* (Cambridge, MA: Harvard University Press).
Hanley, Ryan P. 2004. "Political Science and Political Understanding: Isaiah Berlin on the Nature of Political Inquiry," *American Political Science Review* 98, 327–39.
　2007. "Berlin and History," In *The One and the Many: Reading Isaiah Berlin*, ed. George Crowder and Henry Hardy (Amherst: Prometheus Books).
Hardy, Henry. 1999. "Editor's Preface," in Isaiah Berlin, *Concepts and Categories*, ed. Henry Hardy (London: Pimlico).

2000. "Isaiah Berlin's Key Idea," *Philosophers' Magazine* 11 (Summer 2000), pp. 15–16, online at http://berlin.wolf.ox.ac.uk/writings_on_ib/hhonib/isaiah_berlin%27s_key_idea.html.
2009. *The Book of Isaiah: Personal Impressions of Isaiah Berlin* (Oxford: Boydell Press, in association with Wolfson College, Oxford).
2018. *In Search of Isaiah Berlin: A Literary Adventure* (London: I.B. Tauris).
Harris, Ian. 2002. "Berlin and His Critics," in Isaiah Berlin, *Liberty*, ed. Henry Hardy (Oxford: Oxford University Press), 349–374.
Harris, Robert N. Forthcoming. *Alexander Herzen* (Oxford: Oxford University Press).
Hausheer, Roger. 2003. "Enlightening the Enlightenment," in *Isaiah Berlin's Counter-Enlightenment*, eds. Joseph Mali and Robert Wokler (Philadelphia: American Philosophical Society).
Hawthorn, Geoffrey. 1991. *Plausible Worlds: Possibility and Understanding in the Social Sciences* (Cambridge: Cambridge University Press).
Hayek, Friedrich A. 1960. *The Constitution of Liberty* (Chicago: University of Chicago Press, 1960).
Helvetius, Claude Adrien. 1909 [1759]. *De l'esprit* (Paris: Mercure de France).
Herodotus. 2005. *The Histories*, trans. Aubrey de Selincourt (London: Penguin).
Herzen, Alexander. 1956. *From the Other Shore and The Russian People and Socialism*. Introduction by Isaiah Berlin. Trans. Moura Budberg and Richard Wollheim (New York: Meridian Books).
2012. *A Herzen Reader*, ed. Kathleen Parthé (Evanston: Northwestern University Press).
Hobbes, Thomas. 1996 [1651]. *Leviathan*, ed. Richard Tuck (Cambridge: Cambridge University Press).
Holbach, Paul Henri Thiry, baron d'. 1770. *Système de la nature* (London [sc. Amsterdam]), part 1.
1817 [1770]. *The System of Nature; or, the Laws of the Moral and Physical World*, "done from the original French of M. de Mirabaud [sc. Holbach]" (translator unnamed), 3rd edn (London).
Holmes, Stephen. 1984. *Benjamin Constant and the Making of Modern Liberalism* (New Haven: Yale University Press).
Ibsen, Henrik. 1998. *Peer Gynt*, trans Christopher Fry (Oxford: Oxford World Classics).
Ignatieff, Michael. 1992. Interview with Isaiah Berlin for *The Late Show*, recorded 30 January 1992, broadcast 5 February 1992, BBC2 TV.
1998. *Isaiah Berlin: A Life* (New York: Henry Holt).
Israel, Jonathan. 2001. *The Radical Enlightenment: Philosophy and the Making of Modernity, 1650–1750* (New York: Oxford University Press).
2015. "Leo Strauss and the Radical Enlightenment," in *Reading Between the Lines: Leo Strauss and the History of Early Modern Philosophy*, ed. Winfried Schröder (Berlin: De Gruyter).
Jacoby, Russell. 2005. *Picture Imperfect: Utopian Thought for an Anti-Utopian Age* (New York: Columbia University Press).
Jahanbegloo, Ramin and Berlin, Isaiah. 1991. *Conversations with Isaiah Berlin* (New York: Charles Scribner's Sons).
James, Clive. 1998. "A Guest from the Future. Gaps and Glories in the Legacy of Isaiah Berlin," *Times Literary Supplement*, Sept. 3, 1998

Joll, James. 1979. "Politicians and the Freedom to Choose: the Case of July 1914," in *The Idea of Freedom: Essays in Honor of Isaiah Berlin*, ed. Alan Ryan (Oxford: Oxford University Press).

Kamm, Frances M. 1993. *Morality, Mortality*, vol. 1: *Death and Whom to Save From It* (Oxford: Oxford University Press).

   1996. *Morality, Mortality*, vol. 2: *Rights, Duties, and Status* (Oxford: Oxford University Press).

Kant, Immanuel. 1912 [1784]. "Idee zu einer allgemeinen Geschichte in weltbürgerlicher Absicht" ("Idea for a Universal History with a Cosmopolitan Purpose"). *Kant's gesammelte Schriften* (Berlin: Reimer), vol. 8.

   1970 [1784]. "What is Enlightenment?" In *Political Writings*, ed. Hans Reiss, trans. H. B. Nisbet (Cambridge: Cambridge University Press).

   1991 [1793]. "On the Common Saying: 'This May be True in Theory, But It Does Not Apply in Practice,'" in Immanuel Kant, *Political Writings*, ed. H. Reiss, trans. H. B Nisbet (Cambridge: Cambridge University Press).

   2000 [1790]. *Critique of the Power of Judgment*, ed. Paul Guyer, trans. Paul Guyer and Eric Matthews (Cambridge: Cambridge University Press).

Kateb, George. 1999. "Can Cultures be Judged? Two Defenses of Cultural Pluralism in Isaiah Berlin's Work," *Social Research* 66, 1009–38.

Kekes, John. 1993. *The Morality of Pluralism* (Princeton: Princeton University Press).

   1997. *Against Liberalism* (Ithaca: Cornell University Press).

   1998. *A Case for Conservatism* (Ithaca: Cornell University Press).

Kelly, Aileen. 2001. "A Revolutionary without Fanaticism," in *The Legacy of Isaiah Berlin*, ed. Mark Lilla, Ronald M. Dworkin, and Robert B. Silvers (New York: New York Review Books).

   2013. "A Luminous Personality," in *The Book of Isaiah. Personal Impressions of Isaiah Berlin*, ed. Henry Hardy (Oxford: Boydell Press, 2013).

Kelly, Duncan. 2002. "The Political Thought of Isaiah Berlin," *British Journal of Politics and International Relations* 4, 25–48.

Kennan, George F. 2014. *The Kennan Dairies*, ed. by Frank Costigliola (New York: W.W. Norton).

Keohane, Nannerl O. 2012. *Thinking About Leadership* (Princeton: Princeton University Press).

Khilnani, Sunil. 2009. "Nehru's Judgement," in *Political Judgement: Essays for John Dunn*, ed. Richard Bourke and Raymond Geuss (Cambridge: Cambridge University Press, 2009).

Kipling, Rudyard. 1902 [1886]. *Departmental Ditties and Other Verses* (Chicago: W. B. Conkey).

Kołakowski, Leszek. 2005 [1976]. *Main Currents of Marxism: The Founders-The Golden Age- The Breakdown* (New York: Norton).

Kripke, Saul A. 1980. *Naming and Necessity* (Cambridge, MA: Harvard University Press).

Lamprecht, Sterling P. 1920. "The Need for a Pluralistic Emphasis in Ethics," *Journal of Philosophy, Psychology and Scientific Methods* 17, 561–72.

   1921. "Some Political Implications of Ethical Pluralism," *Journal of Philosophy* 18, 225–44.

Lane, Melissa. 2011. "Constraint, freedom, and exemplar: history and theory without teleology," in *Political Philosophy versus History?: Conextualism and Real Politics*

in *Contemporary Political Thought*, ed Jonathan Floyd and Marc Stears (Cambridge: Cambridge University Press).
Larmore, Charles. 1996a. *The Morals of Modernity* (Cambridge: Cambridge University Press).
　1996b. *The Romantic Legacy* (New York: Columbia University Press).
Laslett, Peter. 1956. "Introduction," in *Politics Philosophy and Society*, 1st Series, ed. Peter Laslett (Blackwell, Oxford, 1956).
Lovejoy, Arthur O. 1948. "On The Discrimination of Romanticism," in *Essays in the History of Ideas*, ed. Arthur O. Lovejoy (Baltimore: Johns Hopkins University Press).
Lukes, Steven. 1998. "Isaiah Berlin: in Conversation with Steven Lukes," *Salmagundi* 120, 52–134.
　2003. *Liberals and Cannibals: The Implications of Diversity* (London: Verso).
　2008. *Moral Relativism* (New York: Picador).
MacCallum, Jr. Gerald C. 1967. "Negative and Positive Freedom," *Philosophical Review* 76, 312–34.
Machiavelli, Niccolo. 1985 [1532]. *The Prince*, trans, Harvey C. Mansfield, (Chicago: University of Chicago Press).
　1996 [1531]. *Discourses on Livy*, trans. Harvey C. Mansfield, Jr. and Nathan Tarcov (Chicago: University of Chicago Press).
MacIntyre, Alasdair. 1981. *After Virtue: A Study in Moral Theory* (Notre Dame: University of Notre Dame Press).
Mackenzie, Alexander Slidell. 1848. *Life of Stephen Decatur* (Boston: Charles C. Little and James Brown).
Macpherson, C. B. 1962. *The Political Theory of Possessive Individualism: Hobbes to Locke* (Oxford: Oxford University Press).
Mali, Joseph. 2012. *The Legacy of Vico in Modern Cultural History: From Jules Michelet to Isaiah Berlin* (Cambridge: Cambridge University Press).
Margalit, Avishai. 1997. "The Moral Psychology of Nationalism," in Robert McKim and Jeff McMahan, eds, *The Morality of Nationalism* (Oxford: Oxford University Press).
　1998. "The Three Faces of Isaiah Berlin," *Times Literary Supplement*, May 29, 1998.
Marx, Karl. 1973 [1859]. "Preface to *The Critique of Political Economy*," in *Selected Works*, vol. 1 (Moscow: Progress Publishers).
　1976 [1867]. *Capital: A Critique of Political Economy*, vol. I (London: Pelican).
Mill, J. S. 1972. *The Collected Works of John Stuart Mill, Volume XV The Later Letters of John Stuart Mill 1849–1873 Part II*, ed. F. E. Mineka and D. N. Lindley (Toronto: University of Toronto Press).
　1974 [1859]. *On Liberty*, ed. Gertrude Himmelfarb (Harmondsworth: Penguin).
Miller, David. 2005. "Crooked Timber or Bent Twig? Isaiah Berlin's Nationalism," *Political Studies* 53:1,100–23; reprinted in *The One and the Many: Reading Isaiah Berlin*, ed. George Crowder and Henry Hardy (Amherst: Prometheus Books).
Momigliano, Arnaldo. 1976. "On the Pioneer Trail," *New York Review of Books*, November 11, 33–38.
Moon, J. Donald. 2004. "The Current State of Political Theory: Pluralism and Reconciliation," in *What is Political Theory?*, ed. S. White and D. Moon (London: Sage).

Moore, Matthew. 2009. "Pluralism, Relativism, and Liberalism," *Political Research Quarterly* 62:2, 244–56.
Morgenbesser, Sidney, and Lieberson, Jonathan. 1991. "Isaiah Berlin," in Edna Ullmann-Margalit and Avishai Margalit (eds.), *Isaiah Berlin: A Celebration* (Chicago: University of Chicago Press).
Müller, Jan-Werner. 2008. "Fear and Freedom: On 'Cold War Liberalism'," *European Journal of Political Theory*, 7:1, 45–64.
    2012. "Value Pluralism in Twentieth-Century Anglo-American Thought," in *Modern Pluralism: Anglo-American Debates Since 1880*, ed. Mark Bevir (Cambridge: Cambridge University Press).
Mulligan, Thomas. 2015. "The Limits of Liberal Tolerance," *Public Affairs Quarterly* 29:3, 277–95.
Myers, Ella. 2010. "From Pluralism to Liberalism: Rereading Isaiah Berlin," *The Review of Politics*, 72, 599–625.
Nagel, Thomas. 2001. "Pluralism and Coherence," in Mark Lilla, Ronald M. Dowrkin, and Robert B. Silvers, eds, *The Legacy of Isaiah Berlin* (New York: New York Review Books).
Nichols, H. G. ed. 1981. *Washington Dispatches 1941–5. Weekly Political Reports from the British Embassy*, ed. H. G. Nichols, with an introduction by Isaiah Berlin (Chicago: University of Chicago Press, 1981).
Nussbaum, Martha. 1992. *Love's Knowledge: Essays on Philosophy and Literature* (Oxford: Oxford University Press).
    2000. *Women and Human Development: The Capabilities Approach* (Cambridge: Cambridge University Press).
    2001. *The Fragility of Goodness: Luck and Ethics in Greek Tragedy and Philosophy* (Cambridge: Cambridge University Press).
    2011. *Creating Capabilities: The Human Development Approach* (Cambridge, MA: Harvard University Press).
O'Brien, Karen. 2016. "Berlin and Montesquieu," in Laurence Brockliss and Ritchie Robertson, eds, *Isaiah Berlin and the Enlightenment* (Oxford: Oxford University Press).
Oakeshott, Michael. 1975. *On Human Conduct* (Oxford: Clarendon Press).
    1991. *Rationalism in Politics and Other Essays*, ed. Timothy Fuller (Indianapolis: Liberty Fund).
Oz, Amos and Fania Oz-Salzberger. 2012. *Jews and Words* (New Haven: Yale University Press).
Pagden, Anthony. 2013. *The Enlightenment: And Why It Still Matters* (Oxford: Oxford University Press).
Parekh, Bhikhu. 2006. *Rethinking Multiculturalism: Cultural Diversity and Political Theory* (London: Palgrave).
Parthé, Kathleen. 2004. *Russia's Dangerous Texts. Politics Between the Lines* (New Haven, Yale University Press).
Patten, Alan. 2010. "'The Most Natural State': Herder and Nationalism," *History of Political Thought* 31:4, 657–89.
Pears, David. 1991, "Philosophy and the History of Philosophy," in *Isaiah Berlin: A Celebration*, ed. Edna Ullmann-Margalit and Avishai Margalit (Chicago: University of Chicago Press).
Pettit, Philip. 1997. *A Theory of Freedom* (Oxford: Oxford University Press).

1999. *Republicanism: A Theory of Freedom and Government* (Oxford: Oxford University Press).
Pocock, J. G. A. 1981. "Virtues, Rights and Manners: A Model for Historians of Political Thought," *Political Theory* 9:3, 357–9.
1985. *Virtue, Commerce, and History: Essays on Political Thought and History, Chiefly in the Eighteenth Century* (Cambridge: Cambridge University Press).
2008. "Historiography and Enlightenment: A View of their History," *Modern Intellectual History* 5, 83–96.
Pollis, Adamantia, and Schwab, Peter. 1980. "Human Rights: A Western Construct with Limited Applicability," in Adamantia Pollis and Peter Schwab, eds, *Human Rights: Cultural and Ideological Perspectives* (New York: Praeger).
Prichard, H. A. 1968 [1912]. "Does Moral Philosophy Rest on a Mistake?" In *Moral Obligation: Essays and Lectures* (Oxford: Oxford University Press).
Rawls, John. 1993. *Political Liberalism* (New York: Columbia University Press).
1999. *A Theory of Justice*, rev. edn (Cambridge, MA: Harvard University Press).
Raz, Joseph. 1986. *The Morality of Freedom* (Oxford: Clarendon Press).
1995. "Multiculturalism: A Liberal Perspective," in *Ethics in the Public Domain: Essays in the Morality of Law and Politics* (Oxford: Clarendon Press).
Reed, Jamie. 2008. "From Logical Positivism to Metaphysical Rationalism: Isaiah Berlin on The Fallacy of Reduction," *History of Political Thought* 29:1, 109–31.
Riasanovsky, Nicholas V. 1992. *The Emergence of Romanticism* (Oxford: Oxford University Press).
Richards, Robert J. 2002. *The Romantic Conception of Life* (Chicago: Chicago University Press).
Richardson, Henry S. 1994. *Practical Reasoning about Final Ends* (Cambridge: Cambridge University Press).
Riley, Jonathan. 2000. "Crooked Timber and Liberal Culture," in Maria Baghramian and Attracta Ingram, eds, *Pluralism: The Philosophy and Politics of Diversity* (New York and London: Routledge).
2001. "Interpreting Berlin's Liberalism," *American Political Science Review* 95:2, 283–95.
2002. "Defending Cultural Pluralism: Within Liberal Limits," *Political Theory* 30:1, 68–96.
2013. "Isaiah Berlin's 'Minimum of Moral Ground,'" *Political Theory* 41:1, 61–89.
Rorty, Richard. 2001. "The Continuity Between the Enlightenment and 'Postmodernism,'" in Keith Baker and Peter Hans Reill, eds, *What's Left of the Enlightenment?: A Postmodern Question* (Stanford: Stanford University Press).
Rosenblatt, Helena, ed. 2014. *The Cambridge Companion to Constant* (Cambridge: Cambridge University Press).
Rosenblum, Nancy L. 1987. *Another Liberalism* (Cambridge: Harvard University Press).
1989. "Pluralism and Self-Defense" in *Liberalism and the Moral Life* (Cambridge, MA: Harvard University Press).
Ryan, Alan. 2012. *The Making of Modern Liberalism* (Princeton: Princeton University Press).
2013. "Isaiah Berlin: The History of Ideas as Psychodrama," *European Journal of Political Theory* 12:1, 61–72.

2015. "Liberalism 1900–1940," in *The Cambridge Companion to Liberalism*, ed. Steven Wall (Cambridge: Cambridge University Press).
Ryle, Gilbert. 1945–6. "Knowing That and Knowing How: The Presidential Address," *Proceedings of the Aristotelian Society* 46 New Series, 1–16.
Sabl, Andrew. 2001. *Ruling Passions: Political Offices and Democratic Ethics* (Princeton: Princeton University Press).
Sainte-Beuve, C.-A. 1853. "Franklin à Passy." *Causeries du lundi*, vol. 7 (Paris: Garnier).
Sandall, Roger. 2001. "The Book of Isaiah," in *The Culture Cult: Designer Tribalism and Other Essays* (Westport CT: Westview).
Satkunanandan, Shalini. 2015. *Extraordinary Responsibility: Politics Beyond the Moral Calculus* (Cambridge: Cambridge University Press).
Schlegel, Friedrich. 1991. *Philosophical Fragments*, trans. P. Firchow (Minneapolis: University of Minnesota Press).
Schuler, Alfred. 1940. *Fragmente und Vorträge aus dem Nachlass* (Leipzig: Barth).
Scott, James C. 1998. *Seeing Like a State: How Certain Schemes to Improve the Human Condition Have Failed* (New Haven: Yale University Press).
Sergeenko, P. A. 1911. *Tolstoy i ego sovremenniki* (Moscow: V. M. Sablina).
Shapiro, Ian. 1989. "Gross Concepts in Political Argument," *Political Theory* 17:1, 73–6.
  2007. *Containment: Rebuilding a Strategy against Global Terror* (Princeton: Princeton University Press, 2007).
  2016. *Politics Against Domination* (Cambridge, MA: Harvard University Press).
Shils, Edward. 1997. *The Virtue of Civility: Selected Essays on Liberalism, Tradition, and Civil Society*, ed. Steven Grosby (Indianapolis: Liberty Fund Press).
Shklar, Judith N. 1957. *After Utopia* (Princeton: Princeton University Press).
  1964. *Legalism: Law, Morals, and Political Trials* (Cambridge, MA: Harvard University Press).
  1998 [1989]. "The Liberalism of Fear," in *Political Thought and Political Thinkers*, ed. Stanley Hoffmann (Chicago: University of Chicago Press).
Skinner, Quentin. 2008. *Hobbes and Republican Freedom* (Cambridge: Cambridge University Press).
Smith, Steven B. 2006. *Reading Leo Strauss: Politics, Philosophy, Judaism* (Chicago: University of Chicago Press).
  2012. *Political Philosophy* (New Haven: Yale University Press).
  2016. *Modernity and Its Discontents: Making and Unmaking the Bourgeois from Machiavelli to Bellow* (New Haven: Yale University Press).
  Forthcoming. "Conservatives and Modernity." In *The Cambridge History of Modern European Thought*, ed. Peter Gordon and Warren Breckman (Cambridge: Cambridge University Press).
Sternhell, Zeev. 2010. *The Anti-Enlightenment Tradition*, trans. David Maisel (New Haven: Yale University Press).
Stevenson, C. L. 1944. *Ethics and Language* (New Haven: Yale University Press).
Stocker, Michael. 1990. *Plural and Conflicting Values* (Oxford: Clarendon Press).
Strauss, Leo. 1953. *Natural Right and History* (Chicago: University of Chicago Press).
  1959. *What Is Political Philosophy? And Other Studies* (Chicago: University of Chicago Press).
  1965. *Spinoza's Critique of Religion* (New York: Schocken Books).

1989 [1961]. "Relativism," in *The Rebirth of Classical Political Rationalism: An Introduction to the Thought of Leo Strauss*, ed. Thomas Pangle (Chicago: Chicago University Press).

Talisse, Robert B. 2012. *Pluralism and Liberal Politics* (New York and London: Routledge).

Talmon, Jacob. 1979 [1951]. *The Origins of Totalitarian Democracy* (New York: Norton).

Tamir, Yael. 1995. *Liberal Nationalism* (Princeton: Princeton University Press).

Taylor, Charles. 1991. *The Ethics of Authenticity* (Cambridge, MA: Harvard University Press).

1997. "Leading a Life," in *Incommensurability, Incomparability, and Practical Reasoning*, ed. Ruth Chang (Cambridge: Cambridge University Press).

1999. "Democratic Exclusion (and Its Remedies?)," in *Multiculturalism, Liberalism and Democracy*, ed. R. Bhargava, A. K. Bagchi, and R. Sudarshan, (Oxford: Oxford University Press, 1999).

2001. "The Plurality of Goods," in Mark Lilla, Ronald M. Dworkin, and Robert B. Silvers, eds, *The Legacy of Isaiah Berlin* (New York: New York Review Books).

Tetlock, Philip E. 2006. *Expert Political Judgment: How Good Is It? How Can We Know?* (Princeton: Princeton University Press).

Thucydides 1972. *History of the Peloponnesian War*, trans. Rex Warner (London: Penguin).

Tocqueville, Alexis de. 2010[1835–40]. *Democracy in America*, ed. Eduardo Nolla, trans. James Schleiffer (Indianapolis: Liberty Fund).

Venturi, Franco. 1952 *Il populismo russo*. Vols. I, II (Rome: Einaudi).

Voltaire. 1877–85 [1771]. "Epître au roi de Danemark, Christian VII, sur la liberté de la presse accordée dans tous ses états," in *Oeuvres complètes de Voltaire*, ed. Louis Moland (Paris: Garnier).

Waldron, Jeremy. 2013. "Political Political Theory: An Inaugural Lecture," *Journal of Political Philosophy* 21:1, 1–23.

Walicki, Andrzej. 1979. *A History of Russian Thought, from the Enlightenment to Marxism*, trans. by Hilda Andrews-Rusiecka (Stanford: Stanford University Press).

2007. "Berlin and The Russian Intelligentsia," in *The One and the Many. Reading Isaiah Berlin*, ed. George Crowder and Henry Hardy (Amherst: Prometheous Books, 2007).

2011. *Encounters with Isaiah Berlin. Story of an Intellectual Friendship* (New York: Peter Lang).

Walzer, Michael. 1973. "Political Action: The Problem of Dirty Hands," *Philosophy and Public Affairs* 2, 160–80.

1983. *Spheres of Justice: A Defence of Pluralism and Equality* (Oxford: Blackwell).

1995. "Are There Limits to Liberalism?," *New York Review of Books*, 42, 28–31.

2013. "Should We Reclaim Political Utopianism?," *European Journal of Political Theory* 12:1, 24–30.

Warner, Aaron W., Morse, Dean, and Cooney, Thomas E., eds. 1969. *The Environment of Change* (New York and London: Columbia University Press).

Weber, Max. 1948a [1919]. "The Vocation of Politics," in *From Max Weber: Essays in Sociology*, ed. H. H. Gerth and C. Wright Mills (London: Routledge).

1948b. "The Vocation of Science," [1917] in *From Max Weber: Essays in Sociology*, ed. H. H. Gerth and C. Wright Mills (London: Routledge).

West, M. L., ed. 1989. *Iambi et elegi graeci ante Alexandrum cantati*, 2nd edn., vol. 1 (Oxford: Oxford University Press).
White, Steven K. 2004. "Pluralism, Platitudes and Paradoxes: Western Political Thought at the Beginning of a New Century," in *What is Political Theory?*, ed. S. White and D. Moon (London: Sage).
Williams, Bernard. 2001. "Liberalism and Loss," in Mark Lilla, Ronald M. Dworkin, and Robert B. Silvers, eds, *The Legacy of Isaiah Berlin* (New York: New York Review Books).
  2005. *In the Beginning was the Deed: Realism and Moralism in Political Argument*, ed. Geoffrey Hawthorn (Princeton: Princeton University Press).
  2006. *Philosophy as a Humanistic Discipline*, ed. A. W. Moore (Princeton: Princeton University Press).
  2013. "Introduction," Isaiah Berlin, *Concepts and Categories: Philosophical Essays*, 2nd edn, ed. Henry Hardy (Princeton: Princeton University Press).
Windelband, Wilhelm. 1998 [1894]. "History and Natural Science," trans. James T. Lamiell. *Theory and Psychology* 8, 5–22.
Wokler, Robert. 2001. "The Professoriate of Political Thought in England since 1914: a tale of three chairs," in D. Castiglione and I. Hampsher-Monk eds, *The History of Political Thought in National Context* (Cambridge: Cambridge University Press).
  2003. "Isaiah Berlin's Enlightenment and Counter-Enlightenment," in Joseph Mali and Robert Wokler, eds, Isaiah Berlin's Counter- Enlightenment (Philadelphia: American Philosophical Society).
  2008. "A Guide to Isaiah Berlin's Political Ideas in the Romantic Age," *History of Political Thought* 29, 344–69.
  2012. "Ernst Cassirer's Enlightenment: An Exchange with Bruce Mazlish," in *Rousseau, the Age of Enlightenment, and Their Legacies*, ed. Bryan Gasrten (Princeton: Princeton University Press).
Wong, David. 1993. "Relativism," in *A Companion to Ethics*, ed. Peter Singer (Oxford: Blackwell).
Yack, Bernard. 2013. "The Significance of Berlin's Counter-Enlightenment," *European Journal of Political Theory* 12, 49–60.
Yumatle, Carla. 2012. "Isaiah Berlin's Anti-Reductionism: The Move from Semantic to Normative Perspectives," *History of Political Thought* 33:4, 672–700.
Zakaras, Alex. 2013a. "A Liberal Pluralism: Isaiah Berlin and John Stuart Mill," *The Review of Politics* 75, 69–96.
  2013b. "Reply to Galston and Crowder," *The Review of Politics* 75, 111–14.

Index

Absolute, 37–38
absolutism. *See* dictatorships; tyranny; totalitarianism
Adorno, Theodor, 133
aesthetics, 49, 157
agency. *See* individual agency
Agnelli Prize, 21
Akhmatova, Anna, 4, 116, 119, 120, 124, 130; Berlin's bond with, 18, 43, 127, 131; "Cinque," 127; "The Guest from the Future," 127; "Requiem," 128
All Souls College, Oxford, 17, 19, 37, 215; Berlin's research fellowship, 43, 125, 202
Alsop, Joseph, 18
America. *See* United States
analytic philosophy, 3, 33–43, 35n4, 44, 50, 81, 219, 256
Annan, Noel, 24, 207n28
Annenkov, Paul, 100n8
anticommunism: Berlin and, 2, 16, 18–19, 20, 21, 97, 109n21, 114–15, 146, 199–200, 251; critique of determinism and, 58; McCarthyism and, 199, 210; negative liberty and, 194. *See also* Cold War
anti-Enlightenment. *See* Counter-Enlightenment
antiquity, 139, 152, 172, 218, 219, 225–26, 227, 233
antirationalism, 62, 134
antireductionism, 46, 180; Berlin and, 3, 35–40, 44–50, 52, 55, 110
anti-Semitism, 13, 142, 143, 179, 183–85, 188, 190, 254
anti-utopianism, 5, 22, 54, 68, 166, 227, 244, 246, 248

Archilochus, 19, 51
Arendt, Hannah, 60, 61, 204
Aristotle, 7, 53, 238n16, 239; *phronesis* concept, 60, 73, 238
Armstrong, Hamilton Fish, 201
Arndt, Ernst Moritz, 176n10, 177
Aron, Raymond, 58
artistic ideal, 141, 157, 161–62, 163, 164
Arundel House School, 49, 182
Attlee, Clement, 29
Austin, J. L., 2, 16, 17; language analysis, 36–43, 45
authoritarianism, 24, 36, 37, 55, 61n18, 128, 135, 160; monism and, 229; positive liberty and, 231. *See also* dictatorships; tyranny
authority, 86, 118, 144, 250
autonomy, 25–6, 28, 87, 149, 178, 188, 207n28, 247–49, 260
Avineri, Shlomo, 255
Ayer, A. J., 17, 37, 38–39, 50; Berlin's differences with, 43, 256; emotivism and, 38n13; linguistic meaning and, 40; logical positivism and, 39, 42; method and, 45; *Tractatus* paper, 41

Bakunin, Mikhail, 54n6, 100, 107, 117, 125, 126, 144
Balfour Declaration (1917), 254
Balliol College, Oxford, 36, 215
Barker, Ernest, 36
Barrett, William, 146; *Irrational Man*, 146
Baudelaire, Charles, 151, 153, 156
Bauman, Zygmunt, *Modernity and the Holocaust*, 133
BBC Radio lecture series, 86, 93, 94, 126, 198

Beard, Charles, 92
Begin, Menachim, 28
Beiser, Frederick, 153
Belinsky, Vissarion, 118, 123, 124, 125, 127, 212
Bell, Daniel, *The Cultural Contradictions of Capitalism*, 223
Beloff, Max, 215
Ben Gurion, David, 126, 181, 185, 186, 187, 255
Bentham, Jeremy, 221, 233
Berdyaev, Nikolai, 129
Berlin, Aline (nee de Gunzbourg, also Halban), 20
Berlin, Irving (songwriter), 18
Berlin, Isaiah: academic career, 12, 17, 28, 37 (*see also* Oxford *headings*); All Souls Fellowship, 43, 125, 202; American close friendships of, 18; American visits of, 17–18, 53, 54, 82, 118–19; anticommunism of, 2, 16, 18–19, 20, 21, 97, 114–15, 146, 199–200, 251; assessments of, 6–7, 21–30, 33; background and early life of, 5, 12, 13–18, 27–28, 182–88; basic beliefs about humanity of, 258–59; biographer of, 30, 128, 182, 195; breadth of interests of, 22; British self-identity of, 20, 30, 181–82, 183; central themes of, 53–57; characterizations of, 11–12; childhood languages of, 170; Counter-Enlightenment and, 22, 138–39, 143–48, 150–51; "crooked timber, bent twig" metaphors and, 12, 23, 29, 98, 166, 179–80, 181, 191, 216, 227; damaged left arm of, 13, 17, 118; death (1997) of, 33; decisive life events of, 16–21; definitions of "good" and, 204–5; Enlightenment and, 12, 23, 91, 127, 134–37, 145, 148, 155; essay medium and, 2, 15; famous dichotomies, 19, 63 (*see also* hedgehog and fox dichotomy); fourfold legacy of, 261–62; golden age for (1950–75), 20–21; Holocaust and, 183–84; honors awarded to, 20, 21, 30, 37, 43, 125, 202; humanism and, 23–24, 29–30, 55, 56, 165; importance to twentieth-century thought of, 33; individual agency focus of, 24, 53, 55, 112–13, 138–39, 140, 143, 146, 198, 206, 207, 208, 211; intellectual development of, 16–19, 36–38, 37n10, 52; intellectual history and (*see* history of ideas); intellectual preoccupations of, 54–55; Jewish identity and, 5, 12, 13–14, 17, 27–28, 116, 131, 143, 170, 171, 175, 179, 181–89, 251–52 (*see also* Israel; Zionism);

knighthood of, 20; languages and, 16, 119, 170; later years of, 52, 127–28, 187–88, 189, 209, 255; legacy of, 52, 148, 159, 250–56, 261; major themes of, 19–20; marriage of, 20; meaning of philosophy to, 45; nationalism concepts of, 102n12, 169–70, 171n5, 172, 173–78; personal qualities of, 6, 11–15; political leanings of, 28–29 (*see also* liberalism); Russian thought and (*see* Russian intelligentsia); temperament of, 15; triple identities of, 5, 12, 13–14, 18–30; twentieth-century historical forces and, 97–98; two concepts of liberty and, 192 (*see also* negative liberty; positive liberty); *Verstehen* (imaginative understanding) and, 47, 48, 52; writings and lectures, 33, 48, 83; *Against the Current*, 23, 98; *The Age of Enlightenment*, 135; "Alleged Relativism in Eighteenth Century European Thought," 147, 241; *The Apotheosis of the Romantic Will*, 150n4, 151, 159, 160, 161; "Artistic Commitment. A Russian Legacy," 126, 130; "The Arts in Russia Under Stalin," 119; BBC Radio lectures, 86, 93, 94, 126, 198; "The Bent Twig: On the Rise of Nationalism," 98, 142n29, 169–70; "Chaim Weizmann's Leadership," 62n22; *The Crooked Timber of Humanity*, 23, 98; "Democracy, Communism and the Individual," 20, 195; "Does Political Theory Still Exist?," 50; *Encyclopedia Britannica* essays, 22, 86; "European Unity and Its Vicissitudes," 150n4, 151; "The Father of Russian Marxism," 100n7, 126; *Fathers and Children*, 127; Flexner Lectures, 84, 86, 138, 202–3; *Four Essays on Liberty*, 24, 28, 209, 213, 217; "Four Weeks in the Soviet Union," 122; *Freedom and Its Betrayal*, 86, 198, 202; "Generalissimo Stalin and the Art of Government (Utis pseud.), 110n22, 121–22; "The Hedgehog and the Fox," 1, 19–20, 51, 62, 125, 212, 238; "Herder and the Enlightenment," 143; "Herzen and Bakunin on Individual Liberty," 126; *Historical Inevitability*, 20, 25, 56, 57; "History and Theory: The Concept of Scientific History," 43n26, 46–7, 87n9; "The Intellectual Life in American Universities," 200–201; "Introduction: Induction and Logic" (lecture series), 40–41; "Jewish Slavery and Emancipation," 130, 189; *Karl Marx: His Life and Environment*,

Index

16–17, 19, 40, 43, 97–98, 99–101, 102, 109, 116, 117, 118, 134, 201; "The Lessons of History," 6, 265–76; "Lev Tolstoy's Historical Scepticism", 125; *Liberty*, 24; "Logical Translation," 44; *The Magus of the North*, 23; "The Man Who Became a Myth," 124; "Marxist versus non-Marxist Ideas in Soviet Policy," 122; "Matter" (unpublished), 44; "Meetings with Russian Writers in 1945 and 1956," 127–28; Mellon Lectures, 23, 151, 152, 157–61; "My Intellectual Path," 48, 98, 176, 230, 232, 233n8; "Nationalism: Past Neglect and Present Power," 98, 169–70; "A Note on Nationalism," 170; *Personal Impressions*, 21, 127, 207n28; *Political Ideas in the Romantic Age*, 84, 92, 93–94, 96, 151, 138, 150n4, 202, 203; "Political Ideas in the Twentieth Century," 85, 92, 115, 121, 201, 203–4; "Political Judgment," 59–61; *The Power of Ideas*, 98; "The Purpose of Philosophy," 45; "The Pursuit of the Ideal," 20, 230, 232–34, 238; "A Remarkable Decade," 126, 212; "A Revolutionary without Fanaticism," 126; "The Romantic Revolution," 150n4, 151; *The Roots of Romanticism*, 23, 150n4, 151, 157, 202; "Russia and 1848," 124; "Russian Populism," 124; *Russian Thinkers*, 18; *The Sense of Reality*, 58–59, 98; "The Silence in Russian Culture," 122, 123; "Soviet Russian Culture," 123; "The Soviet Intelligentsia," 122, 123; *The Soviet Mind*, 122, 123, 128; "The Three Strands of My Life," 128; "Tolstoy and the Enlightenment," 126; *Two Concepts of Liberty*, 1, 5, 19–20, 24, 26, 138–39, 146, 150, 160, 162, 165, 192, 202, 208–9, 212–13, 214, 216–17, 219, 226, 227, 228, 230–31, 235, 244, 250n1; "Verification," 39–40; "A Visit to Leningrad," 120; *Vico and Herder*, 23, 147; *Washington Dispatches 1941–5*, 119; "Why the Soviet Union Chooses to Insulate Itself," 121

Berlin, Marie (née Volshonok) (mother), 13–14, 20, 181, 182, 183, 186
Berlin, Mendel (father), 13, 182
Bernstein, Eduard, 107; *Evolutionary Socialism*, 108
Bevin, Ernest, 197
Bialik, Chaim Nachman, "A Twig Alighted," 181n16
Blok, Aleksandr, 18
Bohlen, Charles, 18, 119, 201
Bolshevik Revolution. *See* Russian Revolution of 1917
Bonald, Louis Gabriel Ambroise, 171
"boo-hurrah" theory (emotivism), 38n13, 39, 49, 50, 219–20
Borgia, Cesare, 66
Bosanquet, Bernard, 36, 86n8
bourgeoisie, 100, 102, 104, 107, 108, 269. *See also* class struggle
Bowra, Maurice, 30
Bradley, F. H., 36
Brentano Franz, 36n5
Britain: Berlin family emigration to, 13–14; Berlin's honors from, 20, 30; Berlin's identification with, 27, 181–82, 183; philosophical trends in, 35, 35n4, 36, 38, 39; political liberty tradition of, 70; representative government of, 227; romanticism and, 151, 153; Russian Studies in, 124; welfare state and, 29, 61, 251; World War II and, 17–18, 71
British Academy, 20
British Embassy, 17–18, 43, 184
British Foreign Office, 118–19, 183, 197, 199n18
British Idealism. *See* Idealism
British Information Services, 18, 43
Brodsky, Joseph, 124
Bryn Mawr College, Flexner lectures (1952), 84, 86, 138, 202–3
Bulgakov, Mikhail, 130
Burgess, Guy, 17, 118
Burke, Edmund, 97, 134, 144, 146, 251; historicism and, 268; nationalism and, 171, 172n7, 173–74, 176
Byron, Lord, 151, 153, 156

Cadogan, Sir Alexander, 195
Calder-Marshall, Arthur, 14–15, 22
Cambridge University, 34, 35, 35n4, 36, 39
capitalism, 103, 107, 108, 109, 193, 199, 214, 223, 269, 275
Carlyle, Thomas, 134, 156
Carnap, Rudolf, 41, 50
Carr, E. H., *Karl Marx: A Study in Fanaticism*, 99
Cassirer, Ernst, *The Philosophy of the Enlightenment*, 132, 138
Cavour, Camillo Benso, Count of, 7, 178
Chateaubriand, François René de, 151, 153, 156

Cherniss, Joshua, 35n2, 39n18, 41n22, 86n8, 99, 156, 199–200, 206n26
Chesterton, G. K., 174
Choi, Naomi, 3
choice: basic freedom of, 12, 24, 25, 26, 27, 28, 252; human capacity for, 55–57, 71, 204–9, 221; Kantian imperative and, 204; Marxist denial of, 112, 113; moral agency and, 74, 273; moral necessity for, 25; political judgment and, 71; positive liberty as threat to, 205, 208; rejection of, 260; state of Israel as, 5, 28, 189, 251–52; among values, 147, 159–60, 232, 237, 240–41, 244, 247–8, 272. *See also* negative liberty
Chomsky, Noam, 187n32
Chukovsky, Korney, 124
Churchill, Winston, 2, 3, 18, 115; visionary leadership of, 63, 64–65, 71, 74–75, 76, 88
civic humanism, 192–93
civil liberties, 197, 219, 226. *See also* human rights
class struggle, 102, 104, 106, 107, 110, 112, 145, 269
Clemenceau, Georges, 178
Clive, John, 72
Cohen, Benjamin, 18
Cold War: Berlin and, 2, 4, 25, 43, 54, 86, 110, 114, 127, 194–200, 208–9; Counter-Enlightenment and, 146; ideological pressures of, 201; intellectual context of, 195–201; liberalism and, 110, 146, 165, 194, 196, 197, 207, 210; liberty in context of, 5, 199, 210–11; Marxism in context of, 109, 109n22; negative liberty and, 194, 230–31; propaganda and, 123; ultimate outcome of, 210
Cole, G. D. H., 214
Coleridge, Samuel Taylor, 151, 156
Collingwood, R. G., 46, 140–41; *The Idea of History*, 140, 147
communism: determinism and, 57–58; ideological roots of, 121, 163, 195; intellectual ammunition against, 197–98; managerialism and, 28; political struggle over, 86; positive liberty and, 211, 230–31; societal control by, 28. *See also* anticommunism; Cold War; Stalinism
Comte, Auguste, 92, 101, 113, 268
Condillac, Étienne Bonnot de, 135
Condorcet, Marquis de, 138, 266–67, 268, 276
Congress for Cultural Freedom, 19
conscience, 104, 192, 226, 227

conservatism, 41n20, 61n20, 128, 186, 223, 240, 244, 246, 251
Constant, Benjamin, 5, 139, 213–14, 224–28; *Adolphe*, 213; *The Liberty of the Ancients Compared with that of Moderns*, 213, 214, 227; *The Spirit of Conquest and Usurpation*, 213, 227
constitutional guarantees, 213, 227
Cook Wilson, John, 36, 37
corporatism, 214
Corpus Christi College, Oxford, 14, 36
cosmopolitanism, 134, 148, 190, 251
Counter-Enlightenment, 4, 33, 56, 132–48, 171, 190, 260; advocates of, 23; Berlin's analysis of, 138–39, 143–48, 150–51; Berlin's popularizing of term, 22, 134; legacies of, 146–47; personalities of, 151
Craiutu, Aurelian, 4, 199
Croce, Benedetto, 140
Crossman, R. H., 17
Crowder, George, 5–6, 150, 155n13, 159, 161, 164n30, 250, 251, 256–57, 259, 260
Cuban Missile Crisis (1962), 54
cultural belonging, 27–28, 142, 253. *See also* national consciousness
cultural diversity, 26–7, 47, 139–44, 177–78, 177n12, 245–48, 249, 253, 261; autonomy in face of, 258, 260; Herder and, 26, 142, 144, 177n12, 178; value pluralism and, 246–47, 256, 257. *See also* multiculturalism
cultural relativism, 146–48, 240–41, 248
cynicism, 54, 65, 67, 114, 122

Decatur, Stephen, 174
Demaratus, King of Sparta, 218, 226
democracy, 63–64, 76, 195, 225, 227; individual greatness and, 73n43; liberalism and, 70, 216
deontology, 250
Descartes, René, 136
despotism. *See* totalitarianism; tyranny
determinism, 3, 4, 56–58, 68, 87, 87nn9,10, 108, 189, 250; Berlin on, 20, 25, 27, 36n7, 56, 57, 112, 253
dictatorships, 25, 38n12, 105, 111, 214, 270
Diderot, Denis, 135
dignity, 25, 29, 108, 113, 143, 165, 188, 189, 203, 235, 250n1
Dilthey, Wilhelm, 45, 56
Disraeli, Benjamin, 22, 98, 143, 171
diversity. *See* cultural diversity; multiculturalism

Index

Dostoevsky, Fedor, 11, 118, 121, 122; *The Brothers Karamazov*, 250n1, 273
Droysen, Johann Gustav, 176n10
Dubnov, Arie, 35n2, 98n2
Dudley, Alan, 110, 197
Dworkin, Ronald, 216, 231

Eban, Abba, 195
egalitarianism. *See* equality
Elliston, Herbert, 114n34, 198, 199
Emerson, Ralph Waldo, 150
emotivism ("boo-hurrah" theory), 38n13, 39, 49, 50, 219–20
empathy, 26, 46n33, 47–8, 52, 117–18, 128; historical, 141, 145
empiricism, 42, 44, 46, 47, 49, 50–51, 198; Counter-Enlightenment rejection of, 144–45; Hume and, 39, 40, 40n20; Idealism vs., 37, 38, 52
Encounter (publication), 19
Encyclopedia Britannica, Book of the Year, 22, 85
Engels, Friedrich, 58, 99, 103, 106
England. *See* Britain
enlightened despotism, 144
Enlightenment, 1, 4, 12, 17, 22, 28, 33, 132–48, 156n14, 171, 173, 188; Berlin's definition of, 138; Berlin's view of, 12, 23, 91, 127, 134–37, 145, 148, 155; Kant's definition of, 132; liberalism and, 247; Marxist thought and, 133, 201; materialists and, 87, 89; monism and, 137, 139; motto of, 132; personal autonomy and, 260; rationalist basis of, 132, 135–36, 155, 163; romanticism's conflict with, 1, 3, 6, 23, 139, 151, 155, 156; scientific method and, 135, 136, 145; twentieth-century debate over, 132–34; universal human rights and, 144. *See also* Counter-Enlightenment
epistemology, 46, 52, 55, 94
equality, 22, 25, 29, 51, 111n25, 113, 137, 177–78, 195; conflicting values and, 232, 233, 235–38; as liberalism's fundamental value, 216
Erasmus Prize, 21
ethics, 1, 3, 35n2, 38, 42, 43, 74–75, 157, 214, 224, 233, 240; "boo-hurrah" theory of, 38n13, 39, 49, 50, 219–20
expressive freedom, 146, 245n33

fact-value dichotomy, 243
fanaticism, 58, 62, 64, 65, 66, 67, 111, 113, 115

fantasia (imaginative insight), 140, 141, 144–45
fascism, 134, 171, 178, 189, 214, 270; ideological sources of, 36, 144, 145–46, 149, 162, 163, 166, 195, 240
Feuerbach, Ludwig, 101n9, 104; "Toward a Critique of Hegelian Philosophy," 37n11
Fichte, Johann Gottlieb, 112, 151, 153, 154, 156, 176n10, 184; Berlin's lecture series and, 198; nationalism and, 36, 171–78, 190; romantic will and, 163; theory of knowledge and, 157–58; theory of self and, 162
"final solution," concept of, 16, 69, 83, 91, 95–6, 231, 233, 237, 247, 275
First International, 100n6
First World War. *See* World War I
Flexner Lectures (1952), 84, 86, 138, 202–3
Foreign Affairs, 85–86, 110n22, 121, 122, 123, 201
formalism, 50
fox. *See* hedgehog and fox dichotomy
France: Germany's resentment of, 180, 254, 268; nationalism and, 178, 267; romanticism and, 153. *See also* Enlightenment; French Revolution; *philosophes*
Franklin, Benjamin, 23n21
Frederick II (the Great), King of Prussia, 268
freedom, 4, 24, 27, 111n25, 198; as absolute, 206–7, 217; ancient vs. modern conceptions of, 217, 218, 219, 225–26, 227; British tradition of, 70; of choice (*see* choice); coercion and, 3, 87, 142, 206; in Cold War context, 5, 199, 210–11; of conscience, 192, 226, 227; constitutional guarantees of, 227; definition of, 217; equality and, 237, 238; expressive, 146, 245n33; Herzen's defense of, 75; hindrances to, 218–19; Hobbes's conception of, 192, 193, 210, 211, 217–18, 219, 221, 226, 227; individual (*see* individual agency); Kant and, 154; liberalism in relation to, 212–28; as relational concept, 193; of religion (*see* religious toleration); romantic concept of, 162, 163, 164; Rousseau and, 206–7; of thought, 137, 221; vulnerability of, 209. *See also* negative liberty; positive liberty
free market. *See* capitalism
free will: determinism and, 56–57; historical impact of, 189; individual choice and, 55–57; Kant and, 56, 154, 165, 166; limits of, 58; romanticism and, 154, 161, 162
Frege, Gottlob, 34

French Revolution, 144, 158n16, 198, 217; lessons of, 265–70, 271, 272

Galston, William, 6, 238, 243n29, 245n33, 247
Gay, Peter, *The Enlightenment: An Interpretation*, 132
Geist (spirit), 37, 102, 141
Gellner, Ernest, 22
German philosophy, 22, 36, 37n10, 38
German romanticism. *See* romanticism
Germany: Enlightenment in, 188; nationalism and, 170, 172–80, 186, 190, 254, 268; political judgment and, 71; socialism and, 269–70; twentieth-century aggression of, 38, 271. *See also* Nazism; World War II
Goebbels, Joseph, 270
Goethe, Johann, 158n16, 176n10
Górres, Joseph von, 177
Graham, Philip, and Katharine Graham, 18
Granovsky, Timofey, 124
Gray, John, 133, 148, 229n1, 237n15, 241n24, 244, 257–58, 259, 260, 261
"great man" theory, 71, 72
Greece, ancient. *See* antiquity
Green, T. H., 36, 38, 38n12, 86n8, 231
Gromyko, Andrei, 119
Guizot, François, 102, 104; *The History of Civilization in Europe*, 102
Gustavsson, Gina, 4–5, 210

Halban, Aline (née de Gunzbourg), *See* Berlin, Aline
Halpern, Alexander, 119
Hamann, J. G., 23, 67, 101, 115, 134, 145, 151, 154, 171, 190, 212
Hampshire, Stuart, 37, 50–51, 67n27, 181, 222
Hanley, Ryan Patrick, 3–4
Hardy, Henry, 1, 3, 33, 55, 184n25, 202
Harris, Robert N., 119
Hart, H. L. A., 220
Hart, Jenifer, 215
Hartmann, Nicolai, 39n18
Harvard University Russian Research Center, 195, 196, 199
Haverford College, 122
Hayek, Friedrich, 5, 136, 194, 198, 198n17, 210
Hayward, Max, 127
Hebrew Bible, 142
Hebrew language, 170, 253
hedgehog and fox dichotomy, 11, 19–20, 74, 76, 125, 186; political leadership style and, 62–5, 76; Tolstoy and, 19, 74, 212, 221; value pluralism and, 19, 51, 238n16
Hegel, Georg Wilhelm Friedrich, 4, 37n11, 51, 90, 176n10, 189, 244, 252; Berlin's view of, 185, 198, 204–5; British Idealists and, 36; dialectic of, 105, 186; fascist ideology and, 36, 38, 38n12; historicism and, 268; Marxism and, 101, 102, 104, 109, 184, 185, 197; monism and, 233; organic metaphor of state and, 36, 174, 176, 253; Spirit concept and, 102
Heidegger, Martin, 133; *Being and Time*, 132
Helvétius, Claude Adrien, 97, 99, 112, 135, 198, 218n17
Herder, Johann Gottfried, 46, 47, 56, 67, 176n10; Berlin's writings on, 2, 22, 97, 101, 115, 139, 147, 182, 184, 190, 253; Counter-Enlightenment and, 134, 144, 151, 190; cultural diversity and, 26, 140, 142, 144, 177n12, 178, 182; Enlightenment and, 156n14; expressive freedom and, 146; historicism and, 134, 268; history of ideas and, 46; imaginative sympathy (*Einfühlung*) and, 96, 140, 141, 182; language and, 141–42; liberalism and, 276; national consciousness and, 147, 172, 172n7, 173, 174, 174n9, 175, 176–77, 178, 190, 253; value pluralism and, 230, 233n8, 234, 236, 239, 241; Vico contrasted with, 147
Herodotus, 139
Herzen, Alexander, 4, 117n7, 118n10; Berlin's identification with, 18, 21–22, 29, 67, 75, 92, 97, 99, 112–18, 124, 125, 126, 128, 131, 201, 209, 212; Tolstoy's description of, 22n17; untranslated memoirs of, 129; works: "Doctor Krupov," 126; *From the Other Shore*, 117, 126; *A Herzen Reader*, 129; "Letters to an Old Comrade," 126; "Letters" to Turgenev, 127; *My Past and Thoughts*, 117–18
Herzl, Theodor, 143, 179, 185, 187
Hess, Moses, 67, 75, 143, 178, 179, 185
Hilton, John, 201
historical context, 239, 239n20
historical inevitability. *See* determinism
historicism, 49n36, 134, 205, 233, 268
history. *See* philosophy of history
history of ideas, 1, 11, 15, 22, 26, 47, 48, 81–96, 261; Berlin's interest in, 3–4, 15, 19, 20, 33, 34, 37n10, 39, 43, 46, 81–84, 96, 153, 171, 202, 212, 215–16, 256; context-specific, 95;

Index

continuities vs. discontinuities and, 82–83, 91–94, 96; essential tools for, 83, 84–90, 96; "final solution" concept and, 16, 83, 91, 231, 275, 275–76; individual thinkers and, 53, 101; justifications for study, 90–96; key figures in, 2, 46; lessons of, 276; Marx and, 99, 110–11; moral imagination and, 95–96; political philosophy and, 84; value of, 81–83, 90–96, 91nn12,13. *See also* political philosophy

Hitler, Adolf, 58, 71, 72, 132, 184, 185
Hobbes, Thomas, 50, 136, 141, 144, 203; conception of liberty and, 192, 193, 210, 211, 221, 226, 227; doctrine of "hindrances," 217–18, 219; *Leviathan*, 192
Holbach, Paul-Henri Thiry, Baron d', 99, 135, 266
Holocaust, 13, 133, 179, 183–84, 204
Home University Library, 17, 98
Horkheimer, Max, 133
Hugo, Victor, 153
human basic goods, 235, 237, 242, 253, 256, 259, 260–61
humanism, 3, 6, 23–24, 26, 29–30, 55, 56, 85; civic, 192–93; romantic, 165
human reason. *See* rationality
human rights, 28, 108, 113, 149, 213–14, 217, 225, 241n, 259; basic human goods and, 259; cultural relativism and, 240; Enlightenment doctrine of, 144; technology and, 272–73
human sciences: Berlin's defense of liberalism and, 49; natural sciences vs., 23, 26–27, 35, 43–48, 56, 60–61, 87, 135, 145, 270–73; philosophy as, 45; scientific method applied to, 3, 136, 266–69, 270; specificity of, 140
human values. *See* value pluralism
human will, 57, 151, 157–58, 161–65
Hume, David, 22, 95, 137–38, 147, 268; empiricism and, 39, 40, 40n20; influence on Berlin of, 95n16; skepticism of, 40n20, 145; *A Treatise of Human Nature*, 139, 145; value pluralism and, 243
Hume's Law. *See* fact-value dichotomy

Ibsen, Henrik, *Peer Gynt*, 174
Idealism, 35–38, 37n11, 52, 68n10, 81n31, 109; as early Berlin influence, 36–37
ideas. *See* history of ideas
identity, 52, 98; public vs. private, 239
Ignatieff, Michael, 12, 30, 98, 128, 182, 183, 195

Ilf, Ilya, 130
Ilin, Ivan, 129
imaginative sympathy, 96, 140, 141, 144–45, 182
individual agency, 108, 165, 193; Berlin's focus on, 24, 53, 55, 112–13, 138–39, 140, 143, 146, 198, 206, 207, 208, 261; conscience and, 192, 226, 227; greatness and, 62–66, 68, 70–75, 73n43; indomitable will and, 157–58; judgment and, 61, 71–77; morality and, 74, 158; nationhood and, 174; Rousseau and, 206; uniqueness of, 26–27. *See also* choice; freedom; free will
individualism, 85, 140, 144, 193, 194, 231, 247
indomitable will, 157–58, 161, 162, 164
intellectuals, 220; Berlin's definition of, 15; nationalism and, 178–79; vs. intelligent member of intelligentsia, 11. *See also* Russian intelligentsia
"Ionian Fallacy," 44, 137
Irgun (Zionist underground), 185
irrationalism, 61, 143–4, 146, 163, 165, 240, 250n2, 268, 270–71
Israel, 12, 22, 185–90, 254–56; Arab population of (*see* Palestinians); establishment of, 54, 142–43, 185; failure of Weizmann's ideals for, 66; human rights and, 28; Jewish law and, 254–55; Law of Return and, 255–56; meaning to Berlin of, 5, 27–28, 116, 171, 186, 187–88, 189, 251–52; occupied territories and, 187; two-state solution and, 187–88, 255. *See also* Zionism
Israel, Jonathan, *The Radical Enlightenment*, 132–33
Italy, 171, 178, 185

Jabotinsky, Ze'ev, 186
Jacobi, Friedrich Heinrich, 134, 145, 151, 156
Jahanbegloo, Ramin, 97, 98, 184, 189; *Conversations*, 128, 129
James, Alice, 199
James, William, 92
Jaspers, Karl, 145
Jena circle, 153–54, 156
Jerusalem, 12, 188–9
Jerusalem Prize (1979), 21, 128
Jevons, Stanley, 103
Jewish identity, 98, 100, 181–88; assimilation and, 142, 143, 181, 184, 253; Berlin and, 5, 12, 13–14, 17, 22, 27, 131, 175, 179, 182; Hebrew language and, 253; Marx and, 22, 98, 100, 102; nationalist movements and,

179, 188, 254–55; nature of, 188; negative liberty and, 190–91; Orthodox Judaism and, 255; persecution and, 142, 179, 183–85, 190, 254; right to choose and, 5, 28, 189, 251–52; secularism and, 143; shared history and, 188, 252; World War II genocide and, 13, 133, 179, 183–84, 204. *See also* anti-Semitism; Israel; Zionism
Joll, James, 72
Joseph II, Holy Roman Emperor, 268
Jowett, Benjamin, 36
Jowett Society, 39
Judaism. *See* Jewish identity
judgment. *See* political judgment; practical judgment
justice, 111n26, 216, 224

Kant, Immanuel, 22, 46, 112, 176n10, 231, 250; autonomy and, 178, 188, 194, 207; Berlin's early exposure to, 16, 37n10, 184; Berlin's views on, 207n28, 250n1; categorical imperative of, 233; "crooked timber of humanity" image and, 12, 23, 29, 166, 180, 216; fact vs. categories distinction and, 46; Enlightenment and, 132; free will and, 56, 165; human dignity and, 108, 204, 250n1; human freedom and, 154; imperative of, 108, 154, 165, 166, 204; judgment concept and, 60; liberal tenets of, 108, 250; monism and, 233; moral law and, 154, 158, 188, 257; nationalism and, 172, 178; negative liberty and, 192; romanticism and, 154, 157–58, 162, 207, 207n28; "What is Enlightenment?," 132
Katyn massacre, 119
Kekes, John, 235n10, 244
Kelly, Aileen, 117
Kennan, George, 5, 18, 194, 196, 201, 205, 250n1; admiration for Berlin, 199, 199n18; prediction of Soviet ultimate failure, 210; psychological analysis of totalitarianism, 203–4
Kennedy, John F., 54
Kerr, Sir Clark, 119
Keynes, John Maynard, 100n7, 220
Kierkegaard, Søren, 156
Kipling, Rudyard, 23
knowledge, 22, 48, 55, 61n19; absolute certainty and, 48; Enlightenment theory of, 135, 137, 155; Fichte theory of, 157–58; humanistic vs. scientific, 135; as "ideology," 145–46; logical positivist view of,

52; natural sciences paradigm of, 23, 45, 271; nature and authority of, 38; romanticism's challenge to, 155, 157–58; unity claim of, 46; virtue and, 155, 157
Kojève, Alexandre, 143
Kołakowski, Leszek, *Main Currents of Marxism*, 114
Korean War, 85
Kripke, Saul, 73n46

laissez-faire, 6, 28, 217, 251
Lane, Melissa, 71–2
language, 4, 36–41, 43, 45, 150; of Berlin's childhood, 170; Berlin's facility with, 16, 119, 129; Berlin's philosophy of, 40–41, 44, 52; evolution of, 253; expressive quality of, 141–42; verification principle and, 40
Larmore, Charles, 150, 257
Laski, Harold, 17
Laslett, Peter, 49, 50
Latvia, 13, 14, 16, 25, 182, 184
leadership. *See* political leadership
Lehi (extreme-right underground), 175
Lenin, Vladimir, 58, 69, 71–2, 100n7, 103–5, 107, 109, 112, 113, 114, 117, 145, 214
Leningrad, 18, 120, 122, 128
Lessing, Gotthold Ephraim, 138
Lewis, C. I., *Mind and the World Order*, 41
liberalism, 1, 212–28, 268; anti-utopian, 5, 22, 54, 165; apolitical, 225–26; Berlin associated with, 25, 28–29, 34, 35, 52, 55, 98, 114n29, 127, 146–47, 150, 164–65, 199, 224–25, 228; Berlin's concept of, 213, 216, 250–56, 276; Berlin's defense of, 49, 261; choice and, 208; Cold War and, 110, 146, 194, 196, 197, 207, 210; Constant and, 227; Crowder's vs. Berlin's case for, 260; defenders of, 49, 76; democratic, 70, 216; discriminatory, 223; fall of Soviet Union and, 128; of "fear," 165, 224; forms of, 223; fundamental values of, 165; imperfection and, 165; influential theorists of, 213; Israel and, 187, 255–56; Kantian basis of, 108, 250; Mill and, 213; national consciousness and, 144, 170–71, 171n5, 251–56; negative liberty basis of, 159, 230–31, 258; nineteenth century and, 200; personal autonomy and, 247; positive/negative aspects of, 206; post-analytic, 50; public vs. private, 223; realism and, 68; Reformation-based vs. Enlightenment-based, 247; romanticism and, 149, 150, 152,

Index

160–61, 164, 165; tradition of, 139; two concepts of, 213–17
libertarianism, 6, 205, 217, 227
liberty. *See* freedom; negative liberty; positive liberty
Likhachev, Dmitri, 116, 129
Likud Party (Israel), 186
linguistic analysis. *See* language
Lippincott Prize, 21
Locke, John, 50, 141, 203, 231; *Letter Concerning Toleration*, 192; *Second Treatise on Government*, 2
logical positivism, 17, 37, 49; Ayer's tenets of, 39, 42; Berlin's critique of, 21, 39, 40, 41, 42, 44–45, 46, 52
Lovejoy, Arthur, 152
Lukes, Steven, 98

MacCallum, Gerald C., Jr., 193, 194
Machiavelli, Niccolò, 2, 7, 22, 54, 66, 67n27, 70, 73, 212; value pluralism and, 230, 233–34, 236, 241
MacIntyre, Alasdair, 133
Maclean, Donald, 119
MacNabb, D. G. C., 37
Macpherson, C. B, 193
Maistre, Joseph de, 2, 23, 97, 115, 144, 151, 198; *Considerations on France*, 144; nationalism and, 171
Malcolm, Angus, 110n23
managerialism, 28
Mandelstam, Osip, 4; *The Prose of Osip Mandelstam*, 126
Margalit, Avishai, 255
marginal utility theory, 103
market economy. *See* capitalism
Marschak, Samuil, 124
Marshall Plan, 54
Marx, Karl, 97–118; absolutism and, 112; appeal of, 101–2, 103, 105; Berlin's view of, 2, 4, 8, 16–17, 19, 22, 40, 43, 54, 85–86, 97–115, 116, 117, 118, 134, 185, 195, 196, 201, 204–5, 210; determinism and, 57, 87; difficult writing style of, 100n7, 167n8; Enlightenment tradition and, 133, 136; fanaticism and, 112; First International and, 100n6; freedom of choice and, 189; French Revolution critique by, 269–70; history of ideas and, 92, 96, 97–111; influences on, 101, 102, 104, 134–35; intellectual contributions of, 101–8, 101n11; internationalism of, 106; lasting influence of, 98, 107n18, 134, 197; limitations of, 50, 96, 106–8; long-term perspective of, 104; monism and, 98, 101n10, 111, 112, 115, 233; morality and, 205; nationalism and, 106–7; organizational skill of, 103; personality and temperament of, 100; *philosophes* as forerunners of, 17, 99; political philosophy and, 103; positive liberty and, 208; Rousseau linked with, 196, 201–2; Russian intelligentsia and, 18; single-mindedness of, 101, 104, 105, 107; successful revolutions and 268–69 (*see also* Russian Revolution of 1917); theory and practice of, 103, 107, 270; three major studies of, 114; works: *The Communist Manifesto*, 97, 103, 105, 108; *The German Ideology*, 105; *Grundrisse*, 84, 99; *Das Kapital*, 98, 100n7, 104, 105, 109, 193. *See also* communism
Marxism. *See* Marx, Karl; communism
materialism, materialists, 55, 87, 89, 96, 134–35, 138, 173
Maurras, Charles, 134
Mazzini, Giuseppe, 92, 178
McBride, Katherine, 202–3
McCarthy, Joseph, 199, 210
Meade, James, 29
meaning. *See* verificationism
Mehring, Franz, 99
Meinecke, Friedrich, 75
Meinong, Alexius, 36n5
Mellon Lectures, 23, 151, 152, 157, 158–59, 160, 161
Mendelssohn, Moses, 138
Menger, Carl, 103
metaphysics, 38, 39, 46, 232
Michelet, Jules, 92, 171, 174, 174n9, 176
Michnic, Adam, 128n25
Mill, John Stuart, 92, 115, 139, 193, 212, 213, 219, 228, 231; history of ideas and, 250n2; individuality and, 247; modern liberalism and, 213; monism and, 233; *On Liberty*, 192, 217, 225
Miller, David, 169n2, 171n4, 5 177n11, 252, 254
Mind Association, Oxford, 39n15
minorities, 247, 251, 253, 254, 260, 270; permanent, 25
moderation, 114, 115
Momigliano, Arnaldo, 147–48
monism: as barrier to good judgment, 76; Berlin's rejection of, 6, 48, 51, 52, 108, 109, 125, 137, 150, 229, 231–32; definition of, 229; differences in goals and practices of,

233; Enlightenment and, 137, 139; ethical, 233; as "final solution," 16, 69, 83, 91, 231, 275–76; forms in Western thought of, 233; hedgehog as metaphoric representation of, 19, 51; historical failures of, 271–72; historicism and, 233; Marxism as, 99, 101n10, 111, 112, 115, 233; perils of, 231; pluralistic thought vs., 3, 4, 51, 55, 216, 229; positive liberty and, 205, 205n25; romantic challenge to, 156–57, 159, 161, 163, 164; Rousseau and, 207; totalitarianism as, 101n10, 161n23

Montaigne, Michel de, 51
Montesquieu, Charles-Louis de Secondat, Baron de, 75, 137, 138, 144, 147, 190
Moor, Karl, 154
Moore, G. E., 34, 35–36, 37, 39
morality, 19, 42–3, 49, 158; authority and, 66; compromise and, 67–68; "final solution" concept and, 231, 233; free will relationship with, 55; individual and, 24, 74, 157–8; judgment and, 48, 74; motivation and, 205; public vs. private, 222; relationship with politics, 54, 67–71, 74; relativism and, 240, 248, 258–59
moral law, 154, 158, 188, 257
moral monism. *See* monism
moral philosophy, 51, 154, 220; "Ionian fallacy" and, 44; monism and, 233; pluralism and, 143, 148, 241; relativism and, 147, 258–59
moral values. *See* value pluralism
Moscow, 4, 13, 17, 18, 118, 119, 120, 121, 122, 127, 129
Mount Holyoke College, 195, 196
Muirhead, J. H., 36
Müller, Adam, 177
multiculturalism, 139, 149, 239n21, 246, 246n34, 247, 253–54, 260. *See also* cultural diversity

Nabokov, Nicolas, 119
Nagel, Thomas, 236–37, 246
Namier, Lewis, 92
national consciousness, 142, 146, 150, 169–71, 180; good and bad forms of, 254; Herder and, 147, 172, 172n7, 173, 174, 174n9, 175, 176–77, 178, 190, 253; liberalism and, 144, 170, 171n5, 251–56; national character and, 138, 139, 148, 175; Zionism and, 188–89, 254–55

nationalism, 5, 21, 22, 98, 102n12, 142, 169–82, 184–85; aggression and, 175; "bent twig" metaphor and, 180, 181, 191; Berlin's four-phase definition of, 173–78; "crooked timber" metaphor and, 180; connotation of for Berlin, 169–70, 171n5, 172; cultural (*see* national consciousness); freedom of choice and, 189; German prototype of, 170; historical development of, 170, 175–81, 190, 253, 268; intellectual ancestry of, 171–72; irrationality and, 268; Jewish identity and (*see* Zionism); major thinkers and, 36, 144, 147, 171–75, 176, 177; Marxism vs., 106–7; Nazism as end-case of, 179; "non-pathological" vs. "pathological," 170, 190; politicization of, 177–78; positive liberty and, 190; romanticism and, 142, 163, 178; spectrum of, 171–72; *völkisch*, 182; Zionism and, 186, 188, 252–53
National Socialism. *See* Nazism
nationhood, 170, 174, 176, 177, 187, 188, 189, 190, 255; Herder concept of, 176, 253
naturalistic fallacy, 159
natural law, 148, 193
natural rights, 193
natural sciences, 55–56; Counter-Enlightenment rejection of, 56, 143, 144–45; as Enlightenment basis, 135, 136, 145; human sciences vs., 3, 23, 26–27, 35, 44, 45, 46–47, 48, 52, 56, 60–61, 74, 87, 135, 145, 266–67, 270–73; knowledge paradigm and, 23, 45, 271; Newtonian revolution and, 198, 265–66; positivism and, 54. *See also* scientific method
Nazism, 13, 16, 34, 50, 71, 204; Jewish genocide and, 13, 179, 183–84, 204; power and defeat of, 270–71; rise of, 171, 172, 179, 185, 269; values of, 242
Nechaev, Sergey, 117
negative liberty, 4, 202, 208–11; Berlin's accounts of, 2, 5, 24, 25, 28, 53, 192, 194, 195, 199, 200, 205, 208–9, 210, 214, 216, 217–18, 230, 248, 251; definitions of, 2, 24, 200, 216, 218; early references to, 192, 193; Hobbes and, 210, 211, 217–18; individualism and, 194; liberalism and, 159, 230–31, 258; libertarian argument for, 194, 227; positive liberty and, 193, 194, 209, 211, 216, 217, 231; Stalinism and, 194; undermining of, 211; value pluralism and, 159, 257–58; Zionism and, 190–91
neo-Kantians, 45

Index

neo-liberalism/neo-conservatism, 217
New College, Oxford, 17, 37, 119
New Deal, 18, 29, 70, 251
Newton, Isaac, 136, 198, 266
New York City, 43, 118, 184
New York Review of Books, 48, 147
New York Times, 110, 195, 196
Nicholas I, Emperor of Russia, 124
Nietzsche, Friedrich, 36, 38, 103, 153, 156, 176n10; anti-Enlightenment and, 133, 134
nineteen-sixties, radicalism of, 20, 127
Novalis, 151, 154
nuclear weapons, 50
Nussbaum, Martha, 260

Oakeshott, Michael, 2, 61–62, 73, 136
Orwell, George, *1984*, 28
Osborne, John, 274
Oslo Accords (1993), 255
Ossian, 141
Ottoman Empire, 219, 222, 253
Owen, Robert, 99
Oxford, Lord, 125
Oxford philosophy: analytical movement and, 3, 33–43, 35n4, 44, 50, 81, 219, 256; Berlin's early engagement in, 33–34; Berlin's transition from, 19, 43, 81–82; development of, 17, 37–40, 43; empiricists and, 38
Oxford Realists (Cook-Wilsonians), 36
Oxford Slavonic Papers, 125
Oxford University: Aristotelian Society, 69n12; Berlin's 1958 inaugural lecture, 19–20; Berlin's retirement from, 20; Berlin's ties with, 12, 14, 17, 28, 36, 37, 182; Berlin's wartime leave from, 17–18, 19, 43, 53, 54, 82, 118–19; Chichele Professorship of Social and Political Theory, 20, 126–27, 192, 214, 224; Gladstone Professorship of Government, 215; Marxists and, 98; political philosophy and, 50–51, 215. *See also* All Souls College; Balliol College; Corpus Christi College; New College; Wolfson College
Oz-Salzberger, Fania, 5
Oz, Amos, 6, 11–12, 187n2

Pagden, Anthony, *The Enlightenment: And Why It Still Matters*, 134
Paine, Thomas, 97
Pakenham, Frank (later Lord Langford), 17
Pale of Settlement, 185
Palestinians, 12, 27, 185, 186, 187–88, 189, 255
Parthé, Kathleen, 4

particularism, 174, 178, 251, 256
Partisan Review, 146
Pascal, Blaise, 2
Pasternak, Boris, 4, 43, 116, 118, 119, 120, 124, 130; Berlin's bond with, 18, 43, 116, 123, 124, 127–28, 131; *Doctor Zhivago*, 123
Pasternak, Josephine, 118, 123
Pasternak, Lydia, 123
paternalism, 135, 137
pattern construction, 88–89
Peace Now, 28, 186
perfection, 164–65, 229, 231, 233, 269, 276
Pericles, 214, 226
personal autonomy. *See* autonomy
personal impressions (*éloges*), 2
personal liberty. *See* individual agency
Petrov, Yevgeny, 130
Pettit, Philip, 193
phenomenalism, 37, 48
philosophes, 11, 17, 87, 89, 99, 139, 156, 180, 268
philosophy of history, 20, 34, 220; Berlin and, 250–51, 253; Collingwood re-enactment theory and, 140–41; as cyclical, 147; determinism and, 3, 4, 56–58, 67–8, 87, 87n9, 87n10, 112, 253; Enlightenment and, 137, 142; French Revolution's outcome and, 268; "great man" theory and, 71, 72; human choice and, 112–13, 189; iron laws of development and, 58; Marxism and, 101–2, 104–5, 106, 107, 110, 269; moral "neutrality" and, 68; pattern detection and, 118n10; teleology and, 142, 253; Vico and, 140
philosophy of language. *See* language
phronesis (practical wisdom), 60, 73, 238
Plamenatz, John Petrov, 220
Plato, 51, 112, 137, 139, 231, 233, 234, 237, 238, 244; Ideal, 112n25, 233; realism, 35–36
Plekhanov, Georgy, 17, 18, 99, 100n7, 109, 114, 117, 201
pluralism. *See* value pluralism
Pocock, J.G.A., 192–93
poetry, Russian, 4, 43, 129
Polanowska-Sygulska, Beata, 128n25
political freedom. *See* freedom
political judgment, 3, 6, 7, 53–55, 58–63, 71–77, 93; competing values and, 239; cultivation of, 75–76, 77; ethics of, 74–75; history of ideas and, 83, 84–89, 96; moral judgment and, 48, 74; pluralistic mindset

and, 76; practical judgment and, 58–59, 62, 73, 77; value of skepticism and, 12
political leadership, 3, 54–77; adaptability and, 66–67; appreciation and, 72–73; "aristocratic" vs. "democratic" styles of, 73n43, 76; charisma and, 268; determinism and, 56–58; dispositional qualities of, 60, 62–63; exemplars of greatness, 63, 64–65, 71, 74–75, 77, 88; good judgment and, 3, 6, 54, 55, 58–63, 61, 71–77, 84; irrationality and, 270–71; moral agency and, 74; moral compromise and, 67–68; nationalism and, 178; personal decency and, 67–71; pragmatism and, 77, 186; styles of, 76; theory vs. practice of, 61, 62, 73; visionary vs. virtuoso, 62–65, 73, 76; wisdom and, 59
political philosophy/political theory: authority and, 86, 144; Berlin and, 2–3, 5, 6, 33, 35, 51–52, 75, 83, 86, 94–95, 97, 126–27, 220–23; central issue of, 86; as context-specific vs. context-transcendent, 94–95; continuities and, 93–94, 96; dangers of ethical monism and, 233; death and revival of, 49–50, 219–20; history of ideas and, 84; "Ionian fallacy" and, 44; irrational state systems and, 270–71; Keynes's view of, 220; liberalism and (*see* liberalism); Marx and, 103; moderation and, 114, 115; morality and, 54; Oxford chair of, 50–51, 215, 224; perennial problems and, 95, 95n15; pluralism and, 221–23; political judgment and, 6–7, 85–86; positive and negative freedoms, 192, 202; principal themes of, 6; Rawls and, 50–51, 220; reformist projects and, 61–62; revival of, 1–3, 220; Rousseau and, 202, 203, 215–16; social planning and, 28–29, 61; Taylor and, 50–51. *See also* liberalism; value pluralism
Popper, Karl, 5, 58, 194, 198, 200, 208–9, 210
popular sovereignty, 213, 226
populism, 191
positive liberty, 4, 5, 24, 25, 162, 202; ancient world and, 217; authoritarianism and, 231; Berlin's definition of, 192, 216; Berlin's view of, 28–9, 162, 163, 164, 195, 205, 216, 217, 251; communist world and, 211, 230–31; Crowder and, 260; dangers of, 205, 208, 210–11, 231; monism and, 205, 205n25; national movements and, 190; negative liberty vs., 193, 194, 209, 211, 216, 217, 231; romanticism and, 162, 163; Rousseau and, 196, 203, 206; tyranny and, 161n23, 162, 164

positivism, 3, 39, 61, 109; Ayer and, 39, 42; Berlin's critique of, 26–27, 54, 55, 61, 74, 250; empirical movements and, 47. *See also* logical positivism
practical judgment, 58–59, 62, 73, 77
practical wisdom (*phronesis*), 59–60, 73, 238
practice vs. theory, 61, 73, 101n11
Pre-Socratics, 44
Price, H. H., 35n4, 37
Prichard, Edward, 18
private sphere, 25, 239; freedoms of, 192, 223, 226
Procrusteanism, 21, 43, 51, 74, 75, 108, 113
proletariat, 98, 101–6, 111, 269, 270. *See also* class struggle
property rights, 217
Proudhon, Pierre-Joseph, 99, 107

Quixote, Don, 205

Rabin, Yitzchak, 187–88
Rachmilevich, Solomon ("Rach"), 16–17, 37n10
racism, 147
"Radical Enlightenment", 133n6
radical student movements, 20, 127
Ramsey, Frank P., 39
rationalism, 35n2; antirationalism and, 22, 61, 134; belief in, 267; Berlin's view of, 136–37, 195–96; Counter-Enlightenment resistance to, 143–44, 145; Enlightenment tradition of, 132, 135–36, 155, 163; Hume's critique of, 137–38, 145; irrationalism and, 144–6, 163, 250n2, 268–9, 270–71; Kant and, 165; Marx and, 269; paternalism and, 135, 137; romanticism and, 154, 155, 157, 250n2; scientific basis of, 61, 135; seventeenth century and, 136, 233
Rawls, John, 50, 216, 220, 224–25, 246; *Political Liberalism*, 224, 257; *A Theory of Justice*, 2, 224, 257
realism, 35–36, 37, 44, 47, 70; cynicism and, 54; respect for, 75; senses of, 47n34, 58–59, 68–69, 83, 84, 86–88, 96, 239; shared, 162
reason. *See* rationalism
reductionism. *See* antireductionism
Reed, Jamie, 35n2
Reformation, 85, 153, 247
relativism. *See* cultural relativism; morality
republican government, 216, 218

Index

Resistance (World War II), 117
revolutionaries, 61, 113, 124, 144, 268, 271–72. *See also specific revolutions*
Riasanovsky, Nicholas, 153
Ricardo, David, 104
Rickert, Heinrich, 45
Riga, Latvia, 2, 13, 16, 25, 30, 143, 181n17, 182, 183, 184
rights. *See* human rights; individual agency; natural rights
Riley, Jonathan, 245n33, 259
Rist, Jean, 117
Romanes Lecture, 127
romanticism, 1, 22, 38, 149–66, 205, 260; artistic creation and, 141, 163; Berlin's analysis of, 4, 5, 22–23, 150–66, 202; Counter Enlightenment and, 134, 139, 145; Enlightenment conflict with, 1, 3, 6, 23, 139, 151, 155, 156; German nationalists and, 177; Herder and, 151, 154, 156, 207, 233n8; humanism and, 165; human will and, 151, 157–58, 161–65; illiberal dangers of, 150, 161n23, 162, 163, 206; indomitable will and, 157–58, 161, 162, 164; inspiration behind, 158n16, 233n8; irrationalism and, 163, 250n2; Kant and, 154, 157–58, 162, 207, 207n28; legacy of, 157–58, 206; major figures of, 151, 153–54; manifestations of, 152; nationalism and, 142, 163, 178; qualities of, 149, 161; transformations from, 153, 155–56; two aspects of, 163–64; tyranny and, 161n23, 162, 163, 164, 165; value pluralism and, 142, 160, 163, 235; voluntarism and, 156, 162
romantic will, 151, 157–59, 161–63
Roosevelt, Eleanor, 195, 196
Roosevelt, Franklin D., 7, 18, 29, 70, 72, 178, 251; Berlin's admiration for, 2, 3, 61, 64; political greatness of, 63–65, 67n26, 69, 76, 88
Rosenblum, Nancy L., 150
Rostropovich, Mstislav, 116
Rousseau, Jean-Jacques, 4, 50, 112, 146, 174, 198, 233; Berlin's interpretation of, 154, 156, 195, 196, 201–2, 202n14, 206–7, 215–16; Marxism and, 196, 201–2; *The Social Contract*, 216; two concepts of liberty and, 194, 203, 206, 216
Royal Institute of International Affairs (Chatham House), 121
Royal Opera House (London), 22
Rumbula forest massacre, 184
Russell, Bertrand, 7, 34, 35, 36, 39, 40; *Roads to Freedom*, 214
Russia: Berlin's identification with, 18, 19, 27, 129, 130, 131, 134, 181–82, 183;Bolshevik Revolution and (*see* Russian Revolution of 1917); intellectual and cultural history of (*see* Russian intelligentsia); Jewish restrictions and, 172, 185; nationalism and, 178–79; Second Congress of Social Democratic Party (1903), 121. *See also* Soviet Union
"Russian Idea," definition of, 128–29
Russian intelligentsia, 11, 116–31; Berlin books series on, 125; Berlin's identification with, 21–22, 124, 235; boomerang effect and, 126; in nineteenth-century, 4, 16, 18, 19, 21–22, 81, 116, 117–18, 124–26, 127, 129–31, 235; in Soviet Union, 4, 18, 43, 116, 119–24, 127, 128, 179
Russian language, 116, 129, 170
Russian Revolution of 1917, 99, 105, 124, 134, 217; aims and effects of, 270, 271; Berlin's witnessing of, 4, 16, 97; Bolsheviks and, 13, 57, 71; February Revolution and, 16
Ryan, Alan, 5, 163
Ryle, Gilbert, 61n19

Sadeh, Yitzhak, 116
Sainte-Beuve, C. A., 23n21
St. Paul's School, 14
Saint-Simon, Henri Comte de, 99, 104, 198, 272
Sakharov, Andrei, 124, 128, 129
Samarin, Yuri, 127
Schalit, Lionel, 16
Scheler, Max, 39n18
Schelling, Friedrich, 151, 154, 156, 162
Schenk, H. G., *The Mind of the European Romantics*, 151
Schiller, Friedrich, 151, 154, 156, 176n10, 191
Schlegel brothers, 151, 154, 156, 158n16
Schleiermacher, Friedrich, 154
Schlesinger, Arthur M., Jr., 18
Schmitt, Carl, 144
Schneersohn Chassidim, 182
Schopenhauer, Arthur, 39n18, 153
science. *See* human sciences; natural sciences
scientific method: application to humanity of, 3, 53, 136, 266–69, 270; Enlightenment primacy of, 135, 136, 145
scientism. *See* positivism

Second World War. *See* World War II
self, 52, 158, 162, 163
self-creation, 146, 158, 164, 252–3
self-determination principle, 270
self-expression, 162, 164
self-realization, 207
Sergeenko, P. A., 22n17
Shakespeare, William, 16, 51
Shamir, Yitzhak, 28
Shapiro, Ian, 5
Sheffer, Harry M., 19, 33–34
Shestov, Lev, 129
Shils, Edward, 65, 65n23
Shklar, Judith N., 25, 49n36, 165, 224, 225, 228
Shneuer Zalman of Liady, 13
Shostakovich, Dmitri, 116
Sidgwick, Henry, 221
Siedentop, Larry, 12
Sinyavsky, Andrei, 130; "Pkhentz," 130
Sismondi, John Charles Léonard de, 104
skepticism, 40n20, 56, 95, 145, 220
Skinner, Quentin, 193, 210
slavery, 218
Smirdin, Alexander, 120
Smith, Steven B., 177n12; *Modernity and its Discontents*, 134
social conservatives, 223
social democracy, 107n18, 108
social engineering, 136
social equality. *See* equality
socialism, 22, 43, 58, 95n15, 98, 100n7, 101, 106, 107, 214, 268, 269–70; utopian, 99, 135; Zionist, 185, 186
social planning, 28–29, 61
social sciences. *See* human sciences
soft despotism, 223, 228
Solzhenitsyn, Alexander, 128
Sophocles, *Antigone*, 239
Sorel, Georges, 23, 144, 145
Soviet Union, 5, 24–25, 85, 119, 204, 206; Berlin's relatives in, 18–19; Berlin's visits to, 17–18, 18–19, 43, 104, 109, 116, 119, 122–23, 127–28; encroachment on Europe by, 197, 208; fall of, 128, 211; intelligentsia of, 4, 18, 43, 116, 119–24, 127, 128, 179; monism and, 229; nationalism and, 179; positive freedom and, 211, 231. *See also* Cold War; Stalinism
Sparta, 218, 226
Spender, Stephen, 19

Spengler, Oswald, 134
Spinoza, Baruch, 112, 136
spirit (*Geist*), 37, 102, 141–42
Stalin, Joseph, 58, 72, 105, 119; Berlin essay on, 121–23, 131
Stalinism, 16, 18, 19, 34, 58, 85–86, 110n23; nationalism and, 179; negative liberty and, 194
state. *See* nationhood
statesmen. *See* political leadership
Steinmetz, Alicia, 5
Stern, Abraham, 185, 187
Stern, Fritz, 73
Stern Gang, 185
Sternhell, Zeev, *The Anti-Enlightenment Tradition*, 133–34
Stevenson, C. L., 38n13
Stirner, Max, 104, 153, 156
Stoics, 217, 225, 228
Strachey, Lytton, 92
Strauss, Leo, 49n36, 143, 146, 252n5; *Natural Right and History*, 193; "Radical Enlightenment" term, 133n6
sufficient reason, principle of, 145
sympathetic understanding. *See* empathy
synthesis, 59, 60, 87–88

Talmon, Jacob, 136, 187, 202, 215
Tamir, Yael, *Liberal Nationalism*, 171n5
Tawney, R. H., 92
Taylor, Charles, 50, 51, 51n41, 238, 239
technology, 60, 133, 266, 269, 272–74
teleology, 194, 250, 253
Tertz, Abram (Sinyavsky pseudonym), 130
Thales of Miletus, 44
theory vs. practice, 61, 73, 101n11
Thoreau, Henry David, 150
Tieck, Ludwig, 154, 156
Times, The (newspaper), "The Fate of Liberty" column, 198
Tocqueville, Alexis de, 7, 73n43, 117, 223, 228
toleration, 137, 165, 246, 247, 257, 274
Tolstoy, Leo, 71, 74, 116, 120, 123, 172, 185; Berlin's works on, 2, 19, 22, 124, 125, 130, 131, 212, 221, 232; description of Herzen by, 22n18; hedgehog and fox metaphor and, 19, 74, 212, 221; *War and Peace*, 123, 125
totalitarianism, 11, 54, 58–59, 221, 225; Berlin's abhorrence of, 16, 18, 25, 34; ideological sources of, 36, 38n12, 48–49, 136, 146, 195; as monism expression,

Index

101n10; psychological analysis of, 203–4; solutions for social problems and, 95; twentieth century and, 34, 136. *See also* Nazism; Stalinism
Treitschke, Heinrich von, 176n10
Trilling, Lionel, 146
Trotsky, Leon, 71, 121, 214, 270
truth, 12, 44, 205, 267
Turgenev, Ivan, 18, 22, 67, 75, 97, 99, 115, 121, 124, 127, 129; *Fathers and Sons*, 127
Turkish *millet* system, 219, 222
tyranny, 5, 113, 143, 149, 214, 217, 220, 225, 228; enlightened despotism and, 144; romanticism and, 161n23, 162, 163, 164, 165; soft despotism and, 224, 228

unfettered will. *See* indomitable will
United Nations: Charter, 54; General Assembly, 196; San Francisco Conference, 119
United States: Berlin's lasting friendships in, 18; Berlin's stays in, 17–18, 19, 43, 53, 54, 118–19, 183, 184, 195, 202; immigration law and, 255; McCarthyism and, 199, 210; New Deal and, 18, 29, 70, 251; nineteenth-century romantics of, 150; representative government of, 227; social conservatives and, 223. *See also* Roosevelt, Franklin D.
universal ends, 242
universal human goods, 242, 253, 259, 260–61
universal values, 148, 162n24, 174, 234–5, 241–42, 248
utilitarianism, 48, 51, 101, 205, 216, 221, 222, 233, 247, 250, 275
Utis, O. (Berlin pseudonym), 85, 110n23, 121, 123
Utley, Thomas, 198
utopianism, 58, 99, 135, 146, 164, 166, 179; absolutist, 54; critics of, 5, 22, 52, 54, 68, 130, 166, 227, 244, 248; pluralism negating, 244, 246, 248; socialist, 99, 104, 135

value judgments, 268
value pluralism, 21, 22, 25–27, 34, 35, 142,143, 144, 149, 229–49, 256–61; analytical-holistic distinction, 236; anti-utopian, 244, 246, 248; Berlin's concept of, 1, 2, 4–5, 6, 11, 16, 19–20, 26, 49, 51–52, 55, 76–77, 108, 111, 112, 148, 150, 156, 159, 165, 199, 213, 216, 217, 221–23, 227, 229–34, 248–49, 250, 251, 256, 257, 261, 273–75; "burdens of judgment" and, 246n35; choices and, 232, 240–41, 244, 273–6; conflict and, 236, 237; core values and, 235–36, 243; cultural diversity and, 47, 139, 181, 256–57; cultural relativism and, 240, 241, 248; defensible vs. indefensible regimes, 261; definition of, 5, 148; four main claims of, 234–40; fox as metaphoric representation of, 19, 51, 238n16; human horizon and, 236, 242–43; Hume's Law and, 243; incommensurability and, 221–22, 223, 237–38, 241, 244, 245, 248; incompatibility and, individual vs. universal values and, 259, 267, 273; liberalism and, 1, 5–6, 15, 33, 149, 150, 159–61, 222–23, 230, 240–41, 244–49, 245n33, 256–61; as local/subjective vs. objective/universal, 234–35; meta-ethical beliefs and, 159; monism vs., 3, 4, 51, 229; moral relativism vs., 258–59; negative liberty and, 159, 257–58; norms implicit in, 243–44; political judgment and, 76; post-Berlinian, 245–48; ranking of values and, 223, 237–8, 241n24, 248; Rawls and, 246, 246n35; romantic theory of, 142, 156, 157, 160, 163, 235; sources of concept, 41n22, 229–30, 230n3, 232–34; subjective/objective ambiguity and, 235; universal level of, 148, 241–43, 248
Verdi, Giuseppe, 22, 178
verificationism, 37, 40, 41, 43; Berlin's opposition to, 46, 48, 52
Versailles Treaty (1919), 270
Verstehen (imaginative understanding), 47, 48, 52
Vico, Giambattista, 26, 45, 47, 56, 67, 96, 151; Berlin's study of, 2, 22, 67, 90, 97, 101, 115, 139, 140–41, 147; Counter-Enlightenment and, 147, 151; Herder contrasted with, 147; historicism and, 134; history of ideas and, 46; imaginative sympathy (*fantasia*) and, 96, 140, 141, 144–45; Michelet and, 174n9; nationalism and, 176; *New Science*, 140; value pluralism and, 26, 230, 233n8, 234, 236, 239, 241; *verum et factum convertuntur* principle, 140
Vienna Circle, 39, 50
virtue, 155, 157
volkish nationalism, 147
Voltaire, 15n6, 136
Vyshinsky, Andrey Yanuar'evich, 196

Wagner, Richard, 176n10
Walicki, Andrzej, 125, 127, 129, 131

Walras, Léon, 103
Walzer, Michael, 67n27, 209, 244, 258, 260
wars, 175, 274
Washington, DC, 118–19, 184
Webb, Beatrice, and Sidney Webb, 17
Weber, Max, 67n27, 92, 230n3
Weidenfeld, George, 125
Weimar Republic, 71
Weizmann, Chaim, 2, 3, 28, 54, 74, 116, 171, 178; failed ideals of, 66; Jewish identity and, 143, 183; political greatness of, 63, 65, 66, 67, 69–70, 72, 76, 85, 88; political pragmatism of, 186; Zionism and, 181, 185, 186, 187
welfare state, 2, 29, 61, 209, 228, 251
will. *See* indomitable will; romantic will
Williams, Bernard, 37, 50, 51, 67n27, 81n2, 237–38, 239n20, 245n33, 246
Wilson, Woodrow, 64, 270
Windelband, Wilhelm, 45
Wittgenstein, Ludwig, 39, 46; *Tractatus Logico-Philosophicus*, 39
Wokler, Robert, 139, 155n13
Wolfskehl, Karl, 14
Wolfson College, Oxford, 20, 127
women's rights, 223
Woozley, A. D., 37

Wordsworth, William, 153, 155
Working Party on Spiritual Aspects of Western Union, 197
World War I, 36, 71, 178, 269; aims/results of, 270, 271
World War II, 1, 63, 68–69, 70, 71, 117, 119; Berlin's political posts during, 17–18, 19, 43, 53, 54, 82, 118–19; effects of, 270–71; Jewish genocide and, 13, 133, 183–84, 204; Soviet nationalism and, 179

Xerxes, 218

Yumatle, Carla, 35n2

Zakaras, Alex, 245n33
Zamyatin, Yevgeny, 130; "On Revolution, Entropy, and Other Matters," 130; *We*, 130
Zionism, 5, 12, 22, 180–81, 185–91; Berlin's belief in, 27–8, 70, 142, 143, 170–71, 185–89, 251–55; as choice, 143, 190; demographic origins of, 185–86, 188; founders of, 179; Jewish experience and, 172; national consciousness and, 188–89, 254–55; uniqueness of, 179; violent extremists and, 185, 187. *See also* Israel
Zoshchenko, Mikhail, 120, 130

Other Volumes in the Series of Cambridge Companions

Gadamer Edited by Robert J. Dostal
Galen Edited by R. J. Hankinson
Galileo Edited by Peter Machamer
German Idealism 2nd edition Edited by Karl Ameriks
Greek and Roman Philosophy Edited by David Sedley
Habermas Edited by Stephen K. White
Hayek Edited by Edward Feser
Hegel Edited by Frederick C. Beiser
Hegel and Nineteenth-Century philosophy Edited by Frederick C. Beiser
Heidegger 2nd edition Edited by Charles Guignon
Hippocrates Edited by Peter E. Pormann
Hobbes Edited by Tom Sorell
Hobbes's 'Leviathan' Edited by Patricia Springborg
Hume 2nd edition Edited by David Fate Norton and Jacqueline Taylor
Hume's Treatise Edited by Donald C. Ainslie and Annemarie Butler
Husserl Edited by Barry Smith and David Woodruff Smith
William James Edited by Ruth Anna Putnam
Kant Edited by Paul Guyer
Kant AND Modern Philosophy Edited by Paul Guyer
Kant's 'Critique of Pure Reason' Edited by Paul Guyer
Keynes Edited by Roger E. Backhouse and Bradley W. Bateman
Kierkegaard Edited by Alastair Hannay and Gordon Daniel Marino
Leibniz Edited by Nicholas Jolley
Levinas Edited by Simon Critchley and Robert Bernasconi
Liberalism Edited by Steven Wall
Life and Death Edited by Steven Luper
Locke Edited by Vere Chappell
Locke's 'Essay Concerning Human Understanding' Edited by Lex Newman
Logical Empiricism Edited by Alan Richardson and Thomas Uebel
Maimonides Edited by Kenneth Seeskin
Malebranche Edited by Steven Nadler
Marx Edited by Terrell Carver
Medieval Jewish Philosophy Edited by Daniel H. Frank and Oliver Leaman
Medieval Logic Edited by Catarina Dutilh Novaes and Stephen Read
Medieval Philosophy Edited by A. S. Mcgrade
Merleau-Ponty Edited by Taylor Carman and Mark B. N. Hansen
Mill Edited by John Skorupski
Montaigne Edited by Ullrich Langer
Newton 2nd edition Edited by Rob Iliffe and George E. Smith
Nietzsche Edited by Bernd Magnus and Kathleen Higgins
Nozick's 'Anarchy, State and Utopia' Edited by Ralf Bader and John Meadowcroft
Oakeshott Edited by Efraim Podoksik
Ockham Edited by Paul Vincent SPADE
The 'Origin of Species' Edited by Michael Ruse and Robert J. Richards
Pascal Edited by Nicholas Hammond

Peirce Edited by Cheryl Misak
Philo Edited by Adam Kamesar
Philosophical Methodology Edited by Giuseppina D'oro and Søren Overgaard
The Philosophy of Biology Edited by David L. Hull and Michael Ruse
Piaget Edited by Ulrich Müller, Jeremy I. M. Carpendale and Leslie Smith
Plato Edited by Richard Kraut
Plato's Republic Edited by G. R. F. Ferrari
Plotinus Edited by Lloyd P. Gerson
Popper Edited by Jeremy Shearmur and Geoffrey Stokes
Pragmatism Edited by Alan Malachowski
Quine Edited by Roger F. Gibson JR.
Rawls Edited by Samuel Freeman
Renaissance Philosophy Edited by James Hankins
Thomas Reid Edited by Terence Cuneo and René Van Woudenberg
Rousseau Edited by Patrick Riley
Bertrand Russell Edited by Nicholas Griffin
Sartre Edited by Christina Howells
Schopenhauer Edited by Christopher Janaway
The Scottish Enlightenment Edited by Alexander Broadie
Adam Smith Edited by Knud Haakonssen
Socrates Edited by Donald Morrison
Spinoza Edited by Don Garrett
Spinoza's 'Ethics' Edited by Olli Koistinen
The Stoics Edited by Brad Inwood
Leo Strauss Edited by Steven B. Smith
Tocqueville Edited by Cheryl B. Welch
Utilitarianism Edited by Ben Eggleston and Dale Miller
Virtue Ethics Edited by Daniel C. Russell
Wittgenstein 2nd edition Edited by Hans Sluga and David Stern